Contemporary Issues in Accounting

Contemporary Issues in Accounting

Edited by

Pang Yang Hoong

ADDISON-WESLEY PUBLISHING COMPANY

Singapore • Tokyo • Seoul • Taipei • Reading, Massachusetts • Menlo Park, California
New York • Don Mills, Ontario • Wokingham, England • Amsterdam • Bonn
Sydney • Madrid • San Juan • Milan • Paris

Cover designed and illustrated by Equinox Art & Design, Singapore
Typeset by Times Graphics, Singapore
Printed in Singapore.

First printed in 1995.

Library of Congress Cataloging-in-Publication Data
Contemporary issues in accounting/edited by Pang Yang Hoong — 1st ed.
      p.   cm.
  Includes bibliographical references and index.
  ISBN 0-201-88900-5 : $35.00
  1. Accounting.   I. Hoong, Pang Yang.
HF5635.C56   1995   95-20860
657–dc20   CIP

Foreword

It is not at all uncommon for a group of scholars to collaborate in producing a book, with each contributing a chapter or two to form the whole. It is, however, quite unheard of for a group of almost two hundred scholars of diverse disciplines to produce a series of fourteen volumes, written contemporaneously and to be launched simultaneously.

The Singapore Business Development Series is an extraordinary endeavour that we at the Nanyang Business School of the Nanyang Technological University volunteered to undertake some two years ago. Among ourselves, the joint effort is affectionately known as the CBW Project – our shorthand for what is more formally termed the Communitarian Books Writing Project.

The CBW Project was borne out of our concern for what we realized was a surprising dearth of information on Singapore, even within Singapore itself. This limited availability of material was a fact that became painfully apparent to those of us in the School who had any kind of involvement with teaching, and was particularly apparent to our non-Singaporean colleagues. Thus from the outset of the Project, we made it our objective to fill as far as was in our capacity, this vacuum of information on our own nation. To this end, we strove to ensure that our series would be as far-reaching and wide-ranging as possible, covering nearly all the major disciplines taught in the nine Divisions of the Nanyang Business School, namely – Actuarial Science and Insurance, Auditing and Taxation, Applied Economics, Banking and Finance, Business Law, Financial and Management Accounting, Human Resource and Quality Management, Marketing and Tourism Management, and Strategy and Information Systems.

It is our sincere desire that our work will be found authoritative, well-researched, diverse yet detailed, by both the student body (undergraduates and graduates) and relevant professional groups inside and outside of Singapore. In addition, we hope that the general reader will find the volumes both informative and interesting.

The usual disclaimer must be made, being that all the authors write in their personal capacities. Individually and collectively, the views they express need not necessarily reflect those of the Nanyang Business School, the various Research Centres within the School, or the larger Nanyang Technological University. Nor need they reflect the views of any other organizations inside or outside of Singapore with which the authors may be associated.

It was our intention that this series of books be produced in time to commemorate Singapore's thirty years of independence as a nation. The books will thus be officially launched at Raffles Hotel, Singapore on the 8th of January, 1996. If any of them seem familiar to readers, it will be because many of the volumes have already made their appearance between July and December of 1995.

As Editor-in-Chief and Dean of the Business School, I would like to place on record my profound appreciation for the communitarian efforts of my colleagues in researching and producing this series. I am extremely proud of their individual input and *esprit de corps*. In addition, I am deeply indebted to our Project Manager, Dr. Soon Lee Ying, for her indefatigable effort in ensuring that all fourteen volumes were completed in time.

My acknowledgments would be incomplete without the inclusion of Professor Lim Chong Yah, the Director of the School's Centre for Accounting and Business Research (SABRE), whose iconoclastic brainchild the communitarian project is. His contribution in this project in all manner and at all times was both invaluable and irreplaceable. My gratitude must also go to the President of the University, Dr. Cham Tao Soon, for his genuine interest and heart-felt encouragement, which saw us through from the beginning of the Project to its end.

To the editors of the fourteen volumes and the one hundred and eighty-four contributors from both within and without of the Nanyang Technological University, I can only convey my heartiest congratulations for a memorable, credit-worthy and certainly praise-worthy communitarian endeavour. Our collegiate venture has indeed borne fruits.

Professor Tan Teck Meng
Editor–in–Chief
Dean, Nanyang Business School
Nanyang Technological University

Preface

The aim of this book is to provide an institutional and historical perspective to some of the more contemporary issues in accounting. The issues covered in the 13 chapters of this book are not meant to be exhaustive or comprehensive, as accounting theory and practice have now become much more complex, and new issues continuously emerge to compete for the attention of accounting academics and practitioners. This is evidenced in the various chapters contained in the book, which deals with contemporary, and, at times, controversial areas such as off-balance-sheet accounting, in-substance defeasance, accounting for new financial instruments and derivatives.

This book has been written with the needs of accounting theory students, researchers and professionals in mind. Wherever feasible, each chapter attempts to examine the issues involved in the local context. This should enhance the usefulness of the volume to accounting students, researchers and professionals in Singapore. Each chapter also attempts to provide a broad and critical overview of the theoretical and empirical research that has been carried out in the field, and, in order to stimulate additional interest among readers, the respective chapters conclude with a section outlining areas for future research. This will enable accounting students and researchers to develop research interests in the various issues contained in each chapter.

It is hoped that the issues raised in each chapter will provide a basis for an active dialogue between the researcher/academic and the accounting professional, as well as others interested in corporate financial accounting and reporting. The book would have achieved its objective if it succeeds in stimulating some interest in accounting research among students and professionals.

Notes on the Contributors

Pang Yang Hoong

Pang Yang Hoong graduated with a BAcc (Hons) from the University of Singapore. She also has a MEcons, majoring in accounting and finance from Monash University. She obtained her PhD in accounting from Queen's University in Canada. Associate Professor Pang is currently Director, PhD (Bus) programme in the Nanyang Business School, Nanyang Technological University (NTU). She is also Editor-In-Chief of the *Accounting and Business Review*. Her publications include *Company Accounting and Finance* (Longman 1990), *Financial Reporting Practices* of *Singapore Incorporated Companies Listed on the Stock Exchange* (Toppan 1989), and articles in local and overseas refereed journals. Her research interests are in the areas of corporate financial reporting, capital markets research and accounting education.

Pearl Tan

Pearl Tan is a Senior Lecturer at the Nanyang Business School. Prior to joining academia, she was an audit manager in an international accounting firm and had considerable experience in financial auditing. She had also performed special investigations work with respect to acquisitions and share issues. Presently she is an honorary consultant to a government office. Her current research interests include the regulation of financial accounting and auditing, international accounting and practical issues in financial accounting.

Andrew Lee

Andrew Lee is the Director of the Centre for Accounting and Auditing Research and Programme Director of the PhD (Banking & Finance) Programme at the Nanyang Business School, NTU. He currently teaches accounting and finance, both at the undergraduate and graduate levels. His research interests are in the area of valuation, corporate finance and the use of accounting information in securities markets.

John J. Williams

John J. Williams was educated in Canada and received his PhD from the Pennsylvania State University in 1978. He has taught accounting at both the undergraduate and graduate levels in several countries. In addition, he was Chairman of the Final Accreditation Examinations Board for the Society of Management Accountants of Canada and was admitted to Fellowship in 1992. Currently, he is an Associate Professor in the Nanyang Business School at NTU where his research interests include accounting theory, behavioural accounting, accounting education and capital markets.

Leong Kwong Sin

Leong Kwong Sin graduated with BAcc (Hons) from the University of Singapore. He obtained his MCom from the University of Canterbury in New Zealand. He has worked in both financial and management accounting areas for a multinational conglomerate. He has also been involved in the computerization of several accounting information systems. He is currently the Head of the Division of Actuarial Science and Insurance in the Nanyang Business School, and Director of the MIT-NTU Collaboration Programme. His current research interests are in the areas of informativeness of corporate financial disclosures and accounting education.

Gillian Yeo Hian Heng

Gillian Yeo Hian Heng's experience was in auditing and financial accounting in a multinational industrial firm before she came to NTU as Senior Lecturer and Director of CREFS. She received her doctoral training majoring in accounting and in capital markets research. She teaches statistical and research methods and financial accounting. Dr Yeo's current research interests lie in the area of capital markets research, financial statement analysis, forecasts and corporate finance.

Joanne Tay Siok Wan

Joanne Tay Siok Wan read for her PhD in the area of international accounting at the University of Exeter, United Kingdom. A published paper based on her doctoral research into measurement of accounting harmonization is now a well-known reference in the area. Dr Tay has been teaching mainly auditing to BAcc undergraduates and MBA (Accountancy) students, as well as supervising MBA and final year research projects in auditing. Her current research focuses on audit judgement, audit qualifications and audit quality.

Peter Lee Lip Nyean

Peter Lee Lip Nyean is currently a Senior Lecturer at the Nanyang Business School, NTU. He teaches advanced financial accounting at the undergraduate level and corporate reporting at the MBA level. His research interest is in corporate accounting policies and financial instruments. Prior to joining the university, his working experience has been in the field of accounting and corporate finance with various organizations including a financial institution, a Big Six firm, an international manufacturing company and a corporate group.

Susan Teo Pin Pin

Susan Teo Pin Pin worked in an international audit firm before joining NTU as Lecturer. This has reflected on her research interests, which include the development of an international auditing harmonization model, the empirical testing of audit quality and the perception of the quality of audit work performed by foreign accounting professionals.

Branson Kwok

Branson Kwok is a Senior Lecturer in the Nanyang Business School and teaches financial management in the undergraduate and MBA pro-grammes. He is the Programme Director of the MBA (Accountancy) Programme. His current research interests include pricing of derivative securities, information economics, audit firm mergers and corporate merger and bankruptcy prediction models.

Lim Ai Bee

Lim Ai Bee is the Accountant of the Department of Finance & Adminis-tration of the Institute of Technical Education ITE. Her research interests are corporate reporting and management accounting systems.

Lee D. Parker

Lee D. Parker is Professor of accounting, finance and management in the School of Commerce at Flinders University in Adelaide, South Australia. He has held previous positions at the Universities of Glasgow, Dundee, Monash and Griffith. He has also been a visiting professor at Case Western Reserve University (Cleveland, Ohio); London School of Economics; University of California (Berkeley); University of Otago (NZ); Kuwait University; University of Mississippi; NTU (Singapore) and University of Alabama. Professor Parker has published over 100 articles and books internationally. He is a past-president of the Academy of Accounting Historians and Fellow of the Centre for Social and Environmental Accounting Research at the University of Dundee (Scotland). In addition he is joint editor of the international research journal, *Accounting, Auditing and Accountability Journal*, and is an editorial board member of eight other research journals in the US, UK and Australia. He teaches, researches and consults in the fields of strategic management, social and environmental accounting, public sector management and accountability, management planning and control, business and professional ethics and accounting history.

Ng Eng Juan

Ng Eng Juan graduated with BEc (first class honours) from University of Malaya and an MBA from University of Southern California. He is a member of the Institute of Certified Public Accountants of Singapore (ICPAS) and a member of the Malaysian Association of Certified Public Accountants (MACPA). Mr Ng has had many years of working experience in an international public accounting firm before joining the academia. He is currently Senior Lecturer in the Nanyang Business School, NTU. Mr Ng's current research interests are in the area of financial accounting theories and practices. Among his publications is a book entitled *Consolidated Accounts – Singapore*, published by Longman in 1992.

Richard Low Siew Siang

Richard Low Siew Siang is a Senior Lecturer in the Nanyang Business School. He teaches business finance in the undergraduate programme. His current research interest is in the informational contents of reported financial statements.

Chung Lai Hong

Chung Lai Hong received her doctoral training in accountancy at the University of Pittsburgh. She teaches managerial accounting in the undergraduate and graduate programmes. Her major research interests include behavioural accounting, group decision making and management planning and control systems. Currently, she is associate editor of the *Accounting and Business Review* and Associate Director of the Centre for Accounting and Auditing Research at NTU.

Contents

1 The Nature of Accounting and Accounting Research

Pang Yang Hoong

1.1 INTRODUCTION

The literature on accounting theory and research has grown exponentially over the past three decades. The number of academic journals in accounting has also seen a geometric growth over this same period. What has developed today is a proliferation of accounting theories, although there is still no comprehensive theory of accounting. These theories have developed from the efforts of individuals, academics as well as practitioners with differing backgrounds, using different approaches to address either a particular aspect of accounting or the concept of accounting as a whole. The accounting literature that has appeared reflects the situation as described by the American Accounting Association's Committee on Concepts and Standards for External Financial Reports (1977):

(1) No single governing theory of financial accounting is rich enough to encompass the full range of user–environment specifications effectively; and hence,
(2) There exists in the financial accounting literature not a theory of financial accounting, but a collection of theories which can be arrayed over the differences in the user–environment specifications.
(pp. 1–2)

This broad spectrum of accounting is reflected in the diverse accounting research that exists in the literature. The purpose of this book is to provide a brief but broad overview of some major issues that confront accounting researchers today. The book contains four parts, each dealing with a different aspect of contemporary accounting research and/or practice.

1.2   RESEARCH IN ACCOUNTING

Part I contains three chapters that deal with research in accounting. In **Chapter 2**, Pearl Tan offers the view that there exists today a gap between academic research in accounting and accounting practice. She attributes this situation to two broad reasons. Firstly, there has been a move away from *a priori* accounting research to that of experimentation or empiricism. This move, in part a product of university-based teaching of accounting and the introduction of doctoral programmes in this field, results in the methodology of research itself being given added importance, so that research tools increasingly become more and more complex. Secondly, accounting research increasingly integrates models and concepts from other disciplines.

One result of this is the advent of what is commonly described as 'market-based research in accounting' or 'capital markets research in accounting' (which is covered in Chapter 3). The natural consequence of this development in accounting research is that academic research in accounting becomes largely divorced from accounting practice. In fact, Abdel-khalik (1983) describes accounting research and accounting practice as 'incompatible twins'. The common complaint is that academic research fails to communicate to practitioners. This is because practitioners feel that academics lack 'real world experience', so that they tend to report research findings that are of little relevance to practitioners. Even if they are relevant, they are gauged in mathematical–technical language that only other academics can understand. In other words, such research writings are written by academics for other academics. Chapter 2 concludes with some suggestions for bridging the existing gap between academic research and accounting practice. This includes a call to accounting researchers to undertake research that is relevant to practice, that is, applied research that guides practitioners in their judgement choice in the face of uncertainty. Education can also be used as a link between research and practice, but ultimately, research must be written in a way that is readable by and understandable to practitioners. Without the establishment of effective communication links, the gap between research and practice will not be bridged, but will continue to be reinforced.

In **Chapter 3**, Andrew Lee reviews one branch of accounting research that has strong links with finance theory, commonly known as capital markets research in accounting or 'market-based accounting research'. This term is commonly used to refer to research in accounting and its relation to capital markets. This body of research in accounting has its roots in the move away from normative research towards empirical research in accounting, and the use of empirical evidence to evaluate the relative superiority of alternative accounting rules. The early studies, beginning with the seminal Ball and Brown (1968) study, attempted to test the claim by normative accounting theorists that accounting income has no informative content because of the diversity of accounting rules adopted for income recognition. Information content is defined in terms of market reactions to the release of such accounting income numbers. The chapter traces the development of this branch of accounting theory and research following Ball and Brown (1968) over the next three decades. It attempts to help the reader develop an understanding of the objectives and motivation underlying such theories, and the implications of such theories of efficient markets on accounting and its role in equity valuation.

While most practitioners have tended to ignore academic research in accounting or to view it with scepticism, there is also a group of accounting researchers who have themselves become disenchanted with the extant academic research in accounting, and have consequently developed a new perspective on accounting research. This school of research is widely known as positive accounting research and is critically reviewed in **Chapter 4** by J.J. Williams.

The main thrust of positive accounting research is to study the factors that determine management's choices of particular accounting practices, the choices made by accounting standard-setters and the development of accounting theory itself. The philosophy adopted by positive accounting theorists is that academic research and accounting theory has failed to impact accounting practice in the past because it has been normative and unscientific. These researchers do not ask which accounting alternative is best, but rather, they ask why accountants have chosen to adopt the particular alternative. Instead of asking how accounting standards should be set, they ask what factors influence the way accounting standards are set. The argument is that if we can understand *why* accounting has developed the way it has so far, then we can predict, or alter its future development. The *why* behind the development of current accounting practices is said to have emerged from the interaction of various interest groups, each with conflicting interests, such as shareholders and investors, auditors, policy setters, consumers of financial information, and management.

Perhaps accounting practitioners may find this school of positive accounting research more meaningful than the traditional approaches to accounting research. However, this line of research has not been very helpful in the attempt to develop one generally accepted accounting theory or framework for accounting. If positive accounting theorists are able to determine not only the economic factors that influence various interested parties to adopt different accounting standards, then they may be able to further their research to help accounting regulators and policy-setters to anticipate how accounting practitioners and members of the financial community will react to proposed accounting changes, and possibly, to predict the economic impacts of such changes.

1.3   FINANCIAL REPORTING AND DISCLOSURE ISSUES

The proliferation of research, some of which is reviewed in the three chapters comprising Part I of the book, has so far failed to yield a comprehensive theory or framework for accounting theory or practice. There are many factors that could help to explain this current state of accounting development. One major factor that has contributed to this inability to agree on a theory or framework for accounting is the increasingly complex and ever-changing business environment within which accountants must work and adapt. This has made the role of the accounting profession in general, and corporate financial reporting in particular, more demanding.

In the past, accounting and its output, the financial statements, served the traditional role of enabling management to report on the results of its stewardship over the assets and resources of the company to the shareholders. Today, the number of stakeholders in the company has grown from the traditional group of shareholders to include potential investors, financial intermediaries and members of the financial community, creditors, employees, the government, auditors and even the general public. Now, financial reporting must serve the multiple and often conflicting needs of these various groups of stakeholders. The task of attempting to balance the needs of these stakeholders is an onerous one for management. This is because the disclosure/non-disclosure of financial information affects resource allocation in the economy. It also gives rise to economic consequences that impact different stakeholders differently. There is also a need to reduce the extent of information asymmetry in capital markets. The case for accounting regulation as a result of this complexity is discussed by Pang Yang Hoong and Leong Kwong Sin in **Chapter 5**. With the increasing complexity in the business environment and the multiple demands made upon financial reporting, the question that naturally emerges is whether the information contained in one set of financial statements is reliable and useful. In **Chapter 6**, Gillian Yeo addresses this issue with a discussion of the common problems faced in present day financial reporting. The chapter evaluates the effectiveness with which current accounting standards in Singapore deal with this problem of relevant disclosure in financial statements, and analyzes the areas where more extensive disclosure is desirable. In addition to mandatory disclosures as provided by accounting standards, the chapter also examines the nature and extent of voluntary disclosures in Singapore.

One question that emerges from the discussion in the chapter is that of information overload. As it is, financial statements today are including more and more information, both mandatory as well as voluntary, in an effort to satisfy the varied demands of interested groups (Leong, Low and Pang, 1988). The sheer volume of information contained in a set of annual reports must surely be a deterrent to readers, particularly unsophisticated readers, as one has to sieve through pages and pages of the report to find the salient information that is needed for a particular decision. Perhaps the alternative to more extensive disclosure lies in preparing separate special purpose reports for each user group, rather than more extensive disclosures, including voluntary disclosures, in a single set of financial statements. For the unsophisticated reader, the answer may lie in the preparation of simplified financial statements. This is an issue that will become increasingly important as Singapore becomes a nation of investors following the privatization of statutory boards such as Singapore Telecom and the Public Utilities Board.

The call for more extensive disclosures in financial statements raises yet another question, that of information quality. In **Chapter 7**, Joanne Tay presents a comparative analysis of the regulation of financial reporting and quality of information in Singapore, Malaysia and Thailand. The analysis reveals a number of differences in various aspects of financial reporting regulation among these countries. These differences help to provide insights into the impact of economic development and regulatory form on the quality of corporate financial reporting. The chapter provides some empirical evidence suggesting that there is a direct correlation between the existence of reporting regulation and the quality of financial reporting.

1.4   ISSUES IN ACCOUNTING THEORY AND PRACTICE

The prevailing argument in the various chapters of the book thus far is that accounting is subject to the influences and demands of an increasingly complex business environment, and that a major challenge for accounting theorists and practitioners is to be able to adapt to these new demands. Whether the accounting profession has been able to do so is reflected in the five chapters contained in Part III of the book, which deals with some contemporary issues that pose a major challenge to accounting theorists and practitioners.

In **Chapter 8**, Peter Lee provides an overview of the issues and accounting development for financial instruments. Over the last two decades, the financial markets have introduced a wide variety of new, innovative financial instruments such as futures, swaps, options, interest rate collars, caps and floors, collaterized mortgage obligations and hybrid bonds among others. Factors that have contributed to the development of these new financial instruments are the deregulation of the financial services industry, increased competition among financial institutions, changes in tax regulations and advancements in computer and information technology.

As these new financial instruments differ in terms of tenure, flexibility, credit risks, transaction costs and cash flow requirements, they give rise to accounting problems of measurement and valuation. In this regard, the accounting profession in Singapore has yet to issue any accounting standard to provide guidance on the measurement and valuation of financial instruments, although the Institute of Certified Public Accountants of Singapore (ICPAS) has recently issued ED 48. As Singapore develops into a global financial centre, these financial instruments will play an even more important role in the financial sector. Accounting must rise to the challenge accordingly.

Two other challenges facing the accounting profession today are the advent of off-balance sheet financing and in-substance defeasance, the topics covered in **Chapters 9** and **10**, respectively. Off-balance sheet financing refers to the funding or refinancing of a company's operations in such a way that under legal requirements and existing conventions, some or all of the finance may not be shown on the balance sheet of the company. The motivation for a company to adopt off-balance sheet financing is quite obvious. It enables the company to avoid showing a liability on its balance sheet, thus improving the debt–equity ratio, implying that the company is more 'healthy'. The immediate challenge facing the accounting profession today is to ensure that companies comply with the fundamental accounting concept of 'substance over form', and to take the necessary steps to reduce the inappropriate use of off-balance sheet financing. The author, Susan Teo, calls upon the profession to provide clearer guidelines to enable the evaluation of the financial impact of new off-balance sheet financing methods as they arise.

An in-substance defeasance occurs when a debtor irrevocably places cash or other assets in a trust to be used solely for satisfying scheduled payments of both interest and principal of a specific obligation. The possibility that the debtor will be required to make future payments with respect to that debt must be remote. The effect of such an arrangement is to enable the company to extinguish the debt from its balance sheet, in many cases with the recognition of an extraordinary gain in its profit and loss statement for the year. The reader may refer to Chapter 10 for the accounting details of this arrangement. The authors, Branson Kwok and Lim Ai Bee observe that, although the accounting profession in the United States has issued FASB Statement No. 76, *Extinguishment of Debt* in 1983, no corresponding standard is forthcoming in Singapore. As Singapore takes its role as a global financial centre, issues such as in-substance defeasance can be expected to become more prevalent. This is an issue that will increasingly confront the accounting profession in the immediate future and will represent yet another challenge to be taken up by the ICPAS and accounting academics in Singapore.

Chapter 11 focuses on yet another area of accounting that has been largely neglected by accounting educators and researchers, and for which little or no guidance has been forthcoming from the accounting profession. Lee Parker examines the role of business and accounting in meeting community concerns about social and environmental accountability and providing such disclosures. While there may be many reasons why companies may be reluctant to make such disclosures, clearly the benefits of doing so will accrue to the planet and to the community in general. Empirical evidence shows that companies have been making social and environmental disclosures over the last two decades, but they have mainly been in the form of narrative qualitative information with only occasional statistics included. The disclosures also tend to focus on human resource development rather than on the impact of company activities upon the environment.

While models for reporting of social and environmental account-ability have been suggested by various researchers in the extant accounting literature, none has so far been adopted by companies or the accounting profession. This may be due to the fact that none of these models incorporate fully the social and environmental requirements that have been placed upon companies by society. Corporate social and environmental accountability is indeed an issue that the accounting profession should place on its agenda so as not to continuously lag behind developments in the business community.

Chapter 12 in Part III provides a review of the practices underlying consolidation accounting as promulgated by the Statements of Accounting Standards (SAS) in Singapore. Ng Eng Juan concludes that the provisions of the accounting standards in Singapore are not consistent with any particular theoretical concept of consolidation, but are instead a combination of the 'parent company concept' and the 'entity concept'. The consequence of not adopting a single concept for consolidation may be reflected in inconsistent practices among companies. The author calls for various amendments to the respective standards so as to enhance comparability of consolidated financial statements in Singapore.

1.5 HISTORICAL PERSPECTIVES IN ACCOUNTING

Part VI of the book provides a historical perspective of two major areas in accounting: depreciation accounting and management accounting. As the final two chapters of this book, these chapters serve the role of reflecting back upon accounting's antecedents, tracing the evolving role of accounting over time to its present role today, and finally, anticipating the direction that accounting will follow in the future.

Chapter 13 traces the historical development of depreciation and depreciation accounting from the early days of railroad accounting to the present. The author, Richard Low Siew Siang, presents evidence highlighting the evolving role of depreciation, including some mistaken notions that depreciation can be regarded as a source of funds. He presents arguments to support the adoption of the straight line method for depreciation within the historical cost context, and shows that this method of depreciation is really a surrogate for determining the decline in value of an asset due to the loss of service potential.

In **Chapter 14**, Chung Lai Hong examines the historical developments of management accounting. In the chapter, she shows that management accounting has gone through several 'paradigm' shifts due to the shifting demands for management accounting information. This has been largely brought about by changes in competition, the transformation of the manufacturing environment, and more significantly, the impact of technological innovations in the workplace, as well as innovations in management practice. While many of these changes have resulted from forces external to the organization, many of these changes have also come from within the organization itself. If management accounting is to remain as a relevant tool for management planning and control, its role must be adapted accordingly so as to accommodate such changes.

What comes through clearly in the last two chapters is the observation that the role of accounting is moulded and shaped by the demands of the business environment as it changes over time. Some of these changes are internal to the organization itself, but many are external to and thus largely outside the organization concerned. These changes are imperative as an organization continuously adapts to changing demands in order to stay competitive. Accounting, as the communication device of the organization, must then also adapt to the new operating and business environments.

1.6   CONCLUSION

In conclusion, it is suggested that accounting as an academic discipline and as a profession cannot operate in isolation from other disciplines and professions. By the very fact that accounting is concerned with measuring and reporting the results of an enterprise's economic endeavour, it must of necessity adopt a multi- and cross-disciplinary approach in order to reflect economic reality. In order to achieve this objective, a three-way approach should be adopted. This involves a change in perspective along the following lines:

(1) Accounting education should take on a more 'applied' perspective. While accounting educators should continue to teach what is desired or 'best' accounting theory and practice, they should also explain what is current accepted practice and how it differs from 'best' practice. Ultimately, accounting students graduate and become accounting practitioners, and then, hopefully, they will show less resistance to reform within the accounting profession and move closer towards the adoption of 'best' practice.

(2) Accounting research, especially academic research in accounting, should endeavour to adopt a rigorous, neutral methodology so that the research findings are objective and defendable. However, the problems that form the subject of academic research should endeavour to be of relevance to practitioners and accounting policy setters. This means that academic researchers should not research within an 'ivory tower' environment, but should make efforts to be aware of the problems facing the profession and the business environment. In addition, although the research methodology adopted should be rigorous and neutral, the research findings should be written in a language that can communicate effectively to practitioners.

(3) Members of the accounting profession should adopt a systematic programme of continuing education. This should not be restricted to professional courses conducted by the profession itself. Accounting professionals should also upgrade their learning in a university environment and attend academic conferences, seminars and workshops, during which the latest research papers in accounting are presented and discussed. Accounting researchers will benefit from feedback provided by practitioners, and accounting practitioners in turn will be able to avail themselves of the contemporary research ideas that interest academics.

The above scenario may be more idealistic than practical. However, if some form of continuous interaction can be achieved among accounting educators, researchers and practitioners for the exchange of ideas, problems and possible solutions, then we will have come a long way towards enhancing accounting as an academic discipline and as a profession.

REFERENCES

American Accounting Association, Committee on Concepts and Standards for External Financial Reports (1977). *Statements on Accounting Theory and Theory Acceptance*. Sarasota, Florida

Abdel-khalik, R. (1983). Accounting Research and Practice: Incompatible Twins? *CAMagazine*, March 1983, pp. 28–34

Ball, R. and Brown P. (1968). An Empirical Examination of Accounting Income Numbers. *Journal of Accounting Research*, Autumn 1968, pp. 159–178

Beaver, W.H. (1989). *Financial Reporting: An Accounting Revolution* 2nd edn. Englewood Cliffs, NJ: Prentice Hall

Leong, K.S., Low S.S. and Pang Y.H. (1985). Quantitative Growth of Information in Corporate Financial Reports. *The Singapore Accountant*, Vol 4, No 8, August 1988, pp. 9–15

Lev, B. (1988). Towards a Theory of Equitable and Efficient Accounting Policy. *The Accounting Review*, January 1988, pp. 1–22

Watts, R. and Zimmerman J. (1986). *Positive Accounting Theory*. Englewood Cliffs, NJ: Prentice Hall

2 The Relationship Between Academic Research and Accounting Practice

Pearl Tan

2.1 INTRODUCTION

The contribution of research to accounting practice has been the subject of much debate. There is no consensus on the usefulness or relevance of accounting research to the resolution of problems in accounting practice. It is not surprising that many practitioners find research articles incomprehensible and irrelevant to the immediate problems of the 'real world'. In many cases, the busy practitioner does not have the time to mull over research articles that do not explain the research and results in a way that he can understand.

The gap between academia and the rest of the accounting world has become noticeably wider during the last three decades. During this period, accounting research had undergone a metamorphosis. Two broad trends explain the change. First, accounting research moved away from its traditional *a priori* mode (derived by reasoning alone) to one of experimentation or empiricism. In empirical research, the researcher does not rely on his prior beliefs or someone else's beliefs or evidence but collects or generates evidence external to his beliefs (Abdel-khalik and Ajinkya, 1979, p. 9). In empirical investigation, the method of research assumes a new importance and inevitably involves the use of statistical or mathe-

11

matical techniques to analyse external evidence. The second significant development in accounting research is the integration of the institutional domain of accounting practice with models and other advances from the 'basic disciplines' such as economics, mathematics and statistics (Ball and Foster, 1982, p. 164). A case in point is the research effort known as 'market-based accounting research' whereby finance theory is used to examine the use of publicly disclosed accounting information by equity investors. In fact, as Lev and Ohlson (1982) pointed out, 'market-based accounting research' was not only a beneficiary of other disciplines but also a benefactor. Research endeavour in this field have contributed to a better understanding of capital market efficiency, the Capital Asset Pricing Model, information economics and regulation.

The use of 'scientific' methods of investigation and the inter-disciplinary approach to accounting research have opened new horizons for researchers. As a result of the more sophisticated and rigorous framework in which accounting research is carried out, the meaning within these papers have become less accessible to persons outside academia. This gives rise to the question of whether accounting research is purely an exercise in intellectual indulgence which has little or no practical value. Peasnell and Williams (1986) believed that academic accountants are paying increasing attention to developments in other disciplines and to fundamental inquiry generally, and are becoming less concerned about making direct impressions on practice.

In addressing the issue of *what is* the relationship between research and practice (a positive question), one can only consider perceptions rather than the real phenomenon. The issue of *what should be* the relationship between research and practice (a normative question) has been the subject of many previous discussions but for which there has been no satisfactory conclusion. For example, Lee (1989) summarized some views on the *expected* relationship between research and practice. One view is that research should be conducted primarily to satisfy the need for knowledge by professional accountants. In other words, academic research should be directed at the solving of problems. Another view is that an interdependent relationship between research and professional practice is essential to reinforce each institution's power and authority in society.

In considering the impact of research on practice, this chapter first looks at the different environment in which researchers and practitioners operate. It then reviews the literature on the relationship between the two and analyses some major perceptions of this relationship. This chapter proposes that a long term perspective be adopted in assessing the relationship and finally discusses the possibility of a solution to the widening gap between research and practice.

2.2 RESEARCH AND PRACTICE – TWO DISTINCT TRADITIONS

It is useful to start this discussion with a definition of the word 'research'. As it is not a technically defined word, a dictionary definition will suffice. Chambers English Dictionary defines research as 'a careful search; . . . a systematic investigation towards increasing the sum of knowledge'. Two elements are important in research. First, the methodology of research is critical. Whether 'systematic investigation' implies 'scientific' methods is an issue for debate, but there is growing support for this view of research. Second, research must contribute to knowledge and the understanding of a particular phenomenon. In this aspect, it is debatable as to whether data-gathering or documentation of particular practices without further analysis is considered as research.

Research can be either pure or applied. Pure research is directed towards an understanding and explanation of fundamental issues, whereas applied research is concerned with the solving of problems. Research goals may be threefold: to describe, to explain and/or to predict. The emphasis given to each goal may vary in a particular research context. Research objectives can also be classified as the understanding of problems (descriptive and predictive models) and/or solving of problems (normative models) (Abdel-khalik and Ajinkya, 1979, pp. 21–22).

2.2.1 Development of academic research in accounting

Although accounting research had its origins in practice, it has proceeded to evolve and develop along a path that is independent of the profession. What caused the shift from professional-based research to a more academically-oriented one? One plausible reason is the advent of university-based teaching of accounting and the introduction of doctoral programs in this subject.

The United States had a long tradition of university-based teaching of accounting and an early emphasis on the rigorous research of a PhD dissertation. The ideals, rules and habits of Germanic scientific scholarship symbolized by a PhD undertaking were embraced by many American universities at the turn of the last century (Cowley, 1939; Peasnell and Williams, 1986). The chronological list of the first issues of research-oriented accounting journals highlights the early entry of the United States into academic research. A sample from the list compiled by Dyckman and Zeff (1984) is included in Table 2.1.

Table 2.1   Chronology of academic accounting journals

Name of journal	First issued	Country of publication
Accounting Review	1926	USA
Journal of Accounting Research	1963	USA
International Journal of Accounting Education and Research	1965	USA
Abacus	1965	Australia
Accounting and Business Research	1970	UK
Journal of Business Finance and Accounting	1974*	UK
Journal of Accounting and Economics	1979	Holland (with significant input from USA)

* This journal originated in 1969 under a different name.

It is interesting to note that even in the United States, there has been a significant shift in accounting research during the last 30 years. The type of articles featured in *Accounting Review* reflects the changing landscape of accounting research. To illustrate, the articles featured during 1970 are compared with those featured in *Accounting Review* during 1993 and are presented in Table 2.2.

Table 2.2   Classification of accounting research in *Accounting Review*, 1970 versus 1993

Main focus of articles	1970		1993	
	Number	%	Number	%
A priori development of theory	24	51	0	0
Analytical development of theory	13	28	9	18
Empirical/experimental research	6	13	40	82
Technical or professional guidance	4	8	0	0
Total	47	100	49	100

From the simple analysis above, it can be seen that *Accounting Review* in 1970 was considerably less quantitative in character than *Accounting Review* in 1993. The *a priori* mode of theory development was prevalent in 1970. Many of the papers were seminal in nature and were by no means trivial in their contribution to accounting research at that time. Theory was also cast in a normative mode and the writers were not averse to prescribing solutions to problems. For example, Wheeler (1970, p. 8) stated that 'normative theory. . . is relevant for accounting, as we are not studying natural phenomena but things over which we have control'.

He saw theory development and empirical studies as providing the basis for determining the 'optimal accounting system' which would provide 'optimal information' for actual decision processes. *Accounting Review* in 1970 also included professionally-oriented articles that commented on practical problems and controversies that arose at that time. Examples included Henry R. Jaenicke's exposition on the accounting for restricted stock plans and deferred stock plans (Jaenicke, 1970) and Valdean C. Lembke's article on accounting for divisive reorganizations (Lembke, 1970). It is fairly safe to say (although this is only *a priori* reasoning) that most articles in *Accounting Review* in 1970 could well have been understood by a practising accountant who was reasonably diligent enough to study their contents. The language was clear, the deduction and analysis can be understood by a diligent accountant and there was less unexplained references to complex mathematical or economic models. Most importantly, accounting research then had the explicit purpose of being 'useful' to practice and sought to be useful by making suggestions that practitioners could understand and evaluate.

Accounting Review in 1993 reflects a vastly different research philosophy from that of 1970. Table 2.2 shows that the emphasis has changed altogether from *a priori* theory development to empiricism and experimentation. The underlying philosophy appears to be that theory is conjectural unless supported by empirical evidence. The objective of accounting research is to produce results that are highly defensible in terms of logic and methods of analysis. Accounting research now employs frameworks and methodologies that are more accessible to an economist or a mathematician than they are to an accountant. Ball and Foster (1982) explained that accounting research is the 'mapping of theory into institutional data'. Accounting provides only the data or subject matter of investigation. The theoretical frameworks within which accounting data is analysed are provided by the 'basic' disciplines of economics, mathematics, statistics and psychology, among others. Accounting research as it is today is inextricably entwined with advances in these disciplines. The articles in *Accounting Review* would therefore appeal to persons who have invested a considerable amount of time in learning the basic disciplines. While most accountants have some knowledge of these basic disciplines from their undergraduate training, they have problems with understanding current research which employ more sophisticated frameworks and methodologies.

Furthermore, as Ball and Foster (1982) pointed out, current accounting research is characterized by strong paradigmatic behaviour where the importance of a research to a particular research community overrides its importance to other parties. In other words, each research community is so loyal to a shared paradigm that they are not concerned with whether their research is meaningful or useful to other research communities or to external parties such as the accounting profession, corporate management, or the investment community. This would suggest that research articles may not even appeal to other members of the research community, let alone accounting practitioners. Thus, there is an apparent conflict of goals. On the one hand, accounting researchers are more concerned with testing a particular research paradigm and less concerned with making impressions on society in general. Accounting practitioners on the other hand are concerned with solving problems and improving practice which in fact calls for more applied or normative research. With the diminishing importance of normative accounting research, there are less incentives for accounting practitioners to read articles in today's academic journals.

Another consequence of paradigmatic behaviour among accounting researchers is that the research articles are written in a manner that is more readily understood by those who share the same research paradigm. As the target audience of academic articles are assumed to be like-minded persons in a particular research community, the writers often do not perceive a need to explain the symbols, models or even the language used to those outside that paradigm. Thus, even if the subject matter pertains to a 'real world' problem and the research has important implications for practitioners, the significance of the research does not penetrate into the practical realm because of the communication barrier.

2.2.2 The practitioner's world

The practitioner's world is complex and academic research, in spite of its sophisticated methodologies and frameworks, does not fully capture the richness of the institutional domain of accounting. Many theoretical frameworks are too stylized and rigid to reflect the multidimensional and dynamic world of the practitioner. Furthermore, paradigmatic loyalty in accounting research does not allow for the integration of competing 'views of the world'. Given that the accounting domain is influenced by economic, cultural, organizational, political, historical and psychological forces, the existing models which are developed within highly focused research paradigms are only partial explanations of accounting phenomena. Thus, for example, an examination of the disclosure practices in a particular sample may invoke an economic model to analyse differential content in financial reporting. Competing explanations may be provided from organizational or cultural theory as well. However, research that employs multiple paradigms are difficult and rare. The linking of highly differentiated paradigms involves a theory of a higher order which can integrate the different views of the world in a logical and coherent manner. Accounting research, as it is, is evolving along highly differentiated paths and the search for an integrated approach seems out of place in today's research environment.

In spite of the information revolution today, accounting practitioners still face considerable uncertainty in their decision-making, particularly in how or even whether they should recognize an accounting event. Since assets and liabilities are defined in terms of probable future cash flows, the accountant must determine whether current transactions have any impact on future cash flows and if so, the quantum of those cash flows at the point of recognition as well as at subsequent points. Uncertainty creates many troubling dilemmas for standard-setters as well as for the practitioner. These uncertainties are often resolved arbitrarily (for example, through conservative accounting rules such as the expending off of research expenses) or through the use of 'best professional judgement'.

Professional judgement is fundamental to the decision-making process of accountants. The most important characteristic of financial reporting, that is, that reports must be 'true and fair' is itself a judgemental concept. 'True and fair' is the *epitome* of professional judgement as it defies precision in definition. The preface to Statements of Accounting Standard (SAS) states that 'whilst members are expected to comply with SAS, it is recognized that the Statements are not intended to be a comprehensive code of rigid rules . . . The Statements on their own cannot supersede a member's professional judgement' (ICPAS, April 1984). The right to exercise professional judgement belongs only to qualified professionals who also willingly subject themselves to a Code of Ethics. Professional judgement distils the years of experience, training and careful discernment into every decision made by the accountant.

In a sense, an accountant is an empiricist in his own right. Both accountants and academics are concerned with obtaining evidence to substantiate assertions. However, the process by which the evidence is analyzed is completely different for each group. While the accounting profession upholds the use of judgement in analysing the evidence, the academic community emphasizes a scientific approach in any investigation. Each of the two subcultures are thus very different in their mindsets. (The scientific approach is not necessarily more superior than the judgemental approach. The use of mathematical and statistical techniques is subject to restrictive assumptions as well. In many empirical tests, information is only partial and the more important hypotheses are often not testable). The different mindsets create a gap between the two communities. If academic writers are not able or are not willing to communicate their research to a professional audience, they will have no impact whatsoever on the mindsets of the practitioners who will not accept the findings on the basis of blind faith.

Mautz (1974) provides a vivid description of the concerns of the practitioner and the environment in which he operates. Most practitioners are likely to agree with his observations. Accounting practice puts relatively heavy weight on technical ability and proficiency. Conceptual skills alone are not sufficient to execute one's tasks competently. Significant time pressures on practitioners require immediate solutions to specific problems. However, quality control is as important as timeliness of decisions. Substantial direct and indirect costs can result from mistakes made by the practitioner. The changing business circumstances increase the complexities of transactions and their effects. The accountant and auditor must, as a matter of necessity, exercise caution and conservatism. Finally, the practising community must convince the larger community and the rule-makers that their procedures and guidelines are authoritative. Given these responsibilities, it would appear that the practitioner will find applied or normative research more useful than pure research. Normative research is, however, on the wane in the research community (Peasnell and Williams, 1986). This trend accentuates the perceived gap between research and practice.

2.2.3 Similarities and contrasts

Having considered the different domain of research and practice, it is useful to summarize some of their similarities and differences. Abdel-khalik (1981) offers some interesting insights into this comparison. The article looks at three components of practice (auditing, standard-setting and corporate accounting) and compares their attributes with those of academic research. The conditions that need to be satisfied in a research effort are not necessarily important in the realm of practice. The three conditions necessary for research as stated by Ijiri (1975) are: novelty or discovery, defensibility and reproducibility, and availability (public dissemination). Abdel-khalik (1981) notes that these conditions do not always hold in the problem-solving realm of practitioners or policy-makers. In practice, it is the 'workability of the solution and the perceived minimization of opportunity cost that count' (Abdel-khalik (1981), p. 162). While problems facing both academicians and practitioners can be novel, the problems in practice are case-specific and involve use of judgement in their resolution. They also require immediate solutions and are less susceptible to the use of rigorous, scientific methods of investigation. Furthermore, the practitioner works with proprietory information and his solutions to problems are not available for public dissemination while the results of the academic researcher must fulfil the condition of availability.

2.3 THE RELATIONSHIP BETWEEN ACCOUNTING RESEARCH AND PRACTICE: COMMON PERCEPTIONS

A survey of existing professional and academic literature does not provide favourable views on the relationship between research and practice.

Generally, the literature attests to the gap between the two and there is a growing school of thought that perceives the major role of accounting research as one of providing justification to preferred alternatives. This section categorizes and analyzes the common perceptions held about the relationship.

2.3.1 Accounting research has little impact on practice

This first perception sees accounting research as lacking relevance and comprehensibility from the perspective of the practitioner and is therefore seldom used to resolve real world problems (see Mautz and Gray, 1970; Zeff, 1972; Wolk and Briggs, 1975; Barden, 1975; and Flint and Shaw, 1981). This conclusion was derived largely from *a priori* reasoning; namely, that the focus and structure of academic research are incompatible with the needs of the practitioner. The focus of academic research is on fundamental issues which have practical significance only in the long term. The output of such research is perceived as not being directly relevant to the immediate needs of practitioners.

The writers also drew their conclusions from personal experiences in actual standard-setting situations. Barden (1975) is an exposition of 'an old practitioner's adventures . . . in the hazy wonderland of accounting research'. A retired partner from the then Ernst and Ernst, Barden was commissioned by the American Institute of Certified Public Accountants (AICPA) to write Accounting Research Study No. 13. He decried first the lack of an authoritative framework of concepts and principles to work with in standard-setting; second, the reluctance of standard-setters to interact and work jointly with academics; and third, the increasingly complex nature of academic writings and the difficulty of the layman to comprehend and interpret them.

There appears to be an inadequate understanding of how standard-setters form their opinions, which factors they consider seriously and which are ignored. Mautz and Gray (1970) observed that even after 10 years of standard-setting experience, the Accounting Principles Board (APB) of the AICPA had yet to establish acceptable research procedures or guidance regarding the directions of desirable research. Many research studies commissioned by the APB and the American Accounting Association (an academic association) on specific problems had very little visible impact on standards subsequently issued to address them.

It is interesting to note both writers' opinion that the lack of a cooperative relationship between research and practice is caused as much by the reluctance of practitioners to use research findings as it is by the inability or unwillingness of academics to formulate the problems in a practical way and to provide persuasive empirical evidence.

Dyckman and Zeff (1984) examined article citations in the text of 20 Financial Accounting Standards Board (FASB) Discussion Memoranda issued during the period 1973–1981. Out of a total of 195 non-negative citations, only 35 citations were attributed to research-oriented accounting journals. They also noted that only 22% of citations in sampled main articles of the *Journal of Accountancy*, the influential professional journal of the AICPA, were attributed to academic writings. If one makes a simplistic assumption that the number of citations indicates the authority of the cited source, it would appear that academic articles have little impact on the policy-making machinery of the FASB and the AICPA.

While this perception of the role of research is a commonly held one, it is at best an opinion which is difficult to refute or support empirically. While the immediate impact of research on practice seems negligible, the tracing of idea through to action is a complex process which cannot be evaluated in the short run. What appears to be a schism between practice and research may not be so. The information dissemination process is a complex and fluid one. This chapter proposes that a long term perspective must be taken of the relationship between research and practice. This perspective is discussed later in the chapter.

2.3.2   Accounting research is a consequence rather than a cause of accounting practice

This school of thought sees research as being a 'servant' of practice. Accounting research is seen as providing *ex post* rationalization of practice and to legitimize existing institutional arrangements (Gambling, 1987; Birkett and Walker, 1972; Flint and Shaw, 1981).

An interesting survey was carried out of 183 articles of *a priori* research (that is, deduced from reasoning and unsupported by empirical evidence) during the period 1965–1975 (Bedford, 1978). Thirty-three articles were discarded from the survey because they employed comparatively less of the deductive reasoning process. Of the 150 remaining articles, 57 confirmed or justified an existing or proposed accounting practice. A further 81 appeared to coexist with new or proposed accounting practice. Only 12 items could be said to precede accounting practice. Bedford thus inferred that *a priori* research does not cover the scope of practical problems observed or deal with practical problems in advance of an authoritative proposal in an effective way.

Birkett and Walker (1972) (herein after referred to as B and W) analysed interest and activity in professional research in Australia during the period 1930–1949. Although this historical case study dealt with specific experiences in a particular time period, there are some valuable lessons to learn concerning the impact of research on practice. Their historical analysis showed that professional research in Australia had a confusing birth. While interest in research was visibly shown by the founding fathers of the Australian profession (such as A.A. Fitzgerald and R.A. Irish), there was confusion as to the objectives of accounting research. Research was perceived as being a process of attaining public acceptance of a new profession. It was perceived that the wider the discussion and criticism, the greater the likelihood of acceptance by the general public.

Since the 1930s, there was already a flurry of research activity in the professional circles in Australia but the product of these efforts seemed minimal. In the final analysis, the accounting standards issued in Australia during 1942–1945 were basically an adaptation of the recommendations of the Institute of Chartered Accountants of England and Wales. There was very little original Australian input into the early standards despite the research activity. The 'slow and laborious' democratic process of attaining general acceptance of accounting principles was replaced by the authoritative imposition of standards of a foreign origin.

B and W observed that the research activity during the period was largely practice-driven. However, the original intention expressed at the Inaugural Commonwealth Institute of Accountants' Annual Lecture at the University of Melbourne in October 1940 was to stimulate research and encourage original contributions to accounting thought. The annual lectures were delivered in all cases by leading practitioners. These lectures were confined to the description of practice and the review of literature in a certain field. They sought to inform and guide on 'best practice' and transmit the experiences of experts but they were rarely critical of existing practices.

The B and W case study highlighted the problems faced by standard-setters and policy-makers who embark on any sort of research activity. The primary problem is in defining the objective of accounting research. Regardless of how one defines the objectives of research, 'justification of practice' and 'value-judgement indoctrination' are rarely accepted as authoritative research goals. However, in the B and W case study, these were effectively the objectives of the professional research endeavour at that time. To have any direct impact on practice, research would have to precede practice rather than follow it (Bedford, 1978). B and W's historical analysis showed that research was constrained by practice and consequently was limited in its contribution to the development of accounting standards in Australia during that period.

It may well be that the problem is one of semantics. The word 'research' is often used very loosely in non-academic circles, without an appreciation of the standards and process of inquiry involved. In many instances, research with a professional orientation is actually a fact-finding exercise to inform or educate on certain aspects of accounting practice. Thus, the well-intentioned research of the Australian institutes in the case study may not qualify as research in the strict sense of the word. For research to have a more fruitful relationship with practice, potential researchers are well-advised to have a sound grasp of research objectives and methodology. An understanding of the capabilities and limitations of research can minimize the frustrations in any research endeavour.

2.3.3   Accounting research is used to legitimize the preferences of vested interests groups

While Birkett and Walker (1972) showed how accounting research is used to legitimize institutional practices, Watts and Zimmerman (1979) explained how accounting theories which employ 'public interests' arguments are used to support the preferences of different interest groups in the policy-making process. This highly controversial article won the AICPA's award for Notable Contributions to the Accounting Literature. The article created a wave of dissenting views from other academics and is a frequently cited article in academia. Although its proposition was contentious, the paper highlighted a potential use of accounting research. Sponsored research, in particular, may be commissioned for purposes of buttressing a preferred position. In this respect, the sponsoring party may be more concerned as to whether the results support its position rather than whether the inferences are reliable (Ball and Foster, 1982).

Watts and Zimmerman (1979) went beyond intuitive thinking by proposing a theory for accounting theories using economic analysis: 'While accounting theories have always served a justification role in addition to information and pedagogic roles, government intervention has expanded the justification role. The predominant function of accounting theories is now to supply excuses which satisfy the demand created by the political process. . . .' (Watts and Zimmerman, 1979, p. 300).

The authors (hereinafter referred to as W and Z) used economics to provide a predictive structure for their analysis. Accounting theory is seen as an economic product for which there is a demand and supply. W and Z also used a theory of political process to explain why accounting theories function the way they do. In a regulated economy, legislation vests powers on the government to distribute wealth among interest groups. They assumed that financial accounting statements perform a central role in these wealth transfers and are therefore affected directly or indirectly in the political process. The setting for W and Z's paper is very much based on the US political system where special interests groups invoke advocacy proceedings to support or oppose legislation affecting them. W and Z proposed that accounting theories which employ 'public interests' arguments are used to support preferences of lobbying groups. Similarly politicians and bureaucrats also use particular theories to justify their actions before their constituencies and the media.

The academic researcher in the W and Z scenario is depicted as the unsuspecting and well-intentioned supplier of 'excuses'. Controversial and contemporary issues arising from proposed legislation create opportunities or demand for research on the issues at hand. Accounting research that bears on topics of current interest are more likely to be read, cited or talked about by practitioners, regulators and teachers. W and Z posited that such a demand will create both pecuniary and non-pecuniary incentives for the pool of academic researchers to supply a wide diversity of theories to support alternative positions.

W and Z proposed that accounting theories will change contemporaneously with or lag new legislation but they will not lead them. They proceeded to test their hypothesis by examining the timing of accounting research relating to three legislation in the United States: the railroad legislation of the 1930s; the Income Tax Acts of the 1800s; and the Securities Acts of 1933 and 1934. They concluded that much of the related literature (depreciation accounting, accrual accounting and investor-orientation) follow rather than precede legislation.

The controversial propositions of the W and Z paper stimulated a wave of subsequent articles that were largely critical of the paper's analysis, methodology and conclusions (Christenson, 1983; Peasnell and Williams, 1986; and Whittington, 1987). In spite of the criticisms, W and Z have distinguished themselves from other commentators in two aspects. First, they have boldly put forth a 'theory' of accounting theory which, if assumptions hold, can explain and predict real world phenomena. The logical and consistent development of their theory, based on certain assumptions, simplifies the very complex interaction of research and practice into concise but comprehensive propositions. Other commentators have refrained from making these generalizations in one bold sweep. While their assumptions can be criticized for their lack of realism, the positive school of research (to which W and Z belong) subscribes to Milton Friedman's F-twist: 'A theory is vindicable if [some of] its consequences are empirically valid to a useful degree of approximation; the "unrealism" of the theory or the assumptions is quite irrelevant to its validity and worth'. Second, W and Z used empirical evidence to support their propositions. Many other commentators derived their conclusions from *a priori* reasoning supported by unstructured and informal observations (see preceding discussion).

In spite of the persuasiveness of their arguments, anomalies exist in the W and Z theory.

- It is not able to explain the voluminous amount of normative research which has no relationship to political stimuli whatsoever. Examples include the theories of Chambers (1966) and Edwards and Bells (1961): there is no apparent legislation to which these scholarly works can be tied. The W and Z theory appears to be one-directional. While there is some truth that government legislation often brings about a flurry of research activity on issues at hand, it is not always true that research will only be carried out because of political stimuli.

- Further, the legislation chosen by W and Z for scrutiny was enacted in the infant years of the accountancy profession and at a time when serious academic research was scant. It would not surprise anyone that academic research and the resultant theories would lag rather than lead this early legislation. The fact that research lags behind legislation does not prove a causal relationship between the two. Peasnell and Williams (1986) also made a pertinent observation that the reward system in the research community today provides incentives for value-free research as opposed to the 'normative-policy prescription' type which can be used to buttress preconceived preferences of interests groups. They cited various studies that show that there is a declining interest among researchers to produce articles of the latter type. This trend would make the W and Z theory redundant. For these and other well-articulated criticisms in dissenting articles cited above, the W and Z propositions, while interesting and thought-provoking, leave many questions unanswered.

2.4 A LONG TERM PERSPECTIVE OF THE RELATIONSHIP BETWEEN RESEARCH AND PRACTICE

2.4.1 The spread of ideas

The spread of ideas is an amorphous and diffusive process. Ideas and knowledge flow through a complex and interdependent network of communications which includes personal, organizational, institutional, societal and global elements. The spread of ideas is not necessarily unidirectional, from academia to profession. Professional research and developments can act as important stimuli for academic research. The relationship between research and practice can never be evaluated within a short timeframe where experiences with research can be confusing and frustrating. Seminal ideas sown in the 'ivory tower' of academic research often find fruition over a long term horizon, if ever at all. The fact that these ideas do not have a wider audience does not imply their uselessness. Kindleberger (1989) suggested that widely accepted ideas are not always the best ones. Conversely, the ideas that are rejected may have the greatest impact eventually. He identified the following types of seminal ideas:

(1) The simple idea, largely ignored or rejected by the profession, which refuses to disappear and keeps making its way.
(2) The powerful idea, buttressed by a wealth of metaphor and widely accepted, that is on the whole misleading.

(3) A concept intuitively understood for years but slow in finding its way into standard analysis, which spreads rapidly once it has been formalized.

(4) The strangely held view, widely accepted, that is right for the wrong reason.

An appreciation of the interface between research and practice must take into account the intellectual history of accounting. Historical analysis provides some evidence of the impact of accounting research on areas in financial reporting. Whittington (1981) is an excellent example of such a historical analysis.

2.4.2   Historical flow of ideas: the case of inflation accounting

In his essay on the role of research in inflation accounting, Whittington traced the propositions mooted during the feverish professional and governmental debates in inflation accounting during the 1980s to academic writings of the 1920s and 1930s. His point was that the theoretical foundations of inflation accounting in its various forms could be traced to early writings.

The concept of Constant Purchasing Power (CPP) can be traced to 1911 when Irving Fisher, an academic economist, advocated the use of general price indices for stabilization purposes. In the 1920s, two principal German writers, Schmalenberg and Mahlberg provided theoretical support for stabilization on a historical cost valuation basis as opposed to the replacement cost system advocated by other writers. At that time, the German economy was suffering from exceptionally high rate of inflation, culminating in the hyperinflation of 1923. The system of CPP adopted in Germany during this period was based on the work of Schmalenberg and Mahlberg. Another seminal work in CPP was the notable work of Henry Sweeney who in 1936 produced the first full statement of the CPP model in English.

The writings of these pioneers found their application in 1973 when interest in CPP accounting rose following the oil crisis. An exposure draft on CPP accounting was issued by the Accounting Standards Committee in the United Kingdom in 1973 (ED 8) and in the United States (APB 3 in 1969 and the FASB Exposure Draft of 1974).

Whittington also traced the origins of replacement cost accounting to academic writings. He identified an early pioneer in Schmidt whose system of replacement cost accounting was published in 1921. Schmidt approached the accounting problem from the standpoint of the business economist and was concerned that pricing decisions should be based upon information that reflects current costs. Schmidt advocated valuation on a replacement cost basis combined with an entity concept of physical capital maintenance. As Whittington pointed out, the concept of profit by Schmidt in this early work was similar to the concept adopted by the Sandilands Report in the United Kingdom in 1975. Schmidt's pioneering idea influenced the work of other writers, notably Limperg who was instrumental in developing the 'Dutch replacement cost school'. Limperg's influence is substantial as evidenced from the implementation of his model by Dutch companies, notably Philips Industries. An adaptation of the replacement cost system as advocated by Schmidt and later writers was implemented in the United Kingdom in the early 1980s.

The case of inflation accounting illustrates the latent application of academic writings. It also illustrates the time lags within knowledge development and between the publication of academic research and the application of that research by practitioners. Similarly, many other aspects of accounting practice can be traced to academic writings. Thus a long term perspective of the 'value' of accounting research should be adopted.

2.4.3 Competing views within academic research

Whittington's study also highlighted the multiple approaches that are advocated by various schools of thought to account for inflation. While the professional bodies preferred the use of CPP accounting, governmental regulators upheld the use of replacement cost accounting. The latter's choice is attributed to a fear that indexation may lead to the institution-alization of inflation in the economy (Whittington, 1981, p. 140).

Academic writings do not always provide a consensus as to the *best* method of accounting. It is very rare that the academic community is completely agreed on any one matter. But it is this very same climate of debate that stimulates the development of original accounting thought. It is also true that a literature that is rich with competing theories also lends itself to political use. It is my view that politicization of accounting offers great stimulus for fundamental research. Research is not a static activity. New research challenges findings of past research, and advancements in research can provide information as to the wisdom of past policies. Competing views, theories, methodologies and conclusions are an essential feature of academic research. Although there is the potential for 'misuse' (for example, as in the supply of 'excuses' for vested interest groups), these alternative views reflect the complexity of the world we live in.

2.5 TOWARDS BRIDGING THE GAP BETWEEN ACADEMIC RESEARCH AND ACCOUNTING PRACTICE

The prescription of an ideal relationship between the two respected institutions of practice and research is difficult. Although both institutions share common concerns and interests and may intersect at some points, their historical development and evolutionary processes have given rise to different objectives and directions for each. To force an artificial relationship between the two is to restrict the capacity for growth in each sphere. It is my opinion that there should be active dialogue and cooperation between academics and practitioners. Interaction should however enhance but not hinder the internal development within each sphere. If external parties demand academics to produce 'usable' research, fundamental research with long run implications will be neglected and the boundary of accounting knowledge will not be extended. Similarly, the research community cannot ignore real life developments. The cloistered outlook of academic researchers must be changed and the academic researcher must consciously include the practising accountant in his audience. In the following discussion, I propose some ways by which the widening gap between research and practice can be narrowed.

2.5.1 Increasing the opportunities for practically relevant accounting research

While the development of knowledge should not be hindered by the pressure to produce 'useful' research, it also goes that knowledge should not always be an end in itself. Academic researchers should also identify issues and problems that are relevant to practice and pursue an innovative research program to assist practitioners in either understanding some practical phenomenon or in the resolution of practical problems. While normative research is considered very unfashionable given the current research philosophy, it is an effective means of bridging the gap between research and academia. As Whittington's study on inflation accounting shows, the academic research that had impact on practice was normative in nature. I have identified some broad areas in which academic research may be practically relevant:

(1) Research that explains or clarifies the complex environment in which practitioners operate. Such research informs on the relationships between and among variables in the accounting environment and helps practitioners to understand and predict outcomes or decisions from particular processes. As accounting is not performed in a 'black box', an understanding of the environment is important to the thinking accountant. For example, market-based accounting research is useful in explaining how disclosed accounting information is used by investors. Another potentially useful research is human information processing which provides some insights for the practitioner into his own judgement forming process. Much of current accounting research informs on the environment. The problem with such research is not in its irrelevance to reality but in the way

in which the methodology, limitations and implications of the research are communicated which makes the research appealing to only a limited group of people.

(2) Applied research that guides accounting practitioners in their judgement forming process in the face of uncertainty. This includes research that proposes a certain framework, model, approach or system which practitioners can apply to solve a problem in a particular situation. An example of this research is the application of finance valuation models in the measurement of financial instruments or the formulation of distress prediction models for determining bankruptcy risk.

(3) Innovative research that proposes alternative methods to existing systems. Academic researchers are well-positioned to think beyond the *here and now*. A fertility of ideas today may bring about a change in practice tomorrow. For example, the case study on inflation accounting shows that alternative accounting systems were mooted long before the ideas were adopted. Inevitably, such research would be normative in nature but they provide the soul to an otherwise purely intellectual endeavour.

2.5.2 Education as the link between research and practice

The role of education is important in the spread of ideas and is an important bridge between academia and practice. University education provides the opportunity and challenge for future practitioners and policy-makers to explore new ideas and developments in their field of knowledge. Unconstrained by practice or habits, students can critically and independently analyse the work of researchers. It has been suggested by many accounting writers that the results of research should be taught in university curriculum alongside the professional subjects (AAA, 1986; Wolk and Briggs, 1975; Sterling, 1973). Whether education has any impact on the mindsets and world views of its participants is not always determinable. However, it can serve as a channel for the flow of ideas. As education is a lifelong process, this exposure to ideas must continue even after one leaves an academic institution. Research on accounting offers a rich array of information and ideas on accounting-related phenomena. It remains for the individual to exploit the wealth of literature that lies before him. The individual must be convinced of the value of research in his professional and personal development. He can assess the value only if he understands the research that he reads. In this respect, communication plays a vital role.

2.5.3   Establishing communication links

Both academics and practitioners have responsibilities in improving the communication links in the spread of ideas. Language, both verbal and symbolic, can accelerate or impede the spread of ideas. In this respect, academic researchers should aim to communicate to a wider audience than their band of like-minded research fellows. This does not imply the sacrifice of research goals or the dilution of research standards. Neither does it suggest that research should emphasize only applied works at the expense of fundamental research. It does mean however that the researcher should communicate the objectives, contributions, limitations, methodologies and findings of the research in a manner that is clear to a reasonably diligent reader. It is only when the veil of intellectual mystique is lifted that research reports stand up to scrutiny and can have an impact on practice. Robert Mautz, a well-known practitioner and researcher, sums it up:

> '... accounting practitioners must refuse to accept that which they do not understand ... Do you really expect an intelligent professional to accept conclusions related to his profession solely on faith, completely ignorant of their meaning? If you cannot or will not explain your research results to him in terms meaningful to him, you can expect no impact whatever'.
>
> Mautz (1978, p. 179)

The reader also has responsibilities. As Abdel-khalik and Ajinkya (1979) pointed out, readers share the responsibility for understanding the research. In other words, the reader must apply diligence in appreciating the methods used, the influence of the method on the outcome, the limitations of a particular methodology and the inferences that can be safely drawn from the results. The reader must not expect any one article or any one researcher to provide a definitive answer to a problem. A basic text on research (such as Abdel-khalik and Ajinkya, 1979) can provide the groundwork for understanding research methodology and for the appreciation of research papers.

Both academics and researchers have to make changes in their mindsets if communication links are to established. These changes, while difficult, can facilitate the flow of ideas across the institutions of practice and research. If no effort is made to improve communications, the two institutions of practice and research can merely co-exist and stand to forgo the enrichment in ideas that a more mutual relationship can bring about.

2.6   CONCLUSION

Accounting is a mature discipline and has undergone changes in both its practice and its methods of inquiry. Although research in accounting had its origins in practice, it developed along a separate path. The growth of empirical research and the incorporation of an interdisciplinary approach have extended the boundaries of accounting research. The apparent divergence of accounting research from accounting practice need not be perceived unfavourably. It indicates that accounting has progressed from being a purely professional subject to one having an academic character as well. Interaction between the spheres of research and practice should enhance but not hinder each sphere's internal development.

This chapter surveys the literature to assess some common perceptions held of the role of research in accounting practice. One perception of research is that it serves to justify existing or preferred practices. The present trend towards non-judgemental academic research gives less opportunity for use in this manner. Another common perception is that research has little impact on practice. This paper proposes that a long term view should be taken of the contribution of research to practice. Historical case studies show that practical guidelines in the present day can be traced to seminal writings from an earlier era. Education is a channel that facilitates the spread of ideas and serves as a link between research and practice. Both practitioners and academics have responsibilities to lubricate the spread of ideas. These responsibilities do not entail the dilution of research standards; neither do they imply the uncritical acceptance of research findings. An incorporation of the other in each institution's mindset can establish better communication links between the two. Such a link can bring about a mutually enriching relationship between research and practice.

REFERENCES

Abdel-khalik, A.R. (1981). How Academic Research should be Restructured for Impact, in Buckley, J.W. ed., The Impact of Accounting Research on Policy and Practice, Proceedings of the Arthur Young Roundtable Conference, pp. 157–185

Abdel-khalik, A.R. and Ajinkya, B.B. (1979). *Empirical Research in Accounting*. Accounting Education Series, 4, American Accounting Association

American Accounting Association, Committee on the Future Structure, Content, and Scope of Accounting Education (1986). Future Accounting Education: Preparing for the Expanding Profession. *Issues in Accounting Education*, 1, 1, pp. 169–195

Ball, R. and Foster, G. (1982). Corporate Financial Reporting: A Methodological Review of Empirical Research. *Journal of Accounting Research*, 20, Supplement, pp. 161–234

Barden, H.G. (1975). The Trouble with Accounting Research. *Journal of Accountancy*, 139, 1, pp. 58–65

Bedford, N.M. (1978). The Impact of *A Priori* Theory and Research on Accounting Practice, in Abdel-khalik A.R. and T.F. Keller eds., *The Impact of Accounting Research on Practice and Disclosure*, Durham: Duke University Press, pp. 2–31

Birkett, W.P. and Walker, R.G. (1972). Professional Ideas on Research in Accounting: Australia, 1930–49. *Abacus*, 8, 1, pp. 35–60

Chambers, R.J. (1966). *Accounting, Evaluation and Economic Behaviour.* Englewood Cliffs, New Jersey: Prentice-Hall

Christenson, C. (1983). The Methodology of Positive Accounting. *The Accounting Review*, 58, 1, pp. 1–22

Cowley, W.H. (1939). European Influences upon American Higher Education. *Educational Record*, Vol XX

Dyckman, T.R. and Zeff, S.A. (1984). Two Decades of the Journal of Accounting Research. *Journal of Accounting Research*, 22, 1, pp. 225–297

Edwards, E.O. and Bell, P.W. (1961). *The Theory and Measurement of Business Income.* University of California Press CA

Flint, C. and Shaw, J.C. (1981). Accounting Research from the Perspective of Practice. In M. Bromwich and A. Hopwood eds., *Essays in British Accounting Research*, London: Pitman

Gambling, T.R. (1987). Accounting for Rituals. *Accounting, Organisations and Society*, 12, 4, pp. 319–329

Jaenicke, H.R. (1970). Accounting for Restricted Stock Plans and Deferred Stock Plans. *The Accounting Review*, 45, 1, pp. 115–128

Ijiri, Y. (1975). *Theory of Accounting Measurement.* American Accounting Association

Institute of Certified Public Accountants of Singapore (1984). *Preface to Statements of Accounting Standard.* Singapore: ICPAS

Kindleberger, C.P. (1989). How Ideas Spread among Economists. In Coats, A.W. and Collander, D.C. eds., *The Spread of Economic Ideas*, Cambridge: Cambridge University Press

Lee, T. (1989). Education, Practice and Research in Accounting: Gaps, Closed Loops, Bridges and Magic Accounting. *Accounting and Business Research*, 19, 75, pp. 237–253

Lembke, V.C. (1970). Some Considerations in Accounting for Divisive Reorganisations. *The Accounting Review*, 45, 3, pp. 458–464

Lev, B. and Ohlson, J.A. (1982). Market-Based Empirical Research in Accounting: A Review, Interpretation, and Extension. *Journal of Accounting Research*, 20, Supplement, pp. 249–331

Mautz, R.K. (1974). Where Do We Go From Here? *The Accounting Review*, 49, 2, pp. 353–368.

Mautz, R.K. (1978). Discussion. In Abdel-khalik, A.R. and Keller, T.F. eds., *The Impact of Accounting Research on Practice and Disclosure*, Durham: Duke University Press

Mautz, R.K. and Gray, J. (1970). Some Thoughts on Research Needs in Accounting. *Journal of Accountancy*, 130, 3, pp. 54–62

Peasnell, K.V. and Williams, D.J. (1986). Ersatz Academics and Scholar-saints: The Supply of Financial Accounting Research. *Abacus*, 22, 2, pp. 121–135

Sterling, R.R. (1973). Accounting Research, Education and Practice. *Journal of Accountancy*, 136, 3, pp. 44–52

Watts, R.L. and Zimmerman, J.L. (1979). The Demand for and Supply of Accounting Theories: The Market for Excuses. *The Accounting Review*, 54, 2, pp. 273–305

Wheeler, J.T. (1970). Accounting Theory and Research in Perspective. *The Accounting Review*, 45, 1, pp. 1–10

Whittington, G. (1981). The Role of Research in Standard-Setting: The Case of Inflation Accounting. In M. Bromwich and A. Hopwood, eds., *Essays in British Accounting Research*, London: Pitman

Whittington, G. (1987). Positive Accounting: A Review Article. *Accounting and Business Research*, 17, 68, pp. 327–336

Wolk, H.I. and Briggs, R.W. (1975). Accounting Research, Professors, and Practitioners: a Perspective. *International Journal of Accounting*, 10, 2, pp. 47–56

Zeff, S.A. (1972). *Forging Accounting Principles in Five Countries: A History and an Analysis of Trends*, Champaign: Stipes Publishing Co

3 Capital Markets Research in Accounting

Andrew Lee

3.1 INTRODUCTION

In the last two to three decades, research in financial accounting has undergone revolutionary changes both as to objectives, methodologies, as well as underlying philosophies. To see this, one need only pick up an issue of *The Accounting Review* of the early 1960s and contrast the papers therein with those of another issue of the late 1980s. Much of the revolution has to do with a shift in research paradigm to one that links accounting in some way to security prices, a body of research that has come to be popularly known as market-based accounting research or capital markets research in accounting.[1]

This chapter presents an overview of that research. The goal is to provide readers with a synopsis of the studies carried out, together with some discussion of the objectives, theory and motivation behind those studies, the lessons learned and the directions, as offered by some researchers, for future research. As such, the presentation is necessarily brief and does not give a detailed account and evaluation of each and

---

[1] The meaning of the term 'market-based accounting research', coined by Lev and Ohlson (1982), is widely understood to mean research in accounting and its relation to capital markets. A less ambiguous term might be 'capital markets research in accounting', which is the term used by Bernard (1989).

every study done using this research paradigm; in fact, many important studies have been excluded.[2]

The overview begins with an examination of the evolution of empirical accounting research in the late 1960s. The thrust then was on the information content of accounting earnings numbers. This was followed some 10 years later by research on the economic consequences of accounting choice. In the 1980s, the focus shifted towards studies on the informational (in)efficiency of financial markets as well as the role of accounting in equity valuation. The state of financial accounting research at the turn of this decade and the disappointment expressed over its contribution to practice and policy-making are then evaluated together with suggestions for future research.

3.2 THE BIRTH OF EMPIRICAL RESEARCH IN ACCOUNTING

Prior to the mid 1960s, research in financial accounting was largely normative, adopting an axiomatic approach to the development of theoretical frameworks. Such were the works of Paton and Littleton (1940), Edwards and Bell (1961), Sprouse and Moonitz (1962), Chambers (1966) and Ijiri (1967), among others. The major concern confronting accountants and regulators then was the extreme diversity of accounting rules and disclosures used by business enterprises in reporting their financial results and position, and the corresponding need, driven perhaps by political considerations (for example, to protect naive investors), to narrow this diversity by restricting firms' choices of accounting rules to those that are deemed superior or optimal. One major issue that accounting standard setters had to contend with then was whether the historical cost accounting model should be abandoned in favour of some current cost model.

The normative approach usually begins with some notion of 'true' economic income or financial position of a firm and accounting rules should attempt to capture that 'truth'. The set of rules that best portrays the 'true' picture of the firm's position would be the preferred or superior set. It is not difficult to see why the normative approach quickly came under heavy criticism, for not only were some of the arguments supporting certain preferred set of accounting rules theoretically deficient but it seemed possible, under the approach, to render just about any set of accounting rules as optimal, sometimes even under the same set of basic postulates. The variety of equally superior rules was seen as a hindrance

---

[2] Interested readers are referred to numerous excellent review papers and books on the literature. See for example, Gonedes and Dopuch (1974), Foster (1980), Lev and Ohlson (1982), Ball and Foster (1982), Brown (1987), Griffin (1987), Beaver (1989, chapter 6), Bernard (1989), Dopuch (1989) and White, Sondhi and Fried (1994, chapter 4).

to accounting's role of attesting to the 'truth', for how could different income figures calculated using different rules be all representative of the 'truth'? As such, financial statements presented must be regarded as meaningless and of no use to investors. In Canning's (1929) words:

> 'What is set out as a measure of net income can never be supposed to be a fact in any sense at all except that it is a figure that results when the accountant has finished applying the procedures which he adopts.'

Alternative accounting rules being incorrigible, the normative paradigm soon fell out of favour in academic circles due to its lack of scientific rigour and testability. Overwhelmed by pressure from theorists, the Accounting Principles Board in the United States believed that research might well be the answer to form a more objective basis for selecting optimal or superior accounting rules.

As Dopuch (1989) describes, it was against this backdrop that the University of Chicago launched its annual accounting research conference series in 1966 with the objective of promoting empirical research in accounting and the use of empirical evidence to evaluate the relative superiority of alternative accounting rules. Empirical research was also facilitated in part by advancements in finance theory (notably the efficient markets hypothesis and modern portfolio and asset pricing theories) as well as by the availability to researchers, for the first time, of machine-readable data on firms' security prices and accounting income numbers. Two years later in 1968, two papers were published in the *Journal of Accounting Research* that soon became two of the most influential papers in accounting: Ball and Brown's (1968) paper on the association between abnormal stock returns and unexpected income and Beaver's (1968) paper on stock price and trading volume behaviour surrounding earnings announcements.

3.2.1 Ball and Brown (1968) and Beaver (1968) studies

The methodology employed by Ball and Brown (1968) and Beaver (1968) was not entirely new; the so-called event study methodology was first used by Fama, Fisher, Jensen and Roll (1969) to assess the information content of stock splits. However, the motivation for the studies was novel, at least at that time.

Ball and Brown attempted to test the claim expounded by normative accounting theorists then that accounting income numbers were meaningless because of the diverse accounting rules available to recognize and record income. By constructing models of what the securities market expected incomes of firms to be, Ball and Brown then investigated how the firm's stock price reacted when those income expectations turned out to be false. An observed revision of stock prices associated with the release of income numbers which deviated from the market's expectations of what those numbers should be would provide evidence that the information contained in those income numbers were useful to investors in their decision-making, and not meaningless as claimed.

The event study methodology used by Ball and Brown essentially involved drawing a sample of firms that announced their annual earnings figures and pooling together these announcements across firms and over time.[3] The announcements were then aligned with respect to their announcement dates, with the announcement date being labeled as time 0 on an event time line. The behaviour of security prices of those firms prior to and after time 0 was then studied. Since factors other than income numbers could potentially affect stock prices, Ball and Brown subtracted from the firms' stock returns a suitable portion that was due to market wide effects. More precisely, Ball and Brown used the market model as the equilibrium model of expected returns to proxy for market wide effects on firms' security prices. The market model of equilibrium expected returns is given by:

$$R_{it} = \alpha_i + \beta_i R_{mt} + \varepsilon_{it}$$

where R_{it} is the stock return on firm i for month t, R_{mt} is the return on some overall stock market index for month t, α_i and β_i are parameters estimated from a regression of monthly stock returns of each firm on monthly returns on the market index using data pertaining to that firm for a suitable number of months prior to month t, and ε_{it} is the residual stock return on firm i for month t after abstracting from market wide effects. The residual stock return obtained as a result of this exercise is popularly known as abnormal or unexpected return.

To estimate how much actual accounting income numbers deviated from the market's expectations of what those numbers would be, Ball and Brown used two alternative models of what the market expected income of each firm to be. In the first model, the year-on-year change in a firm's accounting income was assumed to be dependent on the year-on-year change in average accounting income of all firms (other than the firm whose expected income was being estimated). This involved estimating, by ordinary least squares, the coefficients from the linear regression of the change in, say, firm j's income for year s (ΔI_{js}) on the change in the average income for year s of all firms (other than firm j) in the market (ΔM_{js}) using data up to the end of the previous year (year $t-1$):

$$\Delta I_{js} = \hat{a}_{1j} + \hat{a}_{2j} \Delta M_{js} + \hat{u}_{js} \qquad \text{for } s = 1,2,\ldots,t-1,$$

where the hats denote estimates. The expected year-on-year change in

---

[3] It is now well recognized that pooling announcements across firms and over time introduces the problem of cross-sectional and time series dependence which can potentially lead to misleading inferences (see Collins and Dent, 1984; Bernard, 1987). Nonetheless, Ball and Brown's results have been shown to be extremely robust to methodological refinements aimed at overcoming this problem.

income for firm j in year t is then given by the regression prediction using the change in the average income for the market in year t:

$$\Delta \hat{I}_{jt} = \hat{a}_{1j} + \hat{a}_{2j} \Delta M_{jt}$$

The unexpected income change of firm j for year t is the actual income change minus the expected income change:

$$u_{jt} = \Delta I_{jt} - \Delta \hat{I}_{jt}$$

The second model to estimate unexpected income simply assumed that it equals the year-on-year actual change in income. This is equivalent to assuming that accounting incomes follow a random walk process without drift.[4] Having estimated unexpected incomes, Ball and Brown then partitioned the observations into two groups – those with positive unexpected incomes ('good news'); and those with negative unexpected incomes ('bad news') – and tracked the behaviour of the average abnormal returns of each group around the month of the earnings announcement.

The results obtained in Ball and Brown's study are interesting: in the *month* that a firm announced its annual income numbers, its stock price *increased* on average by about 1% over and above any effect of market wide movement in stock prices if the income announced *exceeded* the market's expectation ('good news'), it decreased on average also by about 1% if the income announced fell short of market's expectation ('bad news'). Ball and Brown therefore concluded that

> 'the information contained in the annual income number is useful in that it is related to stock prices.'

If stock prices moved on the announcement of firms' income numbers, it is likely that investors acted on those numbers, which in turn suggests that those numbers were useful to investors. Accounting income numbers are thus said to possess information content.

Beaver (1968) adopted a similar approach as that of Ball and Brown in that he examined whether investors reacted to earnings announcements as reflected in the volume and price movements of stocks around the time of the announcements. If announcements of earnings are accompanied by unusual movements in trading volume or price changes in the firms' stock, then it suggests that investors do in fact utilize earnings information for their decision-making, implying that earnings numbers have information content. However, while Ball and Brown separated their sample into good news firms versus bad news firms, Beaver was unconcerned with the nature of the news and hence only looked at whether there was a stock price change surrounding announcement of earnings numbers, regardless of the direction of that change. In addition, Beaver also examined whether the earnings announcement had any impact on the volume of stock traded.

---

[4] For an exposition of the random walk process, see for example, Greene, 1993.

Beaver's evidence shows that the average trading volume in the week of earnings announcement is about 33% higher than the average trading volume during non-announcement weeks. This led Beaver to conclude that

> 'investors do shift portfolio positions at the time of the earnings announcement, and this shift is consistent with the contention that earnings reports have information content.'

In addition, Beaver also found that the average magnitude of absolute stock price changes in the week of earnings announcement is about 67% higher than the average magnitude during non-announcement weeks, and similarly concluded that earnings reports appeared to have informational value.

3.2.2 After Ball and Brown and Beaver

The Ball and Brown and Beaver studies ushered in a new research paradigm in accounting and got accounting researchers excited about their prospects for the 1970s. Many papers followed from where Ball and Brown and Beaver left (see for example, Beaver, 1972; Beaver and Dukes, 1972, 1973; among others.) Bernard (1989) describes this period as a bull run of the early 1970s in the market for capital markets research.

The euphoric expectations arose largely from the belief that accounting researchers had now found a rigorous approach by which policy-makers could determine the *desirability* of alternative accounting rules. For instance, Beaver and Dukes (1972) examined the association between stock returns and earnings computed using either the deferral or the flow-through method of accounting for inter-period tax allocation. They found that stock returns were more highly correlated with earnings computed using the deferral method, leading them to conclude that this accounting technique provides more useful information to investors than the flow-through method.

However, this euphoria soon led to pessimism following the publication in 1974 of a study by Gonedes and Dopuch who argued that while it was possible to assess the security price *effects* of alternative accounting rules, there was no conceptual foundation for using security prices to assess the *desirability* of any given set of rules. Consider, for instance, the notion that given a choice of accounting alternatives, the one that triggers the strongest price reaction (that is, has the greatest information content) ought to be the most desirable alternative. Unfortunately, changes in stock prices invariably leave some people better off than others. Thus, deciding which is the best accounting alternative must involve judgements affecting social welfare. In Beaver's (1973) words:

> '[To] find out what method is most highly associated with security prices and report that method in the financial statements . . . is incorrect . . . The choice

among different accounting methods involves choosing among differing consequences ... Hence, some individuals may be better off under one method, while others may be better off under an alternative method ... The issue is one of social choice, which in general is an unresolvable problem.'

The bearish sentiment following Gonedes and Dopuch's (1974) review was shared by many. Among others, Kaplan (1975) suggested that the future of empirical accounting research looked rather bleak, while Bernard (1989) subsequently labelled it the Crash of 1974.

3.3 ECONOMIC CONSEQUENCES OF ACCOUNTING CHOICE

The bearish sentiment took a reversal in the late 1970s when Watts and Zimmerman (1978, 1986) rejuvenated the agenda in capital markets research by the introduction of positive theory in accounting. Researchers recognized that even though they could not assess the desirability of alternative accounting policies, they could potentially assess their wealth effects on various parties, a body of literature known as the economic consequences of accounting choice that expanded rapidly through the early 1980s.[5] Watts and Zimmerman argue that regulators impose mandatory accounting policies on firms to redistribute wealth among constituents with conflicting interests, while firm managers voluntarily switch accounting policies in order to avoid violation of debt covenants, change the political visibility of their firms' operations or alter the intertemporal quantum of managerial compensation they receive. Such actions hinge on the assumption of opportunistic behaviour on the part of self-interested parties.

Early research in economic consequences concentrated on examining stock price effects to *mandated* accounting policies and disclosures. This was particularly evident by FASB's (the United States' Financial Accounting Standards Board) sponsorship of several studies that investigated stock price reaction to proposed accounting regulations. For instance, Dukes (1978) studied the security price effects of FAS 8 on accounting for foreign currency translation, Dyckman and Smith (1979) examined the effects of oil and gas accounting standards, Abdel-khalik *et al* (1981) investigated the economic effects of FAS 13 on accounting for leases and Beaver and Landsman (1983) looked at the information contained in disclosures required by FAS 33 on accounting for price level changes.

Later studies expanded on earlier work by attempting to explain cross-sectional variation in stock price reaction to mandated accounting policy changes by linking the magnitude of reaction to several contracting

---

[5] See for example, Lev (1979), Collins and Dent (1979), Leftwich (1981), Holthausen (1981) and Holthausen and Leftwich (1983). See also Williams (Chapter 4 of this book) for a detailed discussion of positive accounting theory research.

variables expounded by Watts and Zimmerman's positive accounting theory. The studies typically hypothesize that a mandated change in accounting policy could affect firms through its impact on debt covenants, management compensation contracts and political visibility of firms.[6]

However, the rally in terms of economic consequences research did not persist for very long. Soon, researchers discovered that there was little, if any, stock price reaction to most mandated accounting policy changes. While this does not of itself dispute Watts and Zimmerman's theory that accounting policy choice may be motivated by and affect contractual relationships, it does suggest that either the stock price effects of such choice are of secondary importance[7] or that existing methodology then were simply not powerful enough to detect any stock price reaction.

If the impact of mandated policy changes on stock prices is at best small, studies that examine price reaction to *voluntary* accounting policy changes are even more problematic. First, it is extremely difficult if not impossible to determine precisely when investors came to know of a firm's voluntary change of accounting policy; this may well be some time prior to the release of the company's financial report to the public. Hence, not observing any price reaction on the release of the company's financial report detailing accounting policy changes may not necessarily mean that there are no effects; perhaps investors had already learned of the changes before the report was released. On the other hand, even if a price reaction is observed, it is difficult to link it to the factors suggested by Watts and Zimmerman. Researchers often use debt–equity ratio as a proxy for closeness to violation of debt covenants and firm size as a proxy for the firm's political visibility, but such variables may well capture some other factors totally unrelated to Watts and Zimmerman's theory.

3.4   RESEARCH ON EFFICIENT MARKETS

In the mid to late 1980s, however, there came a resurgence of research on the efficiency of financial markets. Market efficiency was a topic that occupied researchers in accounting, finance and economics for many years in the late 1960s and early 1970s. Most of the studies then concluded that the market was efficient in processing information, and that publicly available information such as historical share prices or announcements of corporate events could not be used to earn returns in excess of what could otherwise have well been earned but without any analysis of those past

---

[6] See for instance, Collins, Rozeff and Dhaliwal (1981); Leftwich (1981) and Larcker and Revsine (1983).

[7] Holthausen and Leftwich (1983), in their review of economic consequences research in accounting, hinted that 'accounting choices are [probably] not a major determinant of firm values, relative to other decisions a manager makes.'

prices or financial data.[8] So strong was the mindset about financial markets being efficient that Jensen (1978) believes 'there is no other proposition in economics which has more solid empirical evidence supporting it than the Efficient Market Hypothesis.' In a similar vein, Ball (1988) in his review paper writes that 'within a short time of Fama's (1970) influential survey, the growing body of evidence in favour of the efficient market hypothesis had emerged as one of the most consistent and influential empirical areas in economics.'

However, evidence began to surface in the 1980s that pointed to numerous anomalies in the market – the size effect, the P/E effect and what appeared to be a delayed price reaction to the announcement of accounting earnings by firms. The debate between the efficient markets camp and the irrationality of investors camp heightened with the publication of a fairly substantial amount of evidence that stock prices were excessively volatile (Shiller, 1981, 1984) and that there were abnormal returns to be made from the shrewd use of publicly available information contained in financial statements.

3.4.1 Historical development

Early studies on the efficient market hypothesis essentially considered whether security prices followed a random walk process. These included studies on autocorrelations of daily stock returns (Fama, 1965; Fisher, 1966) and studies on whether filter or technical trading rules were able to generate returns that exceeded those obtainable under a simple buy-and-hold strategy (Alexander, 1961; Fama and Blume, 1966). If the market is informationally efficient in that security prices fully reflect all available information, then past returns cannot be used to predict future returns. This would be the case if autocorrelations of stock returns are zero, or if returns from technical trading rules do not exceed those that could be obtained from an otherwise naive strategy of simply buying all stocks and holding them throughout the investment period.

The general evidence of the early studies was that there was some positive autocorrelation in daily stock returns but that the magnitudes were sufficiently small. It was also found that filter rules such as those commonly employed by technical traders did generate returns in excess of those generated by a simple buy-and-hold strategy, but the frequency of trades and the resultant high transactions costs would likely nullify any positive excess returns that might be obtained from the rules. It appears, therefore, that security prices do reflect fully all information contained in

---

[8] See Fama (1970, 1990) for reviews.

the past history of prices, at least up to the point where the marginal benefits of acting on the information do not exceed the marginal costs (Jensen, 1978).

Work on market efficiency quickly expanded to include studies on whether security prices fully reflect all publicly available information such as those contained in corporate announcements. Research in this aspect mushroomed into a cottage industry now known as event studies.[9] Although Fama, Fisher, Jensen and Roll (1969) pioneered the first event study (on stock splits), it was not until much later that researchers began to examine the implications of such studies for market efficiency. As Fama (1991) later confesses:

> 'the purpose (of the Fama, Fisher, Jensen and Roll, 1969, study) was to have a piece of work that made extensive use of the newly developed CRSP monthly NYSE file[10], to illustrate the usefulness of the file, to justify continued funding. We had no clue that event studies would become a research industry.'

Event studies now occupy a significant portion of the empirical literature in corporate finance. The body of research in this field documented significant stock price reactions to announcements of numerous events related to firms' investment decisions, financing decisions and changes in corporate control. For instance, increases in dividends were generally associated with positive stock price changes and vice versa (Charest, 1978; Ahrony and Swary, 1980; Asquith and Mullins, 1983), new issuance of common stock generally resulted in stock price declines (Asquith and Mullins, 1986; Masulis and Korwar, 1986) and mergers and takeovers generally yielded large gains for shareholders of the target firms (Mandelker, 1974; Dodd and Ruback, 1977; Bradley, 1980; Dodd, 1980; Asquith, 1983).

While most of these studies showed that stock prices appeared to adjust rapidly (within a day) to event announcements, the researchers were generally more concerned with plausible explanations for stock price responses *at the time* of the announcement of the event rather than with the speed of price adjustment, an issue that is potentially more relevant if the objective is to test for market efficiency. A quick response of stock prices to the event within a day or two of its announcement and no systematic response thereafter would be indication that the market efficiently processes the information contained in the announcement and investors cannot trade *after* the event is made public and still expect to earn excess returns (prices would have moved immediately following the announcement).

---

[9] Ball and Brown's (1968) and Beaver's (1968) works were also event studies where earnings announcements by firms constituted the event.

[10] This is a machine readable database of monthly closing prices of all securities traded on the New York Stock Exchange (NYSE). The database is maintained by the Centre for Research in Security Prices (CRSP) at the University of Chicago.

3.4.2 Why bother about market efficiency?

If efficient markets research had concentrated simply on tests of technical trading rules or responses of stock prices to announcements of corporate events, there may not have been as much debate on the subject as there has been. A large part of the debate on market efficiency actually comes from accountants and their research. There are at least three major reasons why accountants who produce financial statement data and investors who use those data are interested in and concerned about whether financial markets are efficient.

First, almost all of the empirical studies in accounting in the 1960s and 1970s since the time of Ball and Brown invariably adopt as a maintained hypothesis the efficiency of markets with respect to publicly available information. When Ball and Brown observe stock price reactions at the time of earnings announcements that are correlated with whether the earnings are favourable or unfavourable and conclude thereupon that earnings numbers are useful to investors, they implicitly assume that investors know how to evaluate earnings information in a rational way and see earnings increases as reflecting true future cash flow increases (and vice versa). Without such an assumption, it would be impossible to draw any conclusion from the empirical result that earnings changes are positively correlated with stock price changes. Indeed, one can conceivably argue that investors may well be irrational, naive or functionally fixated on accounting income numbers so that they (mistakenly) bid prices up upon observing earnings increases even if the increases are entirely cosmetic and devoid of cash flow implications.

Studies on economic consequences of accounting policy choice also assume that markets are efficient and investors process information rationally. If a study on the stock price effect of an accounting policy change reveals no such effect and a conclusion is drawn that the change does not matter to constituent parties, it implicitly assumes that investors can 'see through' the accounting change and know how to disentangle the cash flow effects arising from it.

A second reason why market efficiency is of concern to accountants is that market efficiency implies the substance rather than the form of accounting disclosures may be the more important policy issue. This has vital implications for accounting standards setters. For instance, in an efficient market where prices reflect publicly available information and investors can unscramble cash flow implications of accounting numbers, it does not matter whether an item appears in the footnotes or in the body of the financial statements as long as it is reported somewhere in the annual report.[11]

---

[11] Positive theorists, however, would argue that the format of reporting can make a difference even if the market is efficient. For instance, if inclusion of an item in the financial statements results in shifts in financial variables that are inputs to a contractual agreement, wealth transfers may potentially occur.

Third, the art of fundamental security analysis such as that exemplified by the seminal work of Graham and Dodd (1934) involves the intricate process of using financial statement data to find mispriced securities. In fact, the issue of market efficiency with respect to financial statement information originated in the practice of security analysis. If the market is efficient with respect to publicly available information such as financial reports, then fundamental analysis does not pay. Yet investment houses spend enormous amounts of time and resources pouring through financial information to sieve out mispriced securities. At the same time, accounting standards setters are continually conscious of ensuring that financial reporting meets the needs of this major user group. There is little doubt that financial analysts actually help to make markets efficient for it is through their actions of exploiting mispricing situations that cause prices of securities to converge to fundamental values.[12] But the cumulative body of evidence appears to suggest that it has become increasingly difficult to accept market efficiency as an article of faith, a subject to which we shall now turn.

3.4.3   Efficient markets research in accounting

Because accountants produce a wide array of numbers in financial statements and such statements are publicly available, accounting numbers provide a fertile ground for tests of market efficiency. While event studies in corporate finance generally point to fairly rapid adjustments of stock prices to announcements of such events, numerous studies using accounting information appear to yield results contrary to market efficiency, with findings commonly suggesting that the market seems to underreact to financial statement information at the time it is initially disclosed to the public.

One of the most puzzling evidence inconsistent with the efficient market hypothesis has been the post-earnings announcement drift. Stocks which announce quarterly earnings that exceed market expectations (that is, positive unexpected earnings) tend to exhibit positive abnormal returns and vice versa for as long as six months *after* the earnings announcement date. This suggests that one can apparently earn abnormal returns by buying stocks with high (positive) unexpected earnings immediately after the earnings are announced and correspondingly selling stocks with low (negative) unexpected earnings. Foster, Olsen and Shevlin (1984), following earlier studies, reexamined a trading strategy that involves buying stocks whose unexpected earnings are in the highest decile of all firms for any given quarter and selling stocks whose unexpected earnings are in the lowest decile. They documented a mean annualized abnormal return of

---

[12] See Grossman and Stiglitz's (1980) paradox on the impossibility of informationally efficient markets.

about 25% (before transactions costs) on such a trading strategy. Five years later, Bernard and Thomas (1989) extended Foster *et al's* study and documented a lower but nonetheless substantial abnormal return of 18%.

Evidence on the post-earnings announcement drift is extensive. The drift appears robust across different samples, different time periods and different research designs. There have been more than 15 studies on the drift over the last two decades. These studies are not necessarily independent since many of them involve overlapping samples. But together, they are fairly indicative of the persistence of the phenomenon. What makes the drift phenomenon most puzzling is that it is based entirely on only one accounting measure – earnings. Among the many numbers that accountants produce in financial statements, there is probably no other number that is as widely and extensively reported, quoted and used by the financial community as the earnings number. There is therefore no doubt that earnings numbers are available publicly and at almost zero cost.[13] Moreover, since the anomaly has been publicized for a long time, one would presume that if it were due to market inefficiency, rational investors would have recognized it over time and traded away the inefficiency by now. But the phenomenon remains up to this date as evidenced in the latest studies by Ball and Bartov (1994) and Lee (1993).

Because tests of market efficiency are always joint tests of market efficiency and the equilibrium models of expected returns employed in the tests, there is always a concern in studies such as those relating to the drift that the abnormal returns simply reflect a failure to fully control for risk. However, researchers have over time undertaken much effort in their studies to resolve this issue. For instance, Bernard and Thomas (1989) attempt to evaluate this possibility by characterizing certain features of potential risk omission that would be consistent with the data. They conclude, after intensive scrutiny of the results, that it is difficult to attribute the drift to risk omission alone and that perhaps certain costs are impeding immediate response to earnings announcements or traders are not acting rationally.

If accounting earnings numbers alone can be utilized to earn abnormal returns, can other information contained in financial statements also do the same job, or perhaps even better? Ou and Penman (1989a) test precisely that. They devise a logit earnings prediction model which yields as an output a summary measure based on a large array of financial statement items as inputs:

$$\hat{P}r_{it} = [1 + \exp(-\theta' X_{it})]^{-1}$$

where X_{it} is the vector of accounting variables in the financial statements of firm i for fiscal year t, θ is the vector of estimated coefficient weights

---

[13] The cost, if any, is perhaps equivalent to the price of the daily newspaper.

applied to those variables, and $\hat{Pr}_{it}$ (hereafter called Pr) is an assessment of the probability (from zero to one) of a one-year ahead earnings increase, given the accounting attributes.

The summary measure, Pr, serves as an indicator of the direction of *future* earnings changes. To the extent that future earnings changes affect future stock price changes, knowledge of the former would be useful in predicting the latter.

Ou and Penman's model contains 16 to 18 descriptors (depending on the estimation time period) that include many of the inputs tradition-ally associated with financial statement analysis such as percentage change (over the previous year) in current ratio, percentage change in inventory turnover, percentage change in sales, return on equity, debt–equity ratio and gross margin.

Ou and Penman's strategy involves buying stocks which the model predicts are likely to experience earnings increases (Pr greater than 0.5) in the coming year and selling stocks which the model predicts are likely to experience earnings decreases (Pr less than 0.5). Depending on whether one selects stocks with extreme predicted earnings changes (that is, Pr very close to zero or one) or those with less extreme predictions (Pr very close to 0.5), the strategy yields positive abnormal returns over a two-year period in the region of 27 to 37% for predicted earnings increases and negative abnormal returns of between 2 to 42% for predicted earnings decreases. To be more confident that these abnormal returns are not due to inadequate adjustment for risk, Ou and Penman conducted numerous sensitivity tests using several known proxies for risk such as earnings–price ratios, betas, standard deviation of returns, and even firm size. The results are surprisingly robust to these tests and appear to entertain the possibility that the market underutilizes financial statement information as much as two years into the future.

Other studies indicating market inefficiency abound. Harris and Ohlson (1990) find evidence that the market underutilizes information on book values and estimated present values of oil and gas reserves. Stickel (1991) finds that analysts earnings forecast revisions are predictable based on publicly available information and trading on such predictions yields annualized abnormal returns of about 25%. Landsman and Ohlson (1990) conclude that security prices do not appear to fully impound information relating to pensions contained in footnotes to financial statements.

3.4.4 Accounting changes, window dressing and market efficiency

A major branch of accounting research associated with the study of market efficiency attempts to examine the stock price effects of window dressing activities of firms via voluntary accounting policy changes. In an efficient market, investors can 'see through' attempts by firms to 'fudge' financial statement numbers through the adoption of alternative accounting policies or window dressing techniques that have no implications for future cash flows to the firm. Investors are thus assumed to be rational and sophisticated enough to unscramble the true cash flow implications of accounting data. A firm which switches accounting policies to boost accounting earnings in the current period when in fact they have no cash flow implications should not expect its stock price to increase because investors can 'see through' the accounting change and know how to disentangle the cash flow effects, if any, arising from it. This potential observation has been labeled the 'no-effects' hypothesis as opposed to the alternative called the 'mechanistic' hypothesis (sometimes also referred to as the functional fixation hypothesis). The latter hypothesis is 'mechanistic' in the sense that investors react mechanically to (or are functionally fixated on) accounting income numbers without regard to their underlying cash flow consequences.

Early studies that attempt to discriminate between the 'no-effects' and 'mechanistic' hypotheses are generally fraught with methodological difficulties. Consider, for example, the study by Kaplan and Roll (1972) who examined the stock price effects of firms which voluntarily switch to income-increasing depreciation methods. Watts (1982) uses Kaplan and Roll's study to illustrate that the market can 'see through' accounting changes. For income-increasing switches in depreciation methods, Kaplan and Roll find no stock price reaction *at the time of* announcement of the switch (which they take to mean the first earnings announcement that incorporates the switch). On the face of it, this supports the no-effects hypothesis since the switch in depreciation methods merely boosted accounting income with no tax or other cash flow effects. However, what is disturbing is that Kaplan and Roll's study also show stock prices generally rising during the period approximately nine weeks surrounding the time of the switch and subsequently declining beginning from the 10th week after the switch. Such an observation may well be entirely consistent with investors being temporarily fooled by the cosmetic accounting change as indication of real gain in firm value and realizing their folly only many weeks later.

Whatever the findings, it is difficult to draw any meaningful conclusions from Kaplan and Roll's results for two reasons. First, as mentioned earlier, studies of voluntary switches of accounting policies suffer from the problem of not being able to determine precisely when investors came to know of the accounting switch (investors may well have come to know or infer about the switch from the firm's on-going operating or financial activities rather than on the first earnings announcement that incorporates the switch). Second, Kaplan and Roll's sample is clustered in time, so the observed stock price behaviour of switching firms may have been driven by some confounding event during that period.

Two other major studies on the 'mechanistic' hypothesis also suffer similar difficulty of interpretation as Kaplan and Roll's. Hong, Kaplan and Mandelker (1978) investigated firms which adopted the purchase method versus those which adopted the pooling-of-interest method of accounting for mergers: their study is now regarded as 'far too weak . . . . to detect market inefficiencies even if they did exist' (Bernard, 1989). Biddle and Lindahl (1982) examined firms that switched to LIFO method of accounting for inventories: their results have since been found to be due to an omitted variable bias rather than market inefficiency (see Ricks, 1986). In view of the methodological problems, little work has since been done on whether stock prices react efficiently to voluntary accounting switches (apart from several studies on LIFO switches in the 1980s).

3.4.5   Hand's (1990) study on debt–equity swaps

One recent study that rekindles interest on the subject of market responses to window-dressing activities is Hand's (1990) study on debt–equity swaps. Hand's study has been commended by Bernard (1989) for various improvements that helped overcome the methodological problems of the early studies on accounting switches:

(1) The study explicitly models market behaviour under alternatives to the efficient market hypothesis, including predictions of the timing of reactions of a 'functionally fixated' market and cross-sectional differences in the magnitudes of those reactions.
(2) It explicitly considers information that could be revealed indirectly by the announcement of a transaction or policy.
(3) It explicitly considers the financial statement impact of the accounting event under study and whether it was material.
(4) It uses two-day event intervals rather than monthly data, thereby increasing precision.
(5) It explicitly controls for the impact of other information released during the event window.

The first two improvements cited above probably constitute the most significant contribution of Hand's study. For this reason, it is useful to look at Hand's study in greater detail, in part as an illustration of the kind of innovation that accounting researchers can take pride in.[14]

A brief preview of the historical development of debt–equity swaps is in order. Prior to 1980, firms in the United States were able to realize capital gains arising from repurchasing their debt that were selling in the market at below par and yet avoid paying taxes on those gains. In 1980,

---

[14] Hand's (1990) study won the American Accounting Association's Competitive Manuscript Award for 1989.

however, the law was changed to make those gains (that is, the differences between the par values and the market values of the debt repurchased) taxable.

In 1981, Salomon Brothers, an investment bank, found a legal loophole that enabled a firm to avoid this tax if it issued equity of a market value equal to the market value of the debt repurchased. Such a transaction is known as a debt–equity swap because the firm is swapping existing debt with new equity. The accounting gain from this debt–equity swap (the swap gain) was not taxable as long as the swap was undertaken through a third-party principal acting for his own account, a role fulfilled by an investment banker. Since the swap gain is simply the realization of a previously earned but unrealized capital gain, it is considered a noneconomic event and is referred to as a paper gain. However, the gain was seen both by firms and by the financial press as one of the most important attributes of a swap. In July 1984, the US government closed the loophole by declaring such a gain (the swap gain) taxable too. But in the meantime (that is, from 1981 to 1984), the market for debt–equity swaps soared: during that period, firms used swaps to retire about US$10 billion book value of long term debt and to issue in its place US$7 billion market value of equity.

When a firm undertook a debt–equity swap, the amount of the swap gain almost always became publicly available information on the day of the swap announcement; the magnitude of the gain was either disclosed at the time the swap was announced or executed, or it could be very accurately calculated using publicly available information then. Subsequently, when the firm released its quarterly earnings figures, the swap gain would be disclosed again, this time as part of the reported accounting income for that quarter. For instance, suppose a firm released its earnings figures on 12 April 1982 for the fiscal quarter from 1 January to 31 March 1982. If a swap was announced and executed on 20 February 1982, the swap gain would be disclosed on 20 February 1982 concurrently with the swap transaction, and again on 12 April 1982 as part of reported accounting income for the quarter ended 31 March 1982.

Debt–equity swaps provide a clean test setting to discriminate between the efficient markets hypothesis (EMH) and what Hand terms as the extended functional fixation hypothesis (EFFH). Under the EFFH, the market comprises both sophisticated and unsophisticated investors and stock prices at any point in time are set by the marginal investor who may be unsophisticated. In such a case, stock prices may not fully reflect all available accounting information because the marginal unsophisticated investor is incapable of properly unscrambling the cash flow implications of accounting information. On the contrary, EMH states that stock prices fully reflect all available information and implies that stock prices are set as if *all* investors are sophisticated. In the context of debt–equity swaps, sophisticated investors would have recognized the swap gain at the initial swap announcement. The EMH therefore predicts that there will be no stock price reaction to the reannouncement of the gain as part of the swap quarter's earnings. On the other hand, the EFFH predicts that there will be a reaction to the reannouncement of the gain because unsophisticated investors would not have known about the gain until the earnings announcement, at which time they would have misinterpreted it as a real gain rather as just a realization of a previously unrealized capital gain.

Hand designs his tests so as to control for unexpected earnings excluding the swap gain, since it is reasonable to expect that both sophisticated and unsophisticated investors will also react to the unexpected earnings of the firm that are due to the firm's operations apart from the swap transaction. Hand further adopts the proportion of a firm's stock held by noninstitutional investors as a proxy for the probability that the marginal investor of the firm's stock is an unsophisticated investor. The higher the proportion of a firm's stock held by noninstitutional investors, the more likely the marginal investor of that firm's stock is an unsophisticated investor. Hand finds a significant positive reaction to the swap gain on the date the gain is reannounced as part of the quarter's earnings. Moreover, the magnitude of the stock price reaction to the swap gain is greater for firms with a greater proportion of noninstitutional investors. Hand is careful to qualify his results by adding that 'theoretical issues concerning the equilibrium characteristics of markets containing both sophisticated and unsophisticated investors remain unexplored' in his study. Nonetheless, his findings suggest that the extended functional fixation hypothesis whereby some investors are fooled by cosmetic accounting gains cannot be entirely ruled out.

3.4.6 A new way to think about markets?

The notion that there could be unsophisticated investors in the market in fact occupied the discussion in economics and finance in the 1980s. Shiller (1984), for instance, argues that fashions and fads affect financial markets in much the same way that they affect clothings, food or other aspects of lifestyle. Kyle (1985) and Black (1986) introduce the concept of noise traders who trade in financial markets based on factors other than fundamental values. Noise traders may trade for liquidity reasons[15], or because of some fashionable or faddish idea in the market (such as mutual funds, gold or takeovers) or because they see others trade and decide to join the bandwagon in the hope of making abnormal returns (trend chasers). They may even trade so as to deliberately create a trend for others to follow (see Black, 1990). Or they may trade on the latest (most recent) information about fundamental values but to the exclusion of all

---

[15] Black (1986), however, argues that this reason alone cannot plausibly explain the phenomenal trading volumes we see on financial markets in recent years.

previous information ('recency effect') and in so doing, overreact to the new information (see DeBondt and Thaler, 1985, 1987).

Whatever their reasons, when noise traders trade in sufficient numbers for reasons unrelated to fundamentals, they can cause prices to deviate from fundamental values. Delong, Shleifer, Summers and Waldman (1990) model a market in which noise traders not only cause prices to deviate from fundamental values but do so for a long time, thereby surviving in equilibrium. Noise traders can also earn abnormal returns on average not because they have better information (they have none to begin with) but because their actions create trading risk which they themselves (and all other traders) then take on. Such a concept of risk, which Delong *et al* term noise trader risk, departs from and extends the traditional notion of fundamental or asset risk that is expounded in classical economics and finance.

If noise traders trade and survive in the long run and prices are unbiased estimates of fundamental values for only brief moments of time, it may be no wonder that stock prices do not respond instantaneously and unbiasedly to publicly available information as the recent market efficiency studies have found.

3.4.7 Summary

To be sure, the debate on market efficiency will continue. But as Bernard (1989) puts it, 'progress in this literature will not come easily, because the studies will be difficult to decipher.' Research that presents trading strategies capable of earning abnormal returns may simply fail to properly control for risk, while others that purport to resolve anomalies may simply be based on tests with low power.

Extreme claims should be avoided. For instance, any study that documents profitable trading strategies must recognize that there are indeed sophisticated investors out there who are smart enough to detect fact from fiction and the valuable from the vacuous. Ball (1988) is right in saying that 'stock markets are paradigm examples of competition and thus of 'efficiency' in using information.'

On the other hand, studies that blindly reject profitable strategies in favour of market efficiency must realize that there are also some (unsophisticated) investors out there who can be 'fooled' at least some of the time, or that there are certain perhaps as yet unexplored impediments to exploiting the perceived profits. As an illustration of an extreme claim, Bernard (1989) advises would-be researchers on this subject:

> 'I'm not sure I would risk my research time on the assumption that within a matter of hours, the market can become aware of a possible change in mandated accounting policy, predict the financial statement impacts of the change, determine which firms' bond covenants would be most vulnerable to the change, and estimate the change in expected renegotiation costs.'

In a similar vein, Professor James Ohlson of Columbia University, who has conducted numerous studies demonstrating how the market fails to impound accounting information contained in financial reports, was once posed the classical rhetoric: the market 'sees through' all accounting (gimmicks). To which he responded in a quote taken from Penman (1991): 'I wonder what on earth it sees?'

3.5 ACCOUNTING NUMBERS AND EQUITY VALUATION

While areas such as economic consequences of accounting choice and efficient markets did attract attention of accounting researchers for some time, much of the empirical research in the 1980s continued to be dedicated to examining the role of accounting in equity valuation. The emphasis of this line of research has been geared towards identifying the relation between financial statement variables, such as accounting income, and security prices. However, as several academics later note, the contribution of this research to accounting practice has been limited (see Bernard, 1989; Dopuch, 1989; Lev, 1989).

3.5.1 The price–earnings relation

Research on the role of accounting in equity valuation can be broadly classified into two categories. In the first category, the research objective is to investigate whether and to what extent accounting earnings (and other accounting numbers) are associated with *contemporaneous* movements in security prices (a study of the *explanatory* role of accounting numbers). In the second category, the research objective is to investigate whether and to what extent accounting earnings (and other accounting numbers) can be used to predict *future* movements in security prices (a study of the *predictive* role of accounting numbers). Both cases involve some characterization of a relation that maps accounting earnings (or other accounting numbers) onto stock prices.

Studies examining the association between accounting earnings and contemporaneous movements in stock prices are commonly referred to as association studies. Ball and Brown (1968) can be viewed as the pioneer and most primitive study in this area. Ball and Brown assume a very simple model of the price–earnings relation where stock price changes depend only on the sign or direction of unexpected earnings: positive unexpected earnings are associated with stock price increases while negative unexpected earnings are associated with stock price decreases.

In the ensuing decade following Ball and Brown, hardly any study was done to improve on this naive price–earnings relation until 1979 when Beaver, Clarke and Wright extended the research to investigate not just the sign but also the magnitude of unexpected earnings and its association with stock returns. Even then, Beaver, Clarke and Wright (1979) examined only rank correlations between the magnitude of unexpected earnings and stock returns and avoided any specific functional form on the price–earnings relation.

Beaver, Clarke and Wright used a portfolio approach in their research design whereby firms are assigned to 25 portfolios of approximately equal size based on their relative magnitudes of unexpected earnings. To estimate firms' unexpected earnings, Beaver, Clarke and Wright used two alternative models identical to the ones used by Ball and Brown, except that in the case of the random walk model, a drift term was added. Firms with the lowest (most negative) unexpected earnings are assigned to portfolio 1, firms with the next lowest unexpected earnings are assigned to portfolio 2, and so on until portfolio 25, which contains firms with the highest (most positive) unexpected earnings. For each portfolio, the mean unexpected earnings (over all firms in that portfolio) is then computed. Also computed for each portfolio is the mean abnormal return over a period of 12 months ending in the month in which the annual earnings numbers are assumed to be announced. Beaver, Clarke and Wright assumed this to be the third month of the subsequent fiscal year of the firm concerned. Although not precise, this is the month in which the majority of firms are likely to have announced their annual earnings numbers.

Beaver, Clarke and Wright then examined the rank correlation between the mean unexpected earnings and mean abnormal returns across the 25 portfolios. The test was performed and the rank correlation computed separately for each year. Depending on the model of unexpected earnings used, the average rank correlation (over years) varied between 0.66 and 0.74 (see table 5 of Beaver *et al*). The results suggest that there exists a fairly strong positive association between unexpected earnings and contemporaneous stock returns.

Beaver, Lambert and Morse (1980) extended Beaver, Clarke and Wright's work further by proposing for the first time a specific functional form for the price–earnings relation. In particular, they assumed that stock returns are proportional to percentage changes in earnings:

$$\frac{\Delta P_{it}}{P_{it-1}} = \rho \frac{\Delta E_{it}}{E_{it-1}}$$

where E_{it} is earnings of firm i for year t and ρ is the proportionality factor which Beaver, Lambert and Morse assumed to be constant across firms and over time.

Although Beaver, Lambert and Morse opened the door to a more formal characterization of the price–earnings relation, their study was, however, not motivated by accounting's role in security valuation. In fact, they asserted that only permanent (long run) earnings are relevant to valuation and hence captured in prices, and accounting earnings measure such permanent earnings with error. The consequence of this is that stock prices tend to lead accounting earnings because the former capture cash flow implications of economic events as they occur, whereas the latter capture them only with a lag. Stock prices can therefore be used to predict future earnings, an implication which Beaver, Lambert and Morse then took pains not only to test but also to show how earnings forecasts based on past stock price movements were able to outperform earnings forecasts based on past earnings alone (such as those that use traditional time series models).

Research on the price–earnings relation then took a twist in two ways. First, the assumption adopted by Beaver, Lambert and Morse that the proportionality factor linking stock returns and earnings (which was later termed the 'earnings response coefficient') is constant across firms and over time was relaxed as researchers began to study how this proportionality factor might vary with certain characteristics of the firm, such as the information environment of the firm and the extent to which earnings in the current period are expected to persist in future periods. Second, researchers began to extend the price–earnings relation to include other financial statement variables as well. Examples of these other variables include cash flows and accruals, and inflation-adjusted earnings numbers.[16]

3.5.2 Earnings response coefficients

Kormendi and Lipe (1987) were perhaps the first to improve on the specification of the price–earnings relation by examining how the proportionality factor linking stock returns to unexpected earnings might vary according to how much of the current earnings surprise is expected to persist in future periods (a characteristic later dubbed as 'earnings persistence'). The basic tenet of Kormendi and Lipe's study (and the numerous studies that followed) is that stock returns are related to unexpected earnings (scaled by beginning of period stock price[17]) in a linear form:

$$\frac{\Delta P_{it}}{P_{it-1}} = \gamma \frac{UE_{it}}{P_{it-1}}$$

and that the magnitude of the relation, as measured by γ, varies across firms depending on the persistence of earnings. If investors believe that a

---

[16] Cash flows and accruals will be examined in greater detail in the later section. For inflation-adjusted earnings, readers are referred to the numerous studies done: see Beaver, Christie and Griffin (1980), Beaver, Griffin and Landsman (1982), Bublitz, Frecka and McKeown (1985), Bernard and Ruland (1987), among others.

[17] Christie (1987) shows that beginning of period stock price is the proper deflator to use in studies that regress stock returns on accounting variables.

firm's current earnings surprise (unexpected earnings) will persist in the future (that is, earnings persistence is high), then they will attach a higher value to each dollar of that earnings surprise (that is, a higher γ) and vice versa. Kormendi and Lipe use an autoregressive time series model to characterize each firm's earnings stream and then estimate the firm's earnings persistence as a function of the autoregressive coefficients from the time series model. They find evidence consistent with their hypothesis, that is, firms with higher earnings persistence experience greater stock price responses per unit of current earnings surprise. To some extent, this result is fairly intuitive. One would generally think that stock prices would react more strongly to earnings changes that are expected to be permanent (that is, the new level of earnings is expected to continue in the future) rather than changes that are expected to be only transitory.

The coefficient, γ, has come to be known as the earnings response coefficient. Kormendi and Lipe's study subsequently led to numerous other related studies on earnings response coefficients – notably Collins and Kothari (1989), Easton and Zmijewski (1989), and Biddle and Seow (1991) among others. The overall evidence in these studies show that the earnings response coefficient:

(1) Increases with earnings persistence, growth opportunities and size of the firm (where size is used as an indicator of how well informed investors are about the firm).
(2) Decreases with the risk of the firm and the risk-free interest rate.

Studies on earnings response coefficients, however, soon reached a stage where motivation for the research became questionable for at least two reasons. First, as Bernard (1989) observes, it was unclear whether variables that 'explained' differences in earnings response coefficients across firms and over time were fundamental drivers of the coefficients or were simply correlated with some unidentified omitted factor. Second, researchers were unsure how an appreciation of the factors that 'explained' earnings response coefficients could enhance our understanding of the role of accounting in equity valuation. Knowing how earnings response coefficients vary with the factors does not necessarily tell us how it is to be used to determine equity values.

3.5.3   Cash flows versus accruals

Another branch of research that springs from the early studies on the price–earnings relation is in the area of cash flows and accruals. The accrual process has been the hallmark of modern day accounting for a long time. Naturally, debate among accountants has almost always centered on or culminated in a discussion of whether the accrual process provides useful information about an enterprise's future cash flows and financial performance. Despite numerous (often vociferous) attempts by critics to crucify the accrual process in favour of cash flow accounting, the system has largely survived to this date.

Studies on the information content of cash flows and accruals are aimed at examining two issues:

(1) Whether accounting accruals provide information beyond that which is provided by cash flows from operations.
(2) Whether earnings in the form of cash flows have differential (perhaps stronger) stock price implications compared to earnings in the form of accruals.

On the first issue, studies have generally found that accruals do provide incremental information beyond cash flows from operations (see Rayburn, 1986; Wilson, 1986; Bowen, Burgstahler and Daley, 1987), that is, increases in accruals generally translate on average into upward revisions of investors' expectations about an enterprise's future cash flows. This is despite the fact that accruals are often regarded as being the product of arbitrary accounting rules as well as being highly susceptible to manipulation by managers.

On the second issue, Wilson (1987) finds that the cash and accrual components of earnings taken together provide incremental information to investors beyond that provided by earnings itself. However, Wilson's results also suggest that the market appears to attach a higher value to each dollar of earnings in the form of cash flows than to each dollar of earnings in the form of accruals. The limitation of Wilson's study, though, is that it covers only two quarters. When Bernard and Stober (1989) replicate Wilson's study on a much larger sample of 32 quarters, they do not find a similar result; instead, they find that the stock price implication of a dollar of earnings in the form of cash flows is essentially the same as the implication of a dollar of earnings in the form of accruals.

Bernard and Stober (1989) then examine whether differential stock price implications of cash flows and accruals may be contingent upon the nature of those accruals and their economic context. In particular, they progressively investigate various plausible contextual models whereby an increase in current accruals may represent either 'good news' or 'bad news', depending on whether the increase leads investors to infer that future demand for the firm's goods and services will be higher than previously expected, that current demand is lower than previously expected or that the firm is experiencing problems in collecting receivables. However, they are unable to find any evidence of differential stock price implications. They therefore conclude that either accrual information is largely anticipated by investors prior to the release of the annual report that contains such information, or differential stock price implications of cash flows and accruals require a more contextual characterization than suggested by the models they have examined.

A study that is not directly related to cash flows and accruals but nevertheless examines the information content of accounting data other than bottom line earnings is Lipe (1986). Lipe considers six components of accounting earnings – gross profit, general and administrative expense, depreciation, interest, taxes and other expenses – and their association with contemporaneous stock returns using a simple linear relation. He finds evidence that each of the six components is correlated with and explains variation in stock returns beyond that explained by aggregate earnings or the other five components.

3.5.4   The predictive role of accounting numbers

It is now well recognized in accounting circles that one of the basic objectives of financial statements is to provide useful information to present and potential investors, creditors and other users in assessing the amounts, timing and uncertainty of an enterprise's future cash flows.[18] Since an enterprise's future cash flows has bearing on the future price of its stock through the fundamental valuation principle, the practical implication of the objective from the investors' standpoint is that information in financial statements should help investors predict future stock returns.

Relative to the plethora of studies that examine the explanatory role of accounting numbers (such as the association and event studies discussed in earlier sections), the amount of work done on the predictive role of accounting numbers seems limited. Many of the early studies on the predictive role of accounting were confined to how financial statement information could be used to predict bankruptcy (see for instance, Beaver, 1966; Altman, 1968; Ohlson, 1980) or systematic risk (see Beaver, Kettler and Scholes, 1970; Bildersee, 1975).[19]

Ou and Penman's (1989a) study probably represents the first extensive yet focused attempt to conduct a broad analysis of financial statements with the view to predict stock returns. As described in Section 3.4 earlier, Ou and Penman (1989a) use a logit earnings prediction model to forecast the direction of one-year ahead earnings change and then implement a trading strategy of buying and selling stocks on the basis of that forecast. The direct implication of Ou and Penman's financial statement analysis is that the vast array of information contained in accounting statements can be used to uncover mispriced securities.

---

[18] Statement of Financial Accounting Concepts No. 1, *Objectives of Financial Reporting by Business Enterprises,* Financial Accounting Standards Board, 1978.

[19] The contention, however, has typically been that accounting information may not necessarily predict bankruptcy or systematic risk better than predictors based on market prices (see Aharony, Jones and Swary, 1980; Elgers, 1980).

Perhaps motivated by the results of their prediction study, Ou and Penman (1989b) go on to show that prices actually lag rather than lead information contained in financial statements. This is in stark contrast to Beaver, Lambert and Morse's (1980) view that accounting earnings are 'garbled' signals of value and that prices impound value not only with less error relative to accounting earnings numbers but also earlier in time. Ou and Penman (1989b) compare the ability of prices and appropriate financial statement variables to predict future earnings and find that the price changes that Beaver *et al* (1980) indicate lead earnings are actually poor earnings predictors relative to predictors based on financial statement information. This is so because current prices not only capture contemporaneous earnings changes that are permanent (that is, expected to persist in the future) but also those that are transitory (that is, not expected to persist in the future). Prices are incapable of distinguishing between the two components of earnings changes and hence will not predict future (permanent) earnings well. On the contrary, financial statement information can identify the transitory earnings components and filter them out in the prediction of future earnings.

3.5.5 The state of valuation research at the turn of the decade

Towards the end of the 1980s and the beginning of the 1990s, accounting academics began to review the research work of the last two decades with much trepidation. The review generally casts doubt over the benefit of extant research in accounting and how much it has contributed to advancements in practice. Two reasons have been generally given for this result. The first is the lack of incentives for researchers to undertake risky but more path-breaking research. The second is the general lack of appreciation of accounting research by the constituencies (notice, for instance, how long it took before the constituencies began to understand and appreciate the concept of present value in valuing bonds and other debt-related instruments in the balance sheet). Some of the comments are discussed below.

Lev (1989) in his review paper on the usefulness of earnings and earnings research over the last two decades notes how little accounting research has contributed to the enhancement of earnings usefulness or to accounting policy-making in general:

> 'What is the incremental contribution of the recent methodological improvements in the returns/earnings research to our understanding of how and to what extent earnings are used by investors? What is the contribution of such developments to the enhancement of earnings usefulness or to the deliberations of accounting policymakers? The answer seems to be – very little. To the best of my understanding, recent studies do not reveal a more significant or different role of earnings in security valuation than did the early studies.

Nor do they provide new, deeper insights into how earnings are used or should be used by investors . . . If one considers the persistence research, for example, the idea that investors react differently to the earnings of different firms and that such differential reaction is related to the future implications of earnings (persistence) is not particularly revealing. The important questions of why some earnings innovations are more persistent than others . . . , the impact of accounting techniques on persistence, and the practical issues of operationally identifying the persistent component in earnings upon announcement, are still largely unanswered. It is also doubtful whether recent returns/earnings research provides accounting policymakers with useful knowledge. The benefits of recent research developments in the returns/earnings area are, therefore, questionable, and a reexamination of this research paradigm is called for.'

Lev (1989) also laments on the poor explanatory power (as measured by statistical R^2) of almost all capital markets studies in accounting. He cites a sample of 19 studies done between 1980 and 1988 on the relationship between accounting earnings and stock returns and finds R^2 typically ranging from 1% to 10%, occasionally falling between 10 and 15% and rarely exceeding 20%.[20] Lev concludes that 'while earnings appear to be used by investors, the extent of earnings usefulness is rather limited.' He further suggests that while shortcomings in research methodology as well as investor irrationality (noise trading) may be reasons for the low explanatory power, the low quality of currently reported earnings and other financial variables, due perhaps to biases in the accounting measurement process or manipulation of reported data by managers, cannot be entirely ruled out.

Penman (1992) gives a more pointed response, which generally indicates a failure of capital markets research to address the question of how accounting information can be used to value securities:

'Up to 25 years ago, fundamental analysis was the primary focus of research in investment analysis. Correspondingly, financial accounting research embraced a measurement perspective. Fundamental analysis involves the determination of the value of securities from available information, with a particular focus on accounting information. The measurement approach in accounting evaluates accounting concepts as determinants of asset values that are measures of investment worth. Both endeavours are directed toward a basic, practical question: How does one assess how much to pay for a stock and what is the role of accounting in that assessment?

During the past 25 years, research in academia has been otherwise directed. Both traditional fundamental analysis and accounting measurement theory have been judged as *ad hoc* and lacking the theoretical

---

[20] 'Is an R^2 of 5% really low?' asks Lev (1989) in his footnote 31. Patell (1989), in his comment on Lev's (1989) review paper, quotes Roll's (1988) study who finds that on average some 13% of the variation in stock returns can be explained by contemporaneous marketwide factors and 27% can be explained by specific news releases (which includes all kinds of announcements specific to a stock and not just earnings information or, for that matter, any type of accounting information). The remaining 60% of return variation appears unexplainable. Viewed in this light, it may not be surprising that earnings information ranks so low in explaining stock returns.

foundations required of rigorous economic analysis. "Modern finance" established those foundations but has not brought the theory to the question of fundamental analysis. Rather, it has been preoccupied with relative pricing, an understanding of the relationships between the prices of financial assets under conditions of no arbitrage. Asset pricing models recognize that prices covary, and this has implications for the way they are priced. The prices of derivative securities are evaluated from the price of the relevant fundamental security ... but expressions for pricing the fundamental security have not advanced much beyond the dividend discount formula.

Modern financial accounting research has not produced insights into fundamental analysis either. "Capital markets research" in the tradition of Ball and Brown (1968) has the appearance of being involved in valuation analysis because it documents relationships between prices and accounting numbers. It has, indeed, produced a set of empirical descriptions. However, it embraces .... the "information" perspective .... Under this perspective, prices are assumed to be "efficient" and accounting numbers are evaluated *by reference to prices* for their "information content" .... [F]undamental analysis, in contrast, involves the discovery of price *without reference to price*. For this task, capital markets research is misdirected.' (emphasis added)

In Penman's opinion, our zeal for empirical rigour has gotten us no benefit in terms of how accounting information can be used to determine value. The standard bottom line conclusion in empirical financial accounting studies is that since stock prices are efficient, accounting numbers must be useful to investors if they are found to be correlated with price changes (returns). Beyond that, nothing is mentioned as to how investors *use* those numbers to determine value. Researchers have all along been looking to prices to 'verify' accounting numbers (that is, to show whether the numbers are useful). Penman argues that it should have been the other way round: they should be looking to accounting numbers to 'verify' prices (that is, to show whether the prices are correct). That, in essence, is fundamental analysis.

Penman (1991) goes further to comment:

'One is somewhat embarrassed when teaching a financial statement analysis course in presenting students with a large number of calculations in the form of accounting ratios (the list is little changed from 25 years ago) but giving them no indication as to how to draw them together to project firm value. The "modern" financial statement analysis course is spiced up with insights from finance – "efficient markets", beta, the CAPM, the APT ... Abnormal returns and cumulative abnormal returns ... abnormal performance indices, standardized unexpected earnings, and earnings response coefficients! What is a student – or anyone – supposed to do with these? ...

When you buy or sell a stock, do you want to know about the Arbitrage Pricing Theory? No, you want to know how much the stock is worth.'

Penman's remarks probably epitomizes the ironical state of accounting research at the turn of this decade – we thought we have arrived but we are still far from the destination.

Despite the somewhat dismal outlook, the very same academics have suggested there is hope for the future and have indicated several potential directions for future research, a subject to which we shall now turn.

3.6 POTENTIAL FOR FUTURE RESEARCH

In the opinion of some researchers, the area that holds the greatest potential for future research is that which leads to a better understanding of the role of accounting in valuation. In recent years, some groundwork has already been established in this regard and future work can build on this foundation.

Notably, Ou and Penman (1989a, 1989b) have provided evidence of how information in financial statements can be used to predict security performance. Ou and Penman's search for the set of financial statement variables that can be used to predict future earnings changes and hence stock returns was understandably very mechanical and not supported by any theoretical exposition as to why those variables 'worked'. They did this presumably to avoid any criticism that the variables were chosen with hindsight. Future research may potentially lie in understanding why those variables work the way they do and why certain variables work better than others. This can go a long way to improving our understanding of the accounting process and its role in equity valuation.

Another limitation of Ou and Penman's (1989a) analysis as noted by Penman (1992) himself is that the prediction involves only a probability estimate of the direction of one-year ahead earnings change. It does not, for instance, produce a numerical multiplier that one could then apply to current earnings to infer value, much like the price–earnings multiple. Analysis of how the wide array of financial statement information can be utilized to produce such a numerical multiplier would certainly be useful.

More formal modeling of the valuation process and how accounting signals fit in are also beginning to appear (see for example, Ohlson, 1988, 1989, 1990; Ryan, 1991). One of the major shortcomings of extant literature on valuation is that too much emphasis has been placed on statistical rigour and too little on the theoretical and economic underpinnings of the valuation models used. To obtain a better understanding of the role of accounting in valuation will require knowledge of how the accounting system works and how signals about future values are captured in the accounting process.

Bernard (1989) gives several suggestions on the path to take for future research in this area. First, researchers must end reliance on simple, naive models of valuation, especially those which assume that returns can be explained simply by an additive combination of accounting variables without regard to precisely what those variables communicate about the economic status of the firm. In Bernard's words:

> 'In the area of valuation, a substantial amount of work appears to have been guided by the philosophy that the accounting system produces only one number – earnings – that tracks performance with error. As a result, we have probably overinvested in analyses of the details of the simple returns–earnings regression without considering a richer information set. Even when other information has been introduced, it has almost inevitably been done by adding regressors to that same linear returns–earnings regression and observing how quickly (or slowly) the R-squareds rise; in most contexts, such an approach is naive.'

Second, researchers should consider sacrificing large sample sizes and sophisticated statistics and focus instead on small samples, perhaps within an industry or group of related industries. Small samples can potentially lead to 'less noisy' results and provide a deeper understanding of the relation between accounting variables and equity values.

Lev (1989), noting that the efficient markets framework appears now to be too restrictive, suggests that empirical studies of contemporaneous correlations of accounting variables and stock prices should be extended to include explicit tests of the predictive ability of financial statement information. Studies such as Harris and Ohlson (1990) and Ou and Penman (1989a) are in that direction. Lev (1989) also suggests research on the quality of earnings and on how financial information is actually used by investors. The latter can potentially provide insights as to how improvements in the measurement and reporting of earnings can be done.

In summarizing the implications of empirical research in financial accounting for financial statement analysis, White, Sondhi and Fried (1994) calls for an understanding of the nature of the work of the financial analyst:

> '[A]ccounting research has clearly *not* proven that financial analysis is a futile exercise. On the contrary, it is trying to get a better understanding of its *modus operandi*. While the financial markets have become increasingly sophisticated in recent years, we believe that superior financial analysis is still rewarding. We advance three arguments for this belief:
> (1) An inability to understand the impact of alternative accounting methods places the investor at a competitive disadvantage in a world of increasingly sophisticated analytic techniques. Knowledge of the techniques may give him the advantage.
> (2) Particularly with respect to smaller, less intensively researched companies, market efficiency cannot be taken for granted.
> (3) Recent financial history provides many examples of companies, where, at least in retrospect, the financial markets ignored warning signals, and those left "holding the bag" suffered significant financial losses. Investors in banks and other financial intermediaries are but one example of this phenomenon.'

The prospects for future research in financial accounting are clear. As Bernard (1989) finally notes, 'beyond statistical description of the time-series and cross-sectional properties of accounting numbers, financial statement analysis texts supply little systematic evidence that could help guide a fundamental analysis. I expect that a decade from now, we'll be in a much better position to supply that guidance. And in the process of documenting how accounting numbers can be used, we'll enrich our understanding of accounting itself.'

REFERENCES

Abdel-khalik, A.R. *et al* (1981). *The Economic Effects on Lessees of FASB Statement No. 13, Accounting for Leases.* Stamford, Connecticut: Financial Accounting Standards Board

Ahrony, J., Jones, C.P. and Swary, I. (1980). An Analysis of Risk and Return Characteristics of Corporate Bankruptcy Using Capital Market Data. *Journal of Finance*, 35, pp. 1001–1016

Ahrony, J. and Swary, I. (1980). Quarterly Dividend and Earnings Announcements and Stockholders' Returns: An Empirical Analysis. *Journal of Finance*, 35, pp. 1–12

Alexander, S.S. (1961). Price Movements in Speculative Markets: Trends or Random Walks. *Industrial Management Review*, 2, pp. 7–26

Altman, E.I. (1968). Financial Ratios, Discriminant Analysis, and the Prediction of Corporate Bankruptcy. *Journal of Finance*, 23 (September), pp. 589–609

Asquith, P. (1983). Merger Bids, Uncertainty, and Stockholder Returns. *Journal of Financial Economics*, 11, pp. 51–83

Asquith, P. and Mullins, D.W. (1983). The Impact of Initiating Dividend Payments on Stocholders' Wealth. *Journal of Business*, 56, pp. 77–96

Asquith, P. and Mullins, D.W. (1986). Equity Issues and Offering Dilution. *Journal of Financial Economics*, 15, pp. 61–89

Ball, R. (1988). What Do We Know About Stock Market 'Efficiency'. *Unpublished Manuscript*, University of Rochester

Ball, R. and Bartov, E. (1994). The Earnings Event-Time Seasonal and the Calendar-Time Seasonal in Stock Returns: Naive Use of Earnings Information or Announcement Timing Effect? *Working Paper*, July

Ball, R. and Brown, P. (1968). An Empirical Evaluation of Accounting Income Numbers. *Journal of Accounting Research*, Autumn, pp. 159–178

Ball, R. and Foster, G. (1982). Corporate Financial Reporting: A Methodological Review of Empirical Research. *Journal of Accounting Research*, (Supplement), pp. 161–234

Beaver, W.H. (1966). Financial Ratios as Predictors of Failure. *Journal of Accounting Research*, (Supplement), pp. 71–111

Beaver, W.H. (1968). The Information Content of Annual Earnings Announcements. *Journal of Accounting Research*, (Autumn), pp. 67–92

Beaver, W.H. (1972). The Behaviour of Security Prices and Its Implications for Accounting Research (Methods). *The Accounting Review*, (Supplement), pp. 405–437

Beaver, W.H. (1973). What Should Be the FASB's Objectives? *Journal of Accountancy*, (August), pp. 49–56

Beaver, W.H. (1989). *Financial Reporting: An Accounting Revolution.* Englewood Cliffs, New Jersey: Prentice-Hall

Beaver, W.H., Christie, A.A. and Griffin, P.A. (1980). The Information Content of SEC Accounting Series Release No. 190. *Journal of Accounting and Economics,* (August), pp. 127–158

Beaver, W.H., Clarke, R. and Wright, W. (1979). The Association Between Unsystematic Security Returns and the Magnitude of the Earnings Forecast Error. *Journal of Accounting Research,* (Autumn), pp. 316–340

Beaver, W.H. and Dukes, R.E. (1972). Interperiod Tax Allocation, Earnings Expectations, and the Behavior of Security Prices. *The Accounting Review,* (April), pp. 320–332

Beaver, W.H. and Dukes, R.E. (1973). Delta-Depreciation Methods: Some Empirical Results. *The Accounting Review,* (July), pp. 549–559

Beaver, W.H., Griffin, P.A. and Landsman, W.R. (1982). The Incremental Information Content of Replacement Cost Earnings. *Journal of Accounting and Economics,* (July), pp. 15–40

Beaver, W.H., Kettler, P. and Scholes, M. (1970). The Association Between Market Determined and Accounting Determined Risk Measures. *The Accounting Review,* (October), pp. 654–682

Beaver, W.H., Lambert, R. and Morse, D. (1980). The Information Content of Security Prices. *Journal of Accounting and Economics,* (March), pp. 3–28

Beaver, W.H. and Landsman, W.R. (1983). *The Incremental Information Content of FAS 33 Disclosures.* Stamford, Connecticut: Financial Accounting Standards Board

Bernard, V.L. (1987). Cross-Sectional Dependence and Problems in Inference in Market-based Accounting Research. *Journal of Accounting Research,* (Spring), pp. 1–48

Bernard, V.L. (1989). Capital Markets Research in Accounting During the 1980s: A Critical Review. In: Thomas Frecka (ed.), *The State of Accounting Research as We Enter the 1990s,* University of Illinois, Urbana-Champaign, pp. 72–120

Bernard, V.L., and Ruland, R.G. (1987). The Incremental Information Content of Historical Cost and Current Cost Income Numbers: Time-Series Analyses for 1962–1980. *The Accounting Review,* (October), pp. 707–722

Bernard, V.L. and Stober, T.S. (1989). The Nature and Amount of Information Reflected in Cash Flows and Accruals. *The Accounting Review,* (October), pp. 624–652

Bernard, V.L. and Thomas, J. (1989). Post-Earnings Announcement Drift: Delayed Price Response or Risk Premium. *Journal of Accounting Research,* (Supplement), pp. 1–36

Biddle, G.C. and Lindahl, F.W. (1982). Stock Price Reactions to LIFO Adoptions: The Association Between Excess Returns and LIFO Tax Savings. *Journal of Accounting Research,* (Autumn), pp. 551–589

Biddle, G.C. and Seow, G.S. (1991). The Estimation and Determination of Associations Between Returns and Earnings: Evidence from Cross-Industry Comparisons. *Journal of Accounting, Auditing and Finance,* (Spring), pp. 183–232

Bildersee, J.S. (1975). The Association Between a Market-Determined Measure of Risk and Alternative Measures of Risk. *The Accounting Review,* 50, pp. 81–98

Black, F. (1986). Noise. *Journal of Finance,* 41, pp. 529–543

Black, F. (1990). Bluffing, *Manuscript*, Goldman Sachs Asset Management, New York, December

Bowen, R.M., Burgstahler D. and Daley, L.A. (1987). The Incremental Information Content of Accruals versus Cash Flows. *The Accounting Review*, (October), pp. 723–747

Bradley, M. (1980). Interfirm Tender Offers and the Market for Corporate Control. *Journal of Business*, 53, pp. 345–376

Brown, L.D. (1987). *The Modern Theory of Financial Reporting*. Plano, Texas: Business Publications

Bublitz, B., Frecka, T.J. and McKeown, J.C. (1985). Market Association Tests and FASB Statement No. 33 Disclosures: A Reexamination. *Journal of Accounting Research*, (Supplement), pp. 1–27

Canning, J.B. (1929). *The Economics of Accountancy*. New York: The Ronald Press

Chambers, R.J. (1966). *Accounting, Evaluation and Economic Behavior*. Englewood Cliffs, New Jersey: Prentice-Hall

Charest, G. (1978). Dividend Information, Stock Returns, and Market Efficiency. *Journal of Financial Economics*, 6, pp. 297–330

Christie, A.A. (1987). On Cross-Sectional Analysis in Accounting Research. *Journal of Accounting and Economics*, (December), pp. 231–258

Collins, D.W. and Dent, W.T. (1979). The Proposed Elimination of Full Cost Accounting in the Extractive Petroleum Industry. *Journal of Accounting and Economics*, 1, pp. 3–44

Collins, D.W. and Dent, W.T. (1984). A Comparison of Alternative Testing Methodologies Used in Capital Market Research. *Journal of Accounting Research*, (Spring), pp. 48–84

Collins, D.W. and Kothari, S.P. (1989). An Analysis of the Intertemporal and Cross-Sectional Determinants of Earnings Response Coefficients. *Journal of Accounting and Economics*, (July), pp. 143–181

Collins, D.W., Rozeff, S. and Dhaliwal, D. (1981). The Economic Determinants of the Market Reaction to Proposed Mandatory Accounting Changes in the Oil and Gas Industry: A Cross-Sectional Analysis. *Journal of Accounting and Economics*, 3, pp. 37–71

DeBondt, W.F.M. and Thaler, R.H. (1985). Does the Stock Market Overreact? *Journal of Finance*, (July), pp. 793–805

DeBondt, W.F.M. and Thaler, R.H. (1987). Further Evidence on Investor Overreaction and Stock Market Seasonality. *Journal of Finance*, (July), pp. 557–581

DeLong, J.B., Shleifer, A., Summers, L.H. and Waldmann, R.J. (1990). Noise Trader Risk in Financial Markets. *Journal of Political Economy*, 98, pp. 703–738

Dodd, P. (1980). Merger Proposals, Management Discretion and Stockholder Wealth. *Journal of Financial Economics*, 8, pp. 105–137

Dodd, P. and Ruback, R.S. (1977). Tender Offers and Stockholder Returns: An Empirical Analysis. *Journal of Financial Economics*, 5, pp. 351–374

Dopuch, N. (1989). The Auto- and Cross-Sectional Correlations of Accounting Research. *Unpublished Manuscript*, Washington University

Dukes, R.F. (1978). *An Empirical Investigation of the Effects of SFAS No. 8 on Security Return Behavior*. Stamford, Connecticut: Financial Accounting Standards Board

Dyckman, T.R. and Smith, A.J. (1979). Financial Accounting and Reporting by Oil and Gas Producing Companies: A Study of Information Effects. *Journal of Accounting and Economics*, (March), pp. 45–75

Easton, P.D. and Zmijewski, M.G. (1989). Cross-Sectional Variation in the Stock Market Response to Accounting Earnings Announcements. *Journal of Accounting and Economics*, (July), pp. 117–141

Edwards, E.O. and Bell, P.W. (1961). *The Theory and Measurement of Business Income*. Berkeley: University of California Press

Elgers, P.T. (1980). Accounting-Based Risk Predictions: A Re-Examination. *The Accounting Review*, (July), pp. 389–408

Fama, E.F. (1965). The Behavior of Stock Market Prices. *Journal of Business*, 38, pp. 34–105

Fama, E.F. (1970). Efficient Capital Markets: A Review of Theory and Empirical Work. *Journal of Finance*, (May), pp. 383–417

Fama, E.F. (1991). Efficient Capital Markets II. *Journal of Finance*, (December), pp. 1575–1617

Fama, E.F. and Blume, M. (1966). Filter Rules and Stock Market Trading Profits. *Journal of Business*, (January), pp. 226–241

Fama, E.F., Fisher, L., Jensen, M.C. and Roll, R. (1969). The Adjustment of Stock Prices to New Information. *International Economic Review*, 10, pp. 1–21

Fisher, L. (1966). Some New Stock-Market Indexes. *Journal of Business*, 39, pp. 191–225

Foster, G. (1980). Accounting Policy Decisions and Capital Market Research. *Journal of Accounting and Economics*, (March), pp. 29–62

Foster, G., Olsen, C. and Shevlin, T. (1984). Earnings Releases, Anomalies, and the Behavior of Security Returns. *The Accounting Review*, (October), pp. 574–603

Gonedes, N. and Dopuch, N. (1974). Capital Market Equilibrium, Information Production, and Selecting Accounting Techniques: Theoretical Framework and Review of Empirical Work. Studies on Financial Accounting Objectives, *Journal of Accounting Research*, (Supplement), pp. 48–129

Graham, B. and Dodd, D. (1934). *Security Analysis*. New York: McGraw-Hill

Greene, W.H. (1993). *Econometric Analysis*. New York: Macmillan

Griffin, P.A. (1987). *Usefulness to Investors and Creditors of Information Provided by Financial Reporting*. Stamford, Connecticut: Financial Accounting Standards Board

Grossman, S.J. and Stiglitz, J.E. (1980). On the Impossibility of Informationally Efficient Markets. *American Economic Review*, 70, pp. 393–408

Hand, J.M.R. (1990). A Test of the Extended Functional Fixation Hypothesis. *The Accounting Review*, (October), pp. 740–763

Harris, T.S. and Ohlson, J.A. (1990). Accounting Disclosures and the Market's Valuation of Oil and Gas Properties: Evaluation of Market Efficiency and Functional Fixation. *The Accounting Review*, (October), pp. 764–780

Holthausen, R.W. (1981). Evidence on the Effect of Bond Covenants and Management Compensation Contracts on the Choice of Accounting Techniques: The Case of the Depreciation Switch-Back. *Journal of Accounting and Economics*, 3, pp. 73–109

Holthausen, R.W. and Leftwich, R. (1983). The Economic Consequences of Accounting Choice: Implications of Costly Contracting and Monitoring. *Journal of Accounting and Economics*, (August), pp. 77–118

Hong, H., Kaplan, R.S. and Mandelker, G. (1978). Pooling vs. Purchase: The Effects of Accounting for Stock Mergers and Stock Prices. *The Accounting Review*, (January), pp. 31–47

Ijiri, Y. (1967). *The Foundations of Accounting Measurement*. Englewood Cliffs, New Jersey: Prentice-Hall

Jensen, M.C. (1978). Some Anomalous Evidence Regarding Market Efficiency. *Journal of Financial Economics*, 6, pp. 95–102

Kaplan, R.S. (1975). The Information Content of Accounting Numbers: A Survey of Empirical Evidence. *Symposium on the Impact of Research in Financial Accounting and Disclosure on Accounting Practice*, Duke University, Chapel Hill, NC

Kaplan, R.S. and Roll, R. (1972). Investor Evaluation of Accounting Information: Some Empirical Evidence. *Journal of Business*, (April), pp. 225–257

Kormendi, R.C. and Lipe, R. (1987). Earnings Innovations, Earnings Persistence, and Stock Returns. *Journal of Business*, (July), pp. 323–346

Kyle, A. (1985). Continuous Auctions and Insider Trading. *Econometrica*, 53, pp. 1315–1335

Landsman, W.R. and Ohlson, J.A. (1990). Evaluation of Market Efficiency for Supplementary Accounting Disclosures: The Case of Pension Assets and Liabilities. *Contemporary Accounting Research*, (Fall), pp. 185–198

Larker, D.F. and Revsine, L. (1983). The Oil and Gas Accounting Controversy: An Analysis of Economic Consequences. *The Accounting Review*, (October), pp. 706–732

Leftwich, R. (1981). Evidence of the Impact of Mandatory Changes in Accounting Principles on Corporate Loan Agreements. *Journal of Accounting and Economics*, 3, pp. 3–36

Lee, A. (1993). On Delayed Responses to Earnings Announcements. *Ph.D. Dissertation*, New York University

Lev, B. (1979). The Impact of Accounting Regulation on the Stock Market: The Case of Oil and Gas Companies. *The Accounting Review*, 54, pp. 485–503

Lev, B. (1989). On the Usefulness of Earnings and Earnings Research: Lessons and Directions from Two Decades of Empirical Research. *Journal of Accounting Research*, (Supplement), pp. 153–192

Lev, B. and Ohlson, J.A. (1982). Market-Based Empirical Research in Accounting: A Review, Interpretation, and Examination. *Journal of Accounting Research*, (Supplement), pp. 249–322

Lipe, R.C. (1986). The Information Contained in the Components of Earnings. *Journal of Accounting Research*, (Supplement), pp. 37–68

Mandelker, G. (1974). Risk and Return: The Case of Merging Firms. *Journal of Financial Economics*, 1, pp. 303–336

Masulis, R.W. and Korwar, A.W. (1986). Seasoned Equity Offerings: An Empirical Investigation. *Journal of Financial Economics*, 15, pp. 91–118

Ohlson, J.A. (1980). Financial Ratios and the Probabilistic Prediction of Bankruptcy. *Journal of Accounting Research*, 18, pp. 109–131

Ohlson, J.A. (1988). Accounting Earnings, Book Value, and Dividends: The Theory of the Clean Surplus Equation (Part I). *Unpublished Manuscript*, Columbia University (November)

Ohlson, J.A. (1989). The Theory of Value and Earnings, and An Introduction to the Ball-Brown Analysis. *Unpublished Manuscript*, Columbia University (May)

Ohlson, J.A. (1990). A Synthesis of Security Valuation Theory and the Role of Dividends, Cash Flows, and Earnings. *Contemporary Accounting Research*, (Spring), pp. 648–676

Ou, J.A., and Penman, S.H. (1989a). Financial Statement Analysis and the Prediction of Stock Returns. *Journal of Accounting and Economics*, (November), pp. 295–329

Ou, J.A., and Penman, S.H. (1989b). Accounting Measurement, Price-Earnings Ratios, and the Information Content of Security Prices. *Journal of Accounting Research*, (Supplement), pp. 111–144

Patell, J.M. (1989). Discussion of On the Usefulness of Earnings and Earnings Research: Lessons and Directions from Two Decades of Empirical Research. *Journal of Accounting Research*, (Supplement), pp. 193–201

Paton, W.A. and Littleton, A.C. (1940). *An Introduction to Corporate Accounting Standards*. Chicago: American Accounting Association

Penman, S.H. (1991). Return to Fundamentals. Unpublished paper, University of California, Berkeley

Penman, S.H. (1992). Return to Fundamentals. *Journal of Accounting, Auditing and Finance*, (June), pp. 465–483

Rayburn, J. (1986). The Association of Operating Cash Flows and Accruals with Security Returns. *Journal of Accounting Research*, (Supplement), pp. 112–133

Ricks, W.E. (1986). Firm Size Effects and the Association Between Excess Returns and LIFO Tax Savings. *Journal of Accounting Research*, (Spring), pp. 206–216

Roll, R. (1988). R^2. *Journal of Finance*, (July), pp. 541–566

Ryan, S.G. (1991). Historical Cost Accrual Methods and the Role of Book Value and Earnings in Linear Valuation Models. *Journal of Accounting, Auditing and Finance*, (Spring), pp. 257–287

Shiller, R.J. (1981). Do Stock Prices Move Too Much to be Justified by Subsequent Changes in Dividends. *American Economic Review*, (June), pp. 421–436

Shiller, R.J. (1984). Stock Prices and Social Dynamics. *Brooking Papers on Economic Activity*, pp. 457–510

Sprouse, R.T. and Moonitz, M. (1962). *A Tentative Set of Broad Accounting Principles for Business Enterprises*. New York: American Institute of Certified Public Accountants

Stickel, S.E. (1991). Common Stock Returns Surrounding Earnings Forecast Revisions: More Puzzling Evidence. *The Accounting Review*, (April), pp. 402–416

Watts, R.L. (1982). Does it Pay to Manipulate EPS. *Chase Financial Quarterly*, (Spring), pp. 8–26

Watts, R.L. and Zimmerman, J.L. (1978). Towards a Positive Theory of the Determination of Accounting Standards. *The Accounting Review*, (January), pp. 112–134

Watts, R.L. and Zimmerman, J.L. (1986). *Positive Accounting Theory*. Englewood Cliffs, New Jersey: Prentice-Hall

White, G.I., Sondhi, A.C. and Fried, D. (1994). *The Analysis and Use of Financial Statements*. New York: John Wiley and Sons

Wilson, G.P. (1986). The Relative Information Content of Accruals and Cash Flows: Combined Evidence at the Earnings Announcement and Annual Report Release Date. *Journal of Accounting Research*, (Supplement), pp. 165–203

Wilson, G.P. (1987). The Incremental Information Content of the Accrual and Funds Components of Earnings After Controlling for Earnings. *The Accounting Review*, (April), pp. 293–322

4 Positive Accounting Theory: A Synthesis of Method and Critique

John J. Williams

4.1	Introduction	4.5	Economic-based criticisms of PAT
4.2	An overview of the PAT framework	4.6	Philosophy of science issues
4.3	The foundations of PAT	4.7	Assessing the accomplishments
4.4	Empirical evidence	4.8	Summary and conclusion

4.1 INTRODUCTION

The basic, and first question, that differentiates any discipline from other disciplines is its subject matter. By subject matter we mean the attribute that represents the phenomena studied. Accounting development has historically examined three mutually exclusive data bases as candidates for current practice: historical cost; current value in either an entry price mode or exit price mode; and present value. Choice among these alternatives has occupied accounting theorist's attention for most of the 20th century. Stated normatively, the question is what ought to be the data base represented in the financial accounts and financial statements of reporting entities?

Positive Accounting Theory (PAT) represents a radical departure from this type of normative reasoning. The question is now shifted from what ought to be the subject matter of accounting to what is current practice in terms of the choice of techniques from Generally Accepted Accounting Principles (GAAP). This shift is deemed to be necessary by PAT because the normative approach is alleged to be unscientific.

This chapter addresses the contents of PAT by examining Watts and Zimmerman's publication, *Positive Accounting Theory* (1986). The first part of the discussion considers the theoretical linkages and assumptions that yield the three major hypotheses proposed by PAT. Next, the

69

empirical evidence supporting these hypotheses is summarized and several limitations of the empirical research methodology are examined. The latter part of the chapter synthesizes some of the major critiques of PAT which centres on the economics-based theory of the Chicago School and appeals to various philosophy of science authorities. The chapter concludes with a summary of the major limitations of PAT.

4.2 AN OVERVIEW OF THE PAT FRAMEWORK

Chapter 1 of Watts and Zimmerman's 1986 book develops their view of the role of theory. Three features of accounting theory are crucial in developing this perspective: first, it is stated that the objective of accounting theory is to explain and predict accounting practice; second, this theory is claimed to be potentially non-normative in that it offers no prescriptions for how accounting practice ought to be done; third, accounting theory is deemed to be economics-based and grounded in the use of scientific concepts of theory development. An important consideration which emerges from this conceptual foundation is the complete omission of normative theories of *any* kind, including the array of income determination models such as present value, current entry and exit value models, and inflation models which have been the hallmark of traditional accounting theory development.

The next five chapters focus on the linkage developed between share values (via market prices) and accounting data, beginning with a description of the Efficient Markets Hypothesis (EMH) and Capital Asset Pricing Model (CAPM) in Chapter 2. Chapter 3 builds on the seminal work of Ball and Brown (1968) and Beaver (1968) in surveying the literature on the reaction of stock prices to accounting earnings. The literature on the relationship between changes of accounting method and stock market reaction is the subject matter of Chapter 4. Much of the empirical work surveyed in the chapter is anchored in the initial work of Kaplan and Roll (1972), who utilized the Abnormal Performance Index (API) methodology first proposed by Ball and Brown (1968). Empirical studies using accounting numbers as measures of market risk (that is, beta in the CAPM) and as predictions of failure are the focus of Chapter 5, while the time series properties of accounting earnings are discussed in Chapter 6.

Chapters 7 through 13 constitute the major contribution to PAT. The first four chapters in this set form the bases for Watts and Zimmerman's emphasis on explaining variations in accounting practice across firms and industries, as opposed to the traditional role of accounting which deals with the substantive content of the data base and information underpinning an entity's financial statements. Broadly speaking, the purpose of these specific chapters is two-fold. First, it is essential to the authors' position that a public interest perspective of accounting theory, which simply means favouring disclosure regulation for reasons of improved social welfare, be unequivocally discredited. Second, the authors assume and argue that all persons, notwithstanding politicians or regulators of any type (including standard-setting bodies), are driven by the 'maximizing utility' principle and, hence, always act to promote their own self-interest. Naturally, agency theory as well as the contracting literature provide the foundation for justifying this focus. The result of this theoretical grounding is captured in the new popularized hypotheses stated as follows:

- **Bonus Plan Hypothesis:** *Ceteris paribus*, managers of firms with bonus plans are more likely to choose accounting procedures that shift reported earnings from future periods to the current period (1986, p. 208).
- **Debt/Equity Hypothesis:** *Ceteris paribus*, the larger a firm's debt/equity ratio, the more likely the firm's manager is to select accounting procedures that shift reported earnings from future periods to the current period (1986, p. 216).
- **Size Hypothesis:** *Ceteris paribus*, the larger the firm, the more likely the manager is to choose accounting procedures that defer reported earnings from current to future periods (1986, p. 235).

The latter three chapters in this set survey the literature dealing with empirical tests of accounting choice and contract-related variables, mandated regulation and auditing, respectively.

In Chapter 14, the authors borrow from their controversial 'Market for Excuses' paper (1979) and present two major themes which have antagonised many accounting scholars. Firstly, they submit that they have used the concept of theory germane to science to justify that the objective of accounting theory is to explain and predict accounting practice. The implication here (for the alert reader) is that any theory which lies outside the domain advocated by them is literally a bad thing because it is unscientific. Secondly, however, and directly related to this implication for accounting theory, is that the authors relegate all other theories to the category of the 'market for excuses'. These theories are prescriptive in nature and cover all the pre-mid 1960's accounting literature. Both of these themes underscore the authors' preference for the marketplace, instead of regulation, to govern the appropriate source and grounding of accounting theory.

Finally, in Chapter 15, PAT is evaluated from the perspective of the previous 14 chapters. They admit that the empirical evidence presented and summarised has at least three serious shortcomings: a coherent theoretical base is absent; empirical measures of important contracting variables that are believed to influence accounting choice are inadequate at best; and statistical methods, including analytic problems such as multi-collinearity among various contracting variables, have been problematic.

4.3   THE FOUNDATIONS OF PAT

Accounting choices are the central focus of positive accounting research. This research posits that accounting choices are a function of contracting arrangements that encompass management compensation schemes and lending agreements, in addition to government regulation and political concerns that are directly associated with the use of accounting income numbers. The puzzling issue to those unfamiliar with this literature and its development is why accounting choice plays such a dominant role. The discussion in this section is aimed at providing some insight into this issue.

As a starting point, it is useful to anchor one's thinking to a simple cash flow model of the firm. In economic terms, the value of the firm can be equated to the discounted value of the expected future cash flows over the time horizon or life of the firm. At any point in time, this quantum is equivalent to the familiar concept of present value, or economic value of the firm. The usual assumption in this approach is that, at any point in time, the firm has undertaken optimal decisions regarding the mix of investment, financing and production choices. Part of this efficient set of decisions includes the choice of accounting methods (usually from GAAP) which are utilized to produce the income or earnings number on the firm's financial statements. A second, and critically important assumption, is that these accounting numbers form the basis for extant contracting and decision-making.

Given the above scenario, *any* event which alters the distribution of the firm's cash flows can be described as having an economic consequence because a change in the pattern of cash flows necessarily produces a change in the value of the firm. In fact, the meaning of economic consequences is even broader than this because it also applies to any individual whose wealth is affected because that event impacts their own personal contracting or decision-making. Clearly, if accounting rules are changed, which means that if accounting choices are altered in the production of accounting numbers and there is a corresponding change in the distribution of the firm's cash flows, then accounting choices are said to have economic consequences. To the extent that accounting rule changes impact the wealth of individuals who use the accounting numbers in their own personal contracting or decision-making, economic consequences are also said to exist. The question that arises, however, is what causes the change in cash flows and, hence, gives rise to economic consequences.

The key aspect in this argument is the existence of costly contracting and monitoring. Contracts involve documentation, negotiation, evaluation, and in many instances renegotiation. Contracts also involve monitoring to assess performance and evaluate compliance. In the real business world, these activities are not free. Rather, they involve economic effort and have cash flow implications. Thus, a change in choice of accounting methods initiates more of these contracting activities. In turn, costs are incurred, cash flows are changed, and firm value and individual wealth are correspondingly impacted.

It is important to differentiate the positive accounting research, which is embedded in the economic consequences of accounting choice described above, from earlier accounting research which was also positive, as opposed to normative, in nature. This earlier research is often described in terms of the 'no–effects' hypothesis versus the 'mechanistic' hypothesis.

The **no–effects theory** of accounting choice is related to both the EMH and CAPM. The combination of these two theories together with assumptions of zero taxes and no contracting, transaction or information costs, predicts that publicly announced accounting changes will not be associated with any stock price changes. If an accounting change occurs, the best that the EMH can do is to predict that the stock price might go up or down at the time of change, but there are no implications for any price changes after the change is announced. In other words, prices will reflect the implicit value change but there will be no subsequent price drift up or down.

To predict the direction of a price change associated with an accounting change requires a valuation model, and early research relied on the CAPM as the valuation model. This model suggests that the firm's expected future cash flows and the expected rate of return are the factors that determine the value of the firm. Under this view, a change in accounting procedures involves no cash flow effect. Investors and potential investors alike can costlessly unravel any accounting earnings number. In this world, everyone can recalculate whatever agreements or contracts that currently exist at no cost and, hence, with no cash flow effects. And, under these circumstances, there is no impact on firm value whatsoever. Stated differently, and much to the chagrin of die-hard accountants and managers, accounting numbers are simply irrelevant to firm value in this world. Thus, the situation for accounting numbers here is perfectly analogous to the famous Modigliani and Miller (1958) proposition which indicated the irrelevance of capital structure to a firm's value.

The **mechanistic theory**, on the other hand, predicts that changes in accounting rules or procedures are associated with changes in stock prices. The belief is that stock prices can be managed by manipulations in accounting numbers. Stated bluntly, believers in this view think they are smart and the market is dumb. Accounting is viewed as a monopoly source of information about firm value, and investors are naive and do not have the ability to discriminate between accounting numbers produced by different rules or procedures. In technical terms, this view predicts that abnormal stock returns are correlated with accounting earnings changes even in the absence of no effect on a firm's cash flow. In summary, the mechanistic hypothesis is contradictory to the EMH hypothesis for changes in accounting procedures.

The no–effects theory of accounting choice is not specific about which accounting technique or set of techniques will be adopted by firms or industries. As suggested above, however, economic consequence theories introduce the notion of costly contracting and monitoring. Therefore, accounting choices affect the value of the firm because economic agents act to protect themselves against transfers of wealth. In particular, the types of economic consequences analyzed by Watts (1977), Watts and Zimmerman (1978) and Holthausen and Leftwich (1983), among others, provide useful insights into the nature and importance of costly contracting and monitoring for accounting choice. These are discussed below under the headings of management compensation plans, debt contracts and lending agreements, political visibility and regulation.

4.3.1 Management compensation plans

Accounting choice and management compensation plans are linked in the following manner. Usually, bonus schemes are put in place to provide incentives for managers to reach targeted levels of earnings or returns specified by accounting rules. These schemes explicitly tie the managers wealth to the calculus of reported accounting numbers. Thus, managers can voluntarily choose different accounting rules to present a more favourable earnings number and thereby enhance their own wealth. Alternatively, proposed mandatory accounting changes can compel managers to change their existing set of financing or investment decisions to offset any unfavourable implications on their bonus plan agreements. If such changes in the efficient production set are not optimal, the value of the firm is lowered because of reduced future cash flows.

It is also possible for managers to lobby for or against proposed mandatory accounting method changes. Lobbying behaviour is a costly exercise which consumes resources of the firm and lowers its value. Moreover, with the existence of costly *ex ante* negotiation of contracts before the accounting change and costly *ex post* renegotiation after the mandated accounting change, firm resources are also consumed which impact the firm's value. Thus, potential economic consequences emerge from a change, voluntary or mandatory, in accounting rules.

4.3.2 Debt contracts and lending agreements

Generally, when firms enter into various kinds of borrowing, there is a requirement imposed by lenders that specific conditions must be satisfied. For example, restrictions on individual payments, limitations on the issue of new debt, and prohibiting merger activity are a few of the ways in which accounting numbers can be linked to debt contracts. However, voluntary or mandatory changes in accounting rules can lead to changes in the level of these restrictions. Clearly, the potential for wealth transfer between shareholders and bondholders arises which can impact a firm's cash flows. Again, managers may lobby against the change or realign their investment–financing–production mix, which alters the pattern of cash flows and, therefore, the value of the firm.

It is important to realise that the assumption of costly contracting and monitoring is not sufficient to induce economic consequences. In addition, it is important to remember that both borrowers and lenders are assumed to be rational decision makers. Thus, a second condition for economic consequences to arise is that managers will not engage in behaviour that reduces the value of the firm if it means that human capital value (that is, the amount of wages and bonuses) is simultaneously reduced.

4.3.3 Political visibility

The economic consequences associated with the political factor arises because large firms are visible in the eyes of the public. Therefore, when large companies report unusually large profits, there is an outcry from the public that they are victims of unscrupulous pricing policies. In the case of large foreign firms, the argument is that unfair trade policies create an economic arena where local firms are disadvantaged relative to profitable foreign firms. Politicians seize on such opportunities to transfer wealth to themselves by imposing taxes on such unpopular firms. These taxes may be explicit or implicit. The latter are found in the form of pollution regulations, anti-trust suits, import quotas and tariffs, and a variety of other implicit subsidies.

It should be noted that the causal relationship between the political factor and accounting numbers is not a direct one because the parties with incentives to transfer wealth from the firm to themselves are external to the firm. For instance, if politicians expropriate resources for their own control, they can be used to enhance their image, including the possibility of re-election. Control over these resources can be achieved through any of the legal explicit or implicit taxes mentioned above.

4.3.4 Regulations

Various government bodies use accounting numbers to impose restrictions on firms such as utility companies or banks. In the case of utilities, it is well known that rate bases are calculated with accounting numbers. Changes in accounting numbers can be conveniently incorporated into price increases which induces a shift in wealth from consumers to government. To the extent that consumers wish to become informed or to monitor the utilities' cost function, it is a costly exercise. Forming coalitions or protest groups to lobby politicians is time consuming and involves direct cash resources. Thus, accounting changes, whether voluntary or mandatory, elicit economic consequences because of wealth transfers between consumers and the firm.

4.4 EMPIRICAL EVIDENCE

Three major types of empirical studies have been conducted on the economic consequences of accounting choices:

(1) the impact of accounting choices on stock prices;
(2) the voting and lobbying positions on proposed accounting standards; and
(3) the choice of accounting techniques.

Table 4.1 shows a summary of selected empirical research studies which have received substantial recognition and scrutiny in the accounting literature.

Two systematic relationships are apparent in these results. Firstly, there is consistent evidence that choice of accounting method is dependent on firm-specific factors such as the existence of management compensation plans, leverage and size. Secondly, the evidence appears to be consistent with the predictions of economic consequences theories. However, because of the limited number of studies, a lack of control over different industry effects, the absence of different time period effects, and a concentration of only several accounting issues, it is premature to judge the robustness of the results.

The least powerful set of studies are those which examine the impact of accounting choice on stock prices. Both the study by Collins, Rozeff and Dhaliwal (1981) and the study by Leftwich (1981) focused on mandatory accounting changes (that is, full cost versus successful efforts and purchase versus pooling, respectively) while the study by Holthausen (1981) dealt with the voluntary choices between straight–line versus accelerated depreciation. However, methodological limitations may have hampered the consistency in results and some of these issues are addressed below.

4.4.1 Limitations of empirical research

The literature addresses three major limitations which underpin the economic consequences research: specification of the dependent variable; specification of the independent variables; and the power of tests versus the impact of the accounting choice. Given these broad categories of limitations, it is also important to note that they vary across the three types of studies identified in Table 4.1.

Table 4.1 Summary of empirical research studies

Source*	BNL	D	DSS	LP	ZH	WZ	CRD	H	L
Type of Study**	A	A	A	A	A	B	C	C	C
Accounting Issue***	IC	OG	D	OG	DIP	GPL	OG	D	PP
Variables:†									
(1) Compensation Plan	−88%	NT	NT	NT	+5%	+20%	NT	−25%	NT
(2) Lending Contracts									
(a) Existence	NT	NT	NT	NT	NT	NT	+5%	NT	NT
(b) Dividend constraint	+2%	NT	NT	NT	NT	NT	NT	−68%	NT
(c) Interest coverage	+9%	NT	NT	NT	NT	NT	NT	NT	NT
(d) Leverage	+9%	+9%	+1%	+4%	+5%	NT	−50%	−1%	+2%
(3) Political Visibility									
(a) Size	+94%	NT	+15%	+2%	+1%	+1%	10%	60%	+2%
(b) Concentration	NT	NT	NT	NT	+5%	NT	NT	NT	NT
(c) Capital intensity	NT	NT	NT	NT	+65%	NT	NT	NT	NT

Key: *   BNL (Bowen, Noreen and Lacey, 1981); D (Dhaliwal, 1980); DSS (Dhaliwal, Salamon and Smith, 1982); LP (Lilien and Pastena, 1982); ZH (Zmijewski and Hagerman, 1981); WZ (Watts and Zimmerman, 1978); CRD (Collins, Rozeff and Dhaliwal, 1981); H (Holthausen, 1981); L (Leftwich, 1981).

     **   A = Predicting technique choice; B = Voting and Lobbying; C = Price Studies.

     ***   IC = Interest Capitalisation; OG = Oil and Gas Accounting; D = Depreciation; DIP = Depreciation, Inventory and Pensions; GPL = General Price Level Adjustments; PP = Purchase/Pooling.

     †   % indicates the significance level and + (−) consistent direction of hypothesised effect; NT = not tested.

Those studies in group A in Table 4.1 summarise the choice of accounting method as either 'income increasing' or 'income decreasing' and use a zero/one dummy variable for test purposes. This dichotomisation does not reflect the timing difference across accounting periods and may be a poor proxy for the economic decision being made. A similar problem exists for voting and lobbying behaviour which is also measured on a dichotomous basis. In these types of studies, it is also difficult to deal with variations in the intensity of respondents to a proposed change and some externalities on private agreements among voters are not even observable. By far though, the most critical problem lies with specification of the dependent variable in stock price studies. The reasons concern identification of the event dates and investors' expectations.

Voluntary accounting changes create a problem in this regard because it is difficult to determine the exact date on which specific accounting changes are made. Therefore, looking for abnormal returns around an imprecise event date will more than likely produce no effects. For mandatory accounting changes, expectations are important because this is what is revised to produce any abnormal returns. An unknown element is the extent to which investor expectations may be lagged or deferred relative to a past event. These changes in expectations become incorrigible problems in stock price studies. Furthermore, mandatory changes have the added difficulty that there may be numerous critical dates (that is, events) leading up to the actual official pronouncement of an accounting change. Along such a horizon, there is a continuous revision of probabilities by investors concerning the acceptance of a new accounting rule by the standard-setting body.

Ball (1980) has pointed out that mandatory accounting changes may not be exogenous to the system. If this is the case, then such changes are not random but occur in tandem with other economic events. This possibility presents researchers with a joint hypothesis unless the other economic events can be ferreted out of the price reaction. Likewise, as Holthausen and Leftwich (1983) observe, the assumption for voluntary accounting changes is that the market's probability of change is presumed equal across firms.. Thus, if accounting changes are endogenous (that is, if they are induced by violations in any contracting agreements), then it may be impossible to sort out any economic consequences that may be present, *per se*.

In summary, the exogenous versus endogenous issue involves concurrent events which confound statistical results. One of the advantages of moving to the use of daily and even micro transactions in studying abnormal performance is to try and reduce the contemporaneous information effects. A second problem is the clustering effect which arises when multiple accounting changes occur close together for different firms, thus creating a cross-correlation problem for tests of statistical significance.

Turning to problems associated with the independent variables, it seems that the most serious problem is finding appropriate proxies as measures. Unfortunately, the present state of theory development for economic consequences is completely lacking in detailed specification. Once more, we find that many studies are content to use dummy variables as proxies for the existence of compensation plans, lending agreements and monitoring costs. Foster (1980) gives an example of where the mere existence of bond covenants may be insufficient as an independent variable measure. He notes that some oil and gas firms insulated themselves from the full cost/successful efforts controversy by specifying the accounting method to be used independent of GAAP. Finally, there is much concern over how well the measure of size proxies for the political effect. Holthausen (1981) suggests that different industries appear to bear the brunt of US politics in different decades and size may simply represent an industry effect. Of more concern, though, is the very loose connection between size and political visibility on theoretical grounds.

The final methodological concern may completely prohibit ever finding economic consequences under some circumstances. In the case of stock price tests of economic consequences, the relative wealth effect on firm values from accounting choices may be extremely small. As noted in the literature, these tests are doomed by a low signal to noise ratio. Combined with the problems of precise event dates and investors' expectations, the methodology simply is not powerful enough to detect hypothesised economic consequences. For the other two types of empirical studies, however, not only are there more powerful extant results, but the likelihood of improving upon the proxies for accounting method choices and lobbying behaviour are considerably greater.

4.5 ECONOMIC-BASED CRITICISMS OF PAT

To the uninitiated reader of Positive Accounting Theory, the framework appears to be a neat, coherent package of theory and evidence. Moreover, when various criticisms surface, one wonders why there is subtle, if not blatant, animosity towards the positive school and what the roots of the controversy really entail. Shedding light on this aspect of the research programme underlying the Rochester School is not an easy task because it involves several critical historical developments as well as issues embedded in the philosophy of science. But since PAT has assumed the status of mainstream accounting research in most parts of the world, some of the more cogent economic-based issues are discussed in the following sections of this chapter.

4.5.1 Background

To begin with, the spectrum of accounting theory development from the beginning of the 20th century up to about 1970 was normative in nature. The major works of Canning (1929), Gilman (1939), Paton and Littleton (1940), Vatter (1947), Edwards and Bell (1961), Chambers (1964, 1966, 1967) and Sterling (1970), among others, were all prescriptive in nature and argued what accounting should be rather than what it is. During the 1960s a common understanding in the accounting literature was that corporate accounting reports were a monopoly source of information for pricing shares in the stock market. This led to the idea in some quarters that managers could manipulate earnings numbers and fool the market (that is, the market was not clever enough to sort out manipulated earnings).

These developments led academics to criticise the calculation of earnings under GAAP, sometimes as a protest statement to win support for their favourite normative model. Arguments pointed to the use of historical cost in some cases and current values in other cases with the result that earnings numbers were portrayed as a meaningless quantum. Given this result, it was alleged that stock prices could not be relevant signals for allocating resources among alternative investments (Watts and Zimmerman, 1986).

Against this backdrop, Watts and Zimmerman launched their attack on the normative theorising that underpinned most of the major research through to the end of the 1960s. Firstly, Watts and Zimmerman (1986) argued that positive theory as they present it is 'the economics-based accounting theory that evolved from the use of the scientific concept of theory' (p. 13). In their earlier 1979 article, Watts and Zimmerman characterise normative accounting theorists as responding to the demand for political excuses. Taken together, these two positions infuriated many accountants and researchers alike. For example, Whitley (1988) claims that the positive theory of Watts and Zimmerman is an attempt to 'colonise doctoral programmes in accounting' (p. 643). It also prompted Mouck (1990) to suggest that 'the Rochester school exhibits a tendency toward academic imperialism' (p. 238). Secondly, Watts and Zimmerman readily accept that testing the validity of any theory rests on predictions and not *a priori* assumptions and logical reason. In their view, normative accounting theories are unscientific, are not empirically testable and are value-laden. In Sterling's view (1990), 'Watts and Zimmerman have also adopted and augmented the desire to demolish all theories other than PAT' (p. 100).

4.5.2 The substantive content of PAT

In one of the earliest critiques of Watts and Zimmerman, Christenson

(1983) states that the basic approach of PAT is not concerned with accounting theory, but rather, that it is really a sociology of accounting. This argument is based on Watts and Zimmerman's statement concerning accounting theory: 'The objective of accounting theory is to explain and predict accounting practice' (p. 2). This is an important, if not the fundamental, distinguishing characteristic of PAT *vis-à-vis* all other accounting theories. PAT is not concerned with accounting entities as normally portrayed in accounting teachings and textbooks and, hence, the events and transactions that underlie the GAAP data base but, rather, it 'is concerned with describing, predicting and explaining the behaviour of accountants and managers' (Christenson, 1983, pp. 5–6).

To Watts and Zimmerman, an explanation means providing reasons for observed practice. They state that an accounting theory should be able to give reasons for why certain accounting methods, such as LIFO or FIFO, are used by certain firms. On the other hand, prediction of accounting practice means that the theory predicts unobserved accounting phenomena. In other words, the theory provides hypotheses (that is, tells a story) about particular firm attributes that cause the choice of particular accounting techniques such as LIFO and FIFO. Thus, contrary to the thinking of the accounting novice, PAT does not deal with financial transactions, exchanges, or the substantive nature of accounting entities which are the phenomena of concern in all normative accounting theories. Instead, the focus is on the behaviour of individuals. Christenson (1983) draws an analogy between this theoretical focus and that of chemistry: 'Chemical theory consists of propositions about the behaviour of chemical entities (molecules and atoms), not about the behaviour of chemists' (p. 6).

Sterling (1990) is equally concerned about the total dismissal of substantive accounting phenomena in the PAT framework. Indeed, he uses the metaphor advanced by Francis Bacon (1605) which cautions the student to differentiate between words and matter. According to Sterling, the critical error of Watts and Zimmerman is that:

> 'they have proposed a research program with the objective of explaining and predicting words and numerals without mentioning their correspondence (or lack) to things and events, ... they have fallen in love with pictures (financial statements) without recognizing that they need be images of matter (economic goods)' (p. 101).

As discussed previously, the dependent variable is measured in the PAT framework by observing the use or non-use of a particular accounting technique. Sterling (1990) argues that one cannot observe the decision process which produces the choice of technique but only the result. This is the first question addressed by PAT. The second question pertains to the right-hand side of the equation or the independent variables: 'Why the formulae were selected – what causes practitioners to select various practices' (p. 102). The assumption of PAT is that all of the right-hand explanatory factors are anchored in the utility maximization assumption.

When some of the disappointing results of PAT are highlighted, anti-PAT petitioners submit that the methods of behavioural science might provide a better foundation for explaining the motivation of accounting choice instead of utility maximization. However, proponents of PAT would never submit to such an alternative search. As a result, PAT research is accused of being methods-driven and data-driven, instead of being knowledge-driven or problem-driven.

4.5.3 Utility maximization and the Chicago View

To understand more completely the basis for PAT, it is necessary to outline the origins of the assumptions which Watts and Zimmerman draw upon to support PAT. Both Watts and Zimmerman received their training at the Chicago School of Economics which is why the Rochester School of Accounting is often portrayed as an intellectual offshoot of the Chicago View. Moreover, Milton Friedman, a pillar of the Chicago economic's research program, is famous for heralding the importance of prediction over assumption: 'Truly important and significant hypotheses will be found to have "assumptions" that are widely inaccurate descriptive representations of reality' (1953, p. 14). Watts and Zimmerman (1986) assert that his famous essay *The Methodology of Positive Economics* provided an authoritative inspiration for the methodology of PAT (p. 8).

The essence of the Chicago View has been described by several sources including Reder (1982) and Latsis (1976). A summary of these neoclassical propositions are:

(1) Decision-makers have correct knowledge of their economic situation.
(2) Decision-makers prefer the best available alternative given their knowledge of the situation and the means at their disposal.
(3) Given (1) and (2), situations generate their internal logic and decision-makers act appropriately to the logic of their situation.
(4) Economic units and structure display stable, coordinated behaviour.
(5) The wants and preferences of individuals are autonomous with respect to the market systems.
(6) All decision-makers are motivated only by their narrowly defined self-interest and not by the public interest.
(7) The firm is considered to be a nexus of (explicit or implicit) contracts among self-interested parties.

These propositions imply that regulation is a bad thing, the free market mechanism is a good thing, information is an economic good like any other commodity, Pareto optimality rules the economic universe, and individual behaviour can be explained by the maximization of utility.

However, to generate testable hypotheses, a set of auxiliary hypotheses is required which bears the brunt of evaluation. According to

Lakatos (1970), these latter hypotheses form the 'protective belt' which ensures that the initial propositions remain sacred and unchallenged. Mouck (1990) considers the following five hypotheses to be the most prominent under the PAT framework:

(1) The efficient market hypothesis.
(2) The capital asset pricing model.
(3) Contracting and agency theory.
(4) The theory of rational expectations.
(5) A theory of the political process.

It is important at this point to recall the discussion earlier about the arguments put forth by normative accounting theorists. Their position is that there is a lack of uniformity in accounting methods which enables managers to systematically mislead the markets and that accounting earnings are meaningless. Pro-regulators of accounting seize on these allegations to argue for conformity and compliance of accounting standards. In doing so, their maintained hypothesis is that accounting reports are the only source of information on the firm. However, the mission of PAT is to dampen this view and to demonstrate how the regulation of accounting standards and practice interferes with the efficient allocation of resources. PAT needed a theory which could counter the normative arguments and the EMH was the cornerstone. As Watts and Zimmerman (1986) assert:

> 'the EMH suggests that this sole source hypothesis is unlikely to be descriptive and that the stock market is not systematically misled by accounting earnings' (p. 20).

To overcome the meaningless earnings numbers allegation, PAT needed to have some kind of theoretical linkage between capital asset prices (or firm values) and accounting numbers. The CAPM fills this crucial role.

In the CAPM world, expectations about future cash flows are the basis for the buying and selling decisions of investors. However, in this scenario there are no transaction costs, no costs of contracting and no information costs. Thus, as Watts and Zimmerman note (1986, p. 73) 'without additional assumptions, an accounting change has no implications for stock prices in the CAPM world'. Since information is costly in the real world, PAT assumes a rational expectations theory in which investors will acquire information up to the point where the marginal cost of additional information is equal to the expected value. The latter, of course, is realised in the form of more accurate expectations. Finally, by relaxing the assumption of zero contracting costs and borrowing from the works of Coase (1937) and Jensen and Meckling (1976) which develops the theory of costly contracting and monitoring costs for agency relationships within the firm, PAT is able to link the choice of accounting method to earnings and, thus, to cash flows and firm value. It is this combination of linkages that allows researchers to develop the bonus plan, debt/equity and size hypotheses described earlier.

Sterling (1990) is particularly critical of the utility maximizing assumption which, as he correctly argues, is the 'keystone behavioural assumption, serving as the sole explanation of the motivation of *all* the various parties that select accounting practices as well as the basis for the research programme' (p. 102). In his view, this assumption together with its reasoning contains a number of errors, 'any one of which is sufficient to disqualify it as a basis for a research programme and as an explanation of behaviour' (p. 102).

Firstly, it explains too much since any outcome from behavioural actions can be defended as maximizing utility. Since utility maximization is the explanation for x occurring (when it occurred) and for not occurring (when it did not occur), it explains both x and *not x* and, hence, it explains no behaviour.

Secondly, it is argued that utility maximization is not a falsifiable concept. Popper (1983, p. xx) selected it to illustrate that because it is not falsifiable it is not scientific, and yet Watts and Zimmerman claim that he supports the scientific essence of PAT. As Sterling notes 'It is difficult to imagine a more conspicuously fatal flaw in an appeal to authority' (p. 104).

Thirdly, Sterling suggests that disconfirming evidence in science would normally be subjected to intense scrutiny and references the study by McKee *et al* (1984). They extended and replicated the tests of Watts and Zimmerman (1978) and found PAT to be unimpressive because an alterative predictive model outperforms PAT. Although Watts and Zimmerman (1986) cite that 1984 work, there is no discussion of its findings.

Fourthly, Sterling invokes the reasoning of Reder (1982) who describes the way evidence is interpreted by the Chicago School:

> 'Any apparent inconsistency of empirical findings with implications of the theory, or report of behaviour not implied by the theory . . . [requires] one of the following actions (i) re-examination of the data . . . (ii) redefinition . . . of the variables . . . (iii) alteration of the theory . . . (iv) placing the finding on the research agenda as researchable anomaly. TP [tight prior or Chicago School] implies shunning (iii): i.e., the subject matter of the tight prior [Chicago School] is the adequacy of this approach to theory as an explanation of whatever behaviour is considered as economic . . . TP [Chicago School] adherents — with variation among individuals — focus attention upon (i) and (ii) and, failing a quick resolution of the anomaly, move to (iv) but pay little attention to (iii). By contrast, DP [diverse prior or non-Chicago School] adherents consider all possibilities, varying research strategy with circumstances, but showing no strong pre-disposition to neglect (iii).' (p. 13).

The concern then, with PAT, is that it restricts the kind of research methods that are used and it ignores evidence which does not match the beliefs and assumptions of the researchers.

Finally, Sterling recognizes that Watts and Zimmerman's greatest error is not comprehending that a normative or a prior stance must be taken on what counts as evidence in hypotheses testing. In fact, the nature of what ought to count as acceptable evidence in empirical testing is the very reason for sequencing conceptual work first, followed by the initiation of empirical research. In other words, normative theory is needed to conclude empirical research. Both must exist interactively. The ultimate testimony here comes from Stephen Hawking, one of the great minds of the last 400 years:

> 'Even if there is only one possible unified theory, it is just a set of rules and equations. What is it that breathes fire into the equations and makes a universe for them to describe? The usual approach of science of constructing a mathematical model cannot answer the questions of why there should be a universe for the model to describe . . . If we find the answer . . . it would be the ultimate triumph . . . for then we would know the mind of God' (1988, pp. 174–175).

As a striking example of Reder's (1982) description of the Chicago School's evaluative approach to evidence, Watts and Zimmerman (1986) suggest that the data supporting PAT's hypothesis as presented in their Table 11.3 provides strong evidence for the hypotheses that managers maximize their utility, but the low R^2 of 9% indicates there is plenty of room for improvement in the model. Sterling (1990) counters with the following interpretation:

> 'That is, researchers should seek more ingenious ways to run the test to get their Investigator Ingenuity Index above the unacceptably low 9 per cent. There is no suggestion that the evidence might cast doubt on utility maximization' (p. 107).

While Sterling (1990) is extremely critical of the Chicago School form of economics-based models, there are others with a similar view. These include Tinker *et al* (1982), Whittington (1987), Demski (1988), Whitley (1988) and Boland and Gordon (1992) who all challenge the equilibrium concepts of the Chicago School. Whittington (1987) argues that Watts and Zimmerman (1986) present a biased and unbalanced view of PAT. It is biased in his view because the limitations of EMH assumptions are ignored and the neoclassical assumptions are value-laden. He further argues that Watts and Zimmerman (1986) do not present a balanced view of the philosophy of science issues nor the legitimate contributions of normative accounting theorists.

Demski (1988) is much more sympathetic to PAT and subtly apologises for the bias and unbalanced views which underlie PAT. For example, 'it is important to keep in mind that the rhetoric of perfect markets is a substitute for inadequate theory' (1988, p. 625). Demski (1988) further submits that PAT treats the endogenous as exogenous which means that Watts and Zimmerman's choice of independent variables are totally suspect and, in fact, are not independent at all. Individual choice, which Demski (1988) argues is anchored in the theory of revealed preferences, is inextricably wrapped up with the jointness of choice of accounting method, production, labour, capital and the total organizational arrangement. The problem is that the very phenomena that the independent variable may be trying to explain are governed by that same phenomena and, hence, methodologically the argument is tautological and internal relative to a more primitive identification which requires exogenous factors. For example, what environmental factors are linked to the efficient and simultaneously determined choice of accounting method, debt/equity mix and motivational incentives. This problem reduces the validity of empirical statistical testing to zero.

A third, and extremely cogent observation by Demski, concerns drawing the boundaries around what amounts to the information set and the corresponding linkage between the earnings performance index of the firm and the postulated effect of manager's actions on the value of the firm. The problem here involves the so-called comparative advantage of accounting information (that is, earnings) relative to all other sources of information that could affect earnings. For sure, there are other sources of information and, therefore, to speak of correlations in the above linkage is suspect; at best, Demski argues that the correlations should be partial correlations which recognizes 'the existence of other information (e.g. cash)' (1988, p. 626). Moreover, this means that the analysis should contain conditional probabilities instead of marginal probabilities in the definition of information content. This argument, it should be noted, goes beyond the mere criticism of a 'marginalist approach' to equilibrium arguments which is the thrust of Tinker *et al's* (1982) objection to PAT.

Another boundary problem which is underscored by Demski (1988) is the importance of political activities in understanding regulatory phenomena:

> 'Formal economic modelling of multiperson phenomena uses the notion of equilibrium behaviour. Here, by contrast, we see extensive use of behavioural constructs instead of formal equilibrium analysis' (p. 626).

How can political activity in the larger regulatory arena be reduced to a political cost term internal to the firm without examining equilibrium behaviour in a larger political model? To adduce a single person specification which is required in revealed preference, and assumed in the logic of PAT, from the strategic behaviour of a multiperson political model, is sheer speculation because no formal model currently exists.

Boland and Gordon (1992) pursue the basis for criticising an economics-based accounting theory. In their view the two salient features of this approach are the methodological individualism and the neoclassical maximization hypothesis. Therefore, criticism must be aimed at one of the two or both. Many critics claim that the latter, which is an unshakable foundation of the Chicago view, is not even feasible because it requires knowledge beyond what is logically possible. As if this denunciation were not sufficient to cast doubt on the theoretical proprietary of PAT, Boland

and Gordon (1992) continue with the assertion that 'Methodological individualism poses the larger problem' (p. 148).

What concerns Boland and Gordon here is the hidden assumption of the Chicago School, which has been discussed earlier, that society's welfare is maximized by the maximizing behaviour of each individual agent in the social system. In other words, a condition of universal maximization is simultaneously attained through the maximizing of each individual's utility. As observed by several critics, non-economists may not fully appreciate what this assumption entails. Simply stated, the maximization of utility can only occur under states of equilibrium. We know that a state of equilibrium is identical to saying that the pricing mechanism of supply and demand clears the market. And, it must be further remembered that individual decision-makers always calculate their cost functions with these equilibrium prices in mind. So, in theory, the use of equilibrium prices is perfectly valid if all markets are cleared and, hence, there is equilibrium. What is not valid is the use of equilibrium prices when supply does not equal demand, because in this instance, markets are not cleared and there is no equilibrium.

So, in an equilibrium world, individuals are price takers, all individuals are maximizing their utility and society is in a state of Pareto optimality. Thus, Watts and Zimmerman's entire framework cannot tolerate market failure. The real issue is whether it is valid to assume that all markets are cleared. If they are not, supply does not equal demand and there is disequilibrium. In disequilibrium, decision-makers are not maximizing their utility. So what force will adjust the price to an equilibrium position which, in turn, will clear the market and restore society to an universal equilibrium? Neoclassical economics does not have the answer because it was not designed to explain disequilibrium states. Nor was it designed to explore any behavioural constructs other than utility maximization.

The worst nightmare for neoclassical economists is convincing a decision-maker that they know there is disequilibrium and, moreover, what precise moves are necessary at the margin to restore universal utility. If there ever was a case of incorrigibility and arbitrariness in allocation, this problem wins because of the impossibility of ever knowing the exact externalities of any adjustment from disequilibrium to equilibrium conditions. Invoking costly contracting and monitoring assumptions can never remove the incorrigible jointness of information costs and the change required in dynamic markets to restore equilibrium.

This discussion is particularly relevant to PAT because, as Demski (1988) notes, the important question is 'not how accounting method choices vary through time and circumstance, but why the organization has been designed to motivate this particular behaviour in the accounting domain' (p. 626). It must be recalled that descriptive research involves *how* questions while *why* questions are the domain of theory. The impact of

Demski's (1988) and Boland and Gordon's (1992) analyses is that Watts and Zimmerman appear to provide descriptive theories in PAT even though they *claim* to provide positive explanations. This conclusion is consistent with Sterling (1990), who asserts that Watts and Zimmerman do not deliver what they claim to deliver in PAT.

4.6   PHILOSOPHY OF SCIENCE ISSUES

Much of the criticism of PAT has been initiated under the banner of philosophy of science issues. The papers by Tinker *et al* (1982), Christenson (1983), Lowe *et al* (1983), Whittington (1987), Hines (1988), Whitley (1988), Mouck (1990), Sterling (1990) and Boland and Gordon (1992) all focus on the methodology of science. This is a formidable array of criticism and the reason for such vehement response seems to be the bewildering variety of arguments, statements and justifications offered by Watts separately, Zimmerman separately, the two Watts and Zimmerman papers and the 1986 text.

What needs to be understood by the non-informed reader is that no amount of analysis by these critics can converge on the real methodological approach which characterises PAT. Indeed, one wonders why Watts and Zimmerman went through the laborious process of justifying PAT on all kinds of methodological fronts when, in fact, almost all of them are irrelevant to what PAT is all about. Moreover, Boland and Gordon (1992) explicitly note that the vast majority of these critiques are superfluous to challenging the methodology of PAT. So, perhaps in the final analysis, Watts and Zimmerman's reference to various authorities is a straw man. And since they do not respond in their 1990 summary article to any of these critiques, perhaps the reason is that they are irrelevant to Watts and Zimmerman's actual methodology. In summary, the arguments from the philosophy of science critics are largely based on what they said they were doing whereas, in essence, their methodology is anchored in other arguments.

Despite the apparent diversion from the *a priori* reasoning set up by Watts and Zimmerman, it is nonetheless instructive to review some of the statements made by them and to distil the reasons why the critics took exception to these statements. Following this, an examination of the *de facto* methodology supporting PAT will perhaps be more easily understood.

The odyssey begins with Watts' (1977) discussion of what are confirmable theories from an inductivist point of view. Theory, according to Watts, must meet two criteria: firstly, there must be a set of hypotheses which has been confirmed and, secondly, this set must have been subjected to formal testing. Separately, Zimmerman (1978, 1979, 1980) argues differently. In these papers, Zimmerman appeals to the instrumentalist approach of Milton Friedman and to the positivism ascribed to Paul Samuelson. Initially, it is the views of Watts (1977) that dominate the discussion of methodology in Watts and Zimmerman (1979). Here, theory is defined in terms of 17th century inductivism. In this approach, real world obsevations produce data from which a hypothesis is formed and tested. The hypothesis becomes theory only if there is confirmation from testing. Presumably they believe that this process is positive and not normative because they repeatedly want the reader also to believe that their views are not normative or prescriptive.

By 1986, Watts and Zimmerman unloaded everything from their previous work and more. In the early part of Chapter 1 (p. 8), they try to explain that their view of positive theory is different from the discredited logical positivism of the 1930's. To substantiate this view, they rely on the work of Popper (1963). However, as Boland and Gordon (1992) observe, virtually all of this appeal to Popper is out of context: 'Popper explicitly identifies two groups: "positivist" and "negativists". Popper clearly states that he is a member of the latter group; that is, Popper is not a positivist' (p. 147). After acknowledging the importance of explanation, the reader is puzzled to find Watts and Zimmerman switching a few pages later to a version of Friedman's thinking. Here they admit that some criterion is needed to choose between alternative theories and they opt for the one that is the best predictor 'even if it has a lot of prediction errors' (p. 12).

Sterling, in particular, takes exception to the authorities of Poincare (1905), Passmore (1953), Popper (1959) and Hempel (1965) which are cited for claiming that PAT is scientific theory. After quoting these authorities, Watts and Zimmerman proceed to elaborate on how the concept of theory used in science has traditionally been called positive theory and it is not to be confused with a 'different view of the philosophy of science, logical positivism' (1986, p. 8). In substance, they discredit logical positivism as being scientific.

The irony here for Sterling (1990) is that all four of these authorities are in fact logical positivists:

> 'Poincare is credited with (or blamed for) being an ancestor of logical positivism. Hempel is an avowed logical positivist, having been heavily influenced by Schlick and Carnap, and being well-known for his contributions to logical positivist theories such as the verifiability theory of meaning and the covering law theory of explanation (which is also known as the Popper–Hempel theory of explanation). Similarly, although Popper does not classify himself as a logical positivist, he was influenced by them (and had considerable influence on Carnap), and his *Logic of Scientific Discovery* was published (in German) by the Vienna Circle, the birthplace and long-time home of logical positivism. The article by Passmore (1953) from which Watts and Zimmerman extracted a quotation is a defense of logical positivism' (p. 124).

So it seems that Watts and Zimmerman use logical positivism as support for PAT being scientific and then impeach their own witnesses.

Since much is made of Popper and the methodological rules by which science is said to progress, it is perhaps instructive to digress from other critics of PAT and focus for a moment on this approach to science. Essentially, Popper is concerned with developing a rational theory of the rules of the scientific game. Logical positivism focuses instead on formalising existing scientific knowledge. Popper did not approve of this approach because empirical observations are fallible and, therefore, the epistemological foundations are suspect. The issue here is that through the doctrine of induction, positivists accept the reality of empirical knowledge from the natural world which they claim is irrefutable. Popper viewed this notion of science as unacceptable because experience is always open to re-evaluation and, hence, is contestable and revisable. For Popper, the final arbiter of theories is usefulness which is governed by the objective of decisions.

Whitley (1988) offers four reasons that cast doubt on the formulation of rules which would improve the truth content of scientific theories. Firstly, the Popperian programme does not offer explicit criteria for evaluating observational statements. That is, under what conditions are theories falsifiable in the sense that they do not explain the predictions which occur. Stated differently, are the theories wrong or are the observations incorrect? Without governing criteria, the rules for scientific progress are incomplete. Secondly, it is virtually impossible to develop a single experiment which will decide between two competing theories. Thirdly, there is no common ground for comparing theories over time; as Lakatos (1970) observes, rationality is something that is contingent and contextual. Fourthly, it is unlikely that a community of scholars could be organized around the goal of pursuing absolute truth through a systematic search for falsification.

The application of a philosophy of science programme with the above problems seems of limited value if Watts and Zimmerman are claiming to use it as scientific support for PAT. Whitley (1988) argues that because human science goals are different from natural science, and since social science research is interactive and value-laden, and because meanings and cultural conventions are what constitute social phenomena, the rules of Popper may be totally inappropriate. The outcome is that 'their analysis is seriously flawed and relies on theories of scientific method that are incoherent and inapplicable to accounting research' (p. 643).

Christenson (1983) develops three arguments against the philosophy of science discussion and implications presented in PAT. Specifically, he condemns the use of an outdated philosophy by Watts and Zimmerman which in his view should be called empirical and not positive. Secondly, he also takes issue with their appeal to Friedman (which is prediction-oriented and suppresses explanation). Christenson seems to be arguing that the assumptions underlying equilibrium markets are false which automatically invalidates any claim to prediction. Finally, Christenson is highly critical of the many anomalies which they try and excuse in their results. According to Popper, as Christenson explains, the magnitude of these anomalies would discredit the theory used to produce them and it would not allow for adjustments to the observational data.

Lowe *et al* (1983) pursue similar criticisms of Watts and Zimmerman in their appeal to PAT as being scientific. Firstly, Lowe *et al* argue that the methodology of PAT is seriously suspect in the sense that it is not justified by Watts and Zimmerman. They do not offer any reason for preferring the Popperian approach over others, such as Lakatos (1970). Secondly, Lowe *et al* are concerned that they do not even address what kind of evidence would be necessary to dismiss their theory. This concern has troubled others as well simply because Watts and Zimmerman insist that their method is the only one which is justifiable for generating and assessing knowledge claims in all the sciences.

While the opinion of other critics could be discussed, they either repeat the arguments discussed thus far or twist the critique into an internal debate over their favourite philosophy of science approach. As Boland and Gordon (1992) suggest, such arguments seem futile given the deliberately modest methodology that Watts and Zimmerman actually adopt. Let us examine then what this methodology entails.

Boland and Gordon (1992) nicely capture the simplicity of the Chicago School methodology of Stigler and Becker (1977) which is exactly that of Watts and Zimmerman. Stigler and Becker (1977) argue that a researcher explains phenomena (that is, accounting choice) in terms of utility maximization. The central focus of economic analysis is tied to a decision-maker's objective cost function. Individuals are assumed to never change their tastes or their utility functions. Any changes in behaviour are necessarily explained by a change in the objective cost function. In terms of modelling, the procedure is straightforward: build a model of the cost function, assume all individuals are maximizers and feed the model some data to determine whether the model fits the data. Notice that for anyone to challenge the pivotal role of explanation in this scenario, they would have to provide an alternative model which is a better description of reality or is more useful in making predictions. Watts and Zimmerman do not care at all about verifying (un)realistic assumptions *before* conducting the research. So the view of Watts and Zimmerman by 1990 is that if you think your model is better, test it with some other behavioural assumptions so that the world can compare the models.

4.7 ASSESSING THE ACCOMPLISHMENTS

Demski (1988) considers the sheer novelty of PAT to be one of its unusual strengths. The other unusual strength is that the combination of an under-developed theory and an under-developed set of empirical techniques tells us something about accounting choice which was previously unknown. Although PAT is the state-of-the-art in revealed preference work, Demski is concerned about how this relates to the current mix of regulated, mandated and delegated standard-setting and disclosure reporting. In his view, the long-run success of PAT is linked to these questions of governance.

Watts and Zimmerman (1986) of course, believe that they have contributed significantly to accounting explanation and prediction. They express the optimism that the theory is strong in unravelling the 'confusing mixture of methods' (p. 355). In terms of prediction, they claim that PAT provides useful predictions to investors and analysts because they will not interpret balance sheet and earnings numbers as unbiased estimates of firm value. In their 1990 review of PAT, they further claim that PAT has withstood the test of market failure.

Sterling (1990) is more harsh of the accomplishments of PAT:

> 'In short, Watts and Zimmerman start with the *assumption* that all people act to maximize their utility when selecting accounting methods and after 350 pages they conclude with the *major empirical finding* that managers act to maximize their utility when selecting accounting methods' (p. 128).

This conclusion is not unexpected, beneficial, nor does it contribute to our knowledge of accounting. Other experience, Sterling (1990) notes, has taught us that managers manipulate accounting numbers when it is in their interest to do so. Since PAT ends with this conclusion as a solution, Sterling views it as 'an uninformative restatement of a well-known problem, the place to begin research into ways to solve the problem . . . I assess PAT's addition to knowledge to be nil . . .' (p. 128). In summarising the accomplishments of PAT, Sterling (1990) remarks that

> 'One of the authorities on science cited by W&Z spoke of the fear that the "actual effect of positivism in the social sciences is to lead to the production of a vast quantity of work that boasts of being scientific but is empty and commonplace" (Passmore, 1953, p. 675). In my view that fear has been realized in PAT' (p. 130).

Sterling (1990) of course, is but one voice in the larger community of accounting scholars. One could easily conjecture that if PAT had not been created, then there would be an existing void to be filled by empiricism of some sort and sooner or later someone else would have invented or created the structure espoused by Watts and Zimmerman. If, as Demski (1988) proposes, we were to apply a utilitarian test to PAT, then the conclusion would undoubtedly point to a positive contribution of PAT to our existing stock of knowledge. Obviously, the theory is still in a developmental mode and the statistical techniques are continuously being refined. It would be brutal and hostile, in my opinion, to fault PAT for not providing the ultimate scientific solution (if one exists) to all of our contemporary accounting questions.

There is certainly no doubt that methodological criticisms of PAT have failed the market test in terms of institutional support. As Boland and Gordon (1992) nicely put it, there is nothing wrong with methodological criticism but it is important to understanding why it has failed the market test in the case of PAT. In their view, it is because 'their quality or relevance has not been sufficient to warrant purchase' (p. 164). To be successful, criticism must first emanate from precisely the same paradigm. The paradigm underpinning PAT is neoclassical economics and the assumption of agents operating in perfect markets. Clearly, any worthwhile criticism of PAT must address the issue of the *realism* of this paradigm.

To be sure, real world markets as we encounter them today are not perfect. The fundamental question is 'how close to perfect markets are the manifestations of agents behaviour that we wish to examine'? Watts and Zimmerman assume that sufficient equilibrium prices are available by which the costs and benefits of choosing any accounting method can be calculated. To challenge this assumption by appeal to paradigms external to the neoclassical economic model are invalid, and patently doomed to failure. Whether Watts and Zimmerman, or anyone else, *ought* to be promoting PAT is totally irrelevant to this issue.

4.7.1 Future research opportunities

The theory developed by Watts and Zimmerman has been utilized to develop predictions about the choice of accepted accounting procedures from within the currently defined set of GAAP. This focus needs to be clearly differentiated from predictions about what the set itself is to look like. In other words, predictions about an expanding or restricting set of GAAP is quite different than predictions from within the current set.

Future research can address the issue of the existing set by focusing on the theory's present limitations which include:

(1) Developing better proxy variables to represent contracting and political costs.
(2) Specifying the cross-sectional models.
(3) Collinearity among the contracting variables.

For example, better models that explain cross-sectional variations in the currently existing set of GAAP could benefit managers and lenders. The focus could be on different debt contracts and their respective agency costs. Research here could lead to improvements in the design of contracts for both lenders and managers. Auditors as well could benefit from knowledge of increased predictability. They could use such knowledge to modify audit procedures in cases of earnings approaching the violation covenants of debt contracts.

More intensive research would be required to model the development of the accepted set of procedures rather than managers' choice from within the accepted set. As Watts and Zimmerman note, however, this would be difficult because it would entail modelling the demand for contracts as a monitoring device and comparing the net benefits of alternative methods of monitoring. At the limit, this returns the problem to a comparison of market mechanism versus regulation.

Literally no work has been done on examining the PAT framework in the Singapore context. There is no reason why future research cannot focus on an investigation of contracting costs, compensation plans and political costs using the set of international accounting standards followed by Singaporean companies. Moreover, with the recent mandated disclosure requirement by the Stock Exchange of Singapore concerning E40 and bond–cum–warrant financing, there is a rich opportunity to pursue the above issues. In particular, a shift in the optimal production–investment–financing mix of affected firms in this regard is an immediate and potentially fruitful research opportunity.

4.8 SUMMARY AND CONCLUSION

Watts and Zimmerman have contributed a line of research to accounting thought that is novel and stimulating. Their pursuit is based on the foundations of neoclassical economic theory and is grounded, as most critics would argue, in the weakest of positive methodological approaches to scientific research. Certainly not in dispute, is the observation that they study the behaviour of accountants and accounting practice, and not accounting as an independent art or science form. The domain of accountants and accounting is in no way isomorphic, and it is abundantly clear that any appeal to epistemological sources of scientific truth, verification theories or empirical methods will never make these two domains equal.

Notwithstanding Watts and Zimmerman's choice of paradigms, they appear to have antagonised some scholars by asserting that PAT is scientific, while the study of any other accounting phenomena is unscientific. This sparked rejoinders from the academic community which focused on empirical outcomes and methodological approach. In all fairness, the empirical results to date are weak in terms of statistical support for PAT. However, this suggests that more rigorous and repetitive hypothesis testing is both necessary and potentially fruitful. The debate over methodological approach on the other hand has been a dismal failure.

So, have Watts and Zimmerman wittingly or unwittingly stacked the deck of PAT in their favour? Certainly they have eliminated all alternatives by choosing neoclassical economics to answer their PAT questions which, in fact, are questions from neoclassical economic theory. Moreover, they have insulated themselves from methodological attack within the neoclassical model by challenging other researchers to put forward a better model. They know that unless such an alternative is grounded in neoclassical economic theory, there is no philosophy of science basis for making a comparison. Hence, they are in a no lose situation. Finally, the ideological issue of the merits of society in general versus the self-interest of individual utility maximizers is pre-determined in the PAT model; thus, the latter guarantees universal optimality.

Looking into the future, PAT as a branch of accounting knowledge, has been institutionalised in the education system of most Western countries and in my opinion it will not be easily dislodged. In closing, perhaps the most exciting and challenging avenue for young scholars is to integrate the existing theory and empirical work with the entire governance structure of accounting, including regulation, standard-setting entities, mandated reporting and international harmonisation.

REFERENCES

Ball, R. and Brown, P. (1968). An Empirical Evaluation of Accounting Income Numbers. *Journal of Accounting Research*, pp. 159–177

Ball, R.J. (1980). Discussion of Accounting for Research and Development Costs: The Impact on Research and Development Expenditures. In Studies on Economic Consequences of Financial and Managerial Accounting: Effects on Corporate Incentives and Decisions. Supplement to *Journal of Accounting Research*, pp. 27–37

Beaver, W.H. (1968). The Information Content of Annual Earnings Announcements. In Empirical Research in Accounting: Selected Studies 1968. Supplement to *Journal of Accounting Research*, pp. 67–92

Boland, L.A. and Gordon, I.M. (1992). Criticising Positive Accounting Theory. *Contemporary Accounting Research*, pp. 142–170

Bowen, R.M., Noreen, E.W. and Lacey, J.M. (1981). Determinants of the Corporate Decision to Capitalize Interest. *Journal of Accounting and Economics*, August, pp. 151–179

Canning, J.B. (1929). *The Economics of Accountancy: A Critical Analysis of Accounting Theory*. New York: Ronald Press

Chambers, R.J. (1964). Measurement and Objectivity in Accounting. *Accounting Review*, 39, pp. 264–274

Chambers, R.J. (1966). *Accounting, Evaluation and Economic Behaviour*. Englewood Cliffs, N.J.: Prentice-Hall

Chambers, R.J. (1967). Continuously Contemporary Accounting-Addivity and Action. *Accounting Review*, 42, pp. 751–757

Coase, R. (1937). The Nature of the Firm. *Economica*, 4, pp. 386–405

Christenson, C. (1983). Methodology of Positive Accounting. *The Accounting Review*, pp. 1–22

Collins, D.W., Rozeff, M.S. and Dhaliwal, D.S. (1981). A Cross-Sectional Analysis of the Economic Determinants of Market Reaction to Proposed Mandatory Accounting Changes in the Oil and Gas Industry. *Journal of Accounting and Economics*, March, pp. 37–72

Demski, J. (1988). Positive Accounting Theory: A Review. *Accounting, Organizations and Society*, pp. 626–629

Dhaliwal, D.S. (1980). The Effect of the Firm's Capital Structure on the Choice of Accounting Methods. *Accounting Review*, 55, pp. 78–84

Dhaliwal, D.S., Salamon, G. and Smith, E. (1982). The Effects of Owner Versus Management Control on the Choice of Accounting Methods. *Journal of Accounting and Economics*, July, pp. 41–53

Edwards, E.O. and Bell, P.W. (1961). *The Theory and Measurement of Business Income*. Berkeley: University of California Press

Foster, G. (1980). Accounting Policy Decisions and Capital Market Research. *Journal of Accounting and Economics*, March, pp. 29–62

Friedman, M. (1953). The Methodology of Positive Economics. *Positive Economics*, pp. 3–43

Gilman, S. (1939). *Accounting Concepts of Profit*. New York: Ronald Press

Hawking, S. (1988). *A Brief History of Time*. London: Bantam Books

Hempel, C.G. (1965). *Aspects of Scientific Explanation and Other Essays in the Philosophy of Science*. New York: The Free Press

Hines, R. (1988). Popper's Methodology of Falsification and Accounting Research. *The Accounting Review*, 63, pp. 657–662

Holthausen, R.W. (1981). Theory and Evidence of the Effect of Bond Covenants and Management Compensation Contracts on the Choice of Accounting Techniques: The Case of the Depreciation Switch-Back. *Journal of Accounting and Economics*, March, pp. 73–109

Holthausen, R. and Leftwich, R. (1983). The Economic Consequences of Accounting Choice: Implications of Costly Contracting and Monitoring. *Journal of Accounting and Economics*, pp. 77–117

Jensen, M.C. and Meckling, W.H. (1976). Theory of the Firm: Managerial Behaviour, Agency Costs and Ownership Structure. *Journal of Financial Economics*, 3, pp. 305–360

Kaplan, R. and Roll, R. (1972). Investor Evaluation of Accounting Information: Some Empirical Evidence. *Journal of Business*, pp. 225–257

Lakatos, I. (1970). Falsification and the Methodology of Scientific Research Programmes. In *Criticism and the Growth of Knowledge* (Lakatos, I. and Musgrave, A. eds.), pp. 191–196, Cambridge: Cambridge University Press

Latsis, S.J. (1976). A Research Programme in Economics In *Method and Appraisal in Economics* (Latsis, S.J. ed.), 1–41, Cambridge: Cambridge University Press

Leftwich, R. (1981). Evidence of the Impact of Mandatory Changes in Accounting Principles on Corporate Loan Agreements. *Journal of Accounting and Economics*, March, pp. 3–36

Lilien, S. and Pastena, V. (1981). Determinants of Intra-Method Choice in the Oil and Gas Industry. *Journal of Accounting and Economics*, December, pp. 145–170

Lowe, E., Puxty, A. and Laughlin, R. (1983). Simple Theories for Complex Processes: Accounting Policy and the Market for Myopia. *Journal of Accounting and Public Policy*, pp. 19–42

McKee, Bell, A.T. and Boatsman, J. (1984). Management Preferences over Accounting Standards: A Replication and Additional Tests. *The Accounting Review*, 59, pp. 647–659

Modigliani, F. and Miller, M.H. (1958). The Cost of Capital, Corporation Finance and the Theory of Investment. *American Economic Review*, 48, pp. 261–297

Mouck, T. (1990). Positive Accounting Theory as a Lakatosian Research Programme. *Accounting and Business Research*, pp. 231–239

Passmore, J.A. (1953). Can the Social Sciences Be Value-Free? In *Readings in the Philosophy of Science*, (Feigl, H. and Brodbeck, M. eds.), pp. 674–76, London: Appelton-Century Crofts

Paton, W.A. and Littleton A.C. (1940). *An Introduction to Corporate Accounting Standards*. Chicago: American Accounting Association

Poincare, H. (1905). *Science and Hypothesis*. London: Walter Scott

Popper, K.R. (1956, 1983). *Realism and the Aim of Science*. New York: Rowman and Littlefield

Popper, K.R. (1959). *The Logic of Scientific Discovery*. New York: Harper & Row

Reder, M. (1982). Chicago Economics: Permanence and Change. *Journal of Economic Literature*, pp. 1–38

Sterling, R. (1990). Positive Accounting: An Assessment. *Abacus*, pp. 97–135

Sterling, R.R. (1970). On Theory Construction and Verification. *The Accounting Review*, pp. 444–57

Stigler, G. and Becker, A.C. (1977). De Gustibus non est Disputandum. *American Economic Review*, pp. 76–90

Tinker, A., Merino, B. and Neimark, M. (1982). The Normative Origins of Positive Theories: Ideology and Accounting Thought. *Accounting, Organizations and Society*, pp. 167–200

Vatter, W.J. (1947). *The Fund Theory of Accounting*. Chicago: University of Chicago Press

Watts, R. (1977). Corporate Financial Statements, A Product of the Market and Political Process. *Australian Journal of Management*, pp. 53–75

Watts, R. and Zimmerman, J. (1978). Towards a Positive Theory of the Determination of Accounting Standards. *The Accounting Review*, pp. 112–134

Watts, R. and Zimmerman, J. (1986). *Positive Accounting Theory*. Englewood Cliffs, N.J.: Prentice-Hall

Watts, R. and Zimmerman, J. (1979). The Demand For and Supply of Accounting Theories: The Market for Excuses. *The Accounting Review*, 54, pp. 273–305

Watts, R. and Zimmerman, J. (1990). Positive Accounting Theory: A Ten Year Perspective. *The Accounting Review*, 65, pp. 131–156

Whitley, R. (1988). The Possibility and Utility of Positive Accounting Theory. *Accounting, Organizations and Society*, pp. 631–645

Whittington, G. (1987). Positive Accounting: A Review Article. *Accounting and Business Research*, pp. 327–336

Zimmerman, J. (1979). On the Statement of Accounting Theory and Theory Acceptance. *Proceedings of American Accounting Association*, pp. 1–15

Zimmerman, J. (1979). The Costs and Benefits of Cost Allocations. *The Accounting Review*, pp. 504–521

Zimmerman, J. (1980). Positive Research in Accounting. In *Perspectives in Research*, (Nair, R. and Williams, T. eds.), pp. 107–128. Madison: University of Wisconson

Zmijewski, M.E. and Hagerman, R.L. (1981). An Income Strategy Approach to the

Positive Theory of Accounting Standard Setting/Choice. *Journal of Accounting and Economics*, August, pp. 129–150

5 The Financial Reporting Environment and Its Implications for Accounting Regulation

Pang Yang Hoong and Leong Kwong Sin

5.1 INTRODUCTION

Until the mid 1960s, the objective of financial reporting was stated in terms of fulfilling the stewardship role expected of management (Beaver, 1989). Financial statements were the prime vehicle by which management, as the steward, reported to the shareholders (who supplied the capital) on the manner in which their financial resources had been employed during the preceding year.

However, by the mid 1960s, the stewardship role of financial reporting had given way to a new perspective – that of the informational role of financial reporting, of which financial statements represent an integral but subset of the reporting function.

This move towards an informational perspective can be said to have been the end product of the current financial reporting environment, which has become increasingly more complex. The complexity in financial reporting today has come about because the number of user groups or constituencies who have a stake or a vested interest in the nature of information disclosed has increased over time.

The purpose of this chapter is to examine the intricacies of the reporting environment, the (often competing) informational requirements of the various constituencies, and how the accounting profession has coped with this evolving and increasing demand for information and additional disclosure in financial statements.

5.2   OBJECTIVES OF FINANCIAL REPORTING

The objectives of financial reporting is quite clearly described in the FASB's Statement of Financial Accounting Concepts No. 1 (1978), which states that:

> 'Financial reporting should provide information that is useful to present and potential investors and creditors and other users in assessing the amounts, timing, and uncertainty of prospective cash receipts from dividends or interest and the proceeds from the sale, redemption, or maturity of securities or loans. Since investors' and creditors' cash flows are related to enterprise cash flows, financial reporting should provide information to help investors, creditors, and others assess the amounts, timing, and uncertainty of prospective net cash inflows to the related enterprise.' (page viii)

The Institute of Certified Public Accountants of Singapore (ICPAS) also defines the objective of financial reporting similarly as the provision of information about the financial position, performance and changes in financial position of an enterprise that is useful to a wide range of users in making economic decisions (RAP 1A, para 12).

It is also interesting to note that the FASB, in the same Statement, described the traditional role of stewardship as being subsumed under the informational role of financial reporting, rather than being the primary role as it had been in the past:

> 'Financial reporting is expected to provide information about an enterprise's financial performance during a period and about how management of an enterprise has discharged its stewardship responsibility to owners.' (page ix)

The objective of financial reporting as defined in the FASB Statement above emphasizes two distinct but related roles for financial disclosure.

(1) The first role of financial reporting can be described as facilitating decision-making by various user groups. The predominant user group is the investor group who needs financial information to enable it to make decisions about selling, buying or holding their investments.

(2) The second role of financial reporting is often described as enabling contracting between parties, such as management and investors, by having the payments under the contract (for example, management incentive contracts) defined largely in terms of financial reporting data.

The first role is often termed the 'pre-contracting' role, while the second is called the 'post-contracting' role (Beaver, 1989). These two roles of financial reporting show that financial statement data today serves many (sometimes different and conflicting) users, and that a single set of financial statements must often serve multiple roles. Moreover, the choice of which accounting method and procedure to adopt in preparing the financial statements is indeed a substantive issue as it can have different impacts upon different interest groups.

In RAP 1A, the position adopted by the ICPAS is similar to that adopted by the FASB. It states that financial reporting does not merely serve the role of decision usefulness, it also incorporates the stewardship function. Paragraph 14 states that financial reporting reflects the results of the stewardship of management or the accountability of management for the resources entrusted to it. Those users who want to assess the stewardship of management do so in order to make economic decisions, such as whether to hold or sell their investment in the enterprise or whether to reappoint or replace the management.

5.3   THE SCOPE OF FINANCIAL REPORTING

Accountants tend to define financial reporting as the disclosure or release of financial information about a company within a financial report, which is, in most cases, the annual report. In some instances the term is used in an even more restrictive sense to mean the information that is disclosed in the audited financial statements, which comprise the balance sheet, profit and loss statement and notes to the accounts.

Figure 5.1 (see next page) provides a broad overview of the levels or scope of financial reporting. It shows that financial statements represent only one component of a larger reporting system. It is also interesting to note that financial information about a firm can come from sources outside of the firm, such as analysts' reports, economic statistics and articles about the company.

It should be noted that disclosure about a firm outside of the financial statements serves an important function in financial markets today. Financial intermediaries are in the business to perform such a function. Financial analysts, for instance, conduct private information searches in order to make forecasts of the earnings of a firm. Analysts' reports today contain information about a firm that may not be available in annual reports and are often released to selected clients before the general public has any access to them. They are also generally more timely than annual reports which are prepared only once a year.

In this chapter, financial reporting is defined in the wider context to include the release of financial information beyond what is included in published financial reports.

5.4   USERS OF FINANCIAL INFORMATION

RAP 1A defines the users of financial information to include present and

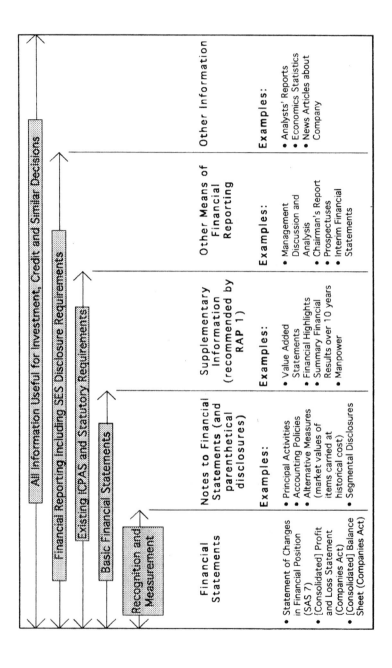

Source: Adapted from FASB's Statement of Accounting Concepts No 5

Figure 5.1   Scope of information in financial reporting

potential investors, employees, lenders, suppliers and other trade creditors, customers, governments and their agencies and the public. Each user group employs financial information to satisfy their own differing needs for information. While it is recognized that there are other sources of financial information besides published financial statements as discussed in the section above, the latter represent one of the main sources of financial information. Companies and the accounting profession are aware of the fact that one set of financial statements are being prepared to attempt to meet the (often differing) needs of these different stakeholders. As will become more apparent later in the chapter, these competing needs among groups of financial information have been largely responsible for inducing a need for the regulation of financial reporting, so as to ensure that financial information is disclosed equitably and in a timely manner.

In general, the users of financial information can be categorized into six major groups: investors, information intermediaries, creditors, regulators, management and auditors. Other users include employees, unions, academics, the financial press and reporting agencies and the public at large. The role and interests of each of these user groups differ, and in many cases, they may even conflict with one another. Moreover, the economic interests of some user groups in financial data are direct, while others have only indirect vested interests in the operations and financial reports of business enterprises. Consequently, financial statement preparers have the difficult task of deciding what information to include in the financial statements so as to best meet the (often competing) needs of these diverse user groups, and ultimately who should bear the costs of such data. The situation is made even more complex by the fact that the information needed by a particular user is dependent on his decision-context which will invariably differ from time to time. The informational characteristics and requirements of each group are described in detail in Beaver (1989) and are summarised below.

5.4.1 Investors

Investors today represent one of the main user groups of financial information. This is because they employ financial information in order to make decisions regarding whether to buy, sell or hold their investments. Investors who are also shareholders are entitled to receive audited financial statements and to attend general meetings of the company. Financial statements are prepared mainly with this user group in mind. However, investors as a group are heterogeneous. They may differ with respect to wealth, access to financial information, and more importantly, the ability to analyse and interpret financial information. These factors have an impact on their demands for financial information. In general, therefore, an investor's demand for information will be dependent on his attitude towards risk, his ability to analyse and use financial information to aid in his decisions and his access to financial sources of information, including financial and/or information intermediaries.

In the finance and accounting literature, investors are classified as being 'informed' and 'uninformed' (Merton, 1987; Grossman and Stiglitz, 1976). This distinction recognizes that as a group, investors have differing abilities and training in accounting, so that there are those who have limited access and ability to understand and interpret financial information, while others, such as investment and portfolio managers and financial analysts, possess the required technical expertise in accounting and financial statement analysis, and are therefore regarded as informed or sophisticated investors.

Some investors who have limited ability to understand and interpret financial information may nevertheless have the opportunity and the financial means to avail themselves of the services of financial intermediaries, such as investment counsellors to whom they can defer a portion of the investment process. Others may avail themselves of the services of information intermediaries, such as financial analysts to whom they can defer a portion or all of the information acquisition and processing of the financial information pertinent to making an informed investment decision. Others, in particular the small investors, may not find the cost of acquiring the services of intermediaries worthwhile relative to the size of their security holdings. As a result, the information demands of individual investors are likely to differ.

Individual investors may also adopt different investment strategies. These investment options in part contribute to the heterogeneity among investors, and in turn, the heterogeneity with respect to the demands for financial information. Beaver (1989) summarizes these investment strategies as taking the following form:

(1) Direct management of their own portfolios or deferral of the investment function to an intermediary;
(2) Use of information intermediaries for the acquisition and processing of information, or dispensing with these services and reliance on their own knowledge and acquisition of information;
(3) Adoption of a diversified versus a non-diversified portfolio;
(4) Adoption of an active versus a passive portfolio management policy.

According to Beaver (1989), an individual investor who uses the services of a financial or information intermediary, would tend to have a reduced direct demand for financial information. In such a situation, the individual investor is shifting his demand for information to an intermediary, who is often regarded in the literature as an 'informed' investor.

Apart from the extent to which the individual investor may defer to intermediaries, they may also differ with respect to investment strategies. Finance theory, or specifically, the mean–variance portfolio theory, states that individual securities are relevant to the investor only in so far as they affect the risk (measured in terms of the variance of return) and the expected return associated with the portfolios (Sharpe, 1978). In the context of the portfolio theory, individual securities are evaluated in terms of their respective contributions to the risk and return of the various portfolios that can be constructed. From this perspective, some aspects of individual security return behaviour may be relatively unimportant to these investors because they can be diversified away. According to portfolio theory, diversification reduces much of the uncertainty or risk associated with holding a single security. In other words, there may be considerable risk involved with regards to the return on a single security, yet through holding a diversified portfolio, much of this risk (termed unsystematic or diversifiable risk) can be eliminated at the portfolio level (Fama, 1976).

In the light of the portfolio theory, the demand for financial information may be dependent on the degree of diversification of the investor's portfolio. The investor is concerned with financial information to the extent that it is useful in assessing the attributes of the portfolio return. For the investor holding a well-diversified portfolio, financial information which helps to assess the overall return of the portfolio will be in demand. However, for the investor who does not choose to hold a diversified portfolio, financial information relating to unsystematic risk may be of greater importance to the investment decision.

Similarly, the demand for financial information may be influenced by the extent to which an investor adopts an active or a relatively passive trading strategy. If a passive trading strategy is adopted, the investor essentially buys and holds a security until it is liquidated for consumption purposes. For instance, the investor may decide to purchase a well-diversified cross-section of securities, such as an index fund, in which case, the direct demand for firm-specific information would essentially be replaced by the demand for market or economy-wide information. On the other hand, an investor who adopts an active trading strategy would continually require information that will permit him to detect mispriced and/or underpriced securities so as to enable continual trading on such information. In short, an active trading strategy involves a concerted effort to take advantage of perceived short term mispricing of stocks and the demand for information will, in the main, be of the kind that helps to predict short term movements in stock prices.

These classifications of investors and their investment strategies are by no means exhaustive nor are they mutually exclusive. However, they do illustrate the fact that investors are indeed a heterogeneous group operating within an environment in which the demand for financial information can be expected to vary across investors, depending on their reliance upon financial and/or information intermediaries, and the specific portfolio and/or trading strategies that they may adopt.

Given the non-homogeneity among investors, it is difficult for financial statement preparers to decide what financial information to provide that will be directly useful to investors. If financial statements are to be prepared for the sophisticated investor, as in the case of the United States, then the preparer of financial statements can assume that the existing set of audited financial statements can be understood by investors. All he needs to do is to find out if the information being included is useful, and if not, what else should be disclosed. However, if financial statements must meet the needs of unsophisticated investors, then it is likely (as many studies have found) that the present set of financial statements do not satisfy the needs of the small investor. The solution may be either to simplify existing financial statements or else to prepare a separate set of simplified set of financial statements that will be understandable to, and useful for, the small, unsophisticated investor.

5.4.2 Information intermediaries

As described by Beaver (1989), information (and financial) intermediaries can be thought of as professionals who develop financial information and aid in its analysis and interpretation. The output of the information intermediaries is therefore also information. These intermediaries take information in their raw form and they transform this information into processed information, incorporating in the process, their ability to understand, synthesize and interpret the raw data. These intermediaries include but are not restricted to financial analysts, bond rating agencies, stock rating agencies, investment counsellors, brokerage firms and portfolio managers. We usually think of these intermediaries as providing a service to consumers of financial information by lowering the cost and/or inconvenience of acquiring such information. In the process, they also help to make the markets more efficient.

According to Beaver (1989), information intermediaries can be viewed as performing three information-related activities:

(1) The search for information that is not publicly available (private information search);
(2) The analysis, processing and interpretation of information for the purpose of prediction (prospective analysis); and
(3) The interpretation of events after the fact (retrospective analysis).

Besides relying on publicly available information, information intermediaries such as financial analysts also gather information from private sources, including management, creditors, suppliers and customers. It has been argued that the activities of these intermediaries help to make the market more efficient because the process of competing analysts searching for information may in part result in security prices that reflect a richer information system (Bernstein, 1975).

Lees (1981) surveyed financial analysts in the United States and found that the sources of information for analysts, in order of importance, were the following:

(1) Interviews with company executives
(2) 10-K's and other reports filed with the SEC
(3) Annual and interim stockholders' reports
(4) Management forecasts, if available
(5) Formal presentations by company executives
(6) Forecasts by other analysts
(7) Press releases concerning the company

Hence, it would appear that these information intermediaries play an important role in the process of acquiring and disseminating information to the investment community. However, the dissemination of information from these intermediaries to the public domain is not a costless process, just as the acquisition of information by these intermediaries is by no means costless. This means that those who avail themselves of the services of these intermediaries, either for convenience or because they are unable to understand and interpret publicly available financial statements them-selves, have to bear the cost of these intermediaries who can be expected to make a profit from their endeavours. They then make decisions by relying on the information and interpretation given by the intermediaries.

It has been argued in the literature that these intermediaries provide a valuable service to investors. Abdel-khalik and Ajunkya (1982) report that the time period before the information acquired by financial analysts is disseminated to the public domain is not trivial. Analysts first provide the information to their select clients who are able to earn abnormal returns by acting on their information. By the time the information is made public, no more abnormal returns are possible. Therefore, it would seem that those investors who do and/or can afford to avail themselves of the services of intermediaries tend to earn higher returns than those who do not or cannot, as they have to rely on their own ability to search for and interpret publicly available information.

As the roles of these information intermediaries are also diverse, the relationship between financial reporting and the information intermediary is by no means simple. At one level, financial reporting provides one source of input factors for the intermediaries. However, if the function of the intermediary is to provide more comprehensive and timely informa-tion, then financial reporting by the company can be regarded as a competing source of information to those users whose information needs are, by and large, provided by the intermediary. The implication of this is that if the small investor and those who rely on financial intermediaries to provide them with financial information are willing to employ these intermediaries, then financial reporting can be modified to ensure that these financial statements contain information that intermediaries want. However, the small investor who cannot afford to pay for an intermediary would be adversely affected.

Information intermediaries such as financial analysts have been considered by the accounting regulators as one of the main users of financial information (FASB Statement of Financial Accounting Concepts No. 1). There has even been an impetus by accounting regulators in the United States towards the provision of financial statements that serve the needs of the 'sophisticated' user, that is, information intermediaries such as financial analysts, to the detriment of the individual (or unsophisticated) investors. There is no corresponding regulation in Singapore requiring the provision of financial statements for the 'sophisticated' user. The Companies Act, in fact, provides that every shareholder has the right to receive a copy of the annual audited financial statements (as well as six-monthly statements for public listed companies). These audited financial statements are prepared to comply with statutory disclosure requirements set out in the Companies Act as well as the various Statements of Accounting Standards (SAS).

5.4.3   Creditors

Creditors as a group include banks as well as suppliers and trade creditors. Banks are interested in financial information that enable them to determine whether their loans and the interest attaching to them will be paid when they fall due. In this connection, they will be interested in information that reflects cash flows and cash commitments as well as the company's ability to generate cash flows in the future.

Suppliers and trade creditors are interested in information that enables them to determine whether amounts owing to them by the company will be paid when due. Trade creditors are likely to require information relating to the shorter term compared to banks, as the credit terms extended by them to the company are likely to be much shorter than the period provided by banks for settlement of a loan or overdraft.

5.4.4   Management

Companies compete with one another for investors' funds in the market. Consequently, they have incentives to provide financial information to the investment community. Management as representatives of their company can also be viewed as agents to whom investors have entrusted the control over a portion of their resources. Hence, the management are expected to report on their stewardship of those resources, and this implies that they have a responsibility to act in the interests of the investors or shareholders. Therefore, a primary role of financial reporting from the perspective of management is to enable shareholders to evaluate their stewardship of resources. This role is also reinforced by the legal liability imposed upon management by securities and company legislation.

In view of the information and operating environment that surrounds management, it is clear that management has a high stake in the financial reporting function. It is also to be expected that management will have incentives to prepare and supply financial information that reflects how well they have performed their stewardship role.

As management are also often compensated on the basis of financial performance, they have the incentive to report financial information in such a manner and within time periods so as to influence their annual compensation favourably (Healy, 1985). The literature reports evidence that management tends to smooth earnings over time, and that accounting policy choices are often made so as to result in smoother earnings trends (Beidleman, 1973). They also exhibit a tendency to disclose favourable information ('good news') much more promptly than unfavourable information ('bad news'), that is, they would attempt to delay the reporting of unfavourable information until delay is no longer possible, as when they are required to file annual returns with the securities commission (Lurie and Pastena, 1975).

The consequence of management's incentives to disclose favourable information while suppressing unfavourable information is that investors may be unable to distinguish between stocks of differing quality to the same extent that they would under fuller and more timely disclosure. This is a major argument in favour of disclosure regulation.

5.4.5   Financial reporting regulators

Financial reporting regulators play an important role in the reporting environment, as they largely determine the nature, the amount and timing of the flow of information from management to the public. In the United States, the primary regulators are the FASB and the SEC, although Congress and other private regulatory agencies can also influence financial reporting requirements (Watts and Zimmerman, 1978). In Singapore, the Companies Act and the Stock Exchange Listing and Disclosure Requirements set out the nature and timing of information to be provided by management on a regular basis, while the accounting profession, namely the Institute of Certified Public Accountants of Singapore (ICPAS), issues standards and provides guidance on reporting and disclosure in financial statements.

The ICPAS is the sole accounting standard-setting body in Singapore. The role of standard setting is performed through the Accounting Standards Committee in conjunction with the Financial Reporting Standards Consultative Committee appointed by the Council of the ICPAS. As the ICPAS is a member of the International Federation of Accountants (IFAC), the promulgations of the IFAC are generally adopted as accepted accounting practice in Singapore unless the particular standard is not applicable to the local context.

In other countries, these regulators also regulate the flow of information from intermediaries to their clients. For example, the SEC has instituted regulation regarding the use of insider information by financial analysts and their clients, essentially prohibiting them to trade on such information (Kripke, 1980). The Securities Industry Act in Singapore also contains regulations regarding insider trading on the Singapore Stock Exchange. Insiders in the Singapore context refer to substantial shareholders, directors and officers of the company and related companies and persons related to these directors and officers.

The role of financial reporting regulation is to ensure that the financial statements and other forms of disclosure provide information that are useful to investors, who are regarded as the main users of financial statements. In the FASB Statement of Financial Accounting Concepts No. 1, the FASB expressly stated that:

> 'The objective stems primarily from the needs of external users who lack the authority to prescribe the information they want and must rely on information management communicates to them.' (page vii–viii).

In a similar vein, the SEC Advisory Committee on Corporate Disclosure (1977) suggested that the purpose of corporate disclosure is:

> 'to ensure the public availability in an efficient and reasonable manner on a timely basis of reliable, firm-oriented information, material to informed investment, and corporate suffrage decision making.' (page D-8)

These stated objectives of reporting and disclosure appear to emphasize the welfare of investors more than that of other user groups like the creditors and employees. In Singapore, the ICPAS adopts a similar position with regard to the objective of financial reporting. In its Recommended Accounting Practice (RAP 1A), the ICPAS states that:

> 'financial statements . . . largely portray the financial effects of past events and do not necessarily provide non-financial information. Financial statements also show the results of the stewardship of management, or the accountability of management for the resources entrusted to it. Those users who wish to assess the stewardship of management or accountability of management do so in order that they may make economic decisions; these decisions may include . . . whether to hold or sell their investment . . . or whether to re-appoint or replace the management.' (Para 13, 14)

This investor orientation appears to tie in with the need to ensure that the market for securities trading is fair so that informational deficiencies due to the lack of adequate disclosure can be prevented. One should note, however, that financial reporting can have effects on resource allocation and capital formation. This objective of financial reporting may not seem to be the main, or one of the main, objectives of financial reporting.

Nevertheless, it is an important aspect of the reporting function and should not be ignored or discounted.

5.4.6   Auditors

The need for management to report on their stewardship of resources as well as the provision of information in a fair and unbiased manner means that there is a need for a 'monitoring' mechanism that is independent of management. The role of the auditor then is to provide an independent review of the operations and financial position of the company, and to make an independent certification as to the 'fairness' of the financial statements. The professional association of auditors and public accountants also provides the standards for disclosure and issues pronouncements regarding new standards and interpretation of standards and disclosure requirements.

In view of the role that the auditor plays, it is expected that the auditor's interests in financial reporting will be to ensure that the welfare of shareholders is not compromised. As with management, this responsibility is reinforced by legislation such as securities and company law setting out the duties and responsibilities of auditors. The Singapore Companies Act provides for the appointment of auditors annually at the Annual General Meeting of members, during which the audited financial statements for the year are presented for members' approval. Therefore, the auditors' responsibility for financial statements is towards shareholders. In addition, the profession has also instituted a system of self regulation through professional codes of conduct and peer review.

A recent development in Singapore is the establishment of audit committees by public listed companies. This is now a requirement by legislation provided in the Companies Act. The functions of the audit committee set out in Section 201B are as follows:

'(a) to review
  (i)   with the auditor, the audit plan;
  (ii) with the auditor, his evaluation of the system of internal accounting controls;
  (iii) with the auditor, his audit report;
  (iv) the assistance given by the company's officers to the auditor;
  (v)   the scope and results of the internal audit procedures; and
  (vi) the balance sheet and profit and loss account of the company and, if it is a holding company, the consolidated balance sheet and profit and loss account, submitted to it by the company or the holding company, and thereafter to submit them to the directors of the company or the holding company; and
(b) to nominate a person or persons as auditor.'

With the addition of the audit committee as a new mechanism of corporate governance, the reporting function is given an added impetus. Financial statements are now reviewed by an additional committee of the board of directors to ensure that the attestation function of the auditor is carried out conscienciously. Investors are seen to have been given added protection through the imposition of this legislation.

5.5   ECONOMIC AND SOCIAL CONSEQUENCES OF FINANCIAL REPORTING

The reporting of financial information can result in various economic and social consequences (Zeff, 1978; Rappaport, 1977). Beaver (1989) summarizes these consequences in terms of the following:

(1) The distribution of wealth among individuals;
(2) The aggregate level of risk and allocation of risk among individuals;
(3) The aggregate consumption and production (for example, effects on the rate of capital formation);
(4) The allocation of resources among firms;
(5) The use of resources devoted to the production, certification, dissemination, processing, analysis and interpretation of financial information;
(6) The use of resources in the development, compliance, enforcement and litigation of regulations; and
(7) The use of resources in the private sector search for information.

These consequences can and often do affect the various interested parties in the financial reporting environment differently. Zeff (1978) remarked that the subject of social and economic consequences 'has become the central contemporary issue in Accounting', and in the article, Zeff provides various instances when the issuance of accounting standards and policies by the accounting regulators actually resulted in various constituencies being adversely affected, and therefore, demanding a voice in the setting of accounting standards. Examples of accounting and reporting issues that have been the subject of the 'economic consequences' debate include the accounting for research and development costs, foreign currency translations, leases, the restructuring of troubled debt, accounting for inflation and relative price changes, and segment reporting.

The discussion in this chapter suggests that the economic and social consequences of reporting can have differing impacts upon different users of financial statements. Consequently, the selection of a financial reporting system and the choice of disclosure policies becomes essentially a social choice. There is unlikely to be a consensus among financial statement users as to the 'best' reporting system. This is because the choice of the 'best' reporting system cannot be made outside of a decision-oriented context, and thus, is likely to be situation-dependent. Moreover, since decisions are ever changing and never constant, no consensus on a single 'best' financial reporting system can be expected to materialize.

In selecting from among reporting alternatives, accounting regulators must make tradeoffs among and between the needs of the various financial statement users. Even within the investor community, the diversities among investors and their preferences for information and trading strategies induce heterogeneous preferences for financial information.

The traditional view espoused by policy-makers, and especially so in Singapore, has been that there is a need to protect small and 'uninformed' investors. This has been motivated by concerns over the information asymmetry in capital markets. The call for regulation to redress such inequities has been generally phrased in (somewhat paternalistic) terms suggesting that uninformed investors are 'at the mercy of market insiders' (Ross, 1979), and that the possibility of fraud is a major moral hazard facing investors.

The response to this plea, especially in the United States, has been that uninformed investors have the means to protect themselves from such moral hazards. For instance, they can minimize trade with the informed, for example, by buying and holding only well-diversified portfolios and not engaging in short run trading strategies (Beaver, 1989). Alternatively, uninformed investors can identify specific groups of insiders, such as managers, and prohibit them by legal or contractual arrangements from trading in the securities of their own firms. In this connection, insider trading laws are by and large effective in protecting the investor community from such insider trades. At the extreme, suspecting gross information asymmetries, uninformed investors may either imitate the actions of the informed investors, or they can withdraw from trading in specific securities or from the stock market altogether (Merton, 1987).

However, Lev (1988) notes that such protective measures are costly to the informed as well as the uninformed investors and even to the economy as a whole. Holding diversified portfolios of securities for the long run only denies investors the benefits of portfolio rearrangements in the light of changed economic circumstances or as their consumption needs and preferences change. Prohibiting managers from owning and trading in the stocks of their own firms effectively eliminates the benefits of owning managerial stocks as a means of aligning the interests of shareholders and managers so as to reduce agency costs. Moreover, if all uninformed investors were to withdraw completely from the market, this will remove from the informed investors the benefits of their costly acquired information, thereby decreasing the incentive for information production. The end result of such action is that the economy will be deprived of the allocational and risk sharing benefits of large and efficient capital markets (Lev, 1988).

The economic consequences of information asymmetry or inequity in capital markets are generally reflected in relatively wide bid–ask spreads, high transaction costs, lower liquidity of traders, thinner volumes of trades, and in general, decreased social gains from trade (Glosten and Milgrom, 1985; Demsetz, 1968; and Mendelson, 1985).

The discussion thus far suggests that there is a need for a mechanism that can mediate between the various needs of the different user groups for financial statements. Such a mechanism should attempt to find a tractable solution to conflicting requirements for information, as well as induce management to disclose information fully and fairly and in a timely fashion. The approach that has been taken in the United States, and in practically every other country has been the regulation of financial reporting.

5.6 WHY REGULATION OF FINANCIAL REPORTING?

The adverse consequences of information inequity or asymmetry in capital markets can be alleviated by removing the major source of inequity – the informational advantage held by informed investors (Lev, 1988). This advantage could be reduced by instituting a policy mandating regular and timely public disclosure of information pertinent to the needs of users, including the uninformed investors. To this end, securities acts, company legislation and stock exchange regulations have mandated the release of annual and periodic financial statements, as well as regular filings of reports with the stock exchanges. Companies legislation and accounting standards and pronouncements regulate the form and content of financial statements, and the independent certification by an auditor adds to these statements the degree of credibility that is necessary to inspire confidence in investors and other financial statement users. This provides for some minimum amount of consistency in the preparation of financial statements and ensures that financial statements disclose certain minimum information regarding the operations and financial position of the company. It also ensures that the welfare of users with limited access to other sources of information about the firms and their operations are adequately protected. Legislation in Singapore has also mandated the establishment of an audit committee of the board with the stated responsibility to oversee the reporting function of management and the attestation function of auditors.

Lev (1988) points out that a policy regulating or mandating public disclosure of accounting information is not assumed to be motivated by an altruistic or politically oriented desire to assist some persons (such as uninformed investors) at the expense of others in a zero–sum sense, as implied in the objective of information disclosure contained in the FASB Statement of Financial Accounting Concepts No. 1. Rather, the motivation for disclosure should be based on the more economically palatable notion that by removing the source of inequity, the generally harmful effects of information asymmetry can be mitigated. With regulation of financial reporting, the protective measures that have been suggested for uninformed investors (Merton, 1987) should then be unnecessary without jeopardizing their welfare.

Lev (1988) suggests that an operational public-interest criterion should be that 'the interests of the less informed investors should, in general, be favored over those of the more informed investors' (p. 13). Such a policy, consistently applied, will contribute to equality of opportunity in financial markets through the decrease in information asymmetries and the increase in the degree of informativeness of prices, thereby alleviating the socially harmful effects of inequity. Lev's suggestion can be implemented partially by providing an alternative set of simplified financial statements alongside the traditional statutory financial statements. These simplified financial statements should be prepared with the 'less informed' investors in mind, so that the information would be presented in a manner that can be readily understood by these less informed investors.

Ultimately, the regulation of financial reporting alone can only provide piece meal solutions to information asymmetry. This is because judgemental decisions must still be made as to which economic consequences and whose interests should be considered as having priority over those of other constituencies. The effective consideration of these substantive issues can only be undertaken through the development of a framework for accounting that jointly recognizes the multiple and complex role of information in a multi-person setting, as well as the explicit recognition of the rationale for regulation as an institutional solution for resolving social choice issues.

5.7 AVENUES FOR FUTURE RESEARCH

This chapter has raised many issues and questions for which further research is warranted. The accounting profession and indeed accounting academics and researchers appear to have abandoned their quest for a theoretical framework for accounting after earlier efforts failed to arrive at fruition. The conclusion arrived at in this chapter is that that the quest should be continued, even though the task is an onerous one. Until a theoretical framework for accounting can be developed within a multi-person, multi-decision setting, accounting practitioners and standard-setting bodies will be forced to adopt piece meal, *ad hoc* solutions to accounting problems as they arise. Such an approach has contributed to the existing state of financial reporting, where accounting standards permit alternative (and sometimes even conflicting) practices in a given situation. Academic researchers should take up the challenge and renew their efforts at developing a unified theoretical framework for accounting.

Research should also be conducted to find ways to operationalize Lev (1988)'s suggestion that information asymmetry can be mitigated by favouring the interests of the less informed investors over those of the sophisticated investors. It was suggested earlier in the chapter that one approach may be to prepare a set of simplified financial statements for these less informed investors. Research could focus on the specific informational needs of this group of investors, and how financial reporting can meet these needs. More importantly, research should aim at determining the form and presentation of these financial statements so that they will be readily understood by less informed investors. A related issue that researchers might also consider is how to provide credibility for this set of simplified financial statements.

Accounting research might also be extended to the question as to how financial reporting can satisfy some (if not most) of the informational needs of different user groups. A partial solution may be to consider whether management is the most suitable agent to provide this financial information. Perhaps the needs of existing and potential investors can best be served by information intermediaries who are in a position to prepare financial reports that would satisfy these investors. Management could then prepare financial statements to satisfy regulatory requirements and the informational needs of creditors and lending agencies.

REFERENCES

Abdel-khalik, A. and Ajinkya, B. (1982). Returns to Informational Advantages: The Case of Analysts' Forecast Revisions. *The Accounting Review,* October 1982, pp. 661–680

Beaver, W.H. (1989). *Financial Reporting: An Accounting Revolution* 2nd edition. Englewood Cliffs, NJ: Prentice Hall

Beidleman, C. (1973). Income Smoothing: The Role of Management. *The Accounting Review,* October 1973, pp. 653–667

Bernstein, L. (1975). In Defence of Fundamental Investment Analysis. *Financial Analysts Journal,* January–February 1975, pp. 57–61

Demsetz, H. (1968). The Cost of Transacting. *Quarterly Journal of Economics,* February 1968, pp. 22–53

Fama, E. (1970). Efficient Capital Markets: A Review of Theory and Empirical Work. *Journal of Finance,* May 1970, pp. 383–417

——, (1976). *Foundations of Finance.* New York: Basic Books

Financial Accounting Standards Board (1978). *Statement of Financial Accounting Concepts No. 1,* Stamford, Conn: FASB

Glosten, L.R. and Milgrom, P.R. (1985). Bid, Ask and Transaction Prices in a Specialist Market with Heterogenously Informed Traders. *Journal of Financial Economics,* March 1985, pp. 71–100

Grossman, S.J. and Stiglitz, J.E. (1976). Information and Competitive Price Systems. *American Economic Review,* May 1976, pp. 246–253

Healy, P. (1985). The Impact of Bonus Schemes on the Selection of Accounting Principles. *Journal of Accounting and Economics*, Vol 7, pp. 85–107

Kripke, H. (1980). Inside Information, Market Information and Efficient Markets. *Financial Analysts Journal*, March/April 1980, pp. 20–24

Lees, F.A. (1980). Public Disclosure of Corporate Earnings Forecasts. *The Conference Board*

Lev, B. (1988). Towards a Theory of Equitable and Efficient Accounting Policy. *The Accounting Review*, January 1988, pp. 1–22

Lurie, A.J. and Pastena, V.S. (1975). How Promptly Do Corporations Disclose Their Problems? *Financial Analysts Journal*, September/October 1975, pp. 55–61

Mendelson, H. (1985). Random Competitive Exchange: Price Distributions and Gains from Trade. *Journal of Economic Theory*, December 1985, pp. 254–280

Merton, R.C. (1987). A Simple Model of Capital Market Equilibrium with Incomplete Information. *Journal of Finance*, July 1987, pp. 483–510

Rappaport, A. (1977). Economic Impact of Accounting Standards — Implications for the FASB. *Journal of Accountancy*, May 1977, pp. 89–98

Ross, S. (1979). Disclosure Regulation in Financial Markets: Implications of Modern Finance Theory and Signalling Theory. In *Issues in Financial Regulation* (Edwards, ed.) New York: McGraw-Hill, pp. 177–202

Securities and Exchange Commission (1977). *Report of the SEC Advisory Committee on Corporate Disclosure*, Washington, DC: U.S. Government Printing Office, November 1977

Sharpe, W. (1978). *Investments*. Englewood Cliffs, NJ: Prentice Hall

Watts, R. and Zimmerman, J. (1978). Towards a Positive Theory of the Determination of Accounting Standards. *The Accounting Review*, January 1978, pp. 112–134

Zeff, S. (1978). The Rise of Economic Consequences. *Journal of Accountancy*, December 1978, pp. 56–63

6 Disclosures That Enhance the Value of Corporate Reports

Gillian Yeo Hian Heng

6.1 INTRODUCTION

The objectives of financial reporting as spelt out by the Financial Accounting Standards Board (FASB) of the United States in its Statement of Financial Accounting Concepts No. 1 (1978) can be summarized as follows:

> 'Financial reporting should provide information that is useful to present and potential investors, creditors and other users in making rational investment, credit and similar decisions. Financial reporting should provide information that is useful to present and potential investors and creditors and other users in assessing the amounts, timing and uncertainty of prospective cash receipts . . .'

The accounting standards body in Singapore, the Institute of Certified Public Accountants of Singapore (ICPAS) stated in its Statement of Recommended Accounting Practice 1 (RAP 1) that:

> 'Financial reporting is essentially a process of communication of information. The success of this communication depends upon the appropriateness of the accounting principles followed in determining net profit or loss and balance sheet values, the degree of disclosure given in the financial statements . . .'

Beaver (1989) summarized the important effects of the disclosure of financial information. Financial information can affect the following:

(1) The distribution of wealth among investors. More informed investors can increase their wealth at the expense of the less informed. Legislation governing disclosure plays an important role in reducing this information asymmetry among investors.
(2) The aggregate level of risk incurred and the distribution of risk among constituencies.
(3) The allocation of investments among firms. Disclosure may alter investors' beliefs about the relative rewards and risks associated with particular securities.
(4) The amount of resources used by the private sector in the search for undisclosed information.

Given the above, it is thus important that financial reporting provides reliable information about the economic reality of the entity. Disclosure of this information is an important factor in the achievement of the efficiency of the capital markets where the securities of these companies are traded.

In Singapore as in all countries, the law lays down the minimum amount of information which management must communicate to investors and the time limits for doing so. The requirements of the law, the Companies Act (Cap. 50), are supplemented by the regulations of the Stock Exchange of Singapore and the accounting standard-setting body in Singapore (ICPAS). The two main types of accounting pronouncements issued by ICPAS are the Statements of Accounting Standards (SAS) and the Statements of Recommended Accounting Practice (RAP). Compliance with SAS is mandatory while compliance with RAP is recommended.

To what extent does present day financial reporting fully achieve its intentions? To what extent have the accounting pronouncements in Singapore facilitated the achievement of these intentions? This chapter aims to provide a discussion on the following issues:

(1) An identification of common problems in present day financial reporting. This includes a discussion of the accounting pronouncements, if any, in Singapore that address these problems and an evaluation of these pronouncements. Where there are no accounting pronouncements in Singapore, pronouncements from the United States and the United Kingdom are used as a basis for discussion.
(2) An analysis of the areas where more extensive disclosure of information is desirable. Arguments justifying the disclosure of such information are included.
(3) An examination of voluntary disclosures in Singapore.
(4) A review of theories relating to management's incentives for voluntary disclosure.

(5) A review of the empirical studies on the different areas of voluntary disclosure.

(6) Conclusion and suggestions for further research.

6.2   SOME COMMON PROBLEMS IN PRESENT DAY FINANCIAL REPORTING

Common problems in present day financial reporting relate to the following:

(1) Adherence to legal form rather than economic substance;

(2) The use of cost rather than value; and

(3) A focus on the past rather than the future.

The above issues were also identified by the Institute of Chartered Accountants of Scotland's publication, *Making Corporate Reports Valuable* (1988). The section below provides a more detailed discussion of some of the above issues and where appropriate, the accounting pronouncements in Singapore that address these issues. An evaluation of these accounting pronouncements is also made. Where there are no pronouncements on a particular issue, the pronouncements from the United States and United Kingdom are used to provide a basis for discussion.

6.2.1   Adherence to legal form rather than economic substance

The focus on form rather than substance attitude has resulted in the prevalence of off-balance sheet financing. Some common examples relate to the following areas:

(1) *Related Party Transactions*
In almost all cases of fraud or misconduct during the past few decades, related parties have played a role. It is easy to use related parties to hide the effects of transactions from those who do not realize the relationship.
The accounting pronouncements in Singapore (SAS 21) on Related Party Disclosures have addressed this issue by requiring all reporting entities to disclose related party relationships in their reports irrespective of whether there have been transactions between related parties. The effects of all significant transactions in which related parties are involved should be disclosed. The nature as well as the types and elements of the transactions necessary for an understanding of the financial statements should be disclosed.

(2) *Associated Companies and Off-Balance Sheet Financing*
In off-balance sheet financing, the total debt of a company increases

but the increased borrowing is not reflected in the financial statements of the company. This enables the company to show better gearing ratios, obtain additional borrowing or have access to additional funds while still maintaining its borrowing limits with its lenders.

The use of associated companies as a means of off-balance sheet financing is common. Through associated companies, losses or debts may be opportunistically shifted off the balance sheet of the investor company. These associate companies are effectively controlled by the investor company.

To address this problem, control (rather than legal ownership) over the activities of another entity should be the dominating factor in deciding whether or not to consolidate, and economic substance rather than legal form should prevail in the presentation of the company's activities and results.

It is good to note that the accounting pronouncement on consolidation in Singapore (SAS 26) requires control rather than mere majority legal ownership as the criteria for consolidation.

(3) *Financial Instruments and Off-Balance Sheet Financing*

In recent years, the increased volatility in financial markets and the changes in the financial services industry have resulted in the use of innovative financial instruments and transactions to manage financial risks. Financial reporting has not kept pace with these financial instruments innovations and as such many financial statement users question whether the information currently provided about financial instruments is adequate. This led the FASB of the United States as well as the International Accounting Standards Committee (IASC) of the United Kingdom to embark on projects on financial instruments and off-balance sheet financing. Both the FASB and IASC projects can be divided into three phases: disclosure, measurement and recognition, and distinguishing between liabilities and equity.

FASB's response to the need for improved disclosure regarding financial instruments resulted in the issue of SFAS No. 105 on *Disclosure of Information about Financial Instruments with Off-Balance Sheet Risk and Financial Instruments with Concentrations of Credit* Risk. The statement requires disclosure about the extent, nature and terms of financial instruments with off-balance sheet risk and related information about credit, market and liquidity risk, as well as information about concentrations of credit risk for financial instruments. IASC's Exposure Draft 48 requires such disclosures for all financial instruments recognized or unrecognized. FASB's focus on financial instruments with off-balance sheet risk (risk of accounting loss exceeding that recognized) is preferred as the focus should be on unrecognized items where losses have not been accounted for. Items recognized would presumably have losses properly accounted for.

The recognition and measurement issues are based on the assumption that all financial instruments regardless of their complexity are made up of a few building blocks or fundamental financial instruments. Complex financial instruments need to be broken down into their fundamental building blocks to determine their economic substance. Understanding and properly accounting for the fundamental instruments is essential to resolving the recognition and measurement problems that arise.

Financial instruments that have the characteristics of both liabilities and equity would have to be reviewed in the light of the definitions of liabilities and equity as specified in the conceptual framework.

At present, there are no accounting pronouncements on financial instruments in Singapore, though IASC's ED 48 is being considered by the profession. Recommended accounting practice RAP 5 on *Off-Balance Sheet Financing and Window Dressing* emphasizes the importance of appropriate accounting in the case of transactions and arrangements involved in both Off-Balance Sheet Finance and Window Dressing. Where inappropriate accounting could mislead, disclosure decisions are inadequate and appropriate accounting must be adopted. RAP 5 also emphasizes the importance of economic substance over legal form in accounting for a transaction. However, RAP 5 tends to be general and more detailed guidelines are needed.

An exposure draft FRED 4 on *Reporting the Substance of Transactions* was issued in 1993 by the Accounting Standards Board of the United Kingdom. The exposure draft sets out general principles covering the following areas: determination of the substance of a transaction, accounting for any resulting assets and liabilities in the balance sheet, disclosures that are necessary, and determination of 'vehicle' companies for transactions that need to be consolidated. Illustrations on how these principles can be applied to specific transaction types such as consignment stock, sale and purchase agreements, factoring, securitized assets and loan transfers are useful. Common features of transactions used in off-balance sheet finance are:

(1) Separation of legal title from the rewards and risks associated with ownership;
(2) A series of transactions used such that their effects are not easily understood; and
(3) Use of options in transactions where it is highly likely that the options are recognized.

The key issue in determining the substance of the transaction is to identify its effects on the assets and liabilities of the entity.

6.2.2 The use of cost rather than value

As a result of the use of cost rather than value, it becomes difficult to judge alternative uses of an entity's resources or how much better off an entity is in this period compared to the previous period. The accounting pronouncements in Singapore require assets to be shown in the balance sheet at depreciated historical cost or at amounts representing current revaluations or revaluations of earlier periods. Valuation of assets is not required to be consistently practised by all firms. As such, sum totals of assets may be meaningless and may not reflect the true financial wealth of the entity at each accounting date.

In the short term, this problem can be addressed by requiring regular revisions. In the long term, the statement of assets and liabilities should be drawn up annually on a value basis. The financial statements should display the financial wealth of the entity at each accounting date. The focus however should be on adopting an appropriate current valuation method and not on general price level adjusted historical cost. Most empirical studies indicate that the relevance of general price level information is either weak or not acceptable. Moreover, inflation is very much controlled in Singapore and is at a low 2% to 3%.

6.2.3 The focus on past rather than the future

Present day financial statements offer little in the way of an evaluation of the future. The balance sheet does not enable the user to judge what alternative uses could be made of the assets, and valuation practices do not show the financial wealth at an entity's command. All the external user receives are comments in the directors' report or chairman's statement. The future cash flow of an entity has to be estimated by the user. The external user therefore has little in a corporate report to help him form a view on the entity's potential future performance and financial position.

To address this issue, a summary of the forecast financial report (profit and loss statement) for at least the coming year could be provided to investors. The summary should be based upon the current methods used in preparing a prospectus, for example, in an issue of shares. The major assumptions used by management in preparing the forecast should be disclosed. Management could also provide a discussion of the differences between the financial forecast disclosed in last year's report and the actual results of the year.

A disclosure of the forecast earnings or earnings per share in the form of a point estimate or range would be very useful. Besides the statement of cash flows for the current year, it will also be desirable for management to have a forecast of the cash flows to come.

Where quantitative estimates of performance are extremely difficult to arrive at, then at least qualitative statements indicating an increase/

decrease in earnings/EPS could be disclosed. Such earnings disclosures could be made not only in the corporate annual reports but could also be disclosed during the financial year in the press or other business publications.

Disclosure of forecasts would provide an improved data base for investors, creditors and other users of financial statements especially with regard to investment and other opportunities. However, there are a number of problems related to the disclosure of corporate financial forecasts. Ijiri (1974) classifies these primary issues as reliability, responsibility and reticence. Reliability relates to the relative accuracy of the forecasts. A number of factors may affect the accuracy of the forecast, for example, the length of the forecast horizon, the nature of the industry in which the company operates (such as volatile industries), the external environment, and the sophistication and experience of the company in producing a forecast. Responsibility refers to the possible legal liabilities of the firms making forecasts and the accountants auditing the forecasts. Given the difficulties associated with identifying and attesting forecasts, Mautz (1974) suggests that accountants should attest to the arithmetic accuracy, the integrity of forecast data, the consistency in application of accounting principles, the adequacy of disclosure, and the reasonableness of assumptions and projections. Reticence refers to the degree of silence on issues that would place the firm at a competitive disadvantage with forecast disclosure.

The empirical evidence has shown that the disclosure of forecasts has definite advantages to investors and the general public. These benefits are discussed in the section on previous research on voluntary disclosures. However, given the difficulties and problems associated with forecast disclosure, it would perhaps be better to have the disclosure of earnings forecasts as non-mandatory for smaller private companies. In the case of larger public listed companies, forecast disclosures should be encouraged.

6.3 AREAS WHERE MORE EXTENSIVE DISCLOSURE OF INFORMATION IS DESIRABLE

The combined requirements of the Companies Act, Stock Exchange listing requirements and the requirements of the accounting profession in Singapore have led to significant disclosures being made about the organization. The arguments for further disclosures, financial or non-financial, must be justified in terms of the additional costs involved versus the resulting benefits for the various user groups.

The following sections provide a discussion of some of the areas where more extensive disclosure of information is desirable. The arguments justifying such disclosure are also addressed.

(1) The overall objectives of the entity and to what extent these are achieved
(2) The economic environment which the entity is in
(3) Exchanges between the entity and its social environment
(4) The human assets of the entity
(5) Market capitalization measures
(6) Cash flow reporting
(7) Value-added reporting

6.3.1   Objectives of the entity

Information relating to the objectives of the entity in present day corporate reports is normally given in very general terms in the Chairman's statement or an equivalent. As such, financial statement users may not be fully aware of the main aims of the entity and to what extent these are being achieved.

To address these requirements, management could formally draw up a Statement of Corporate Objectives and this should be reviewed by the board of directors on a regular basis to evaluate the extent of achievement. An appropriate summary of the statement could be contained in every corporate report issued.

6.3.2   Economic environment

More information can also provided about the environment within which the entity is operating, the state of the markets in which the entity deals in its share of the market, currency management effects, effects of technological changes, and other matters.

Information on these as well as comparative operational statistics should be disclosed as far as possible.

6.3.3   Social accounting

In traditional financial accounting, exchanges between the firm and its social environment are ignored. Social accounting is used to express a corporation's social responsibilities. This means an extension of disclosure into the non-traditional areas such as providing information about employees, products, community service, and pollution prevention and reduction measures. Social accounting is also taken to describe a form of accounting called socioeconomic accounting which measures and discloses the costs and benefits to society created by the production activities of the organization. These social costs and benefits are internalized to determine a more relevant and exhaustive result that represents the socioeconomic profit of the firm.

The justification for providing such disclosures is based on the following arguments:

(1) Effects of the disclosure of socially oriented information on the capital markets;
(2) The moral obligations of the organization as a corporate citizen; and
(3) The concept of organizational legitimacy.

A number of empirical research studies have attempted to assess the relevance to investors of certain social responsibility disclosures by firms by evaluating their effects on security returns. The results of these studies indicate that:

(1) The price behaviour of firms making social disclosures differs from that of firms not making such disclosures (Belkaoui, 1976).
(2) Pollution control records are useful in assessing a firm's total systematic risk (Spicer, 1978).
(3) The information content of a firm's social responsibility disclosure depends on the market segment identified with the firm (Ingram, 1978).

Donalson (1982) indicated that the underlying function of all organizations from the standpoint of society is to enhance social welfare through satisfying consumer and worker interests, while at the same time remaining within the bounds of justice. When they fail to live up to these expectations, they are deserving of moral criticism.

Lindblom (1983) argued that organizations seek to establish congruence between the social values associated with or implied by their activities and the norms of acceptable behaviour in the larger social system of which they are a part. Where these two value systems exist, organizational legitimacy exists to justify the continued existence of the organization.

6.3.4   Human assets of the entity

More information can also be provided in corporate reports about those who manage the entity and on the staff of an entity.

Information can be given about the past experience of directors and senior managers and their past and present directorships. As regards information on staff, it would be desirable if the personnel's contributions to the difference between an entity's market capitalization and its financial wealth can be arrived at in some way. There have been many research papers on the topic of 'human asset accounting' but the efforts of trying to bring the 'human asset' into published financial statements has been rather unsatisfactory.

Monetary measures of human assets include historical cost or acquisition cost, replacement cost, opportunity cost, the compensation model and adjusted discounted future wages. The historical cost or acquisition cost method consists of capitalizing all of the costs associated with recruiting, selecting, hiring, training, placing and developing an employee and amortizing these costs over the expected useful life of the asset. The replacement cost method consists of estimating the costs of replacing the firm's existing human resources. The opportunity cost method as proposed by Hekimian and Jones (1969) establishes human resource values through a competitive bidding process within the firm whereby managers bid for the scarce employees they need to recruit. The compensation model as proposed by Lev and Schwartz (1971) determines the value of human capital as the present value of his or her remaining future earnings from employment. The adjusted discounted future wage method as proposed by Hermanson (1964) values an employee by adjusting discounted future wages by an efficiency factor computed as a ratio of the return on investment of the given firm to all other firms in the economy for a given period.

6.3.5 Market capitalization

It is not the practice to disclose the value that the market places on an entity's issued capital. There could be definite advantages in disclosing the market capitalizations of the company. Users can then make comparisons between that figure and the figure shown in the balance sheet for shareholders' funds and seek explanations of the difference.

The difference can be accounted for by the presence in the entity of a host of interacting and complex qualities such as organization, corporate culture, goodwill, staff morale and trademarks. In addition, the market capitalization figure can be affected by economy-wide or industry-wide factors. It would be helpful if management would comment on the difference between the market valuation and the disclosed financial wealth.

6.3.6 Cash flow reporting

Accrual accounting facilitates the evaluation of management's stewardship and is essential to the matching of revenues and expenses. The efficacy of the accrual system has been questioned, however. Thomas (1969) states that all allocations are arbitrary and incorrigible and recommends the minimization of such allocations. Advocates of cash flow reporting base it on the investors' desires to predict cash flows. A cash flow ratio would be a more reliable investment indicator than the present price–earnings ratio due to the many arbitrary allocations.

Empirical evidence supports the association of both operating cash flows and accruals with abnormal security returns (Rayburn, 1986). This is the case when both cash flows and accruals have information content.

6.3.7 Value-added reporting

The value-added statement like a modified version of the income statement reports the return of the company to a larger group of capital and labour providers. The benefits of including a value-added statement in the company's annual report are (Belkaoui, 1992):

(1) Value-added statements perceive employees as responsible participators in a team effort with management. This may motivate employees to work harder.
(2) Productivity incentives for employees may be based on value added ratios.
(3) Value-added ratios provide better measures of the strength, size and importance of the company.

6.4 VOLUNTARY DISCLOSURES IN SINGAPORE

Recommended accounting practice, RAP 1, on *Standards of Disclosure in Financial Statements*, recommends the following voluntary disclosures: summary of financial results, manpower, financial highlights of the year and value-added disclosures.

Other than the disclosure on manpower and value added statements, the disclosure of past summary of financial results and highlights do not provide new or additional information to users.

The Institute of Certified Public Accountants of Singapore (ICPAS), the Singapore Institute of Management and the Stock Exchange of Singapore hold an Annual Report Award (ARA) competition yearly. The objectives of the ARA as spelt out in the guidelines are:

(1) To encourage full and prompt disclosure of relevant financial and other information;
(2) To encourage the development and use of valid/objective measures of organization performance;
(3) To increase the awareness within the organization of the role of accounting and practices recommended by ICPAS, both mandatory and voluntary;
(4) To increase the awareness of the organization's responsibilities as a corporate citizen; and

(5) To enhance communications between employers and employees so as to create a sense of pride in the organization they work in.

Evaluation of the annual reports is carried out based on the amount of detailed information provided under each section of the annual report. The sections relating to voluntary disclosures of information are:

(1) *Chairman's Statement and Management's Review*
Information to be provided includes:
- (a) special trade conditions or factors of a material nature affecting the year's trading results
- (b) circumstances relating to abnormal or extraordinary items of a material nature
- (c) material changes in the nature of business such as principal activities, geographical diversifications, technological developments and others
- (d) review of divisional activities
- (e) review of economy (economies) and industrial sector of the company

(2) *Indication of Prospects*
Indication of company's earnings prospects together with any material assumptions made, plus corporate plans for the coming year.

(3) *Financial Highlights*
This gives the 'Year at a Glance' presentation for important items like turnover and related data, earnings per share data, return on shareholders' funds, dividends per share and others. Historical data for at least five years in the form of a summary profit and loss account and balance sheet and key financial ratios can be provided.

(4) *Value–Added Statement*
The objective of presenting the value-added statement is to provide users of financial statements with information on the value-added by the operations of the enterprise. The information include value-added from operations and distribution to employees, providers of capital, government and the residual that is retained by the entity. The guidelines also indicate that it would be useful to have the value-added statement extended to incorporate value-added per employee, per dollar of employment costs, per dollar of investment in fixed assets and per dollar turnover.

(5) *Productivity Indicators*
These are measures of efficient utilization of resources. Examples of such indicators using a per employee or per dollar capital employed basis include units produced/sold, traffic/tonnage handled and others.

(6) *Information on Directors, Management and Employees*
   Information on directors, senior managers and employees together
   with key responsibilities.
(7) *Information on Shareholders, Share prices and Turnover*
   An analysis of shareholders by type, size of shareholding,
   geographical location, and others.
(8) *Social Responsibility Reporting*
   Reporting of social activities under the following headings:
   environment, energy, fair business practices, community
   involvement, products and other social responsibility disclosures.

While some companies are already recognizing the need for more
informative disclosures, there is clearly substantial scope for improving the
level of information provided, subject to the constraints of commercial
confidentiality. The attraction of winning the Annual Report Award does
offer strong incentives for companies in Singapore to provide corporate
reports with as much relevant information as possible. Apart from the
award, what other incentives exist for management to make more
informative disclosures?

6.5 THEORIES RELATING TO MANAGEMENT'S INCENTIVES FOR VOLUNTARY DISCLOSURE

6.5.1 Agency theory

Recent theories of the firm in accounting and finance view the firm as a
'nexus of contracts', implicit and explicit, between suppliers of various
forms of production. Many of these contracts are defined and monitored
in terms of accounting numbers. If a firm issues any form of capital to
outsiders (non-managers), an agency relationship exists between the
holders of outside capital (principals) and the managers (agents). An
agency relationship gives rise to 'agency costs' because the agent is
expected to act in his own interest which need not be consistent with the
interests of the principals. This moral hazard problem arises because of
informational asymmetry. Typically, the agent has access to superior
information and will use the information to maximize his self-interest at
the expense of the principal.

If capital markets are characterized by rational expectations as it is
under the efficient market hypothesis, the outside shareholders do not on
average lose from the manager's moral hazard behaviour. These shareholders are price protected as the market price will reflect the anticipated
divergence in behaviour.

Agents therefore have incentives to devote resources to reduce this
divergence in behaviour. The principal can constrain and monitor the

agent's behaviour and the agents can offer to impose certain restrictions on their own behaviour through bonding arrangements (Jensen and Meckling, 1976).

Hence, the higher the level of agency costs, the greater the incentives for managers to employ monitoring. One of the means of such monitoring is through the public disclosure of the firm's information so as to remove the superior information position of the management.

6.5.2   Signalling theory

The management of the firm is assumed to be more informed about the firm than the investors. Assuming financial markets do not fully reflect all information, especially that which is not publicly available, then it is possible for managers to use financial policy decision to convey information to the markets. The first application of **signalling** to finance theory was put forth by Ross (1977). He suggests that what is valued in the market place is the perceived stream of returns for the firm. Hence, changes in capital structure or dividend policy may alter the market's perception of the firm's risk class even though the actual risk class remains unchanged. Managers as insiders who have monopolistic access to information about the firm's expected future cash flows will choose to establish unambiguous signals about the firm's future if they have the proper incentive to do so.

The idea of signalling through capital changes or dividend policy can be extended to accounting choices. Management of high quality firm may be motivated to signal to outsiders that their firm belongs to a more desirable category or quality. The signalling could be done through the public disclosure of some superior information that management has. Management has incentives to publicly disclose the information to potential buyers that leads them to believe that their securities are underpriced.

In general, signalling involves undertaking some action that would be irrational unless the firm belongs to the category of higher quality securities. It may be costly to signal and there is the question of credibility of the evidence. For example, the effectiveness will be affected by the ability of the firm of lower quality to imitate the signalling behaviour and lie about the information they have.

6.5.3   Expectation adjustment hypothesis

King, Pownall and Waymire (1990) provided a framework for future empirical analysis of managers' economic incentives to voluntarily disclose earnings forecasts. The framework is based on the expectations adjustment hypothesis advanced by Ajinkya and Gift (1984) under which managers disclose forecasts to induce a revision in investors' expectations of future earnings.

The relation between transaction costs, information asymmetry and corporate disclosure in secondary security markets is analyzed using the expectations adjustment hypothesis.

Earnings forecasts are released by managers to align investor expectations with their own expectations. Forecast disclosure reduces information asymmetry among investors and leads to reduced transaction costs in the market. These transaction costs include investors' expenditures incurred for private information, the bid–ask spread charged for market-making services and others.

These transaction costs are greater when opportunities to trade on private information are greater. (Copeland and Galai, 1983; Glosten and Milgram, 1985; and Diamond, 1985). If traders expect managers to disclose information, their incentive to acquire costly private information is reduced, so timely public disclosure reduces secondary market transaction costs and improves shareholders' wealth.

A sizeable amount of research literature exists on voluntary disclosures in the United States and in other parts of the world. The section below provides a review of this literature in the various areas of voluntary disclosures.

6.6   PREVIOUS RESEARCH ON VOLUNTARY DISCLOSURE

6.6.1   Disclosure of interim financial reports

Leftwich *et al* (1981) investigated the voluntary submission of interim financial reports by companies in the United States. The objective was to determine if the submission of interim financial reports is a function of variables suggested by the agency theory. They postulate that the demand for interim reporting is a function of the following seven variables: ratio of assets-in-place, size of the firm, leverage ratio for debt, leverage ratio for preferred stock, use of outside directors, reporting frequency 10 years beforehand, and exchange listing. However, the overall results of their research are not strong and do not support the postulated relationships between the economic variables and reporting frequency.

6.6.2   Lease disclosures

Bazley *et al* (1985) examined the factors that influence voluntary lease disclosures in Australia. The paper examines whether a firm discloses its lease obligations prior to the issuance of accounting standards on leases.

The independent seven variables chosen are: size, industry, subsidiary relationship (subsidiaries of American and Canadian parents are more likely to disclose), auditor, Australian Institute of Management competition, management compensation schemes, and borrowing agreements. Applying various univariate and multivariate tests, their study shows that these variables have only modest explanatory power.

6.6.3 Segment reporting

A study on voluntary disclosures of segmental information by Salamon and Dhaliwal (1980), addresses the question of whether small companies should be exempted from certain disclosure requirements by the Securities Exchange Commission in the United States. The results suggest that many large firms voluntarily disclose segmental data whereas small ones do not. The paper also tests the relationship between capital structure and voluntary disclosure. The results show that diversified firms which obtain long term capital externally are more likely to voluntarily disclose segmental financial data than diversified firms which do not. The authors conclude that imposing the same level of disclosure requirements on all firms will impose relatively larger costs on small firms. Firms with larger public and investor interest will disclose financing information even in the absence of mandatory requirements.

6.6.4 Current cost disclosures

Wong (1988) examined the economic factors influencing management's decision to present current cost financial statements in New Zealand. The factors considered are: tax rates, leverage ratios, market concentration ratios, historical return on assets, capital intensity, and firm size. The paper concludes that companies which voluntarily submit current cost financial statements have higher effective tax rates, lower leverage ratios, larger concentration ratios and are more capital intensive. These results suggest that companies subject to higher political costs will make discretionary choices to reduce these costs.

6.6.5 Value-added disclosures

A study conducted by Ariff and Gan (1993) identified whether the management of a firm in Singapore use value-added disclosures (VAS) to reveal information about systematic differences in key characteristics or quality of their firm relative to other firms. Variables suggested by agency theory and signalling theory were identified and these were grouped under size, performance and market value-based ratios. The results suggest that firms making a choice for VAS are significantly different from firms not deciding to do so. The VAS-disclosing firms are generally bigger, perform better and appear to have low price to book values.

6.6.6 Earnings forecasts

The literature on voluntary disclosures of earnings forecasts relate to disclosures made by management of firms in the United States that are outside the corporate annual reports. The majority of these forecasts are released through the press and business publications. The literature can be categorized under the following:

(1) *Management's Motivation to Disclose Forecasts*

The models developed by Verrecchia (1983) and Dye (1985) generally show that in the presence of disclosure-related costs, managers who seek to maximize firm value exercise discretion in disclosing their private information by suppressing bad news and revealing only favourable news. The level of disclosure depends on the costs associated with the disclosure of information.

Trueman (1986) showed that the manager uses the forecast release to provide a signal to investors of his ability to anticipate future changes in the firm's economic environment and to adjust production plans accordingly. The act of the forecast release itself provides investors with favourable information. The timing of the forecast release also affects firm value. The earlier the disclosure of earnings forecasts, the higher the end-of-period market price of a firm's stock.

(2) *Characteristics Of Firms Which Voluntarily Disclose Management Forecasts*

Variables reported as significant in discriminating between voluntarily disclosing firms from non-disclosing firms include:

(a) Earnings variability: disclosing firms have significantly less variability in their earnings per share series (Imhoff, 1978; Cox, 1985).

(b) Firm size: disclosing firms are typically larger than non-disclosing firms (Ruland, 1979; Cox, 1985).

(c) Security analysts' mean absolute relative prediction errors: Imhoff (1978) found that the error in security analysts' forecasts is significantly lower for voluntary forecast disclosure firms than for non-disclosing firms.

(3) *Capital Markets And Management Earnings Forecasts*

Patell (1979), Penman (1980) and Waymire (1984) provided evidence on the extent to which price reactions to management forecasts are associated with information content in management earnings forecasts. The evidence showed that:

(a) Good news (bad news) management forecasts are associated with significant positive (negative) abnormal returns in the days immediately surrounding the date of management forecast publication; and

(b) A significant positive association exists between the magnitude of forecast deviation and the magnitude of abnormal returns in the period immediately surrounding the forecast disclosure date.

In general, the results of these studies show that management forecasts convey new information to the market.

6.6.7   Social responsibility reporting

There are several studies on surveys done to determine the extent of social responsibility disclosure practices of companies in Australia, United Kingdom and United States (Guthrie and Parker, 1990; Hall and Jones, 1991; and Zeghal and Ahmed, 1990). Generally, the results of these studies show that a very high percentage of the large listed companies in these countries publish social information in their annual reports. The themes for disclosure range from human resource disclosures, community involvement, the environment, energy and product disclosures. There are also a number of studies where the authors looked at stock market, report user or firm financial performance responses to social disclosures (Parker *et al* (1989), McGuire *et al* (1988) and Patten (1990)). The results of these studies generally indicate that the perceived need for social accounting varies according to the type of investor. The evidence is still not yet conclusive.

6.7   CONCLUSION AND AREAS FOR FURTHER RESEARCH

For capital allocation to proceed efficiently in our economy, information must be disseminated both promptly and publicly. This applies to financial statements as well as other financial and non-financial information that can affect the perceptions of the value of the company. Financial reports ought to portray economic reality. In this chapter an attempt was made to examine how present day financial reporting can more fully achieve its objectives as laid down by the standard-setting bodies. Some common problems in current financial reporting were discussed and an evaluation of the extent of to which the accounting pronouncements in Singapore have addressed these problems. Areas where more disclosure of information is desirable were identified. However, the arguments for further disclosures, financial or non-financial, would need to be justified in terms of the additional costs involved versus the resulting benefits for the various user groups. In conclusion, the following areas for further research are identified:

(1) Methods to identify the substance of transactions, to recognize and measure these transactions in the financial statements. The area of financial instruments is one where much research is needed.

(2) Research on the usefulness of adopting a current valuation method for financial statements in the Singapore context.

(3) Research on the value of corporate financial forecasts to investors, creditors and other users of financial statements.

(4) Research on the effects of disclosure of supplementary financial reports (social, value-added reports, information on market measures and economic environment) to investors and other users of financial statements.

(5) Research on the factors that motivate management to voluntarily disclose more information, identifying the benefits and costs to them.

REFERENCES

Ariff, M. and Gan, A. (1993). Signalling Explanation for Voluntary Disclosure of Value Added Statement in Singapore. *Securities Industry Review,* October

Beaver, W.H. (1989). Financial Reporting: An Accounting Revolution (2nd ed.). Prentice-Hall

Belkaoui, A. (1976). The Impact of the Disclosure of the Environmental Effect of Organisational Behaviour on the Market. *Financial Management,* Winter

Belkaoui, A.R. (1992). Accounting Theory. Harcourt Bruce Jovanerich Publishers

Copeland T. and Galai D. (1983). Information Effects on the Bid Ask Spread. *Journal of Finance*

Cox, C. (1985). Further Evidence on the Representativeness of Management Earnings Forecasts. *Accounting Review,* October

Diamond D. (1985). Optimal Release of Information by Firms. *Journal of Finance,* September

Donalson, T. (1982). Corporation and Morality. Englewood Cliffs, New Jersey: Prentice-Hall

Dye, R. (1985). Disclosure of Nonproprietary Information. *Journal of Accounting Research,* Autumn

Financial Accounting Standards Board (1978). Statement of Financial Accounting Concepts No. 1. *The Objectives of Financial Reporting* by Business Enterprises, FASB

Financial Accounting Standards Board (1990). Statement of Financial Accounting Standards No. 105: *Disclosure of Information about Financial Instruments with Off-Balance Sheet Risk and Financial Instruments with Concentration of Credit Risk*

Glosten, L. and Milgrom P. (1985). Bid, Ask and Transaction Prices in a Specialist Market with Heterogenously Informed Traders. *Journal of Financial Economics*

Guthrie, J. and Parker, L.D. (1990). Corporate Social Disclosure Practice: A Comparative International Analysis. *Advances in Public Interest Accounting,* Vol. III

Hall, C. and Jones, M. (1991). Social Responsibility Accounting: Myth or Reality? *Management Accounting,* March

Hekimian, J.S. and Jones, J.G. (1967). Put People on Your Balance Sheet. *Harvard Business Review,* January/February

Hermanson, R.H. (1964). Accounting for Human Assets. *Occasional Paper No. 14.* East Lansing, Mi: Bureau of Business and Economic Research, Graduate School of Business Administration, Michigan State University

Imhoff, E. (1978). The Representativeness of Management Earnings Forecasts. *Accounting Review,* October

Ijim, Yuji (1974). Improving Reliability of Publicly Reported Corporate Financial Forecasts, in *Public Reporting of Corporate Financial Forecasts,* (eds). P. Prakesh and A. Rappaport

Ingram, R.W. (1978). An Investigation of the Information Content of (Certain) Social Responsibility Disclosure. *Journal of Accounting Research,* Autumn

Institute of Certified Public Accountants of Singapore (1989). Statement of Recommended Accounting Practice 1A: *Framework for the Preparation and Presentation of Financial Statement, ICPAS*

Institute of Certified Public Accountants of Singapore (1987). Statement of Accounting Standard No. 21: *Related Party Disclosures*

Institute of Certified Public Accountants of Singapore (1990). Statement of Accounting Standard No. 26: *Consolidated Financial Statements and Accounting for Investments in Subsidiaries*

Institute of Certified Public Accountants of Singapore (1987). Statement of Recommended Accounting Practice 5: *Off Balance Sheet Financing and Window Dressing*

International Accounting Standards Committee (1994). Exposure Draft 48: *Proposed International Accounting Standard on Financial Instrument, IASC.*

King R., Pownall, G. and Waymire, G. (1990). Expectation Adjustment via Timely Management Forecasts: Review, Synthesis and Suggestions for Future Research. *Journal of Accounting Literature,* Vol. 9

Leftwich, R., Watts and Zimmerman J. (1981). Voluntary Corporate Disclosure: The Case of Interim Reporting. Studies on Standardization of Accounting Practices: An Assessment of Alternative Institutional Arrangements, supplement to Vol. 19 of *Journal of Accounting Research*

Lev, B. and Schwartz, A. (1971). On the Use of the Economic Concept of Human Capital in Financial Statements. *The Accounting Review,* January

Lindblom, C.K. (1983). The Concept of Organizational Legitimacy and its Implications for Corporate Social Responsibility Disclosure. *AAA Public Interest Section Working Paper No. 7.*

Mantz, R.K. (1974). A View from the Public Accounting Profession, in Public Reporting of Corporate Financial Forecasts (eds). P. Prakesh and A. Rappaport.

McGuire, J.B., Sundgren, A. and Schneeweis, T. (1988). Corporate Social Responsibility and Firm Financial Performance. *Academy of Management Journal,* Vol. 31, No. 4

Parker, L.D., Ferris, K.R. and Otley, D.T. (1989). Accounting for The Human Factor. New York, Prentice Hall

Patell, J. (1976). Corporate Forecasts of Earnings per Share and Stock Price Behaviour: Empirical Tests. *Journal of Accounting Research,* Autumn

Patten, D.M. (1990). The Market Reaction to Social Responsibility Disclosures: The Case of the Sullivan Principles Signings. *Accounting Organizations Society,* Vol. 15, No. 6

Penman, S. (1980). An Empirical Investigation of the Voluntary Disclosure of Corporate Earnings Forecasts. *Journal of Accounting Research,* Spring

Rayburn, J. (1986). The Association of Operating Cash Flow and Accruals with Security Returns. *Journal of Accounting Research*

Ross S.A. (1977). The Determination of Financial Structure. The Incentive Signalling Approach. *Bell Journal of Economics,* Spring

Spicer, B.H. (1978). Investors, Corporate Social Performance and Information Disclosure, An Empirical Study. *The Accounting Review,* January

Thomas, A.L. (1969). Accounting Research Study No. 3. The Allocation Problem in Financial Accounting Theory, (Sarasota, Fl: *American Accounting Association*)

Trueman, B. (1986). Why Do Managers Voluntarily Release Earnings Forecasts, *Journal of Accounting and Economics,* January

Verrecchia, R. (1983). Discretionary Disclosure. *Journal of Accounting and Economics,* December

Waymire, G. (1984). Additional Evidence on the Information Content of Management Earnings Forecasts, *Journal of Accounting Research,* Autumn

Zeghal, D. and Ahmed, S.A. (1990). Comparison of Social Responsibility Information Disclosure Media Used by Canadian Firms. *Accounting Auditing & Accountability Journal,* Vol. III, No. 1

7 The Regulation of Financial Reporting and Quality of Information: A Comparative Analysis of Singapore, Malaysia and Thailand

Joanne Tay

7.1 INTRODUCTION

Corporate financial reporting takes many forms, ranging from press releases and earnings announcements to annual reports. These are important sources of information to investors in public companies and their advisors or proxies, such as financial analysts, stockbrokers and fund managers. As such, the quality of this information is highly important. Corporate financial reporting is thus invariably subject to regulation regarding form, content and timing.

An analysis of corporate financial reporting regulation in Singapore, Malaysia and Thailand is of interest for several reasons. Foreign investors, both within and outside the Association of Southeast Asian Nations (Asean), have shown a great interest in the listed companies in these countries. The Stock Exchange of Singapore (SES) and the Kuala Lumpur Stock Exchange (KLSE) have been established regional equity markets for some time. In contrast, the Securities Exchange of Thailand (SET) has only been growing rapidly since the mid 1980s in conjunction with the booming Thai economy. SET has also been the subject of a planned and consistent development programme overseen by the Thai government, in recognition of the importance of foreign investment, both direct and indirect, in developing the economy.

A number of differences exist in various aspects of corporate financial reporting regulation in these countries. The Companies Acts requirements in Singapore and Malaysia are, on the whole, fairly comprehensive and comparable to similar legislation in countries such as Australia and the United Kingdom. Thailand has a Commercial Code, but the accounting requirements contained in this Code can only be described as basic. Finally, the professional accounting bodies in these countries differ in several aspects, not least the manner in which accounting standards are developed and implemented. A comparison among these three countries could thus yield insights into the impact of economic development and regulatory form on the quality of corporate financial reporting.

This chapter begins by briefly reviewing the research literature, both analytical and empirical, on corporate reporting regulation and the quality of information. This is followed by a description and analysis of the regulatory framework governing corporate financial reporting in Singapore, Malaysia and Thailand. Finally, some empirical evidence on the quality of information provided in the published annual reports of Malaysian, Singaporean and Thai listed companies is examined.

7.2 THE REGULATION OF FINANCIAL REPORTING

7.2.1 Types and forms of regulation

There are many different systems of corporate financial reporting regulation in existence. Some systems are set out by government legislation (such as a Companies Act), others by privately-produced professional accounting standards (such as the Statements of Accounting Standards (SAS) issued by the Institute of Certified Public Accountants of Singapore). Some systems of regulation are national, relating to various forms of enterprises domiciled in a particular country, such as Thailand's Commercial Code. Other systems are international, pertaining to specific types of enterprises operating in different countries, such as the International Standards of Accounting and Reporting for Transnational Corporations produced by the United Nations.

The majority of regulatory systems are a mixture of legal, professional and listing requirements. In some countries, professional requirements have also attained the status of law (for example in Canada, the law requires companies to comply with the accounting standards issued by the Canadian Institute of Chartered Accountants, a self-regulating professional body). It is more usual, however, for a national government to establish a quasi-statutory body to set legally approved accounting standards, such as the Australian Accounting Standards Review Board.

Regulation of financial reporting addresses different aspects of the information produced by companies. The *form* of information to be provided is usually specified, for example, what reports and financial statements must be provided (directors' report, balance sheet etc.) Sometimes the layout of the reports and statements is also prescribed. More importantly, however, the minimum *content* of these reports and statements will be set out. The accounting (valuation) treatment of certain items, such as types of fixed assets, investments or physical stock, may be recommended or required, for example the use of cost and/or net realisable value. Regulation will also set out the *type of information* which must be disclosed, such as the quantum of directors' fees and the amount of interest charges paid during the year.

Regulations also specify the *timing* of the information produced. Such requirements will specify deadlines by which reports have to be filed or the number of times per year that certain information has to be produced (such as quarterly reports). In some countries, the *medium* in which the information has to be announced is also specified, such as a national newspaper. Finally, most regulatory systems will include some form of *monitoring mechanism* to ensure that other requirements have been fulfilled, such as a compulsory audit or a statutory review unit.

7.2.2 Regulation research: focus and difficulties

Research on corporate financial reporting regulation has been voluminous and varied. Many different theories have been drawn on, mainly to argue the issue of more–versus–less regulation (Ross, 1979; Aivazian and Callen, 1983). These arguments have usually taken the form of deductive economic analysis, based on the criterion of Pareto optimality (Watts, 1980; Benston, 1982; Cooper and Keim, 1983).

There have been fewer empirical studies of the effects of creating and operating different regulatory systems (Stigler, 1964; Benston, 1973; Chow, 1983). One obvious reason for this is the conceptual and operational difficulty of measuring the effects of regulation. For example, the direct cost of creating and maintaining the Securities and Exchange Commission (SEC) in the United States, which monitors US listed companies, may be calculated, though with some difficulty. However, when companies are required to produce and/or disclose more information, how would the compliance costs borne by these companies be defined and measured? It is argued that greater information disclosure has benefits for the disclosing companies as well as users, but how are these benefits to be defined: in terms of changes in share prices, stability of share prices, or some other measure? And if increased disclosure lowers the cost of risk capital to disclosing companies, how should this benefit be weighed against the cost of disclosing sensitive information to competitors?

7.2.3   Compliance with regulation

In the more–versus–less regulation debate, the proponents for more regulation assume that companies will comply with regulations once the requirements are established. The proponents of less regulation argue that much of the information which is required by regulation would be provided by companies even in the absence of such regulation. It has been suggested, however, that companies do not in fact comply with all the requirements to which they are subject. It has also been suggested that different sources of regulation may have an impact on compliance with requirements. It is usually believed that the same requirement would elicit a higher compliance rate if contained in the law or a listing manual rather than a professional accounting standard (Tay and Parker, 1990, p. 75). However, much less attention has been devoted to the compliance aspect of regulation. This is an empirical field of research, as it would be necessary to review the information actually produced by companies to ascertain the degree to which companies comply with regulation. The results of such research would be interesting and useful to regulators, given the different costs associated with the different types and forms of regulation.

7.3   THE QUALITY OF CORPORATE FINANCIAL REPORTING

7.3.1   Quantity and quality of information

The quality of information may be evaluated both by the amount and type of information disclosed, and the superiority or inferiority of disclosure and measurement (valuation) methods used in providing the information.

Disclosure has been defined as the 'clear showing of a fact or condition on a balance sheet or other financial statement, in footnotes thereto, or in the audit report' (Kohler, 1957). These facts or conditions are 'economic information relating to a business enterprise, quantitative or otherwise, which facilitates the making of investment decisions' (Choi, 1973, p. 160). Disclosure thus relates to both quantitative information which affects a company's results (for example, the amount of directors' annual remuneration), and qualitative information which does not affect the results but may affect an evaluation of the entire company (such as the extent of directors' shareholdings).

The nature of adequate disclosure has been thoroughly discussed (Buzby, 1974a; Wallace, 1987). It is a relative concept, which will and indeed should vary in different situations, depending upon the audience for whom the disclosure is made, the purpose for which the disclosed information will be used, the quantity of information required by users, the manner in which the disclosure is made, and the timing of the disclosure. Buzby (*ibid*) suggests that the selection of the audience and purpose for evaluating the quality of disclosure should consider which groups and purposes exhibit the greatest use of and dependency on financial statements, as well as the homogeneity and information-processing capabilities of competing groups, and concludes that financial analysts represent the best compromise. This conclusion is implicitly supported by the many disclosure studies which have used the stated information needs of financial analysts to assess the quality of disclosure in financial reports (Baker and Haslem, 1973; Chandra, 1974; Belkaoui *et al*, 1977; Benjamin and Stanga, 1977; Firth, 1978). It also receives direct support from research findings that individual investors rely most heavily upon information from stockbrokers when making investment decisions (Baker and Haslem, *ibid*; Baker *et al*, 1977).

7.3.2 Disclosure indices

Many studies have attempted to measure the level of disclosure of information by using a disclosure index (Singhvi and Desai, 1971; Buzby, 1974b; Barrett, 1976 and 1977; McNally *et al*, 1982; Marston, 1986; Wallace, 1987). Such indices may be thought of as 'approximate model[s] of adequate corporate disclosure' (Singhvi and Desai, *ibid*, p. 130), and may be either weighted or unweighted. Weighted indices are conceptually superior, as they incorporate some evaluation of the quality as well as quantity of information provided. Choi (1973) used both weighted and unweighted versions of the same index to compare disclosure in two different years, and found that the use of weights changed the rankings and even the signs of the differences in disclosure scores. However, the use of alternative indices made no significant difference to his results.

Disclosure indices have been criticized on three counts by Dhaliwal (1980).

(1) The indices used in empirical studies have usually been derived by literature searches or surveys of the information needs of various groups of users of corporate financial reporting. As such, any particular index may be incorrectly specified due to reliance on the *perceptions* of users of their needs, rather than their *actual* needs. This criticism is supported by behavioural research in accounting, which indicates that 'individuals (even experts) have poor insight into their own judgement process ... [and] 'subjective' weights are much more evenly distributed across cues [that is, items] than are statistically derived weights' (Ashton, 1974, p. 728).
(2) Dhaliwal also points out that some index items may be redundant, as each item is scored on the basis that its relative importance to a financial analyst does not change, no matter what other information

is available to him. Dhaliwal suggests that a more appropriate approach would take into account the consideration that 'the significance of any single disclosure item is related to the absence or presence of other disclosure items' (*ibid*, p. 387).

(3) Finally, the use of the index may only be appropriate in a given context, as the relative importance of items changes according to time and situation. Thus, for example, Marston's evaluation of disclosure by Indian and UK companies (1986), using the index originally developed by Barrett (1976) to evaluate disclosure by US, Japanese and European countries, may be valid only in the context of evaluation by a US or European user.

These arguments do not invalidate the use of indices but suggest that more care be taken in index construction and scoring. For example, the criticisms made could be addressed by carefully selecting items which have been consistently identified in studies based on both user perceptions and statistical models. The items included in a particular index may be strictly quantitative in nature and mutually exclusive, so that their importance cannot be diluted by the presence of other items. The context of the evaluation of disclosure should also be considered and specified, for example, an international investor from the United States or United Kingdom reviewing information produced by companies listed in Third World bourses.

7.4 SINGAPORE, MALAYSIA AND THAILAND: THE LEGAL FRAMEWORK

Singapore was a British Crown Colony until 1959, and still owes much of its social, political and administrative framework to British influence. Malaysia's colonial link with the British system is also reflected in many ways in its corporate reporting environment, which is very similar, though not identical, to that in the United Kingdom. Gray *et al* (1984) indicated three international influences on Malaysian financial reporting: the UK (very strong), Australia (strong) and the United States (moderate). In contrast, Thailand was never formally colonized by any of the Western powers; however, its legal system shows some influence from both French and German law.

7.4.1 The law in Singapore

The Companies Act

The Singapore Companies Act was based solely on UK legislation until 1967, when it became more closely modelled on Australian companies legislation (Hwang, 1982, p. 12). Companies are required to prepare accounts which show a *true and fair* view of their financial position and results for the accounting period, and all limited liability companies are subject to a compulsory statutory audit. The auditor has the statutory duty to render an opinion on the *truth and fairness* of the accounts prepared by the company.

A comprehensive Amendment Act was passed in 1987 with far-reaching implications for corporate governance and accounting regulation. In particular, company management is now required to maintain adequate internal accounting control systems, and listed companies and their subsidiaries are required to establish audit committees. These committees, consisting of a majority of non-executive directors, have the statutory duty to communicate with the external auditor during the various phases of his audit, and must also review the scope and work of the internal audit department. The statutory auditor is also required to report to the Minister of Finance if, in the course of his audit, he has reason to believe that serious fraud has occurred. In terms of overall disclosure requirements, however, the Amendment Act's extensive changes to the Ninth Schedule made little actual impact, as they served mainly to include in the Schedule requirements previously contained in the professional accounting standards issued by the Institute of Certified Public Accountants of Singapore (ICPAS).

The Accountants Act 1987

The Accountants Act 1987 took effect in February 1989. As a result, the Public Accountants Board was established to license and discipline practising accountants. The Singapore Society of Accountants, a professional self-regulating body established in 1964, was reconstituted as the ICPAS.

Tax law

As in the United Kingdom, the Singapore tax system does not require conformity between tax and financial accounting. Thus, tax regulations have little impact on corporate financial information.

7.4.2 The law in Malaysia

The Companies Act 1965

The Companies Act 1965 was based principally on the United Kingdom's Companies Act 1929 and Australia's Victoria Companies Act 1961. The

Victoria Act was itself adapted from the United Kingdom's Companies Acts of 1907, 1929 and 1948 (Walton, 1986). The Malaysian Act included the UK 1948 Act's requirement for consolidated accounts, and the Victoria Act's more detailed disclosure requirements for the balance sheet and profit and loss account. In addition, it goes beyond these two pieces of legislation with regards to the scope of the directors' report, with directors being required to take responsibility for asset valuation, unusual items and contingent liabilities. The law also requires the provision of a funds statement as part of the financial statements.

The financial statements which must be filed with the Registrar of Companies under the Act thus consist of the balance sheet, the profit and loss account, the funds statement and the notes to these three documents. The directors' report, a statement signed by two directors that in their opinion the financial statements present a *true and fair view* of the company's financial position and the results for the period, and a statutory declaration by a director or person responsible for the company's financial management on the *correctness* of the financial statements must also be filed.

The Companies Act also imposes a statutory audit requirement for all limited liability companies, regardless of size. The auditor must be approved by the Minister of Finance, usually on the condition that he is a member of the Malaysian Institute of Accountants (MIA), with his principal or only residence in Malaysia. The auditor is required to report on the *truth and fairness* of the financial statements, and the auditor's report and financial statements must be filed together.

The bulk of the reporting requirements imposed by the Act are contained in the Ninth Schedule. These consist mainly of disclosure items, although there are some valuation rules relating to fixed assets. The Ninth Schedule was substantially revised in 1985, which came into effect from 1 February 1986, to include many disclosure requirements which had previously been required only by professional standards.

Another requirement introduced in the 1985 revision of the Companies Act was the registration of all firms of public accountants in Malaysia, and individual partners of such firms, with the Registrar of Companies. Each partner is allocated a registration number, which must be cited in all audit reports.

The Accountants Act 1967

The Malaysian profession is regulated by the Accountants Act 1967, which established the MIA. Until the late 1980s, the MIA's sole activity was the registering of practising accountants. This was important as MIA registration is the basis for determining who is qualified to provide audit and accountancy services in Malaysia. Registration was considered necessary because Malaysian accountants have traditionally had very varied educational backgrounds and qualifications. However, membership in the MIA is usually obtained through membership of other accountancy bodies, principally the Malaysian Association of Certified Public Accountants (MACPA).

Tax law

As in Singapore, the Malaysian tax system does not require conformity between tax and financial accounting. Thus, tax regulations have little impact on the financial information produced by Malaysian companies.

7.4.3 The law in Thailand

Ministerial Regulation No. 2

Ministerial Regulation No. 2 BE 2519 (1976) contains the minimum disclosures to be made in the balance sheet and profit and loss account of various enterprises, including limited liability companies. It came into effect on 1 January 1977, and was the first Thai legislation to have a direct impact on Thai financial reporting. Its requirements remain unchanged till today.

The disclosure requirements vary according to the legal form and type of business in which an enterprise is engaged. The Regulation distinguishes among registered partnerships, companies engaged in commercial banking, insurance, credit *foncier* (hire purchase), financing, securities, warehousing and other types of business, branches of foreign banks and insurance companies, and juristic persons established under foreign laws.

The objective of the Regulation is to ensure that the financial statements issued by different entities conform to similar standards. Conformity was sought in order to raise the standard of accounting, to help both in the development of the equity market and in tax and duty collection. Standardisation of disclosure was thus equated with improvement in financial reporting. However, the Regulation only deals with disclosure, and not with the valuation of items disclosed. Moreover, the disclosures required are quite basic and have never been increased, mainly because the majority of Thai companies are still family businesses, with little or no need for external capital.

The Public Companies Act

The Limited Public Company Act BE 2521 (1978), which came into force at the end of March 1979, was part of the government's efforts to develop the Thai equity market. The Act requires audit of the company's balance sheet and profit and loss account, and the publication of an annual report, containing information about the company, its holdings of shares in subsidiaries and private companies, details of contracts between the company and its directors, and details of directors' holdings of shares or debentures of the company and its subsidiaries. Another requirement is the creation and maintenance of a legal reserve, consisting of transfers of at least 5% of the annual net profit, until the reserve forms at least 25% of registered capital.

The annual report and the audited balance sheet and profit and loss account (in Thai) must be filed with the Registrar within one month of their approval at the annual general meeting. The balance sheet must be published in a national newspaper for at least one day within that period.

Tax law

Conformity between book and tax reporting is required if companies wish to claim the full amount of allowances. This inevitably has an impact on the valuation of depreciating or depleting assets. Given the basic disclosure requirements, the result is that the accounts produced, especially by non-quoted companies, may be of more use for tax purposes than for financial analysis.

The Auditor Act

The Auditor Act BE 2505 (1962) set up the Board of Supervision of Auditing Practices (BSAP), consisting of representatives of the government, the universities and the profession. The BSAP regulates the application for and issue of licences to Authorized Auditors, and maintains a Register of Authorized Auditors. Certification of published accounts may only be carried out by Authorized Auditors, and unauthorized certification will involve imprisonment of up to one year, and/or fines of up to 10,000 baht.

The BSAP functions as part of the Ministry of Commerce. It sets licensing examinations for accountants, which are held every six months in June and December. An examination candidate must have had at least a four-year university education and 2,000 hours in public practice within at least two years.

The BSAP's other main activity is the monitoring of annual financial statements produced by *all* Thai companies (about 50,000 in all) for accounting and auditing compliance with legal and professional requirements. BSAP staff (most of whom are not trained accountants) review a sample of financial statements each year. This process is lengthy, involving examination of the working papers on which the financial statements are based, and interviews with the company auditors and executives if problems arise. In all probability, only a very small proportion of the accounts published each year are examined by the BSAP. However, penalities may be severe. The BSAP issues warnings when it is not satisfied with the financial statements, and may suspend or even revoke the licence of the auditor involved.

7.4.4   Distinguishing features

Legal regulation in Singapore is distinguished by a number of features. Firstly, a statutory audit requirement applies to all limited liability companies, regardless of size. Such companies must produce annual accounts which show a 'true and fair view' of their financial position and results, and the auditor is required to qualify his audit report if the financial statements do not comply with the Companies Act or professional accounting standards. The Companies Act also requires company management to implement an adequate system of internal accounting controls. In addition, listed companies and their subsidiaries must establish audit committees to review the work of both the external and internal auditors.

The Malaysian Companies Act requires all limited liability companies to produce annual accounts which must include a funds statement. These accounts must show a true and fair view of the company's financial position, results and funds flow for the accounting period, and are subject to a statutory audit. In addition, the officer responsible for the accounting records and the company's financial management must make a statutory declaration that the accounts are correct. As in Singapore, the auditor must qualify his report if the accounts do not comply with the law or professional accounting standards.

In Thailand, the format (that is, the order and description) of balance sheet and profit and loss account items is specified in the Commercial Code. Audits are required for all companies, and auditors are expected to qualify accounts which do not comply with the law and accounting standards. The annual reports of companies are scrutinized by the BSAP on a sample basis.

7.5 THE ACCOUNTANCY PROFESSION

7.5.1 Singapore

The Institute of Certified Public Accountants of Singapore (ICPAS)

The ICPAS has about 7,500 members, over 5,000 of whom are non-practising. All members are, however, designated Certified Public Accountants (CPAs) whether they are in public practice or not.

The ICPAS deals solely with professional matters, ethics, standards and professional development. Its main emphasis is on maintaining professional behaviour and quality of work. To this end, a Practice Review programme was implemented from July 1994 to ensure consistent audit quality. A varied Continuing Professional Education (CPE) programme is also offered to members and non-members.

The ICPAS has a relatively high profile and standing in Singapore. It participates in dialogue sessions with the Registrar of Companies and Business, and the Inland Revenue Authority of Singapore (IRAS). In addition, it has a heavy involvement in regional professional matters, such as advising on the establishment of professional bodies and professional training in countries like Brunei and the People's Republic of China.

Professional accounting standards

Prior to 1970, there were no local professional accounting standards, and accounting practices were a mixture borrowed from the United Kingdom, Australia and Canada. In consequence, 'there was little uniformity in accounting practices, even within the same industry' (Hwang, 1982, p. 12). From 1970 to 1977, the Singapore Society of Accountants (SSA), the predecessor body of the ICPAS, issued a series of Bulletins and Statements of Accounting and Auditing Practices. These represented codification of existing practices and requirements of the Companies Act, as well as what the SSA considered best practice in the Singaporean context. These pronouncements were not mandatory, but members were strongly encouraged to follow them. During this period, the Financial Statements Review Committee was formed (see next page).

The SSA joined the International Accounting Standards Committee (IASC) in 1975. In 1977, the Accounting Standards committee was established, with responsibility for setting accounting standards and issuing other technical pronouncements. The Committee reviews International Accounting Standards (IAS) and IASC Exposure Drafts, and recommends these statements for adoption by the ICPAS, either in whole or in part. The ICPAS Council decides on adoption and which companies are to be affected. The statement is then exposed for comment for a period of six months. Implementation is usually effective from the beginning of the following year.

The ICPAS now issues two different types of accounting pronouncements. Compliance by ICPAS members is mandatory for Statements of Accounting Standards (SAS). Statements of Recommended Accounting Practice (RAP) outline best practice, but are not mandatory.

The Financial Statements Review Committee

The Financial Statements Review Committee is by far the largest committee in the ICPAS. The committee reviews financial statements on a continuous basis and draws the attention of members responsible for their preparation, or for reporting on them, to any areas in which the presentation or content falls short of compliance with the law and ICPAS pronouncements. The financial statements reviewed comprise a mixture of accounts produced by public and private companies, prospectuses and gazetted and other accounts. As a result of these reviews, practising members may be referred to the Public Accounting Practice Committee for counselling and follow-up to ensure that higher standards are maintained in future.

The Committee also prepares a report every three years, summarising its findings on non-compliance with disclosure requirements in the financial statements reviewed. This report is circulated amongst all the ICPAS practising members.

7.5.2 Malaysia

The Malaysian Institute of Accountants (MIA) and the Malaysian Association of Certified Public Accountants (MACPA)

The MIA is essentially a statutory body, and much of its efforts have been focused on prosecuting non-registered individuals who have been holding themselves out as accountants. It has also established a review of the by-laws on professional conduct and ethics in order to minimize the extent of government regulation of the profession. As at the end of 1989, the MIA had approximately 5,500 members, of whom about one-third were public accountants.

The MACPA was incorporated in 1958, and had about 1,700 members as at the end of 1989. The Association is active in technical activities such as accounting and auditing standard-setting. In addition, it consults with the relevant authorities in relation to amendments to the

Companies Act, the Listing Manual of the KLSE and banking guidelines. It also has dialogue sessions with the Inland Revenue.

Professional accounting standards

In the early 1970s, the MACPA issued Statements dealing with financial reporting disclosures and the forms of various reports, such as the auditor's report and the accountant's report for prospectuses. Apart from these, there were no professionally developed accounting standards in Malaysia. Financial reporting practice was, for the most part, based on the recommendations or standards of the various foreign professional bodies to which practising Malaysian accountants belonged, mainly the Institute of Chartered Accountants in England and Wales (ICAEW) and the Chartered Association of Certified Accountants (CACA).

The MACPA became a member of the IASC in 1975. Since then, the Association has implemented a systematic process of reviewing, adapting, exposing and ultimately adopting IAS in Malaysia. In addition to IAS, the MACPA has also developed a number of its own accounting standards, called Malaysian Accounting Standards (MAS). These deal with accounting topics of local importance that are not covered by IAS (such as accounting for plantations) and topics for which a particularly Malaysian treatment is required (such as earnings per share and acquisitions and mergers).

Finally, the MACPA also issues Technical Bulletins (TB), which represent the opinion of the Association's Technical Committee in situations where no standards or guidelines have been issued, or where an existing statement requires amplification.

From the late 1980s to the early 1990s, the MACPA and the MIA were parties to a cooperation agreement which provided for joint development and issuance of all technical standards for the accountancy profession in Malaysia. MIA committees reviewed and adopted the standards issued by the MACPA prior to 1987. For the past few years, however, the standard setting activities of the two professional bodies have developed separately. However, both bodies require their members to comply with the standards issued, and to qualify their audit reports appropriately in cases of non-compliance.

Review of Financial Statements

Both the MIA and the MACPA have established separate Financial Statements Review Committees to raise professional standards by under-taking reviews of published statements. These reviews ensure that statements comply with legal and professional requirements. The MACPA Committee focuses on the annual reports of public listed companies, while the activities of the MIA Committee concentrate on unlisted companies. Where a statement shows non-compliance with requirements, the committee will draw the attention of the company and its auditors to the relevant areas.

The work of these two Committees is undeniably very limited, as no more than about 25 annual reports are reviewed in any one year. Moreover, the results of these reviews are not made public, so that pressure for improvement can only be exerted by the professional bodies on their members (rather than company management) with no support from the law, the financial press or public opinion. There have been no reported cases to date of MIA or MACPA members who have been disciplined for failing to ensure that requirements have been met. This suggests either that non-compliance is not significant, or that the procedure is relatively ineffective. However, beyond the statutory audit requirement, neither the legal nor professional framework in Malaysia provides for formal and regular checks on the vast majority of Malaysian companies.

7.5.3   Thailand

The Institute of Certified Accountants and Auditors of Thailand (ICAAT)

Although ICAAT was established in 1948, the accountancy profession was only formally recognized in Thailand in 1962 when the Auditor Act was passed. Membership is open to those who possess an accountancy degree or a diploma or certificate which the Institute recognizes as equivalent, or a BSAP licence to practise as an Authorized Auditor (which is only available to university-educated accountants).

The Institute has about 900 members, working in both the public and private sectors. About 50% are Authorized Auditors licensed by the BSAP. This is a minority of the 1,500 Authorized Auditors in public practice, and the total of 2,800 Authorized Auditors in Thailand. This situation may be due to the fact that ICAAT membership is not required to practise in Thailand. Thus there is no incentive for qualified persons to become or remain members of the Institute. This is reflected in ICAAT's low membership fees (current membership registration fee is 50 baht, and annual fees are 100 baht), which adds to the Institute's funding problems. Although ICAAT has been in existence for nearly fifty years, it still has neither permanent office nor full-time staff.

Professional accounting standards

Thailand is unique among the Asean member states, in that neither ICAAT nor other regulatory bodies have resorted to wholesale adoption of accounting standards issued by other professional bodies, either national or international. Gray *et al* (1984) reported 'significant' IASC influence, and 'moderate' UK influence on Thai financial reporting practice. This can be seen from the list of ICAAT pronouncements, which includes topics not presently covered by UK accounting standards. ICAAT also considers Financial Accounting Standards Board (FASB) and American Institute of Certified Public Accountants (AICPA) pronouncements, and Thai audit reports are couched in terms of *fair presentation, generally accepted accounting principles* and *generally accepted auditing standards.*

ICAAT's accounting sub-committee, comprising members of the Institute, academia, practice and the Ministry of Finance, formulates proposals for new Statements of Financial Accounting Standards (SFAS), and undertakes the technical research for each topic. First drafts are exposed to ICAAT members and interested parties through seminars and hearings, and questionnaires sent to selected individuals to elicit more comprehensive responses. An executive committee collates all the amendments or additions brought up through the exposure process and revises the standard. After approval by the ICAAT Board, the standard is forwarded to the BSAP for official agreement. This is necessary because the BSAP is responsible for monitoring compliance with the standard.

Compliance with SFAS is required by both the BSAP and SET. ICAAT's numerous exposure drafts also have some authority: the BSAP issues warnings to companies which do not comply with the requirements of the drafts.

As at July 1990, ICAAT has issued 15 SFAS: the first five in 1979, one each in 1986, 1987 and 1988, five in 1989 and the last two in January 1990. It also has 21 exposure drafts in issue. This large number of exposure drafts in relation to adopted standards may be due to a lack of resources of finance and manpower, in both setting and enforcing standards, as well as a cautious and conservative approach to standard-setting. However, topics covered by these statements indicate a sophisticated approach to financial reporting, especially in the area of company financing. This may indicate the important influence of the capital market on external financial accounting standards.

7.5.4   Distinguishing features

In Singapore, the ICPAS has issued a comprehensive set of accounting standards, based on IAS. Many of the requirements contained in these accounting standards have now been incorporated into the Companies

Act. The Institute also has a Financial Statements Review Committee, which examines the published accounts of companies on a sample basis each year.

Malaysia has two professional accounting bodies, the MIA and the MACPA, with a fair degree of overlapping membership. The profession has developed a comprehensive set of financial accounting standards, both by developing its own and adapting or adopting relevant IAS. Both the professional bodies have regular, though very limited, review programmes for examining published financial statements.

The Thai professional body, ICAAT, is older than the professional bodies in Singapore and Malaysia, but it is undeniably less well established in terms of membership and activities. This is most clearly seen in the small number of Thai professional accounting standards, which rely on other bodies for enforcement. The derivation of these standards from IAS is also not as apparent as is the case with Malaysian and Singaporean accounting standards. However, the influence of the AICPA is more obvious, especially for listed companies, due to SET listing requirements (see next page).

7.6   LISTING REQUIREMENTS

7.6.1   The Stock Exchange of Singapore (SES)

The SES imposes some, but not many, additional reporting requirements on listed companies. Companies are required to comply with the accounting standards issued by the ICPAS. In addition, in response to government promptings for more stringent regulation of the securities industry, the SES has formulated a corporate disclosure policy that requires companies to make immediate public disclosure of material information in a manner designed to obtain the fullest possible public dissemination. Companies are also expected to clarify or confirm market rumours and unusual market actions, and to refrain from unwarranted promotional disclosure, specifically exaggerated reports and predictions (Framjee, 1987, p. 19).

7.6.2   The Kuala Lumpur Stock Exchange (KLSE)

The KLSE Listing Manual contains various regulations with which member firms and quoted companies comply. The only financial reporting requirement which the Manual imposes on companies is compliance with professional accounting standards and pronouncements, and compliance with the Ninth Schedule of the Companies Act. Thus the KLSE's influence on financial reporting is indirect, through the possible delisting of companies that do not comply with legal and professional accounting requirements.

7.6.3   The Securities Exchange of Thailand (SET)

SET was one of the top 10 performers in world bourses in the late 1980s and early 1990s in terms of growth in market capitalization. The development of the equity market has probably been the most important factor in the development of financial reporting in Thailand. Generally however, SET has not tried to regulate accounting practices directly through the SET Act, but has acted through the Ministry of Commerce and ICAAT. This is because it does not wish to discourage companies from listing by imposing significantly heavier reporting requirements for quoted companies.

In its efforts to promote more widespread ownership and foreign investment, SET has encouraged the development of investor-oriented financial reporting particularly in providing consolidated accounts and more detailed information in the notes. Listed and authorized companies must comply with legal requirements and the SFAS issued by ICAAT. In areas not covered by SFAS, companies must comply with IAS and AICPA prouncements, in that order.

The performance of quoted companies is monitored very closely for any sign of speculative trading. Information concerning listed and authorized companies, or issued by these companies, is screened by the Listed Company Supervision Department. Most of the staff members of this department are accountants, who ensure that all SET rules and regulations regarding information disclosure and report submission are strictly observed. In addition, the staff screen a sample of the published accounts of quoted companies. Sample selection is based on their knowledge of companies experiencing operating difficulties, as well as the reputation of the auditors of the companies.

SET-quoted companies must be audited only by Authorized Auditors included in the SET Register of Approved Auditors. There are currently slightly less than 100 of these individuals. Infringements of SET regulations will result in the issue of an oral or written warning to the company and its auditor. More serious cases would lead to delisting of the company and removal of the auditor from the Register.

7.6.4   Distinguishing features

Unlike the SES and the KLSE, the SET imposes additional reporting requirements on Thai-listed companies. However, this is mainly because Thai legislation has kept basic reporting requirement fairly minimal, and professional accounting standards are not yet comprehensive. SET's Supervision Department also screens published accounts. Listed companies are therefore subject to relatively greater regulation than unlisted companies.

Only a small sub-set of Thai Authorized Auditors are approved to certify the accounts of SET-listed companies. This is another indicator of the closer monitoring of financial information produced by such companies.

7.7   EVIDENCE ON INFORMATION QUALITY

Given the different emphases of the regulatory systems in Singapore, Malaysia and Thailand, the impact (if any) on the financial information produced by companies should be evaluated. Tay (1989) carried out an empirical study on the corporate financial information produced by, among others, listed Singaporean, Malaysian and Thai companies in 1986. The study focused on two aspects of the information: the harmony of accounting methods used, and the quality of the information produced. Quality of information was quantified by a weighted index covering 10 accounting areas.

Table 7.1 shows the ranking of these 10 areas, by the information quality scores, for the three countries, with 1 being the area with the highest score and 10 being the area with the lowest score. There were no significant differences between the Malaysian and Singaporean samples in terms of the rankings of the different areas. Companies in these two samples exhibited high (more than 75%) information quality scores for Earnings Per Share (EPS) fixed assets and tax, and low (less than 50%) scores for leases and pension costs. The Thai sample had similar high information quality scores for EPS and fixed assets, and also for intangibles and R&D. Low scores were exhibited for all the other seven accounting areas. Significant differences exist in the scores between the

Table 7.1   Ranking by information quality scores

	Malaysia	Singapore	Thailand
Accounting Area			
Fixed Assets	2	2	3
Lessee Accounting	10	9	5
Intangibles and R&D	8	8	2
Stock	6	7	4
Pension Costs	9	10	6
Taxation	3	3	10
Group Accounts	4	4	7
Foreign Exchange Translation	7	5	8.5
Funds Statement	5	6	8.5
EPS	1	1	1

Note: 1 = Area with highest information quality score
         10 = Area with lowest information quality score
Source: Tay (1989)

Malaysian and/or Singaporean samples and the Thai sample in three areas: tax, group accounts and foreign exchange translation.

The ranking of high and low disclosure rates in the same 10 accounting areas is shown in Table 7.2. Again, the pattern was similar for the Malaysian and Singaporean samples, but not so for the Thai sample. Taken together, Tay's results suggest a difference in the disclosure pattern between Malaysian and Singapore listed companies on the one hand and Thai listed companies on the other.

Table 7.2   Ranking by disclosure rates

	Malaysia	Singapore	Thailand
Accounting Area			
Fixed Assets	3	3	4
Lessee Accounting	10	8	8
Intangibles and R&D	4	7	3
Stock	7	9	6.5
Pension Costs	9	10	6.5
Taxation	6	5.5	10
Group Accounts	5	4	5
Foreign Exchange Translation	8	5.5	9
Funds Statement	1.5	1.5	2
EPS	1.5	1.5	1

Note: 1 = Area with highest disclosure rate
        10 = Area with lowest disclosure rate
Source: Tay (1989)

7.8 PRELIMINARY CONCLUSIONS AND FUTURE RESEARCH

The analysis of the constituents of the regulatory framework for financial reporting in Singapore, Malaysia and Thailand suggests that the development of regulation in Thailand has not kept pace with the country's economic growth, despite the emphasis on attracting foreign equity investment, developing a greater investor-orientation for financial reporting and statutory provision for monitoring compliance with regulation. Legal reporting requirements are quite basic, due to the traditional debt financing profiles and family-ownership of Thai companies, and professional accounting standards are underdeveloped, due to resource problems. The limited empirical evidence on the quality of the financial information provided by listed companies in these three countries supports this analysis: Thai reporting scores consistently lower than Singaporean and Malaysian reporting.

Very little other work has been done in the area of relating changes in financial reporting practices to changes in the form of regulation. Most of the studies undertaken in recent years have been in the context of European Community (EC) Accounting Directives. The Fourth and Seventh Directives have either introduced into national legislation reporting requirements which were previously included in professional accounting standards, or entirely new requirements. However, the focus of such studies (Emenonyu and Gray, 1992; Archer *et al* 1994) has been on the harmonisation impact of such regulation, that is, the extent to which such regulation has made reporting practices in different EC member states more similar. Only one study has considered quality of information (Tay, 1994). Given the ever increasing importance of financial reporting and the regulation thereof, more research appears to be called for on the impact of forms of regulation on reporting practices.

REFERENCES

Aivazian, V.A. and Callen, J.L. (1983). Core Theory and Uniformity in Accounting: Rationalising the Accounting Rulemaker. *Journal of Accounting and Public Policy*, Vol. 2, No. 2, Winter, pp. 225–237

Archer, S., Delvaille, P. and McLeay, S. (1994). Harmonisation and the Comparability of Financial Statement Items in the Annual Accounts of European Multilisted Companies. *Research Paper in Banking and Finance 94/22*, School of Accounting, Banking and Economics, Bangor: University of Wales

Ashton, R.H. (1974). The Predictive Ability Criterion and User Prediction Models. *The Accounting Review*, Vol. 49, No. 4, October, pp. 719–732

Baker, H.K. and Haslem, J.A. (1973). Informatioin Needs of Individual Investors. *Journal of Acountancy*, November, pp. 64–69

——, Chenhall, R.H., Haslem, J.A. and Juchau, R.H. (1977). Disclosure of Material Information: A Cross-National Comparison. *International Journal of Accounting*. Vol. 13, No. 1, Fall, pp. 1–16

Barrett, M.E. (1976). Financial Reporting Practices: Disclosure and Comprehensiveness in an International Setting. *Journal of Accounting Research*, Vol. 14, No. 1, Spring, pp. 10–26

—— (1977). The Extent of Disclosure in Annual Reports of Large Companies in Seven Countries. *International Journal of Accounting*. Vol. 12, No. 2, Spring, pp. 1–25

Belkaoui, A., Kahl, A. and Peyrard, J. (1977). Information Needs of Financial Analysts: An International Comparison. *International Journal of Accounting*, Vol. 13, No. 1, Fall, pp. 19–27

Benjamin, J.J. and Stanga, K.G. (1977). Differences in Disclosure Needs of Major Users of Financial Statements. *Accounting and Business Research*, Vol. 7, No. 27, Summer, pp. 187–192

Benston, G.J. (1973). Required Disclosure and the Stock Market: An Evaluation of the Securities Exchange Act of 1934. *American Economic Review*, Vol. 63, No. 1, March, pp. 132–155

—— (1982). An Analysis of the Role of Accounting Standards for Enhancing Corporate Governance and Social Responsibility. *Journal of Accounting and Public Policy*, Vol. 1, No. 1, Fall, pp. 5–17

Buzby, S.L. (1974a). The Nature of Adequate Disclosure. *Journal of Accountancy*, April, pp. 38–47

—— (1974b). Selected Items of Information and Their Disclosure in Annual Reports. *The Accounting Review*, Vol. 49, No. 3, July, pp. 423–435

Chandra, G. (1974). A Study of the Consensus on Disclosure Among Public Accountants and Security Analysts. *The Accounting Review*, Vol. 49, No. 4, October, pp. 733–742

Choi, F.D.S. (1973). Financial Disclosure and Entry to the European Capital Market. *Journal of Accounting Research*, Vol. 11, No. 2, Autumn, pp. 159–175

Chow, C.W. (1983). The Impacts of Accounting Regulation on Bondholder and Shareholder Wealth: The Case of the Securities Act. *The Accounting Review*, Vol. 58, No. 3, July, pp. 485–520

Cooper, K. and Keim, G.D. (1983). The Economic Rationale for the Nature and Extent of Corporate Financial Disclosure Regulation: A Critical Assessment. *Journal of Accounting and Public Policy*, Vol. 2, No. 3, Fall, pp. 189–205

Dhaliwal, S. (1980). Improving the Quality of Corporate Financial Disclosure. *Accounting and Business Research*, Vol. 10, No. 40, Autumn, pp. 385–390

Emenonyu, E.N. and Gray, S.J. (1992). EC Accounting Harmonisation: An Empirical study of Measurement Practices in France, Germany and the UK. *Accounting and Business Research*, Winter, pp. 49–58

Firth, M. (1978). A Study of the Consensus of the Perceived Importance of Disclosure of Individual Items in Corporate Annual Reports. *International Journal of Accounting*, Vol. 14, No. 1, Fall, pp. 57–70

Framjee, D.B. (1987). The Requirements of the Stock Exchange of Singapore. *Singapore Accountant*, Vol. 3, No. 10, October, pp. 15–19

Gray S.J., Campbell, S.G. and Shaw, J.C. (1984). *International Financial Reporting: A Comparative Survey of Accounting Requirements and Practices in 30 Countries*, London: Macmillan

Hwang, S.C. (1982). *The International Harmonisation of Accounting Standards and Its Effects on the Development and Implementation of Accounting Standards in Singapore*. M. Econs thesis, Monash University

Kohler, E.L. (1957). *A Dictionary for Acountants*, Englewood Cliffs: Prentice-Hall

Marston, C. (1986). *Financial Reporting in India*, London: Croom Helm

McNally, G.M., Eng, L.H., and Hasseldine, C.R. (1982). Corporate Financial Reporting in New Zealand: An Analysis of User Preferences, Corporate Charactertistics and Disclosure Practices for Discretionary Information. *Accounting and Business Research*, Vol. 13, No. 49, Winter, pp. 11–20

Ross, S.A. (1979). Disclosure Regulation in Financial Markets: Implications of Finance Theory and Signalling Theory. In *Issues in Financial Regulation* (Edwards, F.R. ed.) pp. 177–202: McGraw-Hill

Singhvi, S.S. and Desai, H.B. (1971). An Empirical Analysis of the Quality of Corporate Financial Disclosure. *The Accounting Review*, Vol. 46, No. 1, January, pp. 129–138

Stigler, G.J. (1964). Public Regulation of the Securities Market. *Journal of Business*, Vol. 37. No. 2, April, pp. 117–146

Tay, J.S.W. (1989). *Corporate Financial Reporting: Regulatory Systems and Comparability*. PhD thesis, University of Exeter

Tay, J.S.W. and Parker, R.H. (1990). Measuring International Harmonization and Standardization. *Abacus*, Vol. 26, No. 1, March, pp. 71–88

Tay, J.S.W. (1994). Financial Reporting in the United Kingdom and the Netherlands Before and After the Implementation of the Fourth Directive: Evidence on Harmony, Harmonisation and Quality of Information, paper presented at the *17th Congress of the European Accounting Association*, April

Wallace, R.S.O. (1987). *Disclosure of Accounting Information in Developing Countries: A Case Study of Nigeria*. Ph.D thesis, University of Exeter

Walton, P. (1986). The Export of British Accounting Legislation to Commonwealth Countries. *Accounting and Business Research*, Vol. 16. No. 64, Autumn, pp. 353–357

Watts, R.L. (1980). Can Optimal Accounting Information be Determined by Regulation? In *Regulation and the Accounting Profession* (Buckley, J.W. and Weston, J.F. eds.) pp. 153–162: Lifetime Learning Publication

8 Accounting for New Financial Instruments: An Overview of Issues and Standards Development

Peter Lee Lip Nyean

8.1 INTRODUCTION

In the past two decades, the world has witnessed a financial instruments revolution, a term coined to describe the wide range of new, innovative financial products that have been introduced into the world's financial markets. Examples of some of the innovative financial instruments include hybrid bonds, futures, swaps, various forms of options (including options on futures and 'swaptions'), interest rate collars, caps and floors, collateralised mortgage obligations and other instruments with exotic labels such as DARTS, LYONS and CATS. A variety of factors have stimulated the development of these New Financial Instruments (NFI). Among the more important factors are the deregulation in the financial services industry, increased competition among financial institutions, changes in tax regulations and advancements in computer technology.

There are many reasons why NFIs are developed. Finnerty (1988) analyzed and classified these reasons into 11 categories:

(1) Exploitation of tax asymmetries to produce tax savings (for example, zero coupon bonds, convertible adjustable preferred stock and stripped debt securities).

(2) Reduction of transaction costs (for example, hybrid debt instruments, Euro-commercial paper, mortgage pass–throughs and auction rate notes/debentures).

(3) Reduction of agency costs (for example, interest rate reset notes, puttable common stock and floating rate notes).

(4) Reallocation of risks (for example, interest rate swaps, interest rate futures and exchange traded options).

(5) Enhancement of liquidity (for example, adjustable rate notes and negotiable CDs).

(6) Response to regulatory or legislative changes (for example, currency swaps and maximum rate notes).

(7) Level and volatility of interest rates (for example, interest rate caps/floors/collars, and foreign currency-denominated bonds).

(8) Level and volatility of prices (for example, stock index futures).

(9) Academic work (for example options on futures contract and junk bonds).

(10) Accounting treatment to achieve off-balance sheet benefits (for example, puttable common stock and in-substance defeasance arrangements).

(11) Technological developments (for example, annuity notes and zero coupon convertible debt).

This chapter analyzes the characteristics of NFIs and the accounting implications. The conceptual issues from a financial reporting perspective and the accounting literature are reviewed and the methods of approach to standard-setting by the leading accounting regulatory bodies are examined. The impact of new financial instruments and the accounting for financial instruments in the Singapore context is discussed, and the concluding section briefly discusses the research possibilities on financial instruments.

8.2 CHARACTERISTICS OF NFIs AND THE ACCOUNTING IMPLICATIONS

While NFIs have been developed at an explosive rate, the accounting developments have lagged far behind. One reason is the diversity and complexity of many of the new financial instruments which do not readily fit in with the historical cost-based accounting framework and the system of classifying equity, liabilities and assets. As a consequence, special accounting treatment may have to be adopted for some NFIs. To appreciate the complexity of the accounting problems posed by many of the NFIs, it is important to consider their characteristics, the multiple purposes that they serve and the different ways they can be created.

Financial instruments differ considerably in terms of tenure, flexibility, credit risks, transaction costs and cash flow requirements. Some are highly liquid as they come in standardized contracts which are actively traded on organized exchanges (for example, options and futures contracts). Others are customized to suit the user's requirements and are illiquid (for example, forward contracts). These characteristics influence the accounting for financial instruments (for example, the basis at which financial instruments should be measured for financial reporting purposes).

A number of financial instruments can be and often are used for both speculative or hedging purposes. Examples are futures, swaps, options and forward contracts. Under current generally accepted accounting principles, the accounting for an instrument used for hedging purposes differs from the accounting for the same instrument used for speculative purposes. However, problems can arise when the distinction between hedging and speculation is not precise, particularly among financial institutions.

Financial instruments can be viewed as consisting of bundles of rights and obligations: for example, the right (obligation) to receive (pay) periodic cash payments such as interest, dividends or principal repayments, and the right (obligation) to exchange cash for some other assets. NFIs are continually being created by combining or repackaging the inherent rights and obligations. Some of the ways that NFIs have been created are described below.

(1) **Combining distinct sets of rights and/or obligations into a single instrument.** A convertible bond is one such instrument, combining both equity and debt characteristics. Such compound instruments, as they are called, are attractive to both the issuer and the holder. The issuer enjoys the benefit of lower financing cost in the form of a lower coupon rate compared to a similar debt instrument without the conversion privilege. The holder benefits from the conversion when the stock price rises above the exercise price. When multiple sets of rights are combined into one financial instrument, the result is a heterogeneous compound instrument (for example, a convertible, callable debt instrument that has an equity component, a straight debt component and a call option).

(2) **Combining the rights and obligations of two distinct instruments to create a new or synthesized instrument.** One instrument changes the original characteristics of the other (original) instrument, thus effectively synthesizing the original instrument into a new instrument. Probably the most common example is the interest rate swap. Consider the case of a company with a floating rate debt (the original instrument) that enters into an agreement with another party, whereby it agrees to pay fixed rate interest and receives floating rate interest computed on a notional principal amount that is equal to the principal amount of the floating rate debt. In this example, the original floating rate obligation of the company is changed into a fixed rate obligation by the swap (popularly known as a plain vanilla). Other examples include changing a long-term debt

into a short-term debt by purchasing a put option on the debt. Such synthesized instruments are created for hedging purposes and to reduce borrowing costs.

(3) **Repackaging the rights inherent in a financial instrument to create a new instrument(s).** A good example of this is the Collateralised Mortgage Obligations (CMO) and Real Estate Mortgage Investment Conduits (REMICS)[1] (Parks, 1991, pp. 55–62). The original financial instrument underlying a CMO is the typical fixed rate residential mortgage carrying the right to prepay the mortgage before its maturity. This prepayment option, while favourable to the homeowner, is viewed unfavourably by the banks and other mortgage investors since it increases their risk exposure. Because mortgages have different interest rates and maturities, they can be combined into a pool and repackaged into tranches (or classes of securities) with different interest rates, average lives, prepayment sensitivities and final maturities and offered (often through a trust) to investors with different investment needs. Sometimes, the pool of mortgages is split into two classes of securities: one entitling investors to the Interest Payments Only (known as IO) or the Principal Payments Only (known as PO). In many cases, only a portion of the tranches from a pool of mortgages are offered to investors and the balance is retained by the issuers, but the issuers may retain certain credit, interest rate, prepayment and other risks associated with the portion sold.

(4) **Creating new forms of instruments carrying rights and obligations that are linked to a 'mother' instrument.** These instruments are popularly called derivative instruments and include various types of options and futures contracts. In some cases, these derivatives have spawned other derivatives, as in the case of an option on an option.

Each of the above mentioned methods of creating NFIs poses its own unique accounting problems. For example, compound instruments raise the problem of the appropriate accounting treatment for the separate components embedded in one instrument, while CMOs pose the problem of whether to recognise the transaction as a sale or a financing arrangement.

For some instruments, there could be more than one perspective to the problem. Consider the case of the interest rate swap. Theoretically there are three ways to approach the accounting problem (Nair *et al*, 1990): first, the swap and the original instrument can be viewed as one unit with the swap transforming the original liability into a new instrument; a second approach is to view it as the equivalent of a refinancing which results in a possible gain or loss to be recognised at the inception of the swap (this is analogous to a situation where a variable rate

---

[1] For a more detailed accounts of CMOs and REMICs see Parks (1991).

debt is extinguished and refinanced with a fixed rate debt); a third approach is to view the swap and the original instrument as separate instruments with the accounting issues for each instrument being addressed independently. These different perspectives suggest that there are alternative ways to account for the same instrument.

8.3   MAIN ACCOUNTING ISSUES AND LITERATURE REVIEW

Since the accounting problems posed by new financial instruments are as varied as the instruments themselves, it is beyond the scope of this chapter to examine all the specific issues in detail. The approach adopted here is to group the main issues into the following categories to facilitate their analysis:

(1) Recognition issues
(2) Classification issues
(3) Measurement issues (initial and subsequent measurement)
(4) Derecognition issues
(5) Related financial instruments (hedging relationship)
(6) Disclosure issues

8.3.1   Recognition issues

The Financial Accounting Standards Board (FASB) defines a financial instrument as cash, evidence of an ownership interest in an equity or a contract that is both a (recognized or unrecognized) contractual right of one entity, and a (recognized or unrecognized) contractual obligation of another entity, to deliver (receive) cash or another financial instrument or exchange financial instruments on potentially favourable (unfavourable) terms with another entity (FASB Exposure Draft *Disclosure of Information about Financial Instruments,* 1987, paras. 28–29).

Some financial instruments are quite familiar and their recognition in the balance sheet is straightforward (for example, accounts and notes receivable, trade payables, debentures, ordinary and preference shares). Other instruments which confer contractual rights or obligations entail contentious issues of recognition. Three important issues that will be examined are:

(1) Should financial instruments that are executory in nature be recognized as assets and liabilities, and if so, when?
(2) How should options, which are financial instruments carrying a right (obligation) to exchange other financial instruments on

potentially favourable (unfavourable) terms that is conditional on the occurrence of a future event, be recognized?

(3) Should stock options issued to employees be recognized and when?

Financial instruments that are executory contracts

A contract that entails an unconditional right and obligation to a future exchange of financial instruments is executory in nature because the right and obligation are equally unperformed at the inception of the transaction. Examples of this are foreign exchange forward contracts, financial futures contracts and interest rate swaps.

It has been an accepted accounting practice that executory contracts generally are not recognized in the financial statements at inception. However, the case of finance leases has set a precedent for the recognition of executory contracts (SFAS No. 13 and IAS 17) even though they are partially or wholly unperformed, if certain conditions are met. These conditions are: first, the contract results in a transfer of substantial owner risks and rewards associated with the asset or liability to one party; and second, the contractual rights and obligations are firm and can be reasonably measured. Underlying these conditions is the intention that financial reporting should reflect the economic substance of the transaction rather than its form. The question that follows is: how is the transfer of ownership rewards and risks to be determined?

A key indicator that ownership rewards and risks have been transferred to an entity is that it is probable that future economic benefits from the asset will flow to the enterprise and it is probable that there will be a future outflow of enterprise resources. The contractual rights and obligations in forward contracts, futures contracts and interest rate swap give rise to a future benefit (receipt of another financial instrument or cash) and result in a future sacrifice (transfer of a financial instrument or payment of cash) as a result of a past transaction (the signing of the contract).

In order to be recognized as assets and liabilities, the economic benefits and obligations must be firm and capable of reasonably reliable measurement. Ijiri (1980) defines a commitment as firm if its performance is unlikely to be avoided because of severe penalty for non-execution. Evidence of firm commitments include penalties for non-performance and the payment of an initial deposit. Forward contracts are non-cancellable or are cancellable subject to payment of penalties, as are interest rate swaps while margin deposits are required for financial futures contracts. The values of these instruments are capable of reasonably reliable measurement. Therefore, the rights and obligations of forward contracts and futures should be recognized as assets and liabilities at inception even if they are executory in nature.

Options contracts

Options contracts are instruments whose rights and obligations are conditional on events within the control of one party to the contract. The conditional event is generally the option holder's decision to exercise. Options are divided into two basic types, namely, call and put options.

- A call option gives the holder the right but not the obligation to require the option seller (also called option writer) to sell a specified financial instrument at a specified price (the exercise or strike price) at any time up to the maturity date of the option.
- A put option, on the other hand, gives the holder the right but not the obligation to require the option writer to buy the specified financial instrument at the exercise price within the option period.

Whether the option holder or writer, as the case may be, makes a gain or loss from the option contract depends on the relationship between the spot price of the underlying instrument and the exercise price. The relationships between the spot price of the underlying instrument and the exercise price is represented in Table 8.1 by the following matrix:

Table 8.1   Spot price and exercise price relationship

	Exercise price more than Spot price	Exercise price = Spot price	Exercise price less than Spot price
Call option	Out–of–the–money	At–the–money	In–the–money
Put Option	In–the–money	At–the–money	Out–of–the–money

Unlike futures contracts, the risk–reward ratio for an options contract is one-sided. The maximum loss a holder of an option will incur is limited to the amount he paid for the option (the premium), but his gain when the option is in–the–money may be much higher. The converse holds for the writer of an option. The maximum gain will be limited to the amount of the premium received but the potential loss could be much greater.

The accounting for options would have to take into account whether the entity is a holder or a writer of the option, and the purpose of holding or writing the options (whether for speculative or hedging purposes). The recognition issues relating to options that are transacted for investment or speculative purposes will be discussed here. The accounting issues of options for hedging purposes will be discussed in a later section.

For options that are purchased for investment or speculative purposes, the recognition of the transaction at inception is relatively straightforward, especially if the options contract is traded on an exchange. The amount paid for the rights contained in the option could be considered a reasonable assessment of its fair value at inception and the option is recorded as an asset.

The recognition problem is more difficult for options that are written for speculative purposes. How should the premium received be treated? There are three possibilities:

(1) Recognize the premium as income and record a liability for the financial instrument to be exchanged with an offsetting receivable equal to the exercise price. This treatment does not seem reasonable as it assumes that the option is certain to be exercised.
(2) Recognize the premium as income without recognizing an additional asset and liability. The weakness of this treatment is that it ignores the potential obligation of the enterprise and therefore does not provide a true and fair view of the position of the entity.
(3) Recognize the premium as a liability until the option expires at which point it is included in income. This treatment is in accordance with the prudence principle and is an improvement over the other two methods. However, consideration must be given to the basis of measurement subsequent to the initial recognition.

Stock options

Options issued by a company to employees under an Executive Share Option Scheme (ESOS) provide another problem of recognition in accounting. The salient feature of an ESOS is that selected employees (usually key executives) are given the option for an extended period of time, typically two to five years, to purchase ordinary shares in the company at an exercise price that is usually close to the market price at the date the option is granted.

Although there may be a number of possible reasons for having an ESOS, the basic idea is to provide selected employees with an additional financial incentive to perform. If the company performs well, the share price is likely to rise, in which case the option will be in–the–money, and by exercising the option, the executives will be rewarded for their contributions. The accounting for ESOS has been a thorny issue in the United States where it is widely practised.

If stock option schemes are recognized to have motivational effects, they obviously must convey benefits to the employees. This raises the first conceptual issue of whether any compensation expense needs to be recognized when an entity introduces an ESOS. An argument for not recogising compensation expense is that the firm has not incurred any expense or cash outflow through the issuance of additional shares to the executives. The increase in share capital is likely to result in a dilution of earnings per share but this cost is borne by the shareholders, not the entity. Another objection to recognizing compensation expense is based on the economic consequences of such a move. Small firms, especially those which rely on offering stock options to attract executive talent, may find that they could be put in a disadvantageous position by having to record substantial compensation expense. However, these arguments have not been accepted by the Accounting Principles Board in its APB Opinion No. 25, *Accounting for Stocks Issued to Employees*. The thrust of the standard is that a cost is incurred by the shareholders and the entity which could have issued the additional shares at a higher price to other parties. Therefore, the cost to the entity should be considered as part of its operating costs.

A second and more difficult issue with regard to ESOS is when to recognize the option transaction. There are four possible dates: the date of grant of option, the date when the employee's entitlement to it vests, the date the option becomes exercisable, and the date when the option is actually exercised. These dates are not necessarily mutually exclusive.

Of the four possible dates, the APB considered the grant date as the most appropriate conceptually. At the date of the grant, the entity has incurred a conditional obligation and since the number of shares entitlement and the exercise price are known, the value of the compensation could be reasonably estimated.

8.3.2 Classification issues

Traditionally, the capital structure of a firm is divided into two components: equity (comprising ordinary and preference shares) and debt. The FASB's *Concepts Statement No. 6* (pp. ix and x) defines equity as 'the residual interest in the assets of an entity that remains after deducting its liabilities'. Debt is defined as 'probable future sacrifices of economic benefits arising from present obligations of a particular entity to transfer assets or provide services to other entities in the future as a result of past transactions or events'. Thus, one important characteristic of debt is that payment to debt holders is unavoidable while the characteristic of equity is that holders have a residual claim to firm assets. Classification problems arise when an enterprise issues financial instruments that contain characteristics of both. Examples of such instruments are mandatory redeemable preference shares and convertible bonds. The accounting issues relating to these two types of financial instruments are discussed below.

Mandatorily redeemable preference shares

Mandatorily Redeemable Preference Shares (MRPS) are preference shares that have a fixed or determinable redemption date, are redeemable at the option of the holder, or have conditions for redemption that are beyond the control of the issuer. The current practice of classifying it as equity has attracted the criticism that it emphasises form rather than economic substance. Thus, the accounting problem is how to classify this type of instrument.

The problem has been discussed by the FASB in its 1990 Discussion Memorandum, *Distinguishing between Liability and Equity Instruments and Accounting for Instruments with Characteristics of Both*. Three possible approaches to classify and account for MRPS have been identified by the FASB:

(1) classify either as debt or equity;
(2) create an additional balance sheet category for quasi-equity securities; and
(3) adopt an entity approach in which securities are not classified, but are listed in order of seniority ranking with disclosure of important rights and obligations.

The first approach views the problem as a substance versus form issue. Those who favour classifying redeemable preferred stock as **equity** argue on the ground that it is legal capital. However, many believe that the instrument's underlying characteristic rather than its legal form should dictate its accounting classification. They argue that the underlying characteristic of a MRPS is that the issuer has an obligation to deliver cash to another party on a specified date or on demand. This would suggest that it should be classified as a longterm **debt** (Nair *et al*, 1990a). However, according to Kimmel and Warfield (1993), the problem is not as straightforward as it seems. They point out that an essential characteristic of debt under the current definition of debt is that the debt issuer's obligation to make payments is unavoidable. If the issuer tries to avoid its obligations, debt holders can force it into bankruptcy. Their analyzis of the characteristics of MRPS suggests that holders of MRPS do not have this legal recourse, and as a result, its classification of debt is questionable. In addition, the characteristics of MRPS are heterogeneous rather than uniform in nature, thus compounding the problem of classifying it as debt. On the other hand, classification of MRPS based on equity characteristics is equally problematic because it lies between the debt or equity extremes.

The second approach of creating a separate category of **quasi-equity** in the balance sheet is an adaption of the practice in the banking industry where bank regulators split capital into equity and quasi-equity for the purpose of computing capital adequacy ratio. However, this approach requires relating the characteristics of a MRPS to the (unambiguous) definition of quasi-equity. As Kimmel and Warfield (1993, p. 38) pointed out, given the heterogeneous nature of MRPS, 'creation of this statement element would simply shift the debate from a debt versus equity argument to a debt versus quasi-equity argument and increase the demand for new securities designed to avoid a particular classification'.

The **entity approach**, which is attributed to Paton (1922), eliminates the distinction between debt and equity and therefore avoids the problems of classification. Instead, securities are listed in approximate order of seniority accompanied by adequate disclosures about their rights and obligations. The entity approach is supported by the Modigliani–Miller (MM) model in finance theory. Both Paton and MM argue that the corporate entity rather than its shareholders owns the assets, and income from those assets is not affected by the composition of the firm's capital structure. Thus, the format of the income statement is changed to show the income to the corporate entity while the statement of retained earnings shows how it is allocated among the various providers of capital. Since there is no distinction between debt and equity, the debt–to–equity ratio is irrelevant. This approach represents a fundamental departure in terms of financial reporting and would create a huge problem of acceptance within the financial community. While closing the door on one problem, it also opens the door to a host of new problems, particularly with respect to the measurement and interpretation of income.

The general consensus in the finance community is that the distinction between debt and equity is important and useful for the assessment of financial risk. In view of the problem posed by instruments such as MRPS, it may be necessary to review the current definitions of debt and equity to assess whether the definitions need to be tightened.

Convertible debt instruments

A convertible debt instrument is essentially a debt instrument with an embedded option given to the holder to exchange it for shares. This type of instrument is considered to have both debt and equity characteristics. Generally, an entity is able to issue a convertible debt at a lower interest rate than a similar debt instrument without the conversion privilege. An instrument that is very similar to a convertible debt is a debt issued with detachable warrants. The current practice in the United States is that separate accounting for the components is required only for debt issued with detachable warrants, while convertible debt is to be accounted for in the same way as a straight debt instrument [Accounting Principles Board (APB) Opinion No. 14, *Accounting for Convertible Debt and Debt Issued with Stock Purchase Warrants*, 1969]. Thus, the accounting issue posed by convertible debt instrument is whether the instrument should be classified as debt or as equity entirely, or whether the separate components should be identified and accounted for separately.

The rationale put forward for different accounting treatment of convertible debt and a debt issued with detachable warrants is that in the case of the former, the debt and the conversion option are inseparable and therefore the rights contained in the convertible instrument are mutually exclusive. If the holder wants to exercise his right to convert the debt to equity, he will have to give up his right as a debt holder. Furthermore, determining the value of the two components of the convertible instrument presents a difficult measurement problem. Such a problem does not arise with debt issued with detachable warrants since the values of each component could be objectively determined with reference to market prices that are usually available for separately traded debt and warrants.

The argument of inseparability has been refuted by many writers. The fact that the inclusion of the conversion option in the debt instrument enables firms to issue debt at a lower cost shows that the conversion feature has economic value at the time of issuance, and should be recognized and accounted for separately as equity. If a convertible debt is accounted for in the same way as a debt without the conversion privilege, this would be misleading as borrowing cost is understated and comparability with other entities that issue unconvertible bonds is affected.

The problem is viewed essentially as an allocation problem. If the financial reporting is to reflect economic substance properly, then the value of the transaction should be allocated between separately identifiable items in a single transaction. Such allocations between assets of value in a single transaction have been frequently practised (for example, finance leases are separated into their principal and interest components).

Although it is acknowledged that there is a measurement problem involved in determining the values of the two components, the problem is not insurmountable. Past research such as that conducted by Brennan and Schwartz (1977) has shown that it is feasible to estimate the values of the two components. One approach is to estimate the value of a similar bond without the conversion feature first. The value of the conversion feature is then obtained by deducting from the total proceeds the estimated value of the debt. An alternative approach is to use appropriate valuation models such as the discounted cash flow model and option pricing models to estimate the value of each component separately; the amounts so determined are adjusted on a pro-rata basis so that the sum of the components equals the entire proceeds from the issue of the debt.

8.3.3   Measurement issues

Initial measurement

At the point when financial assets and liabilities are first recognized, how should they be measured? The alternatives include:

(1) cash received or paid
(2) the amount stated in the contract

(3) the market value at the time of recognition, and
(4) expected net future cash flows.

The choice of method of initial measurement is generally more straightforward for transactions involving exchange of cash (monetary exchange transaction) or exchange of asset (non-monetary exchange transaction). In the case of a monetary exchange transaction conducted at an arm's length, the amount of cash paid or received generally reflects the fair value of the asset acquired or the liability assumed. For a non-monetary exchange transaction, the initial measurement could be based on the fair value of the consideration exchanged, which may be determined by reference either to the asset given up or to the asset acquired, whichever is the more evident.

The problem of initial measurement is more troublesome for financial instruments which involve firm commitments to exchange cash or assets at a future date (for example, a forward foreign exchange contract or a futures contract). In this case, should the initial measurement be based on the amount stated in the contract or on the value of the rights and obligations arising from the contract?

Under SFAS No. 52, the FASB considers a forward foreign exchange contract as a separate transaction by itself, and accordingly, the underlying instruments to be exchanged under a forward foreign exchange contract are to be recorded as a receivable and a liability.

The IASC's position, which this writer supports, is that what is recognized as financial asset and financial liability at inception are the rights and obligations to make the exchange in the future, not the underlying instruments to be exchanged. In most cases where the instrument conveys both the rights and obligations which are exercisable simultaneously, such rights and obligations are generally of equivalent value and meet the requirement for offset so that at inception, the net value is nil.

The valuation of stock options, assuming that compensation expense is recognized by the enterprise, provides another difficult initial measurement challenge. At least three different alternatives have been suggested:

(1) value the option using an appropriate option pricing model
(2) value the option based on the fair value of services received, and
(3) take the difference between the market price and the exercise price at the date of the grant of option.

Each of these alternatives has its proponents and critics. The FASB is still wrestling with the problem. In the meanwhile, US companies are following the third alternative, which is required under APB Opinion No. 25. The impact on reported income could vary significantly depending on the choice of valuation method used (Foster III *et al*, 1991).

Measurement subsequent to initial recognition

The basis at which financial assets and liabilities should be measured subsequent to initial recognition, whether at fair value (fair value accounting[2]) or at historical cost, is currently one of the most hotly debated issues. To appreciate the debate, an analysis of the current accounting model is necessary. Under the present historical cost model, a number of bases of carrying financial assets and liabilities in the balance sheet can be used, depending on the purpose of holding the assets or liabilities. Assets and liabilities which are intended to be held to maturity are generally carried in the balance sheet based on their historical exchange prices. Subsequent changes in their fair values generally are not taken into account unless an exchange has occurred or an asset has suffered a permanent impairment in its value. For financial assets (but not liabilities) which are held for trading purposes, either cost or market value could be used.[3] If the latter is used, subsequent changes in fair value of the financial asset would be recognized as gains or losses in the income statement.

The historical cost model has come under heavy criticism recently in the wake of the savings and loans (S&L) institutions and banking crisis in the United States. One criticism of historical cost information is that it provides incentives to financial institutions to manage earnings by resorting to a practice known as **gains trading** in which portfolio managers accelerate income recognition by selling high-yielding loans to record gains, but retain low-yielding loans without writing them down to fair value. This results in a reduction of the overall portfolio yield and a narrowing of the interest spread (or even a negative spread) relative to the cost of funds. If there is substantial mismatch between portfolios of assets and liabilities, the long-term viability of the financial institution could well be jeopardised.

Another instance where the current model could lead to management making decisions that are detrimental to the financial institutions' long run interest is when financial institutions are reluctant to foreclose on problem loans because foreclosure may result in repossessed assets being realised at a loss. (While it is a requirement under generally accepted accounting principles to report probable losses, managers have considerable discretion on the amount of loan provisions.) Thus, by allowing financial statements to overstate the underlying economic value, as in the case of the many banks and S&L institutions which have failed, critics of the current model argued that it has lost its relevance for financial

---

[2] Fair value, mark–to–market and market value accounting often are used as synonyms.
[3] IAS 25, *Accounting for Investments*. However, under SFAS 80 and futures contracts and instruments held for trading purposes have to be marked–to–market. Market value is defined as the amount the financial instrument could be exchanged for in a current transaction between willing parties.

reporting. According to them, fair value accounting has more relevance to investors and regulators than the historical cost model.

Arguments for fair value accounting

The following reasons have been cited to support the use of fair value as a basis for measuring financial assets and liabilities:

(1) Fair value accounting provides more meaningful information to users of financial statements in the following ways:
   (a) It closely reflects the present value of the enterprise's expected future net cash flows, and therefore facilitates comparability between enterprises.
   (b) It provides a basis for evaluating management stewardship by reflecting the effects of decisions made in the period to buy, sell or hold assets and to incur, maintain or discharge liabilities. This is particularly important for assessing the solvency position of financial institutions. Bank regulators will be able to identify much sooner financial institutions which are in trouble.
   (c) It provides insight into a financial institution's interest rate risk, particularly when there are significant mismatched maturities of assets and liabilities during periods of interest rate volatility.
(2) The use of fair value accounting would eliminate many of the accounting problems posed by NFIs. For example, the need for special accounting procedures for instruments used as hedges would be eliminated (see p. 21). In the sale of portions of heterogeneous compound instruments, the use of fair value to determine the value of the various components for derecognition (sale) purpose would minimise the problem of creative loan packaging to achieve accounting gain (see p. 19).
(3) Consistency in measurement is maintained. Assets and liabilities having the same economic characteristics are accounted for consistently in the same way.

Objections to fair value accounting

The adoption of fair value accounting is a fundamental departure from generally accepted accounting practice in the eyes of many accountants as it implies a move towards the economic concept of true income or true value as a basis for measurement for accounting purposes. Those who oppose fair value accounting as the appropriate basis for measuring financial assets and liabilities counter-argue that:

(1) For the majority of financial assets that are intended to be held to maturity and whose carrying values the enterprise will likely recover at maturity, changes in market values need not necessarily be more relevant informationally to the user than changes in the fair value of other non-financial assets. Any fall in value of a financial asset below its cost during the holding period does not affect the enterprise if it is held to maturity or its value recovers subsequently. Thus, if a change in the value of the asset or liability does not affect an enterprise or its cash flows, then such a change may not be relevant to the extent of justifying a change in the measurement atrribute of such asset or liability (Jones, 1988).

(2) While market prices of traded financial instruments would provide a fair basis for determining their economic values, the valuation of non-traded instruments would be subjective, difficult to verify, costly and of limited usefulness due to frequent changes in their values. Although there are financial valuation models which could be used to estimate the values of non-traded financial instruments, these models are often based on theoretical assumptions that are subjective and open to manipulation. Thus, the use of such models would result in reduced reliability of the fair value estimates.

(3) Fair value accounting may not reflect the true values of assets and may in fact be misleading. For example, an enterprise that owns a substantial amount of a particular financial instrument such as quoted shares may not be able to realise the market price if it tried to sell all the shares at once.

In addition to the above arguments against fair value as a basis for measuring financial instruments, there are also persuasive reasons to support the use of other bases than fair value in the current accounting model. Some of these reasons are:

(1) They allow the purpose of acquiring the financial asset or incurring the financial liability to be reflected in the measurement bases.

(2) They avoid undue fluctuations in reported income arising from changes in fair value of financial assets and liabilities which may be unlikely to be realised and could be misunderstood.

(3) The carrying amounts incorporate a reasonable degree of prudence, are reliable and avoid the need to make estimates of fair values.

In view of the complexities of business situations, a shift away from the current accounting model towards fair value as a basis for measuring assets and liabilities is unlikely. If this is the case, then a move to fair value accounting for financial instruments would raise questions of consistency in financial reporting for other assets. This seems to be the reason for the FASB's rejection of market value as the appropriate measurement basis for marketable equity securities in 1975 when it issued SFAS No. 12, *Accounting for Certain Marketable Securities*. In paragraph 29 (a) of the SFAS No. 12, the FASB stated that it excluded consideration of market value alone as the determinant of carrying value as it would give rise to 'pervasive issues concerning the valuation of other types of assets, including the concept of historic cost versus current or realisable value'. While a move to fair value accounting for *all* financial assets and liabilities may be difficult to justify conceptually, the use of fair value as a basis for measurement for certain financial instruments is appropriate. In other words, the issue of measurement for financial instruments need not be an 'all or nothing approach'.

The FASB has issued two standards which require fair value accounting for specified financial instruments. Financial futures contracts which are not designated as hedges are required to be marked–to–market under SFAS No. 80, as are investments held for trading purposes under SFAS No. 115. The FASB's justification for marking futures contracts to market is that changes in fair value have a cash flow effect as futures contracts entail daily cash settlement. For trading securities, the purpose of such assets is to generate profit for an enterprise from their sale. Therefore, changes in their fair values are relevant and should be reflected in the financial statements.

8.3.4   Derecognition issues

The issue of derecognition arises in a number of transactions involving financial instruments, for example, in in-substance defeasance arrangements, sale of receivables with recourse and sale of CMOs. The questions that are addressed here include: firstly, under what circumstances should financial assets and liabilities be offset, and secondly, under what circumstances is it appropriate to derecognize a financial asset or a financial liability that still exists?

Offsetting assets and liabilities

Generally, the practice of offsetting liabilities against assets is discouraged by accounting regulatory bodies. The reason for this, as clearly explained by Solomon, is that it is not a faithful representation of the situation because the risks attaching to the two sides of the transaction are not equivalent (Solomon, 1989, p. 68). In addition, many accountants and writers believe that the practice of offsetting liabilities against assets by a company is a form of manipulative accounting designed to mislead users of financial statements regarding the financial risk of the enterprise (Griffiths, 1986).

There are many situations when the issue of offsetting financial assets and liabilities arises. One situation is where there is a relationship between the values of two instruments. An example is when a business enterprise writes a call option against an equity investment that it owns. If the share price rises, the firm would not benefit from the increase in the value of the investment because the option would be exercised, although it would still receive a fixed amount represented by the proceeds from the exercise. In this situation, it may be argued that by offsetting obligations from the written option (assumed to be treated as a liability) against the equity investment (the asset), it would better represent the relationship between the value of the call option and the value of the investment. Another situation where the issue of offsetting arises is the case of executory contracts such as forward contracts, futures and interest rate swaps where the rights and obligations are recognized as assets and liabilities.

In the accounting literature, two different approaches to the offsetting problem can be identified. Under one approach, which follows from Solomon's statement, it would appear reasonable to offset a liability against an asset if the risks inherent in the asset and the liability are equivalent. The problem is how to determine whether the risks in the asset and the liability to be offset are considered equivalent. One interpretation of equality of risk is that the cash flows are perfectly positively correlated (Buchan *et al*, 1992).

The other approach, one which the standard-setting bodies have taken, adopts a legalistic view to the problem. The IASC proposes that financial assets and liabilities should offset only when two conditions are met: first, when an enterprise has a legally enforceable right to set off the recognized amounts, and second, it intends either to settle on a net basis, or to realise the asset and settle the liability simultaneously (Exposure Draft 48, para. 60). This condition is considered met in the case of instruments like forward contracts, futures contract and interest rate swaps since they result from the same financial instrument, and in general, are extinguished only on simultaneous completion of the contract by both parties on maturity. However, where one party to a contract is bound to deliver a financial asset on maturity of the contract regardless of whether the other party delivers, there should be no right to setoff rights and obligations.

Similarly, the FASB[4] in Appendix B to SFAS 105 indicates that a right of set-off must exist if gain and loss positions are to be netted for

---

[4] Appendix to SFAS 105 refers to APB Opinion No. 10, paragraph 7 and Technical Bulletin (TB) 88–2 as the authoritative literature on offsetting.

interest rate and currency swaps and forward contracts. This requirement has aroused the concern of banks, brokers and dealers as their current practice is to net the gain and loss positions on swaps and forward contracts with different counter parties. Since the FASB considers gain and loss positions on forward contracts and swaps as assets and liabilities in their own rights, the current practice is clearly not conforming with what the standard-setters have in mind. The concern of banks and other financial intermediaries is clearly understandable because if the current practice of offsetting gains and losses is not allowed, they will have to gross up such gains and losses in their balance sheet. This may have an impact on their financial ratios, debt covenants and regulatory capital requirements.

Derecognition of a financial asset

Although there are differences between the sale of receivables and CMOs, both raise the same question when the seller retains a portion of the credit risk: is the transaction a sale or a financing arrangement?

Sales of receivables (or factoring) usually are either on a recourse or a non-recourse basis.[5] There is no dispute that sale of receivables without recourse should be recognized as a sale (the receivables are derecognized even when they still exist) since all risks have been transferred to the purchaser. In the case of sale of receivables with recourse, the situation is controversial regarding the appropriate accounting treatment. The transaction could be classified as a sale, in which case the receivable is derecognized (that is, removed from the balance sheet) or it could be classified as a financing arrangement, in which case the receivable is not removed and instead, a current liability is recognized. The FASB requires that the sale of receivables with recourse be accounted for as a sale together with the recognition of any gain or loss, if all three of the following conditions are met (SFAS 77, para. 5):

(1) The transferor surrenders control of the future economic benefits of the receivables;
(2) The transferor's obligation under the recourse provisions can be reasonably estimated; and
(3) The transferee cannot require the transferor to repurchase the receivables

---

[5] The FASB defines recourse as the right of a transferee of receivables to receive payments from the transferor of those receivables for (1) failure of the debtors to pay when due, (2) the effects of prepayments, or (3) adjustments resulting from defects in the eligibility of the transferred receivables. See SFAS No. 77, *Reporting by Transferors of Transfers of Receivables with Recourse*, p. 7.

If any one of these three conditions is not met, the transaction is to be treated as a financing arrangement. The FASB's stance is that the probable future benefits of the asset (the receivable) is separable from the related inherent risk (uncollectability), and in such cases, a sale should be recorded provided that probable future losses are also provided for. However, this position did not have the unanimous approval of all the Board members. The minority dissenting members pointed out that when the asset is a receivable, the future benefits and the future risk cannot be dissociated since they both flow from the same event, namely the payment or nonpayment of the receivable by the debtor. Furthermore, critics of the standard assert that it encourages the legitimisation of what is actually a form of 'off-balance-sheet financing' (Kieso and Weygandt, 1993, p. 342).

If one views the sale of receivables with recourse from a financial instruments perspective, then the transaction could be viewed as comprising two components: the sale of an unconditional receivable (or series of receivables) with the seller giving the buyer a guarantee of no default. In the event of any default by the debtor(s), the seller will have to make good the guarantee. Provided that the seller's obligation under the guarantee could be reliably estimated (for example, based on the seller's past bad debt experience), the two components could be accounted for separately. Thus, the seller's obligation under the guarantee would be recorded as a liability (or a provision) while the sale of the receivable would be recognized as a sale. This approach is consistent with SFAS No. 77.

A problem similar to sale of receivables with recourse arises in the mortgage financing industry where mortgage loans are repackaged for sale. However, securitisation of mortgage loans presents a more complex issue because the seller may sell only a portion of the receivables (pool of mortgages) and retain not only all the credit risk but other risks as well, such as interest rate and prepayment risks. For example, a financial institution with a pool of fixed interest mortgage loans with a value of $50 million is able to sell a participating interest in $40 million of the loans for $41 million dollars in return for assuming credit risk on the portion sold and for guaranteeing a variable yield that exceeds the fixed rate earned on the loan should interest rate rises. This is another example of a compound instrument: the instrument is made up of an unconditional receivable (payable) and an interest rate swap in the form of a guaranteed variable interest rate.

Under SFAS No. 77, if the three conditions mentioned in the preceding paragraph are met, the transaction would be accounted for as a sale and the seller would recognize a gain, if any, after making a provision for the estimated credit losses. However, the standard does not require any recognition of the value of the seller's obligation under the variable interest rate guarantee. It is, therefore, not surprising that the standard has been criticised for permitting the recognition of accounting gains through creative loan packaging. In order to address this problem, the Emerging Issues Task Force (EITF) came out with Concensus on ETIF Issue No. 88–11 which sought to minimise the gain that could be reported through creative loan packaging by requiring that any credit or interest rate guarantee provided by the seller should be taken into account in the determination of the gain. However, the consensus can be considered only a temporary, partial solution (Lewis, 1991).

Derecognition of a financial liability

The incentive for firms to remove debt from the balance sheet has been widely documented in the accounting literature. Generally, the effect of removing debt is to reduce the firm's debt/equity ratio which is widely regarded as an important indicator of financial viability. A reduction in gearing would reduce the firm's beta and may lead to an increase in the price of the firm's share (Roden, 1987). One method of removing (derecognizing) debt is the in-substance defeasance transaction. In-substance defeasance is an arrangement whereby a firm purchases securities and places them in an irrevocable trust for the purpose of meeting the future repayments of one or more of its long-term debts. The debt and the purchased securities are then removed (netted off) from the balance sheet. The reader is advised to refer to Chapter 10 on In-substance Defeasance for a detailed discussion of the related accounting issues.

8.3.5 Accounting for hedging instruments

A variety of financial instruments are presently used by business enterprises as well as financial institutions to hedge against price risks, including foreign exchange rate and interest rate risks. The instruments that are commonly used for hedging purposes include forward contracts, forward rate agreements, financial futures, options, interest rate and currency swaps, interest rate caps and collars. The essence of hedging is the taking on of a position in a financial instrument that is opposite to an exposed asset, liability, transaction or commitment. The objective of hedging is to transfer risk to those who are willing to assume such risk. If a hedge is perfect, any loss on the exposed item will be exactly matched by a gain on the hedging instrument. However, in practice, it is often difficult to achieve a perfect hedge.

The use of financial instruments for hedging purposes pose accounting problems which require special accounting procedures to which the term **hedge accounting** is given. The need for special accounting procedures stems directly from the shortcomings of the transaction-based, historical cost-driven accounting model. Under this model, because the hedged item and the hedging instrument are measured on difference bases, the losses or gains on the hedged items would be recognized in an accounting period that is different from the offsetting gains or losses on the hedging instruments. This results in fluctuations in reported income, thus giving the impression of an increased exposure to price risk when in fact the exposure has been reduced (Stewart, 1989). The objective of hedge accounting is to reflect some sort of symmetry between the accounting for the hedging instrument and the items being hedged. While the principle of hedge accounting is conceptually appealing, there are several issues with respect to its application which have not been consistently resolved by current standards.

One issue concerns how the level at which exposure and risk reduction is to be determined. There are basically two approaches that have been adopted in the past: a transaction approach and an enterprise approach.

- Under the transaction approach, as adopted in SFAS No. 52, a one–to–one identification is sufficient to establish that a financial instrument effectively hedges a specific exposure.
- In an enterprise approach, as adopted by SFAS No. 80 and the IASC's ED 48, the instrument must reduce overall enterprise risk before hedge accounting procedures could be applied. This means that if a firm transacts in a financial instrument to hedge a position that is already offset by the firm's other positions, hedge accounting cannot be applied as the enterprise risk is not reduced. In fact, in such a situation, the hedging instrument increases rather than reduces overall enterprise risk.

The enterprise approach is conceptually more sound and has the support of a number of commentators (Nair *et al*, 1990; Wishon and Chevalier, 1985; Cummings *et al*, 1987). However, there are other commentators that support the transaction approach for selected hedging instruments. Hauworth and Moody (1987) suggests that based on cost–benefit relationships, a transaction approach should be acceptable for options. Another source of support for the transaction approach came from American Institute of CPAs Accounting Standards Executive Committee (AcSEC).

The next issue that has divided opinions concerns the type of exposure to which hedge accounting should be applied. The contentious area is hedging future transactions. Again, there is inconsistency among current accounting standards. Both SFAS No. 80 and ED 48 permit hedging of anticipated probable future transactions, that is, transactions that an enterprise is highly probable but not obligated to carry out in the normal course of business. SFAS No. 52, on the other hand, permits hedging of future transactions that represent a firm commitment only. Besides future transactions, a firm may also hedge its future incomes. Clearly, the accounting problems are greater if hedge accounting is to be applied to future revenue streams (also called operating exposure). The

FASB did in fact discuss the firm's income for one or more future periods being exposed in SFAS No. 80. However, it is not clear whether the standard applies to such a situation.

Another issue is whether certain types of instruments, in particular cross-hedges and options, should be eligible for hedge accounting. In a cross-hedge, the hedging instrument differs from the hedged item in terms of quality and/or maturity, for example, the hedging of corporate bonds with Treasury bills futures. Because of the differences in the characteristics of the hedging instrument and the hedged item, cross-hedging is more complex than simple hedging because the price risk is replaced by what is called a basis risk which cannot be eliminated completely. Cross-hedges do not quality for hedge accounting under SFAS No. 52 but are allowed by SFAS No. 80 and ED 48. The latter's position seems more reasonable, since if cross-hedges meet the criteria for hedging, there is no reason why they should not qualify for hedge accounting.

The question of whether options used for hedging should be included under hedge accounting arises partly because existing standards that have provisions for hedging do not include options and partly because of the special characteristics of options which affect their effectiveness as hedges. For example, written options are not effective as hedges (to the writer) unless they are deep in–the–money and are expected to remain so. Most writers believe that options which are used as hedges should qualify for hedge accounting if they meet the criteria for designation as a hedge.

The last issue that need to be addressed concerns the accounting for hedging instruments such as forward contracts, futures and options, whose total value are comprised of two components: an intrinsic value and a time value.

- The intrinsic value is the difference between the market value of the item underlying the hedging instrument and the exercise price. The value of this component may increase, decrease or remain unchanged over the life of the instrument.
- The time value is the total market value less the intrinsic value. It could be viewed in the same way as an insurance premium, that is, the cost of protection against risk of loss. Unlike intrinsic value, the value of the time component decreases over the life of the instrument to nil at expiration.

Since the two components exhibit different characteristics, the question arises as to whether they should be separately accounted for. SFAS No. 52 and IAS 21 as well as ED 48 require separate accounting of the time value[6] of foreign exchange forward contracts but this is prohibited for

---

[6] In a foreign exchange forward contract, the intrinsic value is usually zero at inception, so the premium or discount on the forward contract is made up of entirely the time value.

futures contracts under SFAS No. 80. A number of writers consider it meaningful to account for the two components separately (Hauworth and Moody, 1987; Boze, 1990). Under this approach, the time value would be amortised over the life of the hedging instrument and the intrinsic value accounted for as a hedge. However, there is the problem of deciding on the appropriate method of amortisation. Although the straight–line method is usually adopted, this method may not always be appropriate.

8.3.6   Disclosure issues

The importance of information in financial reports for economic decision making is widely recognized. Although there are many groups of users who are interested in accounting information, the FASB in its Concepts Statement No. 1, *Objectives of Financial Reporting by Business Enterprises,* identified investors and creditors as the main user groups whose needs should be the focus of financial reporting. One of the objectives of financial reporting, therefore, is to provide information for 'assessing the amounts, timing, and uncertainty of prospective cash receipts from dividends or interest and the proceeds from the sale, redemption, or maturity of securities or loans' (FASB Concepts Statement No. 1, para 37). However, companies in the past have either not disclosed or inadequately disclosed information on financial instruments transacted by them. As a result, this has led to other regulatory agencies such as the Stock Exchange Commission applying pressure on companies and on the standard-setting bodies to improve the standard of disclosure on financial instrument. In particular, non-disclosure of information on financial instruments with off-balance sheet risk has been the focus of criticism.

Disclosures issues on financial instruments are concerned with two main aspects: what information should be disclosed by companies and whether the information should be disclosed for all financial instruments. Information on financial instruments of interest to investors and creditors are those that would assist them to assess future cash flows and the credit and interest rate risks faced by the enterprises. Such information would include cash receipts and payments, interest rate (nominal as well as effective rates), effective yield, maturity, and fair values of the instruments. The last item is probably the most contentious.

There has been much debate on whether fair value information should be provided on certain financial instruments, particularly those that are non-traded or inactively traded. The main arguments against disclosing fair values for such instruments are the problem of estimating fair values and the probable high cost of providing the information. Even if the fair values can be estimated using appropriate financial models, there is the question of whether they are reliable because of the assumptions underlying these models and the need to exercise judgement.

The FASB's response to these concerns is that it considered the additional relevance of the information outweighs the reliability issue. As part of its research on the feasibility of developing market values for non-traded financial instruments, the FASB asked the Bank Administration Institute to conduct a study among banks to identify the sources of market values for financial instruments. The results of the survey showed that markets exist for many types of financial instruments. Most of the instruments were valued at dealer prices and models were used for those that were traded in fairly inactive markets and were believed by the institution to be underpriced or overpriced.

Financial institutions, particularly banks, are the most affected by any disclosure requirements on financial instruments. On the question of whether information should be disclosed for all financial instruments, the most contentious areas relate to liabilities and core deposits. One argument against fair value disclosures of loans is that such disclosures would be irrelevant and meaningless because financial institutions generally intend to hold and not sell their loan portfolios. However, the counter-argument is that many financial institutions manage their assets and liabilities with the objective of hedging interest and currency risks and this suggests that disclosing fair values for both sides of the balance sheet would be appropriate.

Core deposits present another problem. Core deposits refer to the portion of long-term demand deposits which exhibits an inelastic relationship to interest rate changes. This benefits banks and other depository institutions which use the low-cost core deposit accounts to fund longer maturity investments. Thus, it is argued that core deposits have an intrinsic value, a proposition that seems to be supported by the fact that when financial institutions are sold, the economic value of core deposits is considered in determining the institution's selling price. When interest rate rise, the investment assets' market value is reduced and this implies that the recorded value of core deposit should also be reduced. This poses the problem of determining the appropriate method of calculating changes in the value of core deposits. The FASB viewed it as a non-issue as it considers the intrinsic value of core deposits to be an intangible non-financial asset, and therefore, the question of disclosure of its value does not arise.

There are several ways in which fair value information can be disclosed. One method is to show market values in parenthesis in the balance sheet. Another method is by way of a footnote. This may be done by displaying all fair value information in a single note that reproduces the main captions of the statement of financial position or via a supplemental statement of financial position in which all items for which fair values are available are reported at those amounts (Swenson and Buttross, 1993).

8.4   ACCOUNTING STANDARDS DEVELOPMENT

Prior to 1986, accounting standards-setters led mainly by the FASB, its emerging issues task force, the American Institute of CPAs in the United States, the International Accounting Standards Committee (IASC) and other national accounting standards bodies such as the Accounting Standards Commission (ASC) in the United Kingdom and the Canadian Institute of Chartered Accountants (CICA), have dealt with some of the issues raised by new financial instruments. A number of standards issued by the FASB and the IASC have addressed some of these issues. These standards include:

(1) FASB Standards
    (a) SFAS No. 12, *Accounting for Certain Marketable Securities* (now superseded by SFAS No. 115, *Accounting for Certain Investments in Debt and Equity Securities*).
    (b) SFAS No. 15, *Accounting by Debtors and Creditors for Troubled Debt Restructurings*
    (c) SFAS No. 52, *Foreign Currency Translation*
    (d) SFAS No. 65, *Accounting for Certain Mortgage Banking Activities*
    (e) SFAS No. 76, *Extinguishment of Debt*
    (f) SFAS No. 77, *Reporting by Transferors for Transfers of Receivables with Recourse*
    (g) SFAS No. 80, *Accounting for Futures Contracts*

(2) IASC Standards
    (a) IAS 21, *Accounting for the Effects of Changes in Foreign Exchange Rates*
    (b) IAS 25, *Accounting for Investments*

Generally, the standards listed above covered only specific financial instruments. For example, SFAS No. 52 dealt with foreign exchange forward contracts and swaps but excluded futures and options, while SFAS No. 80 dealt only with financial futures but excludes futures on foreign currencies. IAS 21 covered forward foreign exchange contracts and foreign currency loans that are designated as hedges.

It soon became apparent that the *ad hoc* approach to developing standards for specific instruments was totally unsatisfactory. It was not only an inefficient and slow process but more importantly, the lack of a common framework resulted in a number of inconsistencies between standards (for example, between SFAS No. 52 and SFAS No. 80), and many issues remained unsettled.

Recognising the need for a macro-level approach, and under promptings from other regulatory bodies such as the Securities Exchange Commission, the FASB took the lead by setting up a Financial Instrument Task Force in 1986 to tackle the numerous issues relating to financial instruments. The overall mission of the task force was to 'develop broad standards providing a consistent conceptual basis for resolving financial instrument accounting issues' (Woods and Bullen, 1989). Not long after the initiation of the FASB Financial Instrument Project, the IASC entered into a collaboration with the Canadian Institute of Chartered Accountants (CICA) to embark on a similar venture.

The approaches to standards development taken by the FASB and the IAS/CICA collaboration, however, differ significantly. The FASB breaks down its mission into three phases each of which is expected to take at least a couple of years. In contrast to the FASB's more cautious approach, the IASC/CICA made a bold attempt to deal with the problems in one fell swoop. In 1991, the IASC/CICA issued Exposure Draft 40 *Accounting for Financial Instruments* which proposed to deal with issues relating to financial instruments under one standard. This was superseded by ED 48 in January 1994 after the IASC had considered and accepted some of the many comments it received in response to ED 40. The salient features of the FASB's Financial Instrument Project and the IASC's Exposure Draft, ED 48 *Accounting for Financial Instruments* are analyzed below.

8.4.1 FASB's Financial Instrument Project

In the first phase of its Financial Instruments Project, the FASB focused on improving disclosure of information on all financial instruments. SFAS No. 105 *Disclosure of Information about Financial Instruments with Off-Balance Sheet Risk and Financial Instruments with Concentrations of Credit Risk*, which became effective from 1990, required disclosure of financial instruments which lead to off-balance sheet risk as well as those that carry a concentration of credit risk. This was followed in 1991 by SFAS No. 107 *Disclosures about Fair Value of Financial Instruments* which require firms to disclose market values of all financial instruments, except those specifically excluded, whether they are on-balance sheet or off-balance sheet.

The second and most difficult phase of the FASB's financial instrument project deals with recognition and measurement of financial instruments. To resolve the many issues of recognition and measurement raised by existing and new financial instruments, the FASB adopted a fundamental financial instrument approach that is based on the premise that all financial instruments are made up of a few fundamental instruments or building blocks (Bullen *et al*, 1989). Six tentatively identified fundamental financial instruments are unconditional receivable (payable), conditional receivable (payable), forward contract, option, guarantee or other conditional exchange and equity instrument. All other financial instruments are compounds, which can be analyzed as comprising various combinations of these fundamental instruments. The FASB believe that the key to reaching consistent solutions for the various accounting issues raised by complex instruments and by various relationships between instruments lies in determining how to recognize and measure those fundamental instruments.

A Discussion Memorandum entitled *Recognition and Measurement of Financial Instruments* was issued in November 1991. This was followed by SFAS No. 115 *Accounting for Investments in Debt and Equity Securities* which replaces SFAS No. 12. SFAS No. 115 was issued as a result of pressure from regulators and other quarters about the recognition and measurement of debt securities by financial institutions following the crisis experienced by savings and loans institutions. However, the FASB clearly considered SFAS No. 115 as an interim standard since it does not address all the issues relating to measurement of financial instruments; it addresses only issues related to accounting for certain financial assets without changing the accounting for related liabilities.

The third phase of the project will deal with the accounting issues relating to compound financial instruments with both liability and equity characteristics. A Discussion Memorandum *Distinguishing Between Liability and Equity Instruments and Accounting for Instruments with Characteristics of Both* was issued in 1990.

8.4.2 IASC's ED 48

Although the IASC/CICA collaboration started work later than the FASB, it was the first to come out with a comprehensive Exposure Draft, ED 40 (subsequently replaced by ED 48) *Accounting for Financial Instruments*.

The main features of ED 48 are summarised as follows:

(1) A financial instrument is defined as any contract that gives rise to both a (recognized or unrecognized) financial asset of one enterprise and a (recognized or unrecognized) financial liability or equity instrument of another enterprise. The definition of a financial instrument excludes interests in subsidiaries, associates and joint ventures, and employers' obligations under employee stock option and stock purchase plans. (See Figure 8.1).

(2) A financial asset or financial liability should be recognized in the balance sheet when substantially all of the risks and rewards associated with the asset or liability have been assumed and it can be measured reliably. Therefore, executory contracts which meet these two criteria are recognized in the balance sheet even though they are partially or wholly unperformed.

(3) A financial asset or financial liability should be derecognized when substantially all of the risks and rewards associated with the asset or liability have been transferred to others and the fair value of

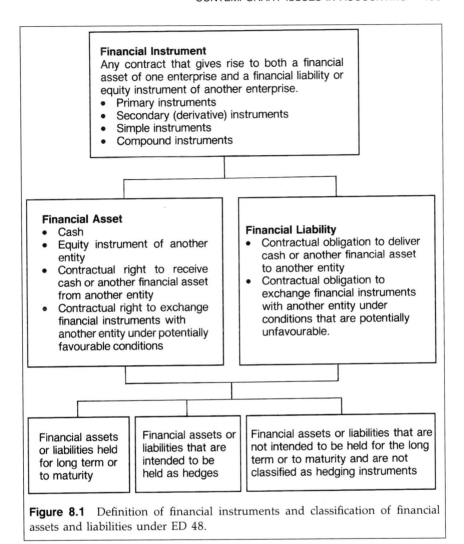

Figure 8.1 Definition of financial instruments and classification of financial assets and liabilities under ED 48.

any risks and rewards retained can be reliably measured; or the underlying right or obligation has been exercised, discharged, cancelled or expired.

(4) Companies that issue compound instruments which have a maturity date and carry the right to convert into an equity instrument of the issuer should account for its components separately at inception.

(5) The principle of substance over form is adopted. Thus, when the substance of a financial instrument is such that it commits the issuer to deliver cash or other financial assets to the holder, the instrument should be classified as a liability regardless if whether the legal form is that of equity or a liability.

(6) A financial asset and a financial liability should be offset, and the net amount reported in the balance sheet when an enterprise has a legally enforceable right to set off the recognized amounts and intends either to settle on a net basis or to realise the asset and settle the liability simultaneously.

(7) A set of benchmark standards is proposed for measuring financial assets and liabilities. Financial assets or liabilities held for long term or to maturity are measured at historical cost. Those items with fixed or determinable repayment schedules should be measured on an amortised basis reflecting their effective yields.

(8) All financial instruments are allowed to be measured at fair value as an alternative measurement standard to the benchmark standards. However, when it is not practical to determine the fair value of a financial asset or financial liability with sufficient reliability, the item should be measured on a cost basis, or, if it has been measured previously at fair value, at the most recently determined fair value.

(9) A set of comprehensive rules for hedge accounting has been proposed which include criteria for identifying a hedge, treatment of gains and losses on hedging instruments and conditions for discontinuation of hedge accounting.

(10) Information about the terms and conditions of financial instruments (whether or not they are recorded in the balance sheet), their exposure to interest rate and credit risks, the fair value of financial assets and financial liabilities carried on a historical cost basis and the accounting policies adopted for recognition and measurement are required to be disclosed.

One of the most significant features of ED 48 is the position of the IASC on fair value accounting. The standard-setters apparently favour the retention of the current model (or at least significant portions of it) but at the same time compromise by allowing, as an alternative, the use of the fair value as a basis of measurement on a comprehensive basis.

There are many similarities between ED 48 and the pronouncements the FASB has issued so far under its Financial Instruments Project (for example, the definition of financial instruments, the disclosure requirements on off-balance sheet risks and the need to disclose fair values of financial assets and liabilities). In addition, ED 48 has also removed some of the differences between the earlier Exposure Draft (ED 40) and extant FASB standards. For example, the criteria for applying hedge accounting are now almost identical with those of SFAS No. 80. However, there are still some areas where ED 48 differs from the FASB's standards issued prior to the establishment of the Financial Instruments Project. These include:

(1) The separate treatment of components of convertible debt required by ED 48 but not by APB Opinion No. 21.

(2) The derecognition of debt under in-substance defeasance arrangements which is not allowed under ED 48 but allowed under SFAS No. 76.

As discussed in the earlier sections, these FASB standards are the subject of much debate. It remains to be seen whether the new standards to be issued under the Financial Instruments Project will introduce changes that are more in line with those proposed in ED 48.

There is no doubt that ED 48 is a long and complex exposure draft that attempts to cover all the main issues posed by financial instruments. As a result, some commentators on the original exposure draft (ED 40) were of the view that it is too ambitious to address all the issues relating to financial instruments in one standard and have suggested that the proposals in the exposure draft be broken into several interrelated IASs that would deal separately with specific issues. However, the IASC does not agree with this proposal and defended its position by arguing that 'the issues cannot be broken apart without the risk of inconsistencies and gaps in coverage' (IASC, Insight, May 1992, p. 15).

8.5 ACCOUNTING FOR FINANCIAL INSTRUMENTS IN THE SINGAPORE CONTEXT

8.5.1 Types of new financial instruments

Since becoming an independent city state in 1965, Singapore has made tremendous progress from an undeveloped island with little natural resources to one of the newly industrialising nations of Asia. As Singapore is also one of the leading financial centres in Asia, financial innovation has made its mark here. However, because of the relatively recent history of Singapore's capital market, its small size and its tax laws, the range of new financial instruments introduced in the Singapore capital market in the past two decades is considerably smaller compared with those in the United States and Europe. These can be grouped into the following categories: derivative instruments, swaps, compound instruments and miscellaneous instruments.

Derivative instruments

One of the earliest derivative instruments is options on stocks which were traded on the Stock Exchange of Singapore (SES) in the early to mid 1970s. However, for various reasons, the volume of transactions in options did not meet the expectations of the SES and options trading was scrapped less than three years after it was introduced. In 1992, the regulatory authorities decided to reintroduce options on stocks on a limited scale. Six stocks have been identified for which options will be traded. At the time of writing, options on four stocks are being traded on the SES.

By far the most successful derivative instruments introduced in Singapore are the financial futures and options traded on the Singapore International Monetary Exchange (SIMEX). SIMEX was established in 1984 as Asia's pioneering financial futures market and has since built up a global reputation for financial innovativeness.

The financial instruments traded on SIMEX include interest rate futures and futures options (Eurodollar, Euroyen and Eurodeutschmarks), currency futures and future options (Japanese Yen, Deutschmarks and British Pound), commodity futures (gold and oil) and equity futures (Nikkei Stock Average futures).

Finally, among the most recent derivative instrument is the covered warrant (for example, the Merrill Lynch Hotel Warrant 95).

Compound instruments

Compound instruments that have been issued by Singapore companies include convertible loan stocks, convertible bonds, bonds with warrants and convertible preference shares. In recent years, the issue of bonds with detachable warrants has become very popular with Singapore companies. One reason is that the coupon interest rates on such bonds are very low, for example, interest rate on DBS Land Ltd's US$75 million unsecured bonds issued in March 1990 was only 1%.

Swaps

Interest rate swaps are transacted mainly by banks and other financial institutions although some large listed companies such as SBS Ltd and Keppel Corporation Ltd have been known to engage in swap transactions.[7] However, as further information on swap transactions is not publicly available, it is difficult to gauge the extent of swap transactions in Singapore.

Miscellaneous instruments

Other new financial instruments that have been introduced include various forms of debt instruments (such as floating rate notes, revolving underwriting facilities, hybrid bonds, adjustable rate bonds and guaran-

---

[7] See SBS and Keppel Corporation annual reports, 1989 and 1987 respectively.

teed bonds), special types of leases (leveraged leases and sale–and–leaseback arrangements), and single premium investment policies (issued mainly by insurance companies).

Future developments

New financial instruments as well as new financial processes will continue to be introduced in Singapore in the face of technological changes and the growing sophistication among the Singapore business and financial communities and investors. However, the rate at which new financial instruments are introduced may well be slower than in the past. Among the new instruments that may be introduced in the future are asset-based securities similar to CMOs or instruments for managing risk and enhancing investment yields (for example, indexed-linked instruments). These types of financial instruments may be given further impetus by the government's policies and efforts to promote equity investments (for example, the liberalisation of the rules on use of CPF funds for investments).

8.5.2 Accounting standards for financial instruments in Singapore

The Institute of Certified Public Accountant of Singapore (ICPAS) is the accounting standard-setting body in Singapore. Statements of Accounting Standards (SAS) issued by ICPAS closely follow those of the IASC. To date, a total of 27 standards have been issued by ICPAS. Of these, three are related to financial instruments: SAS 15 (*Accounting for Leases*), SAS 20 (*Accounting for the Effects of Changes in Foreign Exchange Rates*) and SAS 25 (*Accounting for Investments*).

SAS 20 deals very briefly with foreign exchange forward contracts for hedging and speculative purposes but does not spell out in detail the criteria for application of hedge accounting. SAS 25 deals with the measurement basis of investment securities (equity and debt securities). Investments are classified into current assets and long-term assets. The valuation bases for short-term investments are either market value or the lower of cost and market value. For long-term assets, the bases are either cost or revalued amounts, or in the case of marketable equity securities, the lower of cost and market value determined on a portfolio basis. Investments which are held for the short-term (and classified as current assets) should be held at market value, or the lower of cost and market value.

In addition to the three standards mentioned above, there is a statement of Recommended Accounting Practice (RAP) on the accounting of futures contracts (RAP 4). As the title of the statement implies, the contents of the RAP are recommended guidelines and may not necessarily carry authoritative weight.

It is clear that the ambit of the existing standards is very limited in terms of dealing with the many issues related to financial instruments. As a result, Singapore companies either have to look towards the accounting standards or practices in other countries for guidance or apply their own interpretation of accounting principles when accounting for new financial instruments. Two examples will be used to show how some Singapore companies have dealt with the accounting issues on financial instruments in the absence of specific official pronouncements. These are in-substance defeasance transactions and the issue of bonds with detachable warrants.

- Removal of debt from the balance sheet through in-substance defeasance transactions has been practised in Singapore, although on a much smaller scale than in the United States. At least three listed companies (Singapore Airline Ltd, NOL Ltd and Far East Levingstone Ltd) have disclosed such arrangements in their annual reports. The accounting method adopted by these three companies is consistent with those in the United States (under SFAS No. 76) in that in each case, the defeased liabilities are removed from the balance sheet and reported in the notes as contingent liabilities. One important departure from the US practice is that gains on the transaction are not recognized in income immediately but amortised over the life of the liabilities.

- As regards bonds issued with detachable warrant, the practice among Singapore companies is to account for them as though they were ordinary bonds. In this respect, Singapore companies are not following the United States' practice, where there is separate accounting for the debt and equity components for bonds issued with detachable warrants (but not for convertible bonds). If the US practice of split accounting is adopted, the premium on the equity portion will have to be amortised and charged to income over the life of the bond. From the companies' perspective, there is incentive not to apply split accounting for the separate components, as they will be able to show lower interest expense (based on the coupon rate) and higher profits than would be the case if split accounting were to be adopted. Theoretically, it is possible for a company which does not need external financing to issue bonds with detachable warrants at very low interest rate (such as 1.5%), place the proceeds in risk-free long-term fixed deposits to earn interest at 3.5% per annum and report the difference as net interest income to boost earnings. Of course, in the long run, this may lead to dilution in the earnings per share.

The need for an accounting standard on financial instruments in Singapore is clear cut. As with past IASC standards, Singapore will probably adopt the ED 48 when it is officially promulgated as a standard. Already its predecessor, ED 40, has had some impact on companies that wish to issue bonds with detachable warrants. Under a directive from the Stock Exchange of Singapore, companies that wish to issue bonds with detachable warrants will have to disclose in their circulars to shareholders supplementary information on a proforma basis along the guidelines of ED 40. Some companies have also disclosed the impact of adopting ED 40 requirements for compound instruments in their annual reports.

8.6 IMPLICATIONS FOR RESEARCH

Given the wide range of complex issues presented by new financial instruments (as well as new financial arrangements), it is not surprising that this is one area that is gaining prominence as a hot topic for accounting research. Besides the members of the academic community, the regulatory authorities are also interested in research on financial instruments. For example, the FASB has conducted eight field studies to evaluate how companies affected by SFAS No. 107 accumulate and report financial values for financial instruments. It also asked the Banks Administration Institute to conduct a study to identify the sources banks use to obtain market values for financial instruments.

A substantial portion of research undertaken on financial instruments in the past few years has been of the normative type. This has been very useful in articulating the issues that should be considered in developing accounting standards and in indicating the advantages and disadvantages of various alternatives. While normative accounting research still has a role to play in the current research environment, the focus increasingly is on empirical research especially that conducted under the positive accounting theory framework.

- One potentially fruitful area for accounting research on financial instruments is the impact of alternative measurement bases on a firm's earnings and share prices. In particular, research on whether fair values are more relevant than historical costs to investors and the reliability of models used to estimate fair values would be of great interest to both academicians and standard-setting authorities. This is because relevance and reliability are the two principal criteria for choosing among accounting alternatives.
- Another aspect of financial reporting of financial instruments that needs to be researched is the adequacy of existing financial reporting on financial instruments. Research could explain whether existing accounting and disclosure information on financial instruments is used in analyzing financial reports, how it is used and the extent to which it is used.

- A third area is the economic consequence-type of research. This would provide valuable indications of the impact of accounting regulation on business practices and whether it would influence firms' financing strategies.

What is mentioned above are merely some of the many possible research areas on financial instruments. In Singapore, there is very little research on financial instruments partly because of the reluctance of firms to disclose information. The situation is expected to improve as new accounting standards are introduced requiring greater disclosure.

8.7 CONCLUSION

The development of innovative new financial instruments and financing arrangements in the past two decades has presented a host of challenges to accounting standard setters. These challenges involve difficult and complex issues relating to recognition, classification, measurement and de-recognition of financial assets and liabilities. In order to resolve these issues adequately, a macro-level approach to standards development for financial instruments has to be adopted as the ad hoc approaches in the past have proved unsatisfactory.

Two of the leading standard setting bodies in the world, namely the FASB and the IASC (together with the CICA) have already embarked on a project to develop a standard(s) for financial instruments. Because these projects are undertaken independently and both the regulatory bodies have adopted different approaches, it is important that the standards that are eventually issued promote the cause of harmonisation.

REFERENCES

Brennan, M.J. and Schwartz, E.S. (1977). Convertible Bonds: Valuation and Optimal Strategies for Call and Conversion. *Journal of Finance*, Vol. 32, No. 5, pp. 1699–1755

Boze, Ken (1990). Accounting for Options Forwards and Futures Contracts. *Journal of Accounting, Auditing and Finance*, Vol. 5, No. 4, pp. 627–638

Buchan, M.G., Peasnell, K.V. and Yaansah, R.A. (1992). Netting Off Assets and Liabilities. *Accounting and Business Research*, Vol. 22, No. 87, pp. 207–217

Bullen, H.G., Wilkins, R.C. and Woods III, C.C. (1989). The Fundamental Financial Instrument Approach. *Journal of Accountancy*, Vol. 168, No. 5, pp. 71–78

Cummings, B., Apostolou, N., and Mister, W. (1987). Accounting for Interest Rate Swaps: An Emerging Issue. *Accounting Horizons*, Vol. 1, No. 2, pp. 19–24

Financial Accounting Standards Board (1975). *Accounting for Certain Marketable Securities*. (SFAS No. 12). Stamford, Connecticut: FASB

—— (1976). *Accounting for Leases*. (SFAS No. 13). Stamford, Connecticut: FASB

—— (1977). *Accounting by Debtors and Creditors for Troubled Debt Restructurings.* (SFAS No. 15). Stamford, Connecticut: FASB

—— (1981). *Foreign Currency Translation.* (SFAS No. 52). Stamford, Connecticut: FASB

—— (1982). *Accounting for Certain Mortgage Banking Activities.* (SFAS No. 65). Stamford, Connecticut: FASB

—— (1983). *Extinguishment of Debt.* (SFAS No. 76). Stamford, Connecticut: FASB

—— (1983). *Reporting by Transferors for Transfers of Receivables with Recourse.* (SFAS No. 77). Stamford, Connecticut: FASB

—— (1984). *Accounting for Futures Contracts.* (SFAS No. 80). Stamford, Connecticut: FASB

—— (1985). *Elements of Financial Statements.* (Statement of Financial Accounting Concepts No. 6). Stamford, Connecticut: FASB

—— (1990). *Disclosure of Information About Financial Instruments with Off-Balance Sheet Risk and Financial Instruments with Concentrations of Credit Risk.* (SFAS No. 105). Stamford, Connecticut: FASB

—— (1991). *Disclosures About Fair Value of Financial Instruments.* (SFAS No. 107). Stamford, Connecticut: FASB

—— (1993). *Accounting for Certain Investments in Debt and Equity Securities.* (SFAS No. 115). Stamford, Connecticut: FASB

Finnerty, J.D. (1988). Financial Engineering in Corporate Finance: An Overview. *Financial Management,* Vol. 17, No. 4, pp. 14–33

Foster III, T.W., Koogler, P.R. and Vickrey, D. (1991). Valuation of Executive Stock Options and the FASB Proposal. *Accounting Review.* July, pp. 595–610

Griffiths, I. (1986). *Creative Accounting.* London: Firethorn Press

Hauworth II, W.P. and Moody, L. (1987). An Accountant's Option Primer: Puts and Calls Demystified. *Journal of Accountancy,* Vol. 163, No. 1, pp. 87–97

IASC (1983). *Accounting for the Effects of Changes in Exchange Rates.* (IAS 21)

—— (1985). *Accounting for Investments.* (IAS 25)

—— (1990). *Accounting for Financial Instruments.* (ED 40)

Ijiri Y. (1980). *Recognition of Contractual Rights and Obligations.* FASB, pp. 86–89

Jones, J. (1988). Financial Instruments: Historical Cost v. Fair Value. *CPA Journal,* August, pp. 56–63

Kieso, D.E. and Weygandt, J.J. (1993). *Intermediate Accounting,* 7th ed. New York: Wiley.

Kimmel, P. and Warfield, T.D. (1993). Variation in Attributes of Redeemable Preferred Stock: Implications for Accounting Standards. *Accounting Horizons,* Vol. 7. No. 2, June, pp. 30–40

Lewis, C.E. (1991). Accounting for the Sale of Receivables under EITF Issue No. 88–11. *Journal of Accountancy,* Vol. 171, No. 6, pp. 73–77

Nair, R.D., Rittenberg, L.E. and Weygandt, J.J. (1990). Accounting for Redeemble Preferred Stock: Unresolved Issues. *Accounting Horizon,* Vol. 4, No. 3, pp. 20–30

—— (1990). Accounting for Interest Rate Swaps: A Critical Evaluation. *Accounting Horizon,* Vol. 5, No. 3, pp. 20–30

Parks, J.T. (1991). The ABCs of CMOs, REMICs and IO/POs: Rocket Science Comes to Mortgage Finance. *Journal of Accountancy,* Vol. 171, No. 4, pp. 43–51

Parks, T.J. (1993). FASB 115: It's Back to the Future for Market Value Accounting. *Journal of Accountancy,* Vol. 176, No. 3, pp. 49–56

Patton, W.A. (1922). *Accounting Theory – With Special Reference to the Corporate Enterprise*. New York: The Ronald Press Company

Robert, S.K. (1985). Accounting Developments. *Journal of Accounting, Auditing and Finance*, Vol. 8, No. 3, pp. 67–73

Roden, P.F. (1987). The Financial Implications of In-Substance Defeasance. *Journal of Accounting, Auditing and Finance*, Winter, pp. 79–89

Solomons, D. (1989). *Guidelines for Financial Reporting Standards*, Institute of Chartered Accountants in England and Wales

Stewart, J. (1989). *The Challenges of Hedge Accounting*, Vol. 168, No. 5, pp. 48–56

Swenson, D.W. and Buttross, T.E. (1993). A Return to the Past: Disclosing Market Values of Financial Instruments. *Journal of Accountancy*, Vol. 175, No. 1, pp. 68–78

Wishon, K. and Chevalier L. (1985). Interest Rate Swaps: Your Rate or Mine? *Journal of Accountancy*, Vol. 160, No. 3, pp. 65–84

Woods, C.C. and Bullen, H.G. (1989). An Overview of the FASB's Financial Instruments Project. *Journal of Accountancy*, Vol. 168, No. 5, pp. 42–47.

9 Off-balance Sheet Financing: Impact of Financial Reporting

Susan Teo Pin Pin

9.1 INTRODUCTION

In attempts to show acceptable performance in a competitive marketplace, many firms have resorted to the use of off-balance sheet financing, making it one of the most controversial and debated accounting issues of this decade.

In this chapter, we examine the forms and implications of off-balance sheet financing that are being used. Discussion will cover the nature of off-balance sheet financing, why it is being used, the more common forms of off-balance sheet accounting, the implications of the various forms of off-balance sheet financing on financial reporting and the users of financial statements, and regulatory efforts taken to contain the use of off-balance sheet accounting.

9.2 OFF-BALANCE SHEET FINANCING DEFINED

'Off-balance sheet risks represent disparities between an organisation's reported and actual assets and liabilities. The most significant forms of off-balance sheet risks stem from undisclosed liabilities, such as operating leases. Off-balance sheet transactions offer advantages to businesses seeking to increase cash flows, reduce reported debt, improve financial ratios, and

203

avoid debt covenants. However, off-balance sheet risks are taken at considerable cost to financial statement users. The risks violate the objectives of financial reporting. They reduce the utility and comparability of financial statements. They impair users' ability to assess a company's prospective cash flows and reduce the reliability of statements as reflections of a company's economic resources.' (Morrison, 1993)

In the United Kingdom, Technical Release (TR) 603 defined off-balance sheet financing as:

> 'the funding or refinancing of a company's operations in such a way that, under legal requirements and existing conventions, some or all of the finance may not be shown on its balance sheet.'

Hence, when a company is able to obtain financing (either by borrowing monies or undertaking to pay monies in the future) in such a way that the obligations are not shown as liabilities on the balance sheet, it has used off-balance sheet financing. The immediate advantage of using off-balance sheet financing is quite obvious – the omission of liability that makes a firm's finances look more healthier.

When off-balance sheet financing was first used in financial statements, it was argued that this class of transactions would remove or greatly reduce the liability faced by firms. By matching assets with the liabilities, firms would be freed from future liabilities with regard to the particular liability being removed. If the liability is properly matched with an asset that offers the same cash flow, then firms would have no further concerns about the funding of the liability. Retaining the matched asset and liability in the financial statement may then convey wrong information to users as to the availability of resources. Thus, the rationale for allowing the practice of off-balance sheet accounting was to reflect the perfect matching of assets and liabilities which would lead to the distinguishment of the liabilities. The removal of such items would then improve the truth and fairness of the financial statements.

However, with the passage of time, the lack of risk of recourse has ceased to be the main criterion for exclusion. In fact, many new financial instruments and transactions have evolved with the primary intention of removing liabilities from the balance sheet. It is this group of transactions that exposes the firms to the risk of recourse or other future liabilities that is the important issue in this chapter.

The features of off-balance sheet financing make it especially attractive for firms that are experiencing or expecting financial difficulties, as well as rapidly expanding firms. By removing their existing liabilities, these firms would then be able to raise more funds that they might otherwise not be able to raise, or for which they would have to pay significantly higher interest rates. However, as more firms resort to the use of off-balance sheet financing, it may in turn lead to distrust in the financial information provided by firms and hence reduce the usefulness of financial statements. This potential impact of off-balance sheet financing on the usefulness of financial reporting has made standard-setting bodies take a keen interest in this issue.

In the **United States**, when the standard-setting bodies first encountered the use of off-balance sheet accounting in the early 1960s, the approach taken was to resolve each individual issue as it emerged. (For example, FASB Statement 5 deals with *Accounting for Contingencies*, FASB Statement 13 deals with *Accounting for Leases*, and FASB Statement 76 deals with *Extinguishment of Debt*.) With the completion of the conceptual framework project, the approach taken by the Financial Accounting Standards Board (FASB) in the recent years has been to apply the definitions of assets and liabilities as set out in the framework to determine whether particular transactions should be included in the balance sheet. Hence, the issue of off-balance sheet financing has not been dealt with directly.

However, with new financial instruments and greater sophistication in the financial market, this piecemeal approach may not be effective in resolving problems, as standards tend to lag behind practice. In view of this, the FASB has modified its approach somewhat in its Exposure Draft on *Disclosure about Financial Instruments*, issued in November 1987. In this, an attempt was made to make the standard broad enough to apply to all financial instruments and to resolve current and emerging issues. While this Exposure Draft attempts to ensure that users are informed about the credit risk, future cash flows, interest rate and market value of these instruments, it still does not directly deal with the off-balance sheet issue. A similar exposure draft (ED 48) has been issued by the International Accounting Standards Committee (IASC).

The **United Kingdom** adopted a totally different approach to resolving the issue. In 1985, the Technical Committee of the Institute of Chartered Accountants in England and Wales issued TR 603 to deal with the whole off-balance sheet financing issue in a single attempt. The approach recommended in TR 603 is to try to ensure that financial statements give a 'true and fair view' (that is, substance is more important than form). The onus here is on the preparers of financial statements to ensure that the information provided reflects the essence of the transactions. While this would help ensure that accounting does not lag too far behind practice, there is a level of reliance on the integrity of the preparers of financial statements. Furthermore, as the choice of accounting method in this environment is very judgmental, a wide variety of accounting methods could still be used to account for similar transactions.

In **Singapore**, TR 603 also forms the basis for the Institute of Certified Public Accountants of Singapore's Recommended Accounting Practices (RAP) 5. The emphasis of RAP 5 is also that financial statements should give a true and fair view, and that:

> 'the economic substance of such transactions should be considered rather than their mere legal form when determining their true nature and thus the appropriate accounting treatment.'

While it is not yet clear which of the above approaches would be more effective, the need to restrict the use of off-balance sheet financing is clearly evident. The fact that the use of off-balance sheet financing methods allows firms to effectively borrow and yet not be required to show a corresponding liability makes it very attractive for firms to obtain financing this way. As it becomes more commonly used, its impact on financial statements is also more material and important.

9.3 REASONS FOR USING OFF-BALANCE SHEET FINANCING

Some of the reasons for the popularity of off-balance sheet financing are discussed below.

(1) Removal of debt from the balance sheet improves the quality of the balance sheet and makes further issuance of capital and/or debt possible, often at a lower cost. A firm with a low level of borrowing is generally perceived as financially healthy and strong. This could have the effect of raising the value of the firm's stocks, improving the firm's public debt rating, enhancing its image with the financial press, attracting less sophisticated investors/lenders and qualifying more easily for trade credit.

(2) Loan covenants may impose restrictions on further borrowing by firms (for example, requiring that a certain debt to equity ratio be maintained). Hence, off-balance sheet financing may be the only alternative available to some firms that would not result in the violation of their existing debt covenants.

(3) As the use of historical cost accounting has resulted in an understatement of assets, the use of off-balance sheet financing serves to balance this by understatement of liabilities. Hence, off-balance sheet financing can be equitable. However, this is probably the most dubious of all the reasons, as two wrongs do not necessarily make one right.

(4) The use of off-balance sheet financing may be more informative if the particular transaction or subsidiary in question is very different from the main lines of business. The inclusion of the transaction may cause the financial statement to be not reflective of the activities of the firm as a whole.

(5) Some forms of off-balance sheet financing are arranged so that both parties to the transactions are able to maximize and jointly share some tax benefits. This type of tax planning would result in positive cash flows for both parties and would be one of the rare situations where off-balance sheet financing may actually benefit the shareholders directly.

(6) Financial institutions are subject to legal requirements as to the composition of the assets and liabilities, minimum reserve and capital requirements that must be maintained. By engaging in off-balance sheet transactions, such as the issuance of letters of credit, swaps, future and forward contracts, and banker's guarantees, financial institutions are able to expand their operations without violating the law.

(7) Cost of debt tends to be lower than cost of equity. Hence, the ability to increase debt financing is believed to be a means of lowering the cost of capital. However, increasing the amount of debt would increase risk and that would lead to demand for higher rate of return of both debt and capital. Hence, increasing borrowing beyond a certain level may be viewed negatively by the financial markets. The use of off-balance sheet financing that is not reflected on the balance sheet allows firms to borrow without adverse effects on the cost of capital.

(8) Certain types of off-balance sheet financing may be income increasing or have income smoothing effects. Sales and leaseback agreements allow firms to recognize capital gains, thus resulting in an increase in income reported, and yet retain the use of assets. Inventory repurchase agreements allow the recognition of revenue before the final disposal of the inventories, and can be used to reduce fluctuations and volatility of income.

9.4 METHODS OF OFF-BALANCE SHEET FINANCING

As a result of the perceived advantages of using off-balance sheet financing and also because of new financial market innovations, there are now many different off-balance sheet financing methods in use. The commonly used methods of off-balance sheet accounting include leasing, factoring and securitisation, inventory repurchase, in-substance debt defeasance, interest rate swaps, project financing arrangements, controlled non-subsidiaries, self-financing, consignment stock, contingent liabilities, and other methods.

9.4.1 Leasing

The **financial lease** is one of the most widely used form of off-balance sheet accounting. In this situation, a company acquires the use of an asset by entering into a lease agreement. Since it acquires the use and control of the asset without legal ownership, there is no recording of the asset and the corresponding liability in its balance sheet. However, this kind of scheme, the pioneer of the off-balance sheet financing schemes, can no longer be kept out of the balance sheet with the various standard-setting boards' pronouncements (SSAP 21, FASB Statement 13 and IAS 15). However, some firms have successfully restructured their financing leases to meet the requirements for operating leases and kept them off the balance sheet.

Unlike the financial lease, an **operating lease** can usually be cancelled by the lessee as and when the asset is no longer required. As such, it does not meet the definition of an asset. So unlike a financial lease, there is no requirement to recognize the lease as an asset, as a result of which there is no corresponding liability. While the lessee would prefer the lease to be treated as an operating lease, the option to cancel is usually not favoured by the lessor. In the case where the lessor is primarily the financier, such an operating lease would usually require the lessee to pay a very high penalty for cancellation to prevent premature termination of the lease. There has been a significant increase in the use of such non-cancellable operating lease agreements since the standards on leases were adopted.

9.4.2 Factoring and securitisation

Factoring refers to the selling of debts and accounts receivable to financial institutions at a discount, while securitisation (the mirror image of debt defeasance) refers to the use of debts and accounts receivable as securities to obtain further financing. Upon the receipt of funds, the receivable is then removed from the balance sheet. While this may be the appropriate treatment if the sale is without recourse, sales of receivables are usually with recourse: if the debtor defaults, the bad debt would be borne by the firm and not the financial institution. Hence, there is a need to reflect the possibility of bad debts and the potential liabilities payable to the financial institutions, which is not currently reflected in the balance sheet.

9.4.3 Inventory repurchase

This usually involves a sale of inventory with an option to buy back at maturity. This is often used by businesses that have to hold inventories over a period in time before there is an appreciation in value of the inventories. An example of this transaction is the case of a winery selling maturing wine stocks to a financier. Such a transaction is usually on paper only with no physical movement of the asset (that is, the stock remains at the winery).

The agreement entered into comprises three parts: the sales agreement and two options. There is an option for the winery to repurchase as well as an option for the financier to resell the stocks in the future. When the wine is matured and ready to be sold in the open market, the winery will buy back the wine from the financier. The repurchase price would include an interest element. In such cases, neither the inventories or the loan (option to purchase) would be reflected in the books until the option to repurchase or resell is exercised. Such an agreement provides the funds needed for operation without the need to record the liability as well as the recognition of a gain at the point of sale.

9.4.4 In-substance debt defeasance

This may be used by firms that have issued debentures or have entered into long-term loan agreements with the subsequent rise in interest rates. Here, the firm may place sufficient cash or assets in a trust to pay for both the interest and capital for the long-term loans, and hence remove both the assets and the liabilities off the balance sheet. If the interest rate has risen significantly between the time the original loan was entered into and the creation of the trust, the amount needed in the trust may be much lower than the book value of the loan. By practising in-substance defeasance, the firm not only removes the liability from its balance sheet, it may also report a gain on debt retirement. If a firm can borrow at a low rate of interest and reinvest immediately at a higher rate of interest, it can do instantaneous debt defeasance and recognize the gain immediately.

9.4.5 Interest rate swaps

A firm with a variable rate debt may swap into a fixed rate loan to reduce its exposure to rising interest costs. This swap may increase the amount of interest to be paid as it reduces the interest rate risk. However, as the firm only reports the original loan and not the swap agreement, the increase in interest to be paid is not disclosed and this gives rise to some off-balance sheet financing.

9.4.6 Project financing arrangements

When two or more parties form a new business organization that would be responsible for the building of a new project by owning 50% or less of the new entity, the original parties do not have to consolidate this new business organization. The new business would then borrow more money needed for this project. While the intention is to service the loan out of the proceeds of the project when it is completed, the loan would be guaranteed by the parties forming the new business. As the new business is a separate entity, the guarantee would not be reflected in the financial statements of the original parties, and as a result, there is no increase in liability shown in the financial statements. (If the project had been undertaken by the parties as part of their ongoing operations, the borrowing would have to be reflected as a liability in their financial statements.)

9.4.7 Controlled non-subsidiaries

Where a firm owns only 50% or less of another firm, the second firm is treated as an investment and not a subsidiary in the first firm's accounts. Hence, all the liabilities in the second firm's accounts will not be reflected in the first firm's financial statement. However, most parent companies would still be responsible for the debts of such joint ventures and again the balance sheet would not reflect the true position of the firm. Furthermore, such non-subsidiaries could also be used to obtain more financing for the parent companies without having to show the increased liabilities in the parent company's financial statements.

9.4.8 Self-financing

Under this type of financing, debt is made to look like equity by preselling the value of the assets. This method is often used in construction projects where there is a purchase contract and progress payments are collected even before the completion of the production process. By recognizing that the revenue is being earned during the production process, part of the progress payment collected would be considered earned, and hence no longer a liability in the financial statements.

9.4.9 Consignment stock

Here, the firm obtains stocks which are consigned to it, but the payment for this must be made either immediately upon sale or after it has held the stock for a certain duration. Hence, the manufacturer is effectively financing the operations of the firm, as neither stock nor accounts payable would appear in the firm's financial statements.

9.4.10 Contingent liabilities

These involve transactions for which the obligating event has occurred in the past but the outcome of which is dependent on a future event. If the outcome of the event is difficult to predict or is uncertain, the firm is allowed to defer the recognition of such liabilities until the confirming event occurs.

9.4.11 Other methods of off-balance sheet financing

As a result of increased competitiveness and the tight regulatory controls in the banking sector, more off-balance sheet financing methods are used by banks. These methods (such as standby contracts/letters of credits, forward/future contracts, swaps, options arrangements) enable banks to expand their operations and earn revenue without violating capital structure requirements.

9.5 IMPLICATIONS OF OFF-BALANCE SHEET FINANCING

The primary objective of providing financial statements to external parties is to enable them to make economic decisions. Hence, it is important to consider the impact of off-balance sheet financing on the decisions made by users of financial statements.

While shareholders and creditors are not the only groups of decision makers, they are predominant groups of users of financial information. Furthermore, the majority of the users of financial information use it to aid in making investment decisions. Hence, the implications of off-balance sheet financing is analyzed from the point of view of the capital markets.

It has been suggested that more sophisticated financial statement users are no longer fixated on bottom lines, but would consider the actual accounting facts and make the necessary adjustments when comparing two firms that use different accounting methods. Hence, it has also been argued that it does not matter whether the information is in the balance sheet, or profit and loss statement, or notes to the accounts; as long as the disclosure is adequate, the users of financial statements can still correctly value the firm and its potential earning capabilities.

However, even if we agree that the above argument is valid, there is an implicit assumption that the information needed to make the necessary adjustment is disclosed for users to make the correct decisions. This is not always the case. Often, when off-balance sheet financing is used, the usage is not reflected in the financial statements, but rather is disclosed in the notes to the accounts. Even then, the disclosure tends to be obscure and brief. The information provided may not be sufficient for users to make the necessary adjustments to the financial statements.

The use of off-balance sheet financing could potentially reduce the usefulness of financial statements. Apart from manipulating existing figures, some off-balance sheet financing methods could actually exclude them altogether from the accounts. In such cases, it may be impossible to detect them even after a detailed analysis of the financial statements and the notes to the accounts.

The problem could be even more critical if users are not sophisticated. In this case, disclosure without proper accounting treatment may cause users to make wrong investment decisions, not to mention the situation where the information is not reflected at all, as in the case of off-balance sheet financing.

Leaving important information to footnote disclosures may also create confusion, especially if the note contradicts with information disclosed in the financial statements. The notes to the accounts should be precisely what it says: notes to further explain (not contradict) the numbers included in the accounts. Notes to the accounts should also not be a means for management to protect themselves if things go wrong. Furthermore, the disclosure in the notes tends to be vague, and insufficient information is provided to enable users to make the necessary adjustments needed to compare across firms. Hence, just disclosing the use of off-balance sheet financing as a note of disclosure may not be sufficient.

Also, if the use of off-balance sheet financing in a misleading manner is condoned, then unscrupulous businesses could come up with even more variations of off-balance sheet financing methods to mislead investors. It is therefore important that efforts be made to minimise the use of off-balance sheet financing rather than simply assume that efficient financial markets would be discerning enough to adjust and nullify the effects of off-balance sheet financing.

While most standard-setting bodies are aware of the potential problems and have taken efforts to address the issue, the solutions are still unclear. The difficulties faced by standard-setters may be due in part to flexibility of the standards set thus far. Most current standards recognize that there are differences between firms that require the use of different accounting methods to reflect their performance. Hence, rather than requiring businesses to use one specific method, it reduces the range of acceptable methods, allows firms to choose from these methods and encourages disclosure of choice. This allows firms to report different results for the same set of transactions. Coupled with the vagueness of the terms used, this has made off-balance sheet financing very popular.

While it is not feasible for standard-setters to reissue standards that specify the mandatory use of particular methods for the existing standards, standard-setting bodies still play a vital role in reducing the impact of off-balance sheet financing. By discussing the issues, these boards can increase awareness of their use. Redefining ownership and control could also force firms to reveal some of their off-balance sheet financing transactions.

9.6 REGULATORY EFFORTS

As new methods of off-balance sheet financing continue to evolve, this will continue to pose conceptual and measurement problems for the accounting profession. Adopting the approach of dealing with each new form of off-balance sheet financing as and when it arises is neither efficient nor effective. The more efficient solution would be to devise an all encompassing standard that is more conceptual rather than technical in nature. Such a standard should be broad enough to deal with all possible forms of off-balance sheet financing methods, and would be a longer run solution to these problems.

Steps towards this direction have been already initiated by some standard-setting bodies.

9.6.1 United Kingdom

In the United Kingdom, efforts to curb the use of off-balance sheet item began when the Accounting Standards Committee (ASC) issued a list of guidelines in ED 42 on which items should or should not be treated as an off-balance sheet item. The emphasis was on presenting a 'true and fair' set of accounts.

Some of the guidelines in ED42 are explained below.

- Accounting for substance is explained in the proposed statement as meaning that a transaction's accounting treatment should fairly reflect its commercial effect (para. 1.15).
- This principle should be distinguished from the statement that substance should take precedence over form, or, as it is sometimes put, that economic substance should take precedence over legal form. It is analysis of the commercial effects flowing from the form of special purpose transactions that will lead to an understanding of their substance. Such analysis is essential to the application of the proposed statement (para. 1.16).

Hence, the emphasis is on the need to determine the commercial impact of the transactions and whether they meet the definition of an asset or liability. The approach suggested in ED 42 is set out in para. 13:

> 'A key step in determining the substance of a transaction is to identify whether the transaction has increased or decreased the various assets or liabilities previously recognised in the accounts of the enterprise and whether it has given rise to assets or liabilities not previously recognised.'

The definition of assets and liabilities are set out in para. 14 and para. 22 respectively.

> 'For the purpose of financial statements, assets may be described at a general level as probable future economic benefits controlled by and accruing to a particular enterprise as a result of past transactions or events.' (para. 14)
> 'For the purpose of financial statements, liabilities, including provisions for liabilities, may be described at a general level as present obligations of a

particular enterprise entailing probable future sacrifices of economic benefits by transferring assets or providing service to other entities in the future.' (para. 22)

The requirements of ED 42 are quite similar to the requirements of the FASB Conceptual Framework in the United States. ED 42 also includes a discussion of commonly used off-balance sheet practices.

The efforts begun by the ASC have been continued by a new standard-setting body in United Kingdom, the Accounting Standards Board (ASB). ASB issued (Financial Reporting Standards) (FRS) 3, as well as (Financial Reporting Exposure Draft) (FRED) 3 and 4. In FRS 3, a new profit and loss statement format was given, while FRED 3 and 4 deals with specific off-balance sheet practices such as capital and other financial instruments.

9.6.2   United States

In the United States, besides the conceptual framework that is applicable for all accounting issues, there are also standards dealing with specific off-balance sheet practices (such as SFAS 76 on *Extinguishment of Debt*, SFAS 77 on *Reporting by Transferors for Transfer of Receivables with Recourse*, SFAS 85 on *Yield Test for Determining Whether a Convertible Security is a Common Stock Equivalent*, and SFAS 94 on *Consolidation of All Majority-Owned Subsidiaries*, to name a few).

Besides these specific standards, FASB also issued SFAS 105 in March 1990 on *Disclosure of Information About Financial Instruments with Off-Balance Sheet Risk and Financial Instruments with Concentrations of Credit Risk*. This standard addresses the new financial instruments and attempts to tackle the broad issue of off-balance sheet financing. It requires business entities to disclose more information on their financial instruments to enable investors to better evaluate the financial instruments held and the risks inherent in these instruments. The additional information required under this focuses on the disclosure of two types of risk: credit risk and market risk.

Such disclosure is seen as 'an initial, interim step' in FASB's broad project on financial instruments and off-balance sheet financing. The later phases of this project will address the issues of recognition, measurement and display. Since SFAS 105, the FASB has also issued SFAS 107 on *Disclosure about Fair Value of Financial Instruments*, and Exposure Draft 136B on *Disclosure about Derivative Financial Instruments and Fair Value of Financial Instruments* that discusses the issues of recognition, measurement and display of the required information in the financial statements.

9.6.3 Singapore

As the Singapore Accounting Standards (SAS) are primarily a modification of the International Accounting Standards (IAS), we need to look at the efforts undertaken by the International Accounting Standards Committee (IASC) to better understand the developments in Singapore. To date, there are standards issued to deal with specific issues such as SAS 15 on *Accounting for Leases* and SAS 25 on *Accounting for Investments*. In 1994, IASC issued ED 48 dealing with financial instruments. This is one of the more substantial exposure drafts issued and covers conceptual, measurement as well as disclosure issues.

Here again, the role of professional judgement and the presentation of the transaction to reflect its substance is again stressed.

Paragraph 83 of ED 48 states that:

'Under the benchmark measurement standards, management's intention in entering into a transaction involving a financial instrument is considered the primary factor in determining the substance of the transaction. Intent is the criterion for determining the substance of the transaction. Intent is the criterion for determining the measurement basis to apply to the resulting financial asset or financial liability.'

ED 48 also sets out what should be recognized as a financial liability or asset, when this liability or asset can be removed, as well as when the right to offset a financial liability against a financial asset can be exercised.

'A financial asset or financial liability should be recognised on an enterprise's balance sheet when:
(a) substantially all of the risks and rewards associated with the asset or liability have been transferred to the enterprise; and
(b) the cost or fair value of the asset to the enterprise or the amount of the obligation assumed can be measured reliably.' (para. 19)

'A recognised financial asset or financial liability should be removed from an enterprise's balance sheet when:
(a) substantially all of the risks and rewards associated with the asset or liability have been transferred to others and the fair value of any risks and rewards retained can be measured reliably; and
(b) the underlying right or obligation has been exercised, discharged or cancelled, or has expired.' (para. 27)

'A financial asset and a financial liability should be offset and the net amount reported in the balance sheet when an enterprise:
(a) has a legally enforceable right to set off the recognised amounts; and
  (b) intends either to settle on a net basis, or to realise the asset and settle the liability simultaneously.' (para. 60)

Besides the above, ED 48 also lists widely used financial instruments and the disclosure requirements required of these. The type of disclosure required includes the extent and nature of the financial instrument, the accounting policies and methods, interest rate risk, credit risk, valuation and others.

9.7   CONCLUSION

While the efforts taken by standard-setting boards is a step towards reducing the excessive use of off-balance sheet financing and allows for the evaluation of new off-balance sheet financing methods as they arise, there is some disagreement on whether it is feasible to perform this evaluation based on broad, subjective criteria. It has been argued that the onus should be placed on the preparers and auditors of financial statements to answer open-ended question rather than just meet some criteria which can be circumvented.

Professor Tweedie, the chairman of the ASC, has suggested that the question to ask should be:

> 'If I were on the "outside", and did not have the detailed knowledge of the company's trading performance and ultimate financial position that I have as I look at these accounts, would I be able to obtain a clear and unambiguous picture of the reality from these accounts?'

He then suggested that:

> 'If the picture is poorly painted or worse fails to reflect reality, then the directors have failed to meet the paramount principle of financial reporting – to show a true and fair view – and must return to their canvas until that picture is a faithful representation of the enterprise's state of affairs and profit and loss.'

While Professor Tweedie's views may seem idealistic, it may be just what is needed in this issue. In view of the widespread use of off-balance sheet financing, this issue can no longer be swept under the carpet. Aside from the profession itself, the educational system could also help to increase awareness of the use of off-balance sheet financing. Business schools could include a discussion of it in their accounting courses.

While research into this area is made difficult due to insufficient publicly available data, such research will increase the understanding of the implications of such off-balance sheet transactions and should be encouraged. Work done on this issue can be broadly divided into two main groups.

- The first group tends to focus on possible impacts of reporting requirements for off-balance sheet items (Hunt *et al*, 1993; Motyl, 1993; Munter, 1992; McCarthy, 1992). Here, the emphasis is on the accounting standards and their potential impact.
- The second group attempts to look at the actual usage and impact of off-balance sheet accounting, in particular, the types of off-balance sheet financing that are commonly used, the potential impact of their use on the financial statements and users of financial information (Griffith, 1986; Naser, 1993). While the authors have discussed the off-balance sheet methods used, as well as their expected impact,

the nature and the motivation for the use of these methods have made research in this area very difficult.

There is an urgent need for more work in this area to increase the knowledge base on how firms actually use off-balance sheet methods. Perhaps an alternative approach in building a knowledge base is by studying firms that have used these methods to gain a better understanding on why they chose these methods, how the methods were implemented, and the impact of these method on their operations, financial statements and the market value of the firm. (Terry Smith has made a major contribution using this approach in his book *Accounting for Growth*.) As firms may be reluctant to discuss such issues, archival research looking at firms that have been liquidated may be the approach to adopt for this type of study.

In conclusion, while steps have been taken to increase awareness of the impact of off-balance sheet accounting as well as to discourage its use, the solution to the problem is still not obvious. We can expect to see an increased use of such accounting practices as the market becomes more competitive. Until a definitive solution is found, users of financial statements should pay more attention to the notes to the accounts, where information concerning off-balance sheet practices may be found.

REFERENCES

Accounting Standards Committee (1988). *Accounting for Special Purpose Transactions* (ED 42). London: ASC

Berton, L. (1983). Loose Lenders: Many Firms Hide Debt to Give Them an Aura of Financial Strength. *The Wall Street Journal*, December 13

Dieter, R. and Wyatt, A.R. (1980). Get It Off the Balance Sheet. *Financial Executive*, January

Financial Accounting Standards Board (1994). Exposure Draft on *Disclosure about Derivative Financial Instruments and Fair Value of Financial Instruments*. April 1994. Stamford, Connecticut: FASB

Financial Accounting Standards Board (1987). Exposure Draft on *Disclosure about Financial Instruments*. Stamford, Connecticut: FASB

Financial Accounting Standards Board (1975). *Accounting for Contingencies* (SFAS 5). Mar 1975 Stamford, Connecticut: FASB

Financial Accounting Standards Board (1976). *Accounting for Leases* (SFAS 13). Nov. 1976 Stamford, Connecticut: FASB

Financial Accounting Standards Board (1983). *Extinguishment of Debt* (SFAS 76). Nov. 1983 Stamford, Connecticut: FASB

Financial Accounting Standards Board (1983). *Reporting by Transferors for Transfer of Receivables with Recourse* (SFAS 77). December 1983 Stamford, Connecticut: FASB

Financial Accounting Standards Board (1985). *Yield Test for Determining Whether a Convertible Security is a Common Stock Equivalent* (SFAS 85). March 1985 Stamford, Connecticut: FASB

Financial Accounting Standards Board (1987). *Consolidation of All Majority-Owned Subsidiaries* (SFAS 94). October 1987 Stamford, Connecticut: FASB

Financial Accounting Standards Board (1990). *Disclosure of Information About Financial Instruments with Off-Balance Sheet Risk and Financial Instruments with Concentrations of Credit Risk* (SFAS 105). March 1990. Stamford, Connecticut: FASB

Financial Accounting Standards Board (1992). *Disclosure about Fair Value of Financial Instruments* (SFAS 107). March 1992, Stamford, Connecticut: FASB

Gillespie, Ian, ed. (1989). *Readings in Off Balance Sheet Finance*. The Money Managers Library, London: Eurostudy

Griffith, I. (1986). *Creative Accounting*. London: Sidgwick & Jackson

Hunt, J.H., Monticciolo, D.A. and Belur, A.R. (1993). The New Era in Bank Portfolio Management. *Journal of Fixed Income*, September 1993

International Accounting Standards Committee (1994). *Financial Instruments* (ED 48). London: IASC

Mathews, M.R. and Perera, M.H.B. (1991). Creative Accounting. In *Accounting Theory and Development*, London: Chapman & Hall

McCarthy, E.M. (1992). FASB: Upcoming Implementation Issues. *Journal of Corporate Accounting and Finance*, Fall 1992

Morrison, E.R. (1993). Off-balance Sheet Risks: What Are They and Why is Disclosure Important? *Journal of Accounting Education*, Fall 1993

Motyl, K. (1993). ASB Sets Sights on Off Balance Sheet Financing. *Accountancy Age*, Feb. 25, 1993

Munter, P. (1992). Disclosure of Information About Financial Instruments: The Requirements of SFAS 105 and 107. *Journal of Corporate Accounting & Finance*, Fall 1992

Naser, K.H.M. (1993). *Creative Financial Accounting*. New York: Prentice Hall

Smith, T. (1992). *Accounting for Growth*. London: Random House

The Institute of Chartered Accountants in England and Wales (1985). *Off-balance Sheet Finance and Window Dressing* (TR 603). London: ICAEW

The Chartered Association of Certified Accountants (1988). *Off-Balance Sheet Financing (ACCA Certified Research Report 10)*. London: ACCA

10 In-substance Defeasance – Accounting Practice and Issues

Branson Kwok Chi Hing and Lim Ai Bee

10.1 INTRODUCTION

Accounting gimmick, paper gain, year-end window dressing, cosmetic accounting, give-away to bondholders, cute accounting, illusory earnings and balance sheet cosmetics – these were some of the criticisms to in-substance defeasance from accounting academics, practitioners and the press (see Hand *et al*, 1989, Appendix A). Reacting to the highly controversial practice by Exxon and Kellogg in 1982 and fearing an avalanche of the questionable accounting treatment, the Securities Exchange Commission (SEC) imposed a moratorium on in-substance defeasance. The ban was subsequently lifted after the adoption of FASB Statement No. 76 by the Financial Accounting Standard Board (FASB).

In this chapter, we provide readers with the background of the events leading to the strong reaction of the SEC in 1982 and the adoption of the FASB Statement No. 76 by the FASB. We also discuss relevant accounting issues and review the benefits and costs of in-substance defeasance of debt (hereinafter called in-substance defeasance). We then offer some suggestions for further research as concluding remarks of this chapter.

10.2 EXTINGUISHMENT OF LONG TERM DEBT

When there is favourable movement of interest rate, a company often finds it attractive to retire its fixed interest rate long term debt. Usually, the debt can be extinguished/defeased by the company in the following manner:

(1) called for redemption if the debt is callable,
(2) reacquired in the open market if it is traded in the open market,
(3) retired through debt-to-equity swap or
(4) its future payments are paid in full and the company is legally released.

These are **legal debt defeasance/extinguishment** whereby the debtor is legally released from all future financial obligations. However, in some circumstances debt can be *economically* but not legally defeased. An existing debt can be considered defeased/extinguished in-substance for reporting purposes under FASB Statement No. 76 if:

'The company, the debtor, *irrevocably* places cash or other essentially risk free monetary assets in a *trust solely* for satisfying the debt and the probability that the debtor will be required to make further payment is *remote*'. (emphasis added)

10.3 THE US EXPERIENCE

In 1982, Exxon bought US$312 million of government securities and placed these risk-free securities in an irrevocable trust. The proceeds, both interest and principal payments, from the government securities were designed to meet Exxon's financial obligations of US$515 million in long term debts to its creditors. This was a simple business transaction and was in itself neither controversial nor objectionable. However, what the critics objected to was Exxon's rather unusual accounting treatment of the transaction. As a result of the above arrangement, Exxon removed the US$515 million long term debts from its balance sheet and reported an after-tax gain of US$132 million.[1] The effects of this accounting practice, known as in-substance defeasance, on the financial statements were quite obvious – it cleaned up the balance sheet and consequently provided better debt ratios and a higher income figure.

The reaction to Exxon's accounting treatment was swift. In-substance defeasance was deemed by many of its critics to be inconsistent with the generally accepted accounting concept of extinguishment of

---

[1] In June 1982, Kellogg 'defeased' US$75 million of long term debts by paying cash and liquid assets of US$65.5 million to a third party to assume the financial responsibilities of servicing the debts. This method is not the focus of our study as it is not the 'normal' in-substance defeasance allowed by the FASB Statement No. 76.

liabilities or debts. Some corporations with existing long term debts which were issued during a period of low interest rates might like to 'copy' the same act to gain similar favourable balance sheet and income effects. Fearing a possible avalanche of in-substance defeasance[2], the SEC imposed a moratorium on the practice in August 1982 pending a decision from the FASB. The FASB approved the accounting practice by a vote of four to three and issued FASB Statement No. 76, *Extinguishment of Debt*, in November 1983. The new accounting standard specifies the condition for 'valid' in-substance defeasance and proper accounting treatment of the transaction. The standard was unanimously approved by the SEC and the Commission lifted its moratorium on in-substance defeasance in December 1983. In 1984, the FASB issued Technical Bulletin No. 84–A and 84–4 to explain the technical issues relating to in-substance defeasance.

Since the approval of in-substance defeasance accounting in the United States, many large corporations such as Black and Decker, Merrill Lynch, Marine Midland and USX have defeased their long term debts (Mielke and Seifert's appendix (1987) contains a list of companies that have defeased debts.) The accounting practice has also gained acceptance by companies outside of the United States. Australian corporations like Pioneer, North Broken Hill, Comalco, James Hardie, Petersville and NCL were also reported to have adopted in-substance defeasance (Whittred and Zimmer, 1990). Lee and Tan (1994) report that some Singapore companies like SIA, NOL and Far East Levingston Shipbuilding Ltd have also extinguished some of their debts through in-substance defeasance. Specifically, the study reports that NOL and SIA extinguished debts of S$368.766 million and S$3,007.3 million respectively during the period covered by their financial reports of 1990–91. These amounts are quite significant given the size of the companies.

10.4 IN-SUBSTANCE DEFEASANCE: AN EXAMPLE

To understand the mechanics of in-substance defeasance, it may be helpful to look at the following example:

ABC Incorporated issued US$1 million, 11-year callable bonds at par at t_0. The bond carries a coupon rate of 10% per annum and the annual interest payments are payable at the end of each year (t_1, t_2, . . , t_{11}). It is now exactly one year after the company issued its bonds (we are at t_1) and the interest rates are at an unusually high level[3]. At t_1, the yield of 10-year 12% coupon

[2] Mielke and Seifert (1987, p. 65) reports that defeasance in the tax-exempt market, where tax-exempt debentures specifically allowed the borrower, usually municipality government (and not corporation), to be released from its obligation by depositing sufficient cash or government securities to generate cash flow required to pay all interests and principal, has been used many years before 1982.

[3] The 'favourable' increase of interest rates is a necessary condition for reporting a gain through in-substance defeasance.

government securities is 15% per annum.[4] What are the options available to ABC Incorported if it wishes to extinguish its US$1 million bonds prematurely using its US$850,000 'idle' cash?

As the bonds are callable, ABC Incorporated can redeem its bonds through call. However, this is time consuming and costly as the company generally would suffer a loss in the redemption due to high call premiums which are usually attached to callable bonds. The call premium represents cost of extinguishment of the bonds and should be recorded as a loss (APB Opinion No. 26 and FASB Statement No. 4).

The other options are debt–equity swap, if possible, or acquiring the bonds in the open market. Both methods are also time consuming and costly as an investment banker is generally required for a debt–equity swap. Moreover, there is no guarantee that the bondholders will sell the bonds back to the company in the open market. However, buying back the bonds in the open market is more favourable than the debt–equity swap because if there is an increase in interest rates, the company is likely to report a gain if it repurchases its bonds in the open market.

In-substance defeasance[5] requires the company to spend a total of US$849,436.94 (refer to Table 10.1 for the computation) to buy the 10-year 12% coupon (of US$1 million par value) government securities. This amount represents the sum of the present value of a 10-period annuity of US$120,000 (annual administrative cost of the trust is assumed to be US$20,000 per annum) and the present value of the principal amount of US$1 million payable in 10 years. The cashflows are discounted at 15% per annum. The firm will then transfer the government securities to an irrevocable trust. At the end of each subsequent year (that is, from t_2 to t_{11}), the trust will pay the US$100,000 interest to ABC Incorporated's bondholders and use US$20,000 to meet its annual administrative cost from the interest received on the government securities. At the end of the 10-year period at t_{11}, the trust will use the principal amount of the government securities to meet the principal repayment of the bonds. This arrangement ensures that the financial obligation of the company towards its bondholders will be met over the duration of the bonds.

The following journal entries are made at t_1 for the in-substance defeasance of the US$1 million debts.[6] The firm is also required to disclose the fact of the defeasance (general description of the transaction and the amount of the debt that is considered extinguished at the end of each period) in the notes to the accounts as long as the debt remains outstanding.

---

[4] For simplicity, let us assume that ABC Incorporated has just paid its bondholders the annual interest of US$100,000.
[5] In this example, as in cases involving in-substance defeasance, we assume that 'legal' defeasance of debts is neither allowed by nor provided for in the debt covenant.
[6] The journal entries are consistent with the requirements of FASB Statement No. 76. Whittred and Zimmer (1990) uses a trust clearing account to effect the defeasance.

Table 10.1 Computation of the market value of the government securities

Time:	Interest (12%)	PVIF (15%)	Present Value
t_2	$120,000	0.86957	$104,347.83
t_3	$120,000	0.75614	$ 90,737.24
t_4	$120,000	0.65752	$ 78,901.95
t_5	$120,000	0.57175	$ 68,610.39
t_6	$120,000	0.49718	$ 59,661.21
t_7	$120,000	0.43233	$ 51,879.31
t_8	$120,000	0.37594	$ 45,112.44
t_9	$120,000	0.32690	$ 39,228.21
t_{10}	$120,000	0.28426	$ 34,111.49
t_{11}	$120,000	0.24718	$ 29,662.16
	PV of interest		**$ 602,252.24**
PV of Principal ($1,000,000)			$247,184.71
Total PV of Interest and Principal			**$849,436.94**

	Dr	Cr
Investment in government securities	$849,436.94	
Cash		$849,436.94
Bonds payable	$1,000,000	
Investment in government securities		$849,436.94
(Extra) Gain on extinguishment of bonds payable		$150,563.06

This is relatively straightforward and is a less costly option. In the process, the firm removes the entire US$1 million debt from its balance sheet and it also reports a gain of US$150,563.06 for the financial year.

10.5 THE ISSUES INVOLVED IN IN-SUBSTANCE DEFEASANCE

Critics see in-substance defeasance as an accounting gimmick, nothing more than balance-sheet cosmetics for hiding poor operating performance, as a way to dress up one's balance sheet and a give-away to bondholders.[7] The general scepticism towards the new accounting method is best reflected in Blumstein (1984)'s description of the practice.

[7] The opinions were expressed by *Institutional Investor* (March 1984), Chaney (1985) and *ABA Banking Journal* (September, 1984) as quoted by Hand *et al* (1989). And the last quote, 'shareholders should be suspicious of management that engages in this transaction because of the give-away to bondholders in order to report higher earnings per share', was attributed to Professor Roman Weil (Blumstein, 1984).

'The name is somewhat forbidding . . . but the pitch is easy: pay off large amount of old, cheap debt with smaller amounts of new bonds that pay high interest rates and, *through some accounting magic*, report extra profits and *clean up the balance sheet'*. (emphasis added)

The issue clearly is 'can the liability be considered extinguished when the debtor sets aside an essentially risk-free government securities in an irrevocable trust for its repayment?'

In the context of in-substance defeasance, Canning's (1929, pp. 55–56) concept of liabilities is the most appropriate.

'A liability is a service, valuable in money, which a proprietor is under an existing *legal* (or equitable) *duty* to render a second person (or set of persons) . . .'. (emphasis added)

One could also summarize the characteristics of an accounting liability as reflected by APB Statement No. 4 (1970) on *Basic Concepts and Accounting Principles Underlying Financial Statements of Business Enterprises* and Statement of Financial Accounting Concepts No. 6 (FASB (1985) as follows: first, a duty exists, second, the duty is virtually unavoidable, and third, the event obligating the enterprise has occurred (Wolk *et al*, 1989). These characteristics of a liability apply to the debtor both before and after the in-substance defeasance. Not withstanding the setting aside of an essentially risk-free asset by the debtor in an in-substance defeasance[8], the debtor still has a legal duty to pay the bondholders interest and principal in the future. The debt is not (legally) defeased and a liability still exists. The reservations of the opponents to in-substance defeasance are succinctly expressed by Messrs. Kirk (chairman of the FASB in 1983), March and Mosso, the three dissenters from FASB Statement No. 76 as follows:

'[We] do not believe that extinguishment of debt accounting and resultant gain or loss recognition should be extended to situation where the debtor is not *legally released* from being the primary obligor under the debt obligation'. (emphasis added)

Supporters of the practice, on the other hand, argue that a debt is extinguished if either the debtor is relieved of primary liability of the debt by the creditor[9] or it is *probable* that the debtor will not be required to make future payments (FASB Statement No. 76, emphasis added). If a debtor places an essentially risk-free asset in an irrevocable trust to be used solely for paying scheduled interest and the repayment of principal, the supporters claim it is unlikely that the debtor will be required to make

---

[8] Sometimes, (legal) *defeasance* through setting aside some assets to a third party to assume the financial obligation to debtholders is specificially provided for and allowed in the debt covenants. In this situation, setting aside the required assets legally releases the debtor from being the primary obligor under the debt obligation. Removing the (legally) defeased debt from the balance sheet is considered an appropriate extinguishment of debt. However, in cases dealing with in-substance defeasance, legal defeasance is not specifically provided for in the debt covenants.

[9] This is the normal way of extinguishing a debt and is nothing controversial.

any future payments to the creditor. In-substance defeasance in essence releases the debtor economically, albeit not legally, from being the primary obligor. The argument of 'substance over form' may have persuaded the majority of the members of the FASB into supporting FASB Statement No. 76. FASB Statement No. 76 requires the debtor in an in-substance defeasance to place cash or monetary assets that are essentially risk-free in an irrevocable trust to be used solely to make the scheduled payment of the debt. The asset must be denominated in the same currency in which the debt is payable. For debts denominated in US currency, the standard requires that the essentially risk-free monetary asscts shall be limited to:

(1) Direct obligations of the US government;
(2) Obligations guaranteed by the US government; and
(3) Securities that are backed by US government obligations as collateral under an arrangement by which the interest and principal payments on the collateral generally flow immediately through to the holder of the securities. (FASB Statement No. 76, para. 4a)

The monetary assets held by the trust (according to para. 4b of FASB Statement No. 76)

> 'shall provide cash flows (from interest and maturity of those assets) that approximately *coincide*, as to *timing and amount*, with the scheduled interest and principal payments on the debt that is being extinguished'. (emphasis added)

The statement also requires the recognition of the trustee fee as cost to be included in determining the amount of funds required by the trust. The defeasance can only apply to existing debts. Instantaneous defeasance, whereby the debtor issues debt in a foreign country where the market interest rate is much lower than the domestic risk-free rate and immediately defeases the foreign debts using the required domestic government securities, is not permitted in the United States (FASB Technical Bulletin No. 84–4). The gain or loss in an in-substance defeasance is considered an extraordinary item.

There are equivalent in-substance defeasance accounting standards in Canada, New Zealand and Australia. The Canadian standard, however, treats gain or loss due to in-substance defeasance as a component of income before extraordinary income (Kieso *et al*, 1986). The Australian standard (AASB 1014) allows instantaneous in-substance defeasance if 'it is highly improbable that the reporting entity will be required to assume again the primary obligation for the debt servicing requirements' (para. 10, AASB 1014; Whittred and Zimmer, 1990). Presently the International Accounting Standard Committee (IASC) has not issued any accounting standard on in-substance defeasance. However, Exposure Drafts E40 and E48 issued by IASC adopt very stringent requirements for extinguishment of debts or liabilities and they do not permit in-substance defeasance of debt (Lee and Tan, 1994).

10.6   THE BENEFITS OF IN-SUBSTANCE DEFEASANCE

The main benefits of in-substance defeasance are, as often claimed by its critics, an increase in earnings and a cleaning up of the balance sheet (that is, an improvement in the debt/equity ratio). Cleaning up the balance sheet, as suggested by some financial managers, may enable the company to receive improved credit terms (Roden, 1987). Improvement in the debt/equity ratio is particularly important as it enables the company to reduce restrictions imposed by restrictive debt covenants written in terms of debt ratios. Hand *et al* (1989) find that defeasing firms on average are more highly levered firms. They suggest that some firms might have defeased debts to avoid the restrictions of debt covenants. The same study also finds evidence of income-smoothing by the firms.

In-substance defeasance can also serve as defensive tactics against a hostile takeover by removing the target company's 'crown jewel', the excess cash on hand (Roden, 1987). Favourable treatment by the taxation authorities in the United States was also cited as one of the benefits (Davis *et al* 1991). The presence of accounting (earning) based management compensation schemes may in some cases induce management to carry out in-substance defeasance. Johnson *et al* (1989) report a high (but not significant) correlation between management compensation tied to earnings and defeasing debt resulting in large profits.

In a survey of the financial reports of 46 companies which had defeased debts for the fiscal years ending between 1 January 1982 and 31 December 1985, Mielke and Seifert (1987) find that most companies reported gains (average increase of 8.32%), improvements in current ratio (average change of 6.13%) and debt/equity ratio (average change of 2.42%) due to defeasance of debts. The results are not unexpected. The critics of the accounting treatment have been saying this all along. However, the same study also reports a rather startling observation that 'comparing the rate of return on investment for the defeasance to each company's after-tax cost of debt it suggests that defeasance is not a particularly good investment' (p. 74).

Would cleaning up the balance sheet through in-substance defeasance led to more favourable credit rating from loan officers of financial institutions? In an experiment on commercial loan officers with at least two years of lending experience, Davis *et al* (1991) reports that 'the use of defeasance or debt retirement to increase earnings and reduce debt/equity ratio does not appear to significantly affect loan officers' decision making' (at p. 70). Loan officers look at the fundamentals! Overall, the empirical studies do not seem to have conclusively established the expected gain from in-substance defeasance of debts.

10.7   THE COSTS OF IN-SUBSTANCE DEFEASANCE

In addition to the direct cost of trustee fees, there are some hidden costs to in-substance defeasance, such as wealth transfer from shareholders to bondholders and adverse information cost.

The risk to bondholders as to the uncertainty of interest and principal payments are eliminated when the payments are backed by risk-free assets placed in an irrevocable trust. The risk of the 'in-substance defeased' debts are eliminated at the expense of the existing shareholders – wealth transfer from the shareholders to the bondholders. Wealth transfer in an in-substance defeasance was the subject of two empirical studies. Both Hand *et al* (1989) and Johnson *et al* (1989) report significant positive bond price reactions to announcements of in-substance defeasance. Both studies confirm the gains to the holders of the in-substance defeased bonds. However, the expected negative share price reactions were not significant in Johnson *et al* (1989) due to a possible size parity between the value of defeased debt and those of the equity. Hand *et al* (1989), however, attribute the negative share price reactions to possible contaminating information effect of earnings announcements.

The negative stock price reactions observed by Hand *et al* (1989) may also be due to the negative signalling effect of the in-substance defeasance announcements. The purchase of risk-free government securities is a zero net present value (NPV) investment. Investors may interpret the announcement of an in-substance defeasance of debt as a signal from the firm that it does not have any positive NPV projects or investment opportunities. This interpretation is consistent with the results in Mielke and Seifert (1987) that defeasance is not a particularly good investment. It appears that the equity market recognizes some of the hidden costs of in-substance defeasance of debt.

10.8   SUGGESTIONS FOR FURTHER RESEARCH

It is rare that an accounting method adopted by a few corporations should have aroused so much debate and controversy. The actions by Exxon and Kellogg resulted in a strong reaction from the SEC and also generated heated debates in the accounting community, particularly amongst the members of the FASB. The debates centred on the following issues: first, whether an in-substance defeasance constitutes extinguishment of debt, and second, the benefits and costs of in-substance defeasance. The first issue was settled – though to many critics, still unresolved – by the FASB when it issued Statement No. 76 and the unanimous decision of the SEC to support the position of the FASB. However the benefits and costs of in-substance defeasance would still be the subject of further analytical and empirical studies.

Both Hand *et al* (1989) and Johnson *et al* (1989) document the (expected) positive bond price reactions to announcements of in-substance defeasance. Both studies are extremely well-designed. We must, however, caution that any further attempt to study the bond price reactions using the same approach – albeit with a more recent and larger sample – would merely add another piece of evidence confirming the hidden cost of in-substance defeasance – wealth gain to the bondholders. The risky bond is 'transformed' into a riskless bond through in-substance defeasance. The contribution of another bond price study is therefore likely to be limited.

The results of the event studies on the stock price reactions to the announcements of in-substance defeasance are not conclusive. Johnson *et al* (1989) report insignificant stock price reactions while Hand *et al* (1989) report reliably negative reactions. However, the magnitude of the stock price reactions of Hand *et al* (1989) is 'several times larger than the actual or predicted bond price reactions' (p. 86). In addition to recognizing the negative impact of loss due to wealth transfer from the shareholders to the bondholders, the market infers a decrease in the firm's future cashflows.

The inconsistency of the share price reactions could be due to many factors. One obvious factor that contributes to the inconclusive result of Johnson *et al* (1989) is, as highlighted by the authors, due to the size parity in the market value of the defeased bonds and those of equities. Often the total value of the defeased bonds is small compared with the total value of the equity of the firm. For a given amount of wealth transfer to bondholders, the loss in value per share is often too small to be detectable by any statistical measure. The mixed or inconclusive results may also be due to the information effect of confounding events. The critics have argued, correctly in many cases, that the main effect of in-substance defeasance is in the increase of reported profit. It is, therefore, likely that in-substance defeasance and an increase in reported profit are announced at the same time. An announcement of the 'unexpected' increase in profit may induce a positive stock market reaction which may 'contaminate' the pure effect of in-substance defeasance.

The equity market's reaction may also be due to investors' perception that first, the firm does not have any positive NPV investment opportunities, second, management is engaging in self-serving behaviour due to accounting-based compensation scheme, third, in-substance defeasance is a defensive mechanism against an imminent hostile take-over attempt, and fourth, the defeasance is an effective way to avoid restrictive debt covenants, and that in future it is likely to lower the borrowing cost of the firm. The first two perceptions would likely induce negative market responses while the last two may cause the market to revise the firm's value upwards (Shad, 1976). The different effects of these factors would likely render the empirical research on equity market reaction to in-substance defeasance inconclusive.

A more fruitful area would be in analytical research which specifically take benefits and costs of in-substance defeasance into account when modelling management's accounting choice behaviour.[10] The analytical research could potentially identify conditions of 'shareholder's wealth increasing (decreasing)' in in-substance defeasance. The derived conditions may, in turn, provide us with a basis for partitioning the sample into more 'homogeneous' groups. Using homogeneous sub-samples in empirical research will mitigate – though not completely eliminate – the effects of confounding factors on the empirical results of stock market reaction to in-substance defeasance.

One important research question remains – what are the reasons or factors which cause a firm to defease its debt? Logit and Probit models[11] can be used to predict firms that engage in in-substance defeasance, that is, the defeasing firms. The results from the prediction models can be used to identify the reasons why firms defease their debts and also serve as a proxy for the market expectation of the likelihood that a firm may defease its debt. This proxy will enable us to identify 'surprise' announcements for studying stock market reactions to 'surprised' in-substance defeasance announcements.[12]

Mielke and Seifert (1987) in a survey of the financial reports of the defeasing firms document the extent of gains – higher profit, lower current and debt/equity ratios – in in-substance defeasance. A similar study to see if in-substance defeasance gives rise to same benefits in other countries such as Australia and New Zealand can also be carried out. Since there are only three documented cases of in-substance defeasance in Singapore, it is not feasible to carry out similar research in Singapore. Rather, a case study (through interviews) may give us more insight into the reasons why the Singapore companies defeased their debts. Another feasible study on the benefits of in-substance defeasance may be through an experiment to explore whether decisions of financial statement users are affected by in-substance defeasance of the defeasing firms. Davis *et al* (1991) include only loan officers in their sample. We suggest that the subjects of the experiment be expanded to include 'common' financial statement users like investors, analysts and portfolio managers.

10.9 CONCLUSION

The reaction to in-substance defeasance by Exxon and Kellogg was strong and swift. The accounting issue was settled by the FASB with its

---

[10] Ball and Smith (1992) contains a number of articles on factors affecting accounting policy choice. It is a very good reference for researchers interested in this area.

[11] For a discussion on the Multiple Discriminant Analysis, Logit and Probit models, please refer to Kwok, Lim and Wang (1992) and Kwok and Lim (1994).

[12] For an example of an empirical research which explicitly incorporated the result of a predicting model as market expectations into an event study model, please refer to Loudder, *et al* (1992).

Statement No. 76 which endorsed the accounting treatment. However, empirical studies on the benefits and costs of in-substance defeasance have so far produced mixed and often inconclusive results. This may be due to the effects of some possible confounding factors and events. Controlling the confounding factors and events could potentially improve the significance of the empirical results of the market reaction studies. We also believe that further attempts to study empirically the reasons and benefits of in-substance defeasance by using prediction models like Logit and Probit analyses and experiments would provide us with some interesting results.

REFERENCES

Australian Accounting Standards Board (1989). *Set-off and Extinguishment of Debt* (AASB 1014), Melbourne, June 1989

Ball, R. and Smith, Jr., C.W. (1992). *The Economics of Accounting Policy Choice.* New York: McGraw-Hill

Blumstein, M. (1984). Pros and Cons of Defeasance. *The New York Times,* 12 January

Canning, J.B. (1929). *The Economics of Accountancy.* Ronald Press

Davis, L.R., Lovata, L.M. and Philipich, K.L. (1991). The Effect of Debt Defeasance on the Decisions of Loan Officers. *Accounting Horizons,* June 1991

Financial Accounting Standards Board (1983). *Extinguishment of Debt* (FASB Statement No. 76), Norwalk: FASB November 1983

Hand, J.R.M., Hughes, P.J. and Sefcik, S.E. (1990). In-substance Defeasance – Security Price Reaction and Motivations. *Journal of Accounting and Economics,* 13, pp. 47–89

International Accounting Standards Committee (1991). *Financial Instruments* (Exposure Draft E40), London: IASC, September 1991

International Accounting Standards Committee (1994). *Financial Instruments* (Exposure Draft E48), London: IASC, January 1994

Johnson, J.M., Pari, R.A. and Rosenthal, L. (1989). The Impact of In-Substance Defeasance on Bondholder and Shareholder Wealth. *Journal of Finance,* September 1989

Kieso, D.E., Weygandt, J.J., Irvine, V.B. and Silvester, W.H. (1986). *Intermediate Accounting.* 2nd Canadian edn. Toronto: John Wiley and Sons

Kwok, C.H., Lim, A.B. and Wang Y.G. (1992–93) *The Application of Discriminant Analysis and Logit Analysis in predictions of Financial Distress of Banks/ Financial Institutions: Issues and Comparisons.* Working Paper Series, Centre for Research in Financial Services

Kwok, C.H. and Lim, A.B. (1994). Logit and Probit Models. *Unpublished MBA Lecture Notes,* Nanyang Technological University, April 1994

Lee, P. and Tan, P. (1994). E40, Financial Instruments: Implications for Financial Reporting in Singapore. *Singapore Management Review,* January 1994

Loudder, M.L., Khurana, I.K., Sawyers, R.B., Cordery, C., Johnson, C., Lowe, J. and Wunderle, R. (1992). The Information Content of Audit Qualifications. *Auditing: A Journal of Practice and Theory*, Spring 1992

Mielke, D.E. and Seifert, J. (1987). A Survey on the Effects of Defeasing Debt, *Journal of Accounting, Auditing and Finance*, Winter 1987

Mosich, A.N., Larsen, E.J., Lam, W.P. and Johnston, D.R. (1988). *Intermediate Accounting*. 5th Canadian edn. Toronto: McGraw-Hill

Roden, P.F. (1987). The Financial Implications of In-substance Defeasance. *Journal of Accounting, Auditing and Finance*, Winter 1987, pp. 79–89

Shad, John S.R. (1976). The Financial Realities of Mergers. In Stewart C. Myers, ed. *Modern Developments in Financial Management*. Hinsdale: Dryden Press

Wittred, G. and Zimmer, I. (1990). *Financial Accounting: Incentive Effects and Economic Consequences*. 3rd edn. Melbourne: Holt, Rinehart and Winston

Wolk, H.I., Francis, J.R. and Tearney, M.G. (1989). *Accounting Theory: A Conceptual and Institutional Approach*. 2nd edn. Boston: PWS Kent

11 Social and Environmental Accountability: International and Asian Perspectives

Lee D. Parker

11.1 INTRODUCTION

Social and Environmental Accounting and Accountability have been the subject of experimentation, practical application, research and writing in the accounting literature for at least two decades. Indeed, examples of corporate social disclosures can be found in such countries as the United States, United Kingdom and Australia as far back as the late 19th and the early 20th centuries. By way of stark contrast, this area of endeavour has been barely referred to in undergraduate and graduate accounting programs and has attracted very little attention from accounting regulators and accounting researchers. This neglect has arguably arisen from accountants' focus upon profit and cash flow and also accountants' general view of social and environmental accountability as being an unfamiliar concern, difficult to quantify, defying financial measurement, and with its 'green' image, outside their area of responsibility. As whole national communities and governments have progressively 'gone green' and begun to demand accountability for and reporting of the social impact of organizations, these sentiments are now being revealed as grossly in error.

For the task of assisting corporations and other organizations to meet the demands of social and environmental regulators, both in terms of action and reporting of outcomes, the accounting profession is still relatively ill-equipped due to its failure to recognize the growing importance of this area and to prepare for it. Nevertheless, a considerable wealth of studies and practical as well as theoretical research works are available to those who wish to take up this challenge. This chapter provides an introduction to this burgeoning field of activity and is designed to be of assistance to students, researchers and practitioners alike. It will consider the role of business and accounting in meeting community concerns about social and environmental accountability, and will review the rationales offered for corporate social and environmental disclosures as well as critiques of such arguments and justifications. Some proposed models of social accounting and environmental accounting will be outlined along with an introduction to the question of environmental sustainability and accountability. The important role of social and environmental auditing will then be examined, followed by a review of the available evidence on disclosure practices and reactions to such disclosures in the marketplace and among lobby groups. Finally this chapter will reflect upon experiences and implications of social and environmental accountability issues and practices in the Asian region.

11.2   SOCIAL AND ENVIRONMENTAL ACCOUNTING DEFINED

Before discussing the potential role for business and accounting in meeting community requirements for social and environmental accountability, it is appropriate to briefly review just what various interested parties conceive social and environmental accountability to be. This is an issue which itself is fraught with variety and potential confusion. This author has previously reviewed the variable terminologies and concepts that have been applied in this field (Parker, 1986 and 1992). They include terms such as social responsibility disclosure, social accounting, societal accounting socioeconomic accounting and social audit. The term 'social accounting' appears to be the most widely used of these terms. An extensive analysis of the literature on definition and terminology has revealed a profusion of terminology that has given a somewhat false impression of confusion about the nature and meaning of the accounting and reporting activity being discussed. Across all these terms and their various definitions, a number of major characteristics were commonly cited by their authors. These were:

(1) Assessing the social impact of corporate activities;
(2) Measuring the effectiveness of corporate social programs;
(3) Reporting upon the organization's discharge of its social responsibilities;

(4) External and internal information systems allowing comprehensive assessment of all corporate resources and impacts (both social and economic).

Some differentiation in emphasis between the terms employed can be found, for instance, with respect to 'corporate social disclosure' which emphasizes the reporting function and 'social audit' which includes an emphasis upon the examination and verification of the credibility of social impact information. More recently, Mathews (1993) has further illuminated and differentiated elements of what he calls 'socially responsible accounting', within which he discusses social responsibility accounting, total impact accounting, socioeconomic accounting, social indicators accounting and societal accounting.

This chapter employs the term '**social and environmental accountability**' based on the major common characteristics already identified above. Arguably, environmental accountability has always been contained within the general definition of social accounting, but is now given greater prominence as a subset of social accounting in the light of the great upsurge in the environmental concern among communities and governments worldwide. The word 'accountability' is employed to represent a broader scope than the task of collecting, analysing, measuring and designing reports containing social impact information. It is intended to include the communication and validation of reported information supplied by organizations to all significant interested parties. This allows us to consider pressures for changes and additions to report design and content, the community's reactions to the information supplied, and the intersection between corporate, government and community social agendas.

For the purposes of this chapter, accounting for social and environmental impact might best be described as the publication by an organization of information that will allow interested parties to evaluate that organization's performance in terms of its social impact, both positive and negative. This encompasses both the social impacts of normal organizational activities as well as the social impacts of specific socially-oriented programmes. It involves the development of appropriate information systems as well as their effective communication to interested parties (Parker, 1992).

11.3 A ROLE FOR BUSINESS AND ACCOUNTING

11.3.1 An accounting role?

The role of accountants in the practical development of social and economic accounting on British evidence appears to be somewhat restricted. Bebbington *et al* (1992) discovered this in an extensive mail questionnaire survey administered to financial directors of the top 1,000 companies in the United Kingdom.

- While 21% of responding companies indicated that they undertook disclosures of environmental matters in financial statements, accountants did not appear to rate their involvement in such exercises very highly. They also reported low involvement in screening investments and in undertaking investment appraisals. Outside these more traditional areas, in activities such as environmental review of waste, environmental impact assessments, examination of environmental policy and review of sustainable development, accountants' involvement was even less.
- In contrast to this low level of involvement in environmental accountability matters, 61% of respondents to the survey agreed or strongly agreed that environmental issues should involve accountants and 40% agreed or strongly agreed that accountants should contribute to the environmental sensitivity of their companies.
- More than 80% agreed that there would be an increase in environmental legislation in the future while 52% of respondents agreed that disclosure of environmental information is a matter for legislation.

Thus, it appears that accountants are unwilling to disclose information without legal pressure but at the same time fully expect that pressure for disclosure to eventuate. Gray *et al* (1992) concluded that there appeared to be a contradiction between accountants' positive attitude to their own future involvement in environmental matters and their willingness to take action. This was held by the researchers to be largely attributable to the lack of education and training in social and environmental accountability for accountants to prepare them for taking such action.

In the United States, Gray *et al* (November, 1993) have also observed that environmental accounting largely takes the form of accounting for contingent and other liabilities, land remediation, business risk and other provisions. Voluntary environmental reporting of wider scope occurs relatively infrequently. Gray *et al* (1993) argue that in the litigious atmosphere of the United States, the definition of environment appears to have been restricted to a financial one without the discursive negotiation of the nature of environment that can be found in the United Kingdom and continental Europe. They argue that if environmental accounting and reporting is to be strictly confined to the traditions of conventional accounting, then the concept of environment will be a very narrow and controllable one to suit the restricted conventions of conventional accounting methods. Allied to the potential problems for social and environmental accountability that may be occasioned by such an approach is the potentially problematic focus of most accountants' attentions. It is increasingly being argued that accountancy is often perceived to be a routine, objective, technical activity which in fact has quite far reaching implications not always recognized by accountants themselves. An alternative view is that accounting represents a social art that reflects and constructs the social world, with major implications for activities such as plant closures, wealth distribution, innovation, resource usage, labour relations and organizational interaction with the environment. The problematic nature of accountants' focus is that it is dominated by traditional economic thinking which is primarily concerned with property rights and prices. However, ecological issues such as the quality of air, the usage of the sea and the pollution of rivers are matters over which property rights do not exist.

Economic thinking about the world tends not to take into account social and environmental impacts. Instead, it is based upon severe simplifications and restricted assumptions about the operation of society and organizations. People are conceived of as rational economic beings, ethical issues are treated as implicit and simplistic, economic growth is seen to be automatically desirable, technology is presumed to be neutral and efficiency is understood primarily from a cost minimization point of view. Accountants tend to approach problems in society largely from the point of view of costs, prices and values, with money being the universal medium. Accordingly, accountants are tempted to derive a price for all aspects of nature and society even when this is impossible or irrelevant. The foregoing arguments are put most cogently by Gray and Bebbington (1992) who also argue, however, that pragmatically, there may be ways of mitigating accountants' current impact on society and environment and instead employing accounting to assist organizations to achieve a much greater degree of social and environmental accountability.

11.3.2 Business responses to society demands

Internationally, societies and governments have been demanding much greater attention by businesses to their social and environmental impacts. This is best evidenced by high profile developments such as the Valdez Principles. The massive Valdez oil spill that occurred in Alaska in 1989 resulted in the formulation of a set of principles known as the **Valdez Principles** by a coalition of environmentalists and other social interest groups which included managers of major investment and pension funds. This is a voluntary code of conduct which provides a framework for guiding and evaluating companies' execution of their environmental responsibilities (Sanyal and Neves, 1991). These broad principles cover such areas as protection of the biosphere, sustainable use of natural resources, reduction and disposal of waste, use of energy, risk reduction, marketing safe products and services, damage compensation, disclosure of hazards to workers and the community, appointment of environmental directors and managers and assessment and annual audit. These principles have achieved enormous profile internationally. While the environmental goals set by these principles may be regarded as potentially costly and technically difficult to achieve, many companies involved in activities relating to the environment are becoming aware of and beginning to consider their future strategies towards meeting at least some dimensions of these principles.

In the European Union (EU), such issues are also high on the political agenda. Polls have indicated a significant increase in the already high levels of European public concern about the environment and their policy-makers are responding. The momentum of EU has not been slowed by economic recession and the great number of environmental protection policy proposals in this area is said to pose an unprecedented managerial challenge to European businesses (Wilkes, 1992). In the first six months of 1992, there were 10 such proposals formally adopted, 13 newly published proposals under formal consideration, three new proposals being drafted and 21 new proposals under consideration for possible legislative enactment later in the decade. Wilkes (1992) argues that European businesses face both challenges and opportunities with respect to their environmental responsibilities. The challenge is that management practices will be increasingly placed under the regulators' microscopes while at the same time, the new green markets represent a high growth area for businesses positioned to take advantage of them (for example, the pollution abatement sector). Benefits may also accrue to companies that become 'first movers' in that by adapting their environmental performance to tighter controls at an early stage, they may be able to sell their equipment and knowledge to other organizations that follow.

Similar social and legal pressures for improved environmental and social responsibility by businesses have been building in the United States (Pizzolatto and Zeringue, 1993). Polls taken in here have also revealed a much greater consumer awareness of the need for environmental protection. Many American companies are also listing environmental preservation as a top priority. Congress has been under pressure to impose stricter environmental regulations which has resulted in the passage of the Clean Air Act, for instance. In addition, the United States has federal laws that regulate hazardous waste disposal with these being administered by the Environmental Protection Agency. Thus, the social obligations of businesses in United States are increasing with laws that are likely to become even more stringent. Again, many companies are turning the environmental issue into a business opportunity by developing new products and services and new markets that respond to environmental issues. These include non-hazardous substitutes, waste reduction procedures and recycling processes.

Shrivastava (1992) has described the characteristics of the early phase of green strategies adopted by industries as follows:

(1) Initially, most corporate actions tend to respond and conform to government regulations.

(2) Subsequent to the above compliance response, product designs are changed and new products proliferate to take advantage of green consumerism.

(3) Companies making environment friendly changes in their activities may have initially undertaken these for public image benefits but subsequently begin to see competitive advantages in such activities.

(4) Environmental programs shift from being considered merely as compliance expense items to becoming revenue-generating opportunities.

(5) Corporate attitudes have begun to shift from the confrontational and defensive attitudes of the 1970s to a more cooperative and participative attitude in working with media, labour, government and communities in sharing risk-related information and resolving conflicts.

Roberts (1992) has observed in the United Kingdom that by the 1980s, many of the larger multinational firms (such as in oil and chemicals industries) were beginning to apply the environmental lessons they had learned from their overseas contracts through the use of environmental impact assessments and environmental auditing. Subsequently, international and national business organizations adopted and promulgated broad principles that emanated from this early work. Nevertheless, there still appear to be companies in the United Kingdom which are alternatively ignoring social and environmental issues, treating the matter as simply a public relations exercise, integrating such issues into their health and safety activities, treating the issues as part of Total Quality Management (TQM) or approaching environmental and social issues as a strategic issue in its own right. Gray and Bebbington (1991) nevertheless argue that the majority of these corporations are continuing to act as if environmental matters are a passing fad. The tendency is to follow legal regulations and public opinion with a compliance attitude that environmental issues are now significant and must be addressed but, on the other hand, are not necessarily critical and do not require proactive strategies beyond the requirements of existing legislation and regulations.

Overall, it would appear that business has begun to respond to social and government pressures for greater social and environmental accountability. Business organizations presently occupy a zone where they are highly conscious of the costs of complying with legislation and cleanup costs. On the other hand, there are sectors who are also beginning to recognize business opportunities in taking a more proactive stance. Surveys reveal conflicting messages from businesses such that there is a considerable gap between stated aspirations concerning social and environmental accountability and responsibility, and actual performance. The response is present and growing but it remains largely reactive to social and government pressure (Gray *et al*, 1993).

11.3.3   The potential for business and accounting involvement

The potential for further business involvement in social and environmental accountability is clearly considerable. The impetus for sustaining the current momentum will clearly come from a number of influences. Companies who take a lead in adopting strategies for enhancing their social and environmental responsibility may well be followed by others who see them as an example. The increasing importance and status of environmental audits compared with financial audits or incorporated within them will assist in raising the profile of social and environmental issues and in stimulating companies to include such issues among their other profit and cash flow priorities. Businesses are also seeing increasing opportunities for revenue generation in producing and marketing environmental friendly products, providing equipment and services to industries seeking to restrict their pollution levels, and managing waste products. Legislation continues to proliferate with increasing potential penalties that may apply to directors and other officers of offending companies. At the same time, social pressures appear set to encourage organizations to adopt voluntary codes of social and environmental good behaviour, realizing that energy conservation and waste reduction can actually be economically as well as environmentally beneficial (Buck, 1992).

What potential involvement, however, can be envisaged for the accounting profession? Adams (1992) argues that for the accounting profession to contribute in this area, there should be the following:

(1) Agreed definitions of what is to be measured and why.
(2) The technology to measure and capture the required data.
(3) Systems to record it and controls to ensure that corrective actions are taken when required.
(4) Reporting systems to convey performance measurement data to those who require it.
(5) An audit that can attest to the reliability of the data reported.
(6) A willingness to accept estimates when precise cost apportionment is not possible.

Meeting such requirements presents major challenges which must somehow be met. Gray and Bebbington (1992) point out that the traditional annual report, despite its difficulties, does make things visible. The dominance of financial data in annual reports has the effect of raising the profile of financial matters. Hence, with greater inclusion of energy costs, waste disposal costs and environmental investment expenditures as major disclosure items, accounting can be used to raise the general awareness of environmental and social activities of the organization, that is, making such factors more visible. Annual reports internationally already do make some (but variable) disclosures in these areas. Evidence of this will be referred to later in this chapter.

A range of opportunities exist for the accounting profession to contribute to corporate social and environmental accountability (Adams, 1992). This includes:

(1) Sponsoring research into the interface between environment, finance and corporate accountability.
(2) Incorporating social and environmental responsibility requirements into professional ethics standards.
(3) Assisting in the development of environmental auditing methodologies and monitoring compliance with environmental reporting standards.
(4) Encouraging the educational and professional development process to include consideration of social and environmental issues.

Gray *et al* (1993) suggest five phases for the accountant's role in helping organizations to become more environmentally (and socially) sensitive:

(l) The existing accounting system can be modified to identify environmentally related areas of expenditure (for example, energy, waste, packaging and legal costs).
(2) Environmentally negative elements of the existing accounting system need to be identified and ameliorated (for instance, in relation to investment and performance appraisal).
(3) The accounting system needs to become more forward looking in relation to the changing environmental agenda (such as, changing payback periods as energy costs change, anticipating potential contingent liabilities, costing of greener financing).
(4) Changing the external reporting function to reflect aspects of environmental costs and producing non-financial reports of environmental strategies.
(5) Developing new accounting and information systems that cater not just for financial performance but also for social and environmental performance.

11.4 RATIONALES AND CRITIQUES

A variety of rationales have been advanced for the practice of social and environmental accounting and accountability. Advocates have seen it as attempting to identify the social costs and impact of organizational activity in order to encourage organizations to internalize their external impacts. They argue that this expresses the traditional stewardship concept expanded beyond the marshalling of economic resources to include taking up responsibility for making net positive contributions to social welfare.

On the other hand, corporate management may be more attracted to rationales that social accounting should be undertaken as a means of justifying company activities, to anticipate or avoid pressure for change, to foster and improve public image and consumer response (thereby improving long run profits), or simply to satisfy the various socio political demands invoked by labour, the community and regulatory authorities. Whatever rationales for social and economic environmental accounting are adopted, the choice is related to the perspective adopted by the report producer or advocate (Parker *et al*, 1989). Contrasting perspectives include:

(1) Capitalist versus socialist
(2) Shareholder versus other special interest groups
(3) Internal report user versus external report user
(4) Free marketeer versus radical leftist
(5) Corporate defender versus corporate critic

A variety of differing views about the appropriate rationale for social and environmental accounting may be implied by these differing perspectives. For example, the capitalist may see it as an exercise in pacifying outsider concerns about corporate activities in order to preserve operations and profits, while the socialist may see it as a means of society imposing greater control over anti-social corporate activities. Internal report users may treat social accountability as involving management requirements for corporate activities, while external report users may see it as an extension of the traditional financial accountability and reporting system. The free marketeer may view social accounting as a voluntary response to demands for information in the marketplace, while the radical leftist may regard the same activity as a simple smoke screen designed to veil and preserve management prerogatives.

11.4.1   General criticisms

Attempts at social accounting over the past two decades have been subject to some general criticisms, namely, impracticality, limited progress, public relations bias and the efficient market.

Some critics regard social accounting as suggesting impractical technologies that move accounting beyond its traditional financial transactions boundaries. Such critics have considered the costs of trying to devise appropriate measurement and reporting systems to outweigh a set of what they perceive to be relatively intangible benefits. Certainly, there has been criticism of the slow rate of progress in terms of practical accountability and reporting systems that can be utilized in corporations and other organizations. Others have alleged that the existing attempts at social accounting have exhibited characteristics of a public relations or marketing exercise, with attempts to manipulate corporate image in accentuating positive social performance and suppressing information concerning negative social impacts. Finally, some adherents to the theory of free/efficient capital markets argue that social accounting is unnecessary and unlikely to influence the moral climate of business. They argue that the market has already taken social information about a corporation into account and will have reacted before any such reports are issued. The latter argument is problematical in that market mechanisms do feature imperfections such as imperfect knowledge, factor divisibility and mobility, imperfect competition, disregard of future generations, disregard of equity considerations and an inability to accommodate the need for public goods (Parker *et al*, 1989).

11.4.2 Legitimacy Theory

One theoretical rationale for social accountability has been that of **organizational legitimacy** (Mathews, 1993). This argues that organizations seek to establish congruence between their activities and implied social values with the norms of acceptable behaviour in the social system of which they are a part. Thus organizational goals, methods of operation and output seek to conform with societal norms and values. Ultimately, the organization must conform to the requirements of society to ensure social approval and thus its continued existence. Accordingly, an enlarged social accounting or accountability system may be essential for the continued approval of the organization's operations by society.

11.4.3 Social Contract Theory

A broader but related theoretical rationale for social and environmental accountability is that of the **social contract**. This argues that any business organization operates in society through a social contract, either expressed or implied. The social contract involves the survival and growth of the organization depending upon it delivering some socially desirable ends to society in general and upon its distribution of economic, social and political benefits to the groups from which it derives its power. Thus, an organization must constantly meet the tests of legitimacy and relevance by demonstrating that society requires its services and that groups benefit from its rewards and have society's approval. Through the social contract theory, social accounting may be justified as a technique or set of techniques of data collection and disclosure that enables society to evaluate the social performance of the organization to determine whether it is both legitimate and desirable (Mathews, 1993). Within the framework of social contract theory, Gray, Owen and Maunders (1988, 1991) have argued for a theoretical rationale of **compliance-with-standard**. This argues that a contract exists between an organization and society through law. Therefore, a duty of accountability is owed to society by organizations who are responsible for accounting for the extent to which they have complied with laws (such as pollution, health and safety, toxic hazards). Thus, law is viewed as the rules of the game in which the organization chooses to play and becomes the terms of the social contract between society and the organization. On this basis, accountability is built and social and environmental accountability is justified and structured. Social and environmental reporting therefore seeks to demonstrate the extent to which the organization has met the responsibilities imposed upon it (that is, how well it has kept to the rules of the game). In this way, society determines the rules of accountability rather than the reporting organization.

11.4.4   Decision-usefulness

A further theoretical rationale for social and environmental accounting has been proposed as **decision-usefulness** (Parker, 1986, 1991). This may also be seen as a variant which bears a relationship to or may be accommodated within the concepts of social contract and compliance-with-standard. Corporate social critics have contended that social accounting can serve three major purposes:

(1) Providing a comprehensive view of the organization and its resources
(2) Providing a constraint upon socially irresponsible corporate behaviour
(3) Providing positive motivation for the corporation to act in a socially responsible manner

To this end, social and environmental accounting may be developed with a view to providing decision-useful information to all interested parties including corporate management, shareholders, employees, customers, the general community and government regulators. It attempts to identify interested parties and their decision needs, whereas the social contract and compliance-with-standard approaches seek to render account to the wider audience without necessarily attempting to specify what their variety of specific decision needs may be. All of these perspectives adopt an evolutionary approach to the development of social and environmental accountability and seek to pursue development largely via the path of regulation, be it private regulation, public (legal) regulation or a combination of both.

11.4.5   Organizational change

A further theoretical rationale advanced for corporate social and environmental accountability has been based upon Laughlin's (1991) **model of organizational change**. In Laughlin's model, no change is described as inertia.

- First order change (**Morphostatic**) can occur in the form of rebuttal in which the organization seeks to deflect or externalize a jolt from outside in order to return to its previous state of inertia, or in the form of reorientation where an outside disturbance cannot be rebutted but has to be accepted and internalized into the workings of the organization but is done in such a way that the real heart of the organization is basically unaffected.
- Second order change (**Morphogenetic**) takes the form either of colonization where change is forced on an organization in a manner that infiltrates change through the design, subsystems and interpretative schemes of the organization as a whole, or as evolution where change is chosen by the organization rather than being forced upon it with the result of a common organizational vision based upon shared values through free and open discourse.

This model has been adapted to social and environmental accountability by Gray and Collison (1991) and Gray *et al* (Nov. 1993). They have developed a matrix concerning business posture and the environment in which the perceived state of the physical environment is mapped against business response. This is represented in Table 11.1 below.

Table 11.1 Business posture and the environment

	Perceived state of the physical environment		
Business Response	A Greening as a 'passing fad'	B Environmental issues are significant but *not* critical (Perceived as 'rebuttable or 'reorientable')	C Natural environment *is* in crisis (Perceived as requiring 'colonising' or 'evolution')
1. Do nothing **Inertia**	OK	Perhaps lose business? Catch up costs? Legal problems?	CRISIS (No natural environment)
2. Follow law and public opinion **Morphostatic**	Costs and advantages	OK	CRISIS (Perhaps delayed? No natural environment)
3. Aim for sustainable business **Morphogenetic**	CRISIS (Probably out of business)	Costs and advantages	OK?

Source: Gray and Collison, 1991; Gray *et al*, Nov. 1993

11.4.6 Deep ecology

With specific reference to environment, Maunders and Burritt (1991) have developed a '**deep ecology**' **perspective** for environmental accounting. They argue that ecology considers the interrelationships between all species and matter and argue that there are important direct and indirect links between accounting information and ecological effects. The direct link can be traced through some conventional problems of accounting while an indirect link can be traced through economics. Economics has been linked to ecology via concepts of eco-development, that is, ecologically sound economic development strategies and sustainable development. With economics and ecology linked in this way, accounting and ecology may be linked via economics as an intervening variable.

11.4.7 Radical critique

From the above brief reviews, it is apparent that a variety of theoretical perspectives have developed in order to support accountants' and others' future research and development of social and environmental accountability systems. Nevertheless, such perspectives have been subject to criticism from supporters of the **radical approach**.

In the vanguard of such critiques was Puxty (1986, 1991) who has argued that social accounting is a simple extension of the role of traditional accounting which reflects the interests of the dominant power groups in society. In his view, if it is treated as a sub-set or extension of conventional accounting, social and environmental accounting becomes a continuation of distorted communications, legitimization of power and domination by institutional forces that govern accounting, and represents the self-interests of the holders of capital. Other critics such as Tinker *et al* (1991) argue that many of the above theoretical perspectives represent 'middle-of-the-road' approaches to corporate social accounting and are based upon philosophies of relativism, quietism and pluralism: that is to say such theories are concerned about what is politically pragmatic and acceptable rather than socially just or likely to succeed in rectifying social ills. They suspect these theories of being philosophically relative in contending that one person's view is as good as another's and that their pragmatism may hide a conservative political agenda. These critics fear that such theories may preserve the status quo. Instead they propose a counter-theoretical position that the middle ground is a contested terrain that shifts over time with social struggles and conflicts. What represents middle ground may change with changes in social circumstances and conflicts. Accounting then may not simply serve as a neutral, objective reporter of social and environmental impact but may be integral to reproducing and changing the social relations of the status quo. Such radical critiques are based on a radical position that has been summarized by Mathews (1993):

(1) The market must be de-emphasized or abolished as a device for allocating resources.
(2) Corporations are owned and operated in a way that is designed to establish and exploit power relationships.
(3) The accounting profession is engaged wittingly or unwittingly in maintaining the status quo by attaching itself to the owners of capital to the exclusion of labour.
(4) The accounting profession engages in mystifying the processes of accounting in order to exercise power.
(5) Accountants are ignorant of the extent to which their discipline is both socially constructed and socially constructing.
(6) Accounting must be changed to take account of social relationships in a much wider manner.
(7) Accountants must consciously take sides in social conflict.
(8) Social accounting as presently being considered is deficient because it considers only additional disclosures and externalities but does not envisage a change in the ownership of capital and is based on a modification of the status quo.

Social accounting has thus far been evolutionary rather than revolutionary and therefore is considered from the radical perspective to be inadequate and obstructionist.

11.5   ACCOUNTING, REPORTING AND SUSTAINABILITY

Moving beyond consideration of the potential role of business and accounting with respect to social and environmental accountability and having considered the potential theoretical rationales for accounting for and reporting upon social and environmental impact, it is appropriate to consider present possibilities for such accounting and reporting activity. To this end, a variety of accounting models that have been advanced to date will be reviewed and specific consideration will be paid to the challenges of accounting for environment and environmental sustainability.

11.5.1   Accounting models in review

The most elementary of basic approaches to social accounting was put forward during the 1970s and 1980s. This is the **inventory approach** as shown in Table 11.2 (Parker, 1977; Parker *et al*, 1989). This is a narrative listing that includes descriptions and some costs where they are available. On one hand, it provides a certain level of detail about activities but, on the other hand, it lacks quantification of social impacts.

A potential advancement on the inventory approach is provided by the **outlay cost approach**. An example appears in Table 11.3

Table 11.2   Inventory approach

Beta Ltd
Social Responsibility Report
Year ended 30 June 19X8

(1)   **Employment**
Positive
Expanded operations have provided 826 jobs in the past 12 months.
Minorities employed now constitute 15% of the company workforce.
Retirement counselling has commenced in the past year in all divisions.
Negative
Fluctuating demand has caused periodic layoffs in certain sections of production personnel.
Poor industrial relations still persist in division A.

(2)   **Community**
Positive
Improvement of local parkland has been financed by the company in the past year.
Two executives were loaned for short periods to advise on the development of a new community centre in division C's area.
Charitable contributions were made to the following institutions: X, Y, Z
Negative
Inner city neighborhood around division A in need of redevelopment.
Program to subsidize vocational training for youth has had poor response.

(3)   **Product**
Positive
Quality control procedures have been improved.
Investment in expansion of customer complaint handling section has been doubled over the past year.
Warranty conditions and coverage on two products have been expanded and improved
Negative
Customer complaints about product servicing increased considerably over the past year.
Certain aspects of division B's export product appear to be unsafe and must be re-examined.

(4)   **Environment**
Positive
$26,000 invested in new water pollution treatment plant for division A.
Some old plant buildings in division A have been painted to improve visual effect in its inner city location.
Negative
New air pollution control equipment installed in division B now fails to meet new State pollution control requirements.

Source: Parker, 1977; Parker *et al*, 1989

(Parker, 1977; Parker *et al*, 1989). Only items for which costs have been ascertained are included. This allows comparison of expenditures between years and social categories. An open question is whether both voluntary expenditures and regulatory required expenditures should be distinguished and whether cost outlays are commensurate with social benefits.

Table 11.3 Outlay cost approach

<table>
<thead>
<tr><th colspan="3">Alpha Ltd
Social Responsibility Report
Year ended 30 June 19X8</th></tr>
<tr><th>*Personnel outlays*</th><th>*19X7*</th><th>*19X8*</th></tr>
</thead>
<tbody>
<tr><td>Superannuation contribution</td><td>$504,276</td><td>$625,384</td></tr>
<tr><td>Long term leave provided for</td><td>210,125</td><td>235,468</td></tr>
<tr><td>Worker compensation insurance premiums</td><td>17,515</td><td>19,200</td></tr>
<tr><td>Accident prevention and medical service</td><td>26,726</td><td>32,598</td></tr>
<tr><td>Holiday pay</td><td>876,524</td><td>992,686</td></tr>
<tr><td>Christmas bonus</td><td>26,000</td><td>27,000</td></tr>
<tr><td>Discounts on company products</td><td>4,820</td><td>6,790</td></tr>
<tr><td>Donations for marriages and births</td><td>580</td><td>720</td></tr>
<tr><td>House rental subsidies</td><td>2,600</td><td>3,200</td></tr>
<tr><td>Company sports group subsidies</td><td>800</td><td>700</td></tr>
<tr><td>Plant safety competition</td><td>500</td><td>400</td></tr>
<tr><td>Canteen costs</td><td>12,800</td><td>14,200</td></tr>
<tr><td>Work clothes and protective equipment</td><td>2,600</td><td>4,300</td></tr>
<tr><td>Apprentice training</td><td>38,700</td><td>42,220</td></tr>
<tr><td>Supervisor training</td><td>8,700</td><td>7,600</td></tr>
<tr><td></td><td>$1,769,266</td><td>$2,012,466</td></tr>
<tr><td>*Consumer outlays*</td><td></td><td></td></tr>
<tr><td>Meeting complaints</td><td>2,600</td><td>4,200</td></tr>
<tr><td>Warranty corrective work</td><td>11,260</td><td>8,720</td></tr>
<tr><td>Research and development</td><td>42,000</td><td>26,000</td></tr>
<tr><td>Consumer education</td><td>1,200</td><td>1,800</td></tr>
<tr><td></td><td>$57,060</td><td>$40,720</td></tr>
<tr><td>*Environmental related outlays*</td><td></td><td></td></tr>
<tr><td>Air pollution control</td><td>4,720</td><td>10,560</td></tr>
<tr><td>Noise pollution control</td><td>6,200</td><td>2,320</td></tr>
<tr><td>Landscape and architectural improvement</td><td>500</td><td>4,300</td></tr>
<tr><td></td><td>$11,420</td><td>$17,180</td></tr>
<tr><td>*Community service outlays*</td><td></td><td></td></tr>
<tr><td>Donations to charitable institutions</td><td>490</td><td>570</td></tr>
<tr><td>Subscriptions to associations</td><td>1,200</td><td>1,300</td></tr>
<tr><td>Subsidies to local sports</td><td>200</td><td>450</td></tr>
<tr><td></td><td>$1,890</td><td>2,320</td></tr>
<tr><td>**Total outlays**</td><td>$1,839,636</td><td>$2,072,686</td></tr>
</tbody>
</table>

Source: Parker, 1977; Parker *et al*, 1989

One possibility for trying to place greater emphasis on social outcomes or benefits is explored by the **social program and management report** as shown in Table 11.4 (Parker, 1977; Anderson, 1978; Parker *et al*, 1989). This report highlights selected social impact categories or programs, showing outlay costs for components of the program, program objectives, and a brief evaluation of the extent to which results have met objectives. The evaluation is much in the nature of program budget reports, including a combination of qualitative and quantitative information.

Table 11.4   Social program management report

Program Description: Health and safety in the workplace.
Program Objectives: To reduce incidence of employee suffering through accident and sickness

Outlay costs:	1985	1986
Safety at work training	$12,000	$13,500
Installation of accident prevention equipment	21,000	18,200
Anti-smoking education	—	5,400
Safety officer salary and entitlements	35,000	37,000
Nursing staff and provisions	97,000	112,000
Total	$165,000	$186,000

Results
- Man-hours lost through accidents reduced from 2,650 (1985) to 2,220 (1986).
- Man-hours lost through illness reduced from 3,295 (1985) to 2,982 (1986).
- Number of employees smoking has been reduced from 326 (45%) in 1985 to 245 (34%) in 1986.
- Anti-smoking education has had a good initial impact but further reductions are yet hoped for. Illness is still a significant problem and new health education programs are planned. Accidents have reduced appreciably although not in direct relationship to expenditure in that area. Alternative approaches to the problem are under consideration.

Source: Parker, 1977; Anderson, 1978; Parker *et al*, 1989

The **cost–benefit model**, as shown in Table 11.5 (Committee on Social Costs, 1975; Demers and Wayland, 1982; Parker, 1977; Parker *et al*, 1989) attempts to employ a greater degree of monetary quantification in assessing social benefits as well as social costs. However, a range of problems may also be encountered in this model, with some benefits being described in terms of outlay costs, leaving the problem of estimating actual beneficial social impact still unresolved. Costs may include effects of action taken and of actions not taken so that the report may include a mixture of cost outlays, cost changes, cost savings to outside parties and costs expended by outside parties.

Table 11.5 Cost–benefit approach

PSI Ltd
Social Responsibility Report (Year ended 30 June 19X8)

Social benefits

To employees

Increases in pay	$14,260	
Increases in company contributions to superannuation, long service leave, holiday pay	9,820	
Employee training	12,265	
Job enrichment program	6,240	
Tertiary course subsidies	4,200	
		$46,785

To consumers

Price reductions on sales of products benefiting from increased productivity of new process	3,480	
Decrease in repair charges to consumers (compared with 19X7)	2,970	
		$6,450

To community

Wages paid for new created	26,400	
Increased taxes paid by company	5,760	
Donations to charities	1,100	
Equipment and facilities hired for use by outside groups	720	
Training of handicapped workers	4,695	
		$38,675

To environment

Cost of landscape gardening around manufacturing plants	13,240	
Cost of painting old building exteriors	9,870	
Cost of installing air pollution control devices	26,400	
		$49,510
Total social benefits		$141,420

Social costs

To employees

Work-related injuries and illness	6,580	
Postponed cost of new safety devices	2,820	
Unpaid overtime worked	8,526	
		$17,926

To consumers

Reduced resale value on two products now rendered obsolete	26,500	
Cost of additional safety feature not added to one product (for this year's sales volume)	9,280	
		$35,780

To community

Increase in public facilities and services used	2,485	
Wages lost through layoffs	24,268	
		$26,753

To environment

Cost to local government of detoxifying local water supply	2,526	
Cost of non-renewable resources used	22,326	
Estimated cost of waste dumped	3,397	
		$28,249
Total social costs		$108,708

Net social benefits generated by company for year ended June 19X8		$32,712

Comprising		
Net Social Benefits to Employees	$28,859	
Net Social Costs to Consumers	(29,330)	
Net Social Benefits to Community	11,922	
Net Social Benefits to Environment	21,261	
		$32,712

Source: Committee on Social Costs, 1975; Demers and Wayland, 1982; Parker, 1977; Parker *et al*, 1989

Another version of the cost–benefit approach can be found in the **social impact statement model** developed by Estes (1976) as shown in Table 11.6. This is reviewed by Mathews (1993) who observes that the majority of entries in this statement are in terms of present cash flows off-setting payments made to society against payments received from society.

Table 11.6   Social impact statement

The Progressive Company Year ended 31 December 19X1	$	$	$
Social benefits			
Products and services provided		xxx	
Payments to other elements of society			
Employment provided (salaries and wages)	xxx		
Payments for goods and other services	xxx		
Taxes paid	xxx		
Contributions	xxx		
Dividends and interest paid	xxx		
Loans and other payments	xxx		
		xxx	
Additional direct employee benefits		xxx	
Staff, equipment, and facility services donated	xxx		
Environmental improvements		xxx	
Other benefits		xxx	
Total social benefits			xxx
Social costs			
Goods and materials acquired		xxx	
Buildings and equipment purchased		xxx	
Labour and services used		xxx	
Discrimination		xxx	
In hiring (external)	xxx		
In placement and promotion (internal)	xxx		
		xxx	
Work-related injuries and illness		xxx	
Public services and facilities used		xxx	
Other resources used		xxx	
Environmental damage		xxx	
Terrain damage	xxx		
Air pollution	xxx		
Water pollution	xxx		
Noise pollution	xxx		
Solid waste	xxx		
Visual and aesthetic pollution	xxx		
Other environmental damage	xxx		
		xxx	
Payments from other elements of society			
Payments for goods and services provided	xxx		
Additional capital investment	xxx		
Loans	xxx		
Other payments received	xxx		
		xxx	
Other costs		xxx	
Total social costs			xxx
Social surplus (deficit) for the year			xxx
Accumulated surplus (deficit) 31 December 19X0		xxx	
Accumulated surplus (deficit) 31 December 19X1		xxx	

Source: Estes, 1976; Mathews, 1993

One of the earlier and more comprehensive attempts to design a social accounting model was provided by Linowes (1972) in the form of a **socioeconomic operating statement**. This is reproduced in Table 11.7. It shows the impact of the organization in terms of relations with people, relations with the environment and relations with product. In each of these categories, improvements are summarized and netted off against detriments. However, it provides no estimate of cost/benefit to the environment in the future, the costs referred to being current actual or opportunity costs to the organization.

Table 11.7   Socioeconomic operating statement

	X Corporation	
	Year ending 31 December 19X1	
(1)	Relations with people	
	A Improvements	$
	1 Training program for handicapped workers	10,000
	2 Contribution to educational institution	4,000
	3 Extra turnover costs because of minority hiring program	5,000
	4 Cost of nursery school for children of employees voluntarily set up	11,000
	Total improvements	30,000
	B Less detriments	
	1 Postponed installing new safety devices on cutting machines (cost of the devices)	14,000
	C Net improvements in people actions for the year	16,000
(2)	Relations with environment	
	A Improvements	
	1 Cost of reclaiming and landscaping old dump on company property	70,000
	2 Cost of installing pollution control devices on Plant A smokestacks	4,000
	3 Cost of detoxifying waste from finishing process this year	9,000
	Total improvements	83,000
	B Less detriments	
	1 Cost that would have been incurred to relandscape strip-mining site used this year	80,000
	2 Estimated costs of installing purification process to neutralize poisonous liquid being dumped into stream	100,000
		180,000
	C Net deficit in environment actions for the year	97,000
(3)	Relations with product	
	A Improvements	
	1 Salary of vice-president while serving on government Product Safety Commission	25,000
	2 Cost of substituting lead-free paint for previously used poisonous lead paint	9,000
	Total improvements	34,000
	B Less detriments	
	1 Safety device recommended by Safety Council but not added to product	22,000
	C Net improvements in product actions for the year	12,000
Total socioeconomic deficit for the year		69,000
Add Net cumulative socioeconomic improvements as of January 1 19X1		249,000
Grant Total net socioeconomic actions to 31 December 19X1		180,000

Source: Linowes, 1972; Mathews, 1993

Another attempt to account socially using traditional accounting methodology was experimented with in the early 1970s by the Abt organization employing what it termed the **constituent impact approach**. The key impact areas were employees, customers, community and the general public with items measured in monetary terms and reported in a balance sheet and income statement format. Examples are provided in Tables 11.8 below and 11.9 next page.

Table 11.8 Abt model of social and financial balance sheet items

---

Social and Financial Balance Sheet Items: 19X3

Assets
Staff: Staff on payroll
      Training costs (net of obsolete training)
Organization: Research and development
               Child care
               Social audit
Use of public goods: Public services paid for through taxes (net of consumption)
Financial and physical assets: As per traditional financial balance sheet

Liabilities and equity
Staff: Wages payable
Organization: Borrowing
Public: Environmental resources used through pollution (such as paper,
      electricity, commuting)
Financial liabilities: As per traditional financial balance sheet
Stockholders' equity: As per traditional financial balance sheet
Society's equity: Net increase/decrease in social assets

Source: Parker *et al*, 1989

Another example of traditional accounting format can be found in a **statement of funds flow** developed by Dilley and Weygandt (1973) and shown in Table 11.10. This is a statement of funds flow for socially relevant activities for a power utility company with the majority of items listed having an actual or potential effect on the environment. As Mathews (1993) observes, all costs listed are actual and current, with future costs and benefits not evaluated except in current terms.

Another form of model, based on inputs and outputs has been proposed by Dierkes and Preston (1977). As shown in Table 11.11, it is focused on the environmental impact of decision-making with **social cost figures** being used for the purposes of government regulators, as a basis for negotiation between parties, and to provide social costs in the form of effluent charges levied against the cause of the pollution.

Some researchers have advocated a **technical standards approach** to social accounting, requiring an organization to report on the extent to

Table 11.9   Abt model of social and financial income statement items

---

Social and Financial Income Statement Items: 19X3

Benefits (income)
To company/stockholders: Revenues
Federal/State/local services consumed
Environmental resources used through pollution
To staff: Salaries, career advancement, vacations and holidays, health and life insurance, sick leave, parking, food services, quality of workspace, child care, credit union
To clients/general public: Value of contract work, staff overtime worked but not paid, Federal/State taxes paid by company, contributions to knowledge (publications)
To Community: Local taxes paid
Environmental improvements

Costs (expenditures)
To company/stockholders: Salaries, training, contract costs, overheads, vacations and holidays, improvements to work environment, Federal/State/local taxes paid, health and life insurance, sick leave, food services, child care, interest payments, school tuition reimbursement, income foregone on paid-in capital
To staff: Opportunity cost of total time worked, absence of retirement income plan, layoffs and involuntary terminations, inequality of opportunity, uncompensated losses through theft
To clients/general public: Costs of contracted work, Federal/State services consumed, environmental resources used through pollution
To Community: Local services consumed

Net income
To company/stockholders: To clients/general public
To staff: To community
Total net social income
Total net social and financial income

Source: Parker *et al*, 1989

which its social performance in statutory defined areas matches acceptable performance as defined by established standards. This reflects the compliance-with-standards approach that has been advocated by Gray, Owen and Maunders (1988, 1991). The approach, the format of which is shown in Table 11.12, focuses on providing non-monetary quantified and accountability-oriented information that is practical and cheap to prepare as well as relevant and understandable.

Inspection of the foregoing tables demonstrates that attempts at providing innovative models for corporate social and environmental accountability have been quite widespread and have a history of

Table 11.10   Statement of funds flow

Statement of funds flow for socially relevant activities 1971	
Environmental	$
Installation of electrostatic precipitators (Note 1)	26,000
Construction of power plants (Note 2)	2,089,000
Construction of transmission lines (Note 3)	35,000
Electrical substation beautification (Note 4)	142,000
Incremental cost of low-sulphur coal (Note 5)	33,670
Conversion of service vehicle to use of propane gas (Note 6)	3,700
Incremental cost of underground electrical installations (Note 7)	737,000
Incremental cost of silent jackhammers (Note 8)	100
Environmental research	
Thermal 17,000	
Nuclear 1,955	
Other 38,575	
Subtotal	57,530
Total environmental funds flow	3,124,000
Other benefits	
Charitable contributions	26,940
Employee educational and recreational expenditure (Note 9)	6,000
Total other benefits	32,940
Total 1971 funds flow socially relevant activities	31,156,940
As a percentage of 1971 operating revenues 7.9%	
As a percentage of 1971 advertising expenses 8.5%	

Notes to funds statement

1 The company will complete installation of two electrostatic precipitators in 1973. Costs in 1971 totalled $26,000.

2 The company is building power plants which will begin operation in the middle to late 1970s. Incremental cash costs of environmental controls installed in these plants during 1971 totalled $2,089,000.

3 The company is constructing a high-voltage transmission line from another community to the company's service area. Environmental cash costs resulting from wider spacing in line towers $35,000 in 1971.

4 The company constructed a new substation in 1971 with an enclosed structure rather than open exposure of the electric transformers. The cost of this enclosure along with landscaping of existing substations totalled $142,000 in 1971

5 The company used approximately 150,000 tons of coal during 1971 for electric power generation. Low-sulphur-content coat comprised 8.6% of this coal consumption with the remaining 91.4% being coal of higher sulphur content. The low-sulphur coal cost approximately $2.61/ton more than the high-sulphur coal.

6 Motor vehicles fuelled with propane gas contribute substantially less air pollutants to the atmosphere than gasoline-fuelled vehciles. During 1971 the company converted nine more of its fleet of 115 vehicles to use propane gas. The cost of this conversion was $3,700. Seventeen company vehicles are now operated on propane gas.

7 Underground installation of electric transmission lines has increased since environmental attention has focussed on the aesthetic pollution of poles and wires. During 1971 the company installed underground electric transmission lines, which cost $737,000 more than putting the same lines above ground.

8 Jackhammers used by the company are, with one exception, of the normal noise-polluting type. One jackhammer purchased during 1971 with noise controls costs $100 more than the regular jackhammers

9 The company reimburses employees for educational expenditures and provides recreational opportunities such as the annual company picnic. Such expenditure amounted to approximately $6000 in 1971

Source: Dilley and Weygandt, 1973; Mathews, 1993

Table 11.11 Environment and social cost

Factor	Input (Commitment)			Output (Performance)		
	Description	Measure	Further information	Description	Measure	Further information
Energy	Research and development	D.No. $		Consumption – total	$.$ per	
	Savings measures	D.$		oil	sales	
	Policy and goals	D.No. ($ or %)		gas	$ per unit	
				coal		
				other	output	
				Re-use waste heat	$% of total consump- tion	
Air pollution	Policy and goals	D.No		Noise level (nearest house)	dB A	Comparison with Standards
Water pollution	Research and development	D.No $		Air pollution by pollutant	W W/P	
Solid waste	(by pollutant or waste)			Water pollution by pollutant	W B.o.D	
Noise	Control equipment	S.D. % of total investment		Water charges	$	
	Recycling equipment	% increase in production cost		Solid/semi-solid dumped	S.W	
				Solid/semi-solid sold	$.W	
				New by-products	D.S.$	
				Complaints	No	
				Lawsuits	No.$	
Despo- liation of landscape	Policy and goals	D.No D.$	% production costs	Complaints Lawsuits	No No. $	
	Rehabilitation (landscaping)					
	Beautification	D.$ size area despoiled size area reclaimed				
Raw materials	Policy and goals	D.No		Type	W.%.S	
				Waste	W.%.$	
				Use of recycled materials	W.%.$	
	Research and development substitution recycling	D.No $				
Packaging	Research and development	D.No.$		Returnable	W.%	
				Waste	W.%	
Transport	Modal policy	D		Energy use	S.W	
				Pollution	(as above)	

Notes:

Consideration may also be given to the use of scarce non-renewable resources, and the use of renewable but long term resources such as trees

No = Absolute quality. Could mean both staff and beneficiaries

$ = Cost in applicable currency

% = Proportion or percentage in terms of applicable denominator

D = Description of policy measure, goal, activity; Fr = Frequency of activity; T = Length of time applicable to activity; W = Weight; S = Sales; P = Product; A = Assessment

Source: Dierkes and Preston, 1977; Matthews, 1993

Table 11.12   Technical standards social accounting format

	Pollution Standards Report			
	Standard source	Standard	Variance this year	Variance last year
Air pollutants	X	Y	Z	Z
Water pollutants	X	Y	Z	Z
Noise pollutants	X	Y	Z	Z

General performance comments: (narrative)
X = regulation and issuing body
Y = actual statistics measured
Z = favourable/unfavourable variance from standard

Source: Schreuder, 1979; Parker *et al*, 1989

development stretching back to the early 1970s. They represent a wide variety of approaches, ranging from attempts to retain the traditional financial accounting format, to models based on a more general economic methodology, through to more statistically oriented material that focuses on physical inputs and outputs. However, few examples of their actual application in business organizations or other organizations presently exist. Certainly they provide the opportunity for making a crude but initial beginning. Nevertheless, much remains to be done in terms of developing measurements and reporting formats that will do justice to the accountability that is required.

11.5.2   Environmental accounting

General international community concerns about environmental pollution and environmental preservation appear likely to stimulate greater interest in and pressure for social and environmental accounting formats that are capable of practical application and reporting. It is notable that after the Alaskan oil spill caused by the *Exxon Valdez*, firms in the same industry, as represented by a sample from the petroleum segment of the Fortune 500, significantly increased their environmental disclosures (Patten, 1992). The estimated clean-up costs of this disaster exceeded US$1.25 billion and has raised questions about how the accounting profession should account for something like the Valdez oil spill and whether accountants should recognize liabilities for potential oil spills that can occur, for example when a shipping company is regularly shipping such material on particular routes. As Rubenstein (1990) points out, current accounting practices suffer from two major problems in relation to environmental accountability:

(1) They do not account for the full costs of production including costs of consuming natural resources such as air, water and fertile land.

(2) Accounting rules penalize rather than encourage the environmentally responsible enterprise.

The more a company spends on prevention and clean-up, the less are its reported earnings. Environmental accounting is called for in order to:

(1) Identify the limits of a company's insurance coverage for clean-up costs and related claims.
(2) Encourage responsible corporate behaviour with respect to prevention rather than clean-up.
(3) Record the cost of consuming resources rather than simply because of purchasing them.
(5) Recognize the obligation for environmental protection imposed by existing legislation.
(6) Recognize specific, identifiable contingent liabilities for the clean-up of existing toxic wastes.

With respect to waste management, Laughlin and Barangu (1991) point out that the way in which accounting systems are set up within companies can affect whether waste reduction, reuse or recycling opportunities are implemented. They argue that in most companies, the costs of raw materials, labour and supervision and capital depreciation are charged against a particular production area within the company, while in many others, waste disposal costs are charged as corporate overhead expense. Yet within-plant waste reduction, reuse or recycling can generate direct savings in terms of raw material costs and avoidance of waste disposal costs. Gray *et al*, (1993) have identified three main ways in which organizations are attempting to account for waste. The simplest approach recognizes total actual and potential costs of waste management on a corporate-wide, activity or site basis. The second approach is based on non-financial accounting and employs a recording and communicating information system that reports the physical quantities of waste. These two methods of accounting can be used in conjunction with one another. The third and most sophisticated approach uses an environmental index devised to monitor waste production upon which is based a comprehensive waste accounting system that charges all waste management costs (such as, costs of disposal, insurance, gaining consent, emergency procedures, spillage) back to line management. This employs a 'polluter pays principle' for each functional area of the organization (including research and development, and service units).

Another major aspect of accounting for the environment involves accounting for energy. Gray *et al*, (1993) pose the first step as separating out energy costs in the basic accounting and costing systems. Their survey work suggests that while this appears to be an elementary step, less than 50% of large companies have a system that accounts for energy separately from other costs; fewer still recharge those costs to activity centres but rather treat them as part of general overhead cost. The counting for energy by separating out energy costs and charging them to those areas that incur them begins a process of raising the profile of energy costs in the minds of both employees and management. However, energy conservation cannot be fully achieved by accounting for energy only in terms of cost. Energy units must be accounted for, otherwise through process changes or fuel switches, total costs may appear to fall while in fact energy efficiency may have decreased. One possibility for assisting in this area is to trace energy inputs via a shadow accounting system based on energy units such as therms, BTUs, tons of coal equivalent or other units to inform policy-making. Thus book-keeping entries currently denoted in monetary terms could also be designated in terms of the units of energy contained in their production.

The question of social and environmental reporting has largely been recently couched in terms of 'green' reporting or environmental reporting. Proponents vary from advocating a method that may lead to longer term business performance improvement to one that represents a compliance-with-standards approach. Blaza (1992) suggests that environmental re-porting in the future should go beyond a compliance-led process to one that identifies opportunities and benefits on which management can base long term business plans. Ing (1922) suggests that management should clearly establish the organization's objectives for green reporting and transmit those objectives to all who are responsible for producing the appropriate report. The content and presentation style must also relate to the target audience, although as with financial reporting, they are not always easy to specifically identify. The mode of publishing also bears consideration in terms of the extent to which environmental reports, like financial reports, should be published in the public media, organizational publicity material and annual reports. Environmental reporting will also necessarily involve both qualitative and quantitative data, including both financial and statistical material. Gray *et al*, (1993) suggest practical steps towards both financial and non-financial environmental accounting and reporting. Their suggestions are summarized in Tables 11.13 and 11.14.

Such practical reporting innovations make environmental impacts of the organization more visible to and more easily understood by report readers. Accounting and reporting for the environment, however, cannot be carried out entirely effectively within the conventional financial reporting format. Table 11.14 therefore outlines some of the steps that maybe undertaken for non-financial environmental accounting and re-porting. Obviously this represents a potential for very sizeable and significant reports. Clearly then, each organization must decide what aspects are most significant and the depth and volume of material that is most appropriate to secure effective communication to interested parties. As already indicated earlier in this chapter, despite two decades of social reporting debate and analysis, the number of fully developed examples of actual and practicable social and environmental reporting are still rela-

Table 11.13 Suggested practical approach to financial environmental accounting and reporting

The United Nations recommendations
- disclosure of accounting policies
- cost of current environmental expenditure
- environmental expenditure capitalized in the period
- liabilities, provisions and reserves
- contingent liabilities
- tax effects
- grants received

Develop disclosure with the auditor in mind
- reconsider provisions for remediation and abandonment
- provisions for inventory, accelerated depreciation, new investments, etc
- actual and provided-for legal costs

Make the environment more visible
- disclose energy (including transport) costs
- disclose waste handling and disposal costs
- disclose legal compliance costs
- consider packaging costs
- consider the disclosure of environmental fines

Source: Gray *et al*, 1993

tively few. As Gray *et al* (1993) point out, until minimum standards are set and agreed upon, this form of reporting will remain experimental. There are plentiful examples as shown already from which organizations may already draw in order to produce such reports. While recognizing the benefits which may flow to organizations who choose to account for and report on this area of their operations, it nevertheless remains a likely reality that more widespread reporting will initially come from the increasing imposition of environmental control standards and regulations and from government regulations covering other areas of social accountability, such as human resources management, community impact and service, social program involvement, as well as environmental impact.

11.5.3 Accounting for sustainability

One further emerging subject of discussion deserves mention here. This pertains to the questions of sustainability. The best introduction to accounting and corporate reporting for sustainability has been provided by Gray (1991) and Gray *et al* (1993). Generally, **sustainability** is defined in terms of ensuring that development meets the needs of the present

Table 11.14   Steps in environmental accounting and reporting

POLICY

1 Statement of environmental policy (or steps being taken). The Valdez Principles or ICC are the current state of the art.
2 Steps taken to monitor compliance with policy statement.
3 Statement of compliance with policy statement.

PLANS AND STRUCTURE

1 Structural and responsibililty changes undertaken in the organization to develop environmental sensitivity (for example, VP of environment, committees; performance appraisal of line managers).
2 Plans for environmental activities – introduction of Environmental Impact Assessment; Environmental Audit; Projects; Investment Appraisal criteria; etc.
3 Talks with local green groups; plans to work with community etc.

FINANCIAL

1 Amount spent on environmental protection – capital/revenue; reaction to/anticipation of legislation; voluntary/mandated; damage limitation/proactive (enhancement) initiatives.
2 Anticipated pattern of future environmental spend – to meet legislation, as voluntary; capital/revenue.
3 Assessment of actual and contingent liabilities (such as 'Superfund' type problems); impact on financial audit; impact on financial results.

ACTIVITY

1 Compliance with standards audits, procedures for, results of and issue of compliance with standards report.
2 Environmental audit and issue of summary/results.
3 Physical units analysis on materials, waste and energy.
4 Analysis of dealings with regulatory bodies/fines/complaints
5 Awards/commendations received.
6 Analysis of investment/operating activity influenced by environmental considerations.
7 Analysis/description of voluntary projects undertaken (such as tree planting, schools liaison).

SUSTAINABLE MANAGEMENT

1 Identification of critical, natural sustainable/substitutable, and man-made capital under the influence of (not necessarily 'owned' by) the organization.
2 Statement of transfers between categories.
3 Estimates of sustainable activities.
4 Estimates of 'sustainable costs' which would have to be incurred to 'return the organization (and thus future generation) to same position as they were in before the activity'.
5 Assessment and statement of input/output resource-flows and changes therein

An alternative or complementary reporting form might recognize the different dimensions of environmental impact – such as resources used, emissions, waste, energy; products; transport; packaging; health and safety, toxic hazards, biosphere, built environment; visual environment; community interaction.

Source: Gray, *et al*, 1993

without compromising the ability of future generations to meet their own needs. This basic notion is a generally agreed one internationally but its precise meaning and potential operationalization causes considerable disagreements. The difficulty is based on the fact that given some predetermined acceptable level of life on earth, the extent to which that level is achievable (that is, sustainable) is arguably unknown. Further, there is the question of sustainable for whom? Do we mean sustainable for all existing species or just humans? Other questions that remain to be debated include the manner in which sustainability should be sought (such as, whether economic growth and higher consumption are essential to general wealth and technology sustainability or whether this will only accelerate environmental degradation)? Further questions include the length of time over which sustainability should be aimed for and the level at which governments, corporations and other groups should take responsibility for this issue. Sustainability has been discussed for operationalization purposes in terms of a constancy of natural capital stock. The capital available to humanity in this sense falls into three categories:

(1) Critical natural capital — elements of the biosphere that are essential for life and for which sustainability must remain inviolate (such as the ozone layer and a critical mass of trees).
(2) Other natural capital (sustainable, substitutable or renewable) — elements of the biosphere which are renewable (such as non extinct species and woodlands) or for which reasonable substitutes can be found (such as energy from renewable sources).
(3) Artificial capital – elements created from the biosphere which are no longer part of the natural ecology (such as machines, building and roads).

The key point to be remembered about artificial capital is that it is usually created at the expense of natural capital. To avoid a terminal decline of natural capital, some way of managing sustainability must be found. As part of this exercise, reporting for sustainability requires statements about the extent to which corporations are reducing or increasing the options available to future generations. Gray *et al*, (1993) suggest two approaches – the inventory approach and the sustainable cost approach. The **inventory approach** is concerned to identify, record, monitor and report (probably in non-financial terms) the different categories of natural capital and their depletion or enhancement. An illustration of how this might be done is provided Table 11.15.

The **sustainable cost approach** is simple in theory but may be difficult to undertake in practice. It would essentially involve calculating the amount of money that an organization would have to spend at the end of an accounting period to place the biosphere in the position it was at the

Table 11.15 Inventory of X Corporation's sustainability interactions

CRITICAL NATURAL CAPITAL
Ozone depletion: The level of CFC use/emission for 1991 was XXX (1990, YYY). The corporation is committed to total elimination of CFCs by 1995 and HCFCs by 1997. Tropical hardwood: The corporation has eliminated all use of tropical hardwood in its own processes (1990, YYY used). Supplier audits have established that all hardwood use by suppliers is from sustainably managed sources as accredited by ABC & Co. Greenhouse gases: .... (See also Compliance-with-standards report on emmissions) Critical habitats/species: ....

NON-RENEWABLE/NON-SUBSTITUTABLE NATURAL CAPITAL
Oil and petroleum products:
Product 1 – use, comparative figures, plans for reduction or substitution, funds or efforts expended to provide substitutes;
Product 2 – ditto, etc.
Other minerals and mineral products:
    etc.

NON-RENEWABLE/SUBSTITUTABLE NATURAL CAPTIAL
Energy usage: Use details, change in usage, plans to change, efforts towards renewable sources.
Disposal of wastes: Levels of wastes produced and types, changes and plans. Efforts towards (a) discovery and access to new sources of resource (typically minerals) and (b) extending longevity of use, repairability and recycling might appear here.
    etc.

RENEWABLE NATURAL CAPITAL
Timber products: use, harvesting, recycling, etc.
Species exploitation; ditto.
Habitat destruction/remediation.
Leisure and visual environment, built environment, water, air, noise, etc.

Source: Gray *et al.* 1993

start. It is a notional procedure based on costs rather than values and would appear in the income statement as notional reduction in profit or notional addition to operating expenditure. A third suggestion for reporting for sustainability is the resource flow input/output approach as illustrated in Table 11.16. While it does not directly report sustainability, it allows the reader to assess resource usage and ultimately the sustainability of the organization's activities.

Table 11.16   Resource flow statement for XYZ Lodge Ltd (extract)

INPUTS	LEAKAGES			OUTPUTS
	loss/theft			
brought f/d	*breakages*	*emissions*	*wastes*	*carried f/d*
Building				Building
Fixtures	Deterioration			Fixtures
Furniture				Furniture
Fittings				Fittings
Furnishings	Deterioration			Furnishings
Sheets				Sheets
Crockery	Breakages			Crockery
etc.				etc.
additions to				
non–consumables				
Repairs				
New sheets			packaging	
New crockery			packaging	
etc.				
consumables				
Meat			scraps	
Groceries			packaging	2,700
Canned food			cans	bed-
Canned drink			alu cans	nights
Milk			bottles	
Bottled drink			bottles	
Cleaning materials		sewage	plastics	
Electricity		heat		
Oil		gases, heat		
Gas		gases, heat		
Car miles		gases		
Laundry		water		
etc.				Profit/loss
				Taxation
				paid

As far as possible all inputs, leakages and outputs would be described and/or quantified

Source: Gray *et al*, 1993

11.6   SOCIAL AND ENVIRONMENTAL AUDITING

Having reviewed the role of business and accounting and the theoretical rationales for social and environmental accountability, followed by a brief examination of accounting and reporting models, this chapter now turns to the question of social and environmental auditing. Just as financial reporting requires the attestation of expert third parties (that is, auditors) to provide source credibility to the information produced by report producers, so some form of social and environmental auditing is and will be required for credible corporate social and environmental accountability. This question is now briefly considered.

11.6.1 Social auditing

Given that social accounting disclosure is not produced in great quantities by most organizations, relatively few samples of social auditing exist. Gray, Owen and Maunders (1987) have found that very few organizations have an external audit of their social accounting disclosures and that most social audits are undertaken by organizations representing consumer or labour groups. Examples in the United Kingdom are audits conducted by Social Audit Limited, Counter Information Services, and monitoring activities by local authorities and some arms of government. Government tends to monitor social performance in fields such as race relations, sexual discrimination, air and water pollution, health and safety at work, consumer protection, employee rights and public protection.

The nature and scope of social audit has not been as yet precisely defined. It is an audit that goes beyond conventional accounting principles and practices and focuses on providing independent commentary on the availability or absence of information concerning an organization's impact on society ranging from employees to customers to the local community and the wider society. It therefore attempts to embrace not only economic and monetary variables but also social ones and attempts to increase organizations' accountability (Geddes, 1992; Gray *et al*, 1993). External social audits began in the 1960s and early 1970s in the United States (as seen in Ralph Nader and the consumer movement) and the United Kingdom (for instance, Social Audit Limited and Counter Information Services). These various self-appointed external organizations covered a range of social agendas including the assessment of quality, value for money and ethical basis of supply of goods and services to consumers, implication of corporate strategies for worker health and safety and for environmental pollution, and the environmental impact of corporate activities. In the United Kingdom there were also a number of social audits conducted as part of the anti-closure movement when a wave of industrial plant closures occurred in various regions of the country. These audits were designed to expose the consequences of such closure on the local economy. Social audits were also conducted in defence of cuts to public sector size and activity and as a reaction against centralizing pressures which began to encroach on local government autonomy. Social audit has also included community-based audits concerned with the provision of local public services (Geddes, 1992).

- In the United Kingdom, Social Audit Limited was established to demonstrate that a full social audit was feasible. It set out to publish data covering an organization's interaction with employees, consumers, community and the environment with a view to making it accountable in a broader sense than simply financial. It published the *Social Audit Quarterly* which included reports on organizations such as Tube Investments Limited, Cable and Wireless, Coalite and Chemical, Avon Rubber Company Limited. General reports on armaments and industry and social costs of advertising also published.
- Counter Information Services was a more radical organization concerned with empowering labour. It published 'Anti-Reports' which covered organizations such as Rio Tinto Zinc, Courtaulds, Consolidated Gold Fields, British Leyland, Ford Motor Company, Unilever, as well as reports on South Africa, nuclear technology and women in society. (Gray *et al*, 1993).

Depending upon the issues being examined, social audits can employ a variety of methodologies. In attempting to show the impact of organizational activities on local economies, social audits may be based on some kind of Keynesian multiplier showing a combination of employment, income and expenditure multipliers that reflect economic impact on the local community, both direct and indirect. Another group of social audits may examine more qualitative and less easily quantifiable issues, for instance, considering the number of jobs, wages and conditions of work produced by government or private sector organizations. This may even include attempts at assessing illness and death associated with unemployment caused by plant closures. Another form of social audit may be concerned to find ways in which publicly provided services can meet people's needs more effectively. Focusing, for example, on health and welfare needs of the community, the social audit might try to identify people's needs, how far they are being met and what changes could be made to meet them more effectively. These brief comments point to both the changing role and focus of social audits over time and the difficult question of appropriate and practical methodologies. In some senses, the focus of social auditing has changed. It originally focussed upon evaluating corporate social responsibility but has now changed into a more explicitly political activity. For example, some more recent social audits have assessed community effects of deindustrialization or have been employed to defend public sector organizations against privatization (Geddes, 1992).

11.6.2 Environmental audit

Another developing subset of social auditing is that of environmental auditing. This is akin to an internal management audit but it conducts an environmental impact review of the entire operation of an organization or part of that operation. It has become a specialist service offered by an increasing array of organizations (Ing, 1992). Environmental auditing is a term that covers a range of different activities which include:

(1) Environmental impact assessment
(2) Environmental survey
(3) Environmental review, monitoring and surveillance
(4) Environmental investigation
(5) Eco-audit
(6) Independent attestation of environmental information

A more detailed review of the these types of environmental audit is provided by Gray et al (1993).

Environmental impact assessments were first developed in the United States and then spread throughout Canada, Australia, Holland, New Zealand, Japan, the United Kingdom and beyond. This audit is a process that tries to identify and predict the impact of a new development on the environment, to mitigate this is where feasible and to monitor actual impact. They are applied to projects which require some form of planning permission, particularly where there is an anticipated impact on the environment. They are intended to guide planners in decision-making on new initiatives. Many companies have developed experience in this form of audit which can be undertaken in-house by large organizations or through external consultants. Industry experience as well as technical, legal and scientific knowledge are required. An outline of this process is provided in Table 11.17.

The environmental survey is the simplest type of environmental audit. It is directed towards orienting the organization to environmental issues, identifying actual and potential areas of environmental impact, and laying out an agenda for future environmental audits and better environmental management. The elements of a simple initial environmental survey are outlined in Table 11.18. At the more sophisticated level, an environmental audit contains a number of key elements that are listed in Table 11.19.

Environmental auditing is clearly a major growth area in organizational activity worldwide. It represents a direct response to the 'greening' of communities and governments in their concern about the quality of our total environment. The review of environmental impact, the comparison of environmental impacts against regulated standards, and the investigation of potential environmental impacts of future project proposals each require different approaches and various levels of expertise in law,

Table 11.17 Information in an environmental impact assessment

(1) A description of the proposed project and, where applicable, of the reasonable alternatives for its siting and designs;
(2) A description of the environment that is likely to be affected;
(3) An assessment of the likely effects of the proposed project on the environment;
(4) A description of the measures proposed to eliminate, reduce or compensate for adverse environmental effects;
(5) A description of the relationship between the proposal and the existing environmental and land-use plans for and standards of, the affected area; and
(6) An explanation of the reasons for the choice of the preferred site and project design rather than of the 'reasonable' alternatives.

All this information would, in addition, need to be published in a form which the public can understand, to ensure effective public participation.

Source: Elkington, 1982; Gray *et al*, 1993

engineering, environmental and other source disciplines. As Power (1991) points out, we must avoid the temptation to capture environmental audit purely within the scope of traditional financial auditing expertise. While frameworks and approaches that have been developed for financial auditing purposes may offer useful contributions to the field of environmental auditing, the scope and related expertise required for the conduct of effective environmental audits go well beyond the confines of traditional financial auditing.

11.7 DISCLOSURE PRACTICES AND REACTIONS

While formal models of social accounting and reporting remain at an elementary stage of development, quite a range of studies have nevertheless revealed a variety of disclosure practices and trends internationally. The types and formats of corporate social and environmental disclosure practices that have been identified by survey studies will now be briefly reviewed. This will include reference to studies of marketplace reactions to such disclosures.

11.7.1 Social and environmental disclosure experience

Quite a number of studies have examined the incidence of social and environmental disclosures, predominantly in corporate annual reports.

- In a study of the largest 100 companies listed on the Sydney Stock Exchange in Australia, Trotman (1979) found an increased incidence

Table 11.18   The beginner's environmental survey

Step 1. Get started: asking for assistance if necessary.

Step 2. Draw a systems flow of the organization: Identifying the major categories of inputs, outputs and leakages.

Step 3. Provide a detailed itemization of the elements in Step 2: identifying the products and materials and the activities to which they relate. Pick up additional items involved along the way.

Step 4. Review each item with a view to minimization: refuse, reduce, reuse, recycle, substitute.

Step 5. Assess financial costs and benefits (if any): what can the organization realistically afford?

Step 6. Identify crucial business factors: what are the Issues on which you feel you cannot compromise – where the environment loses out to the business?

Step 7 Draw up a detailed plan of action

Step 8. Review progress at board meeting or equivalent

Step 9. Refine the organization: identify (as appropriate) people, house-keeping/office; processes, products/services; emissions and wastes; and repeat on side and/or business basis.

And do not forget . . .

Step 10. Identify existing and potential law, industry standards, consents as appropriate: the smaller organization relies here upon its trade association and related journals and trade magazines. This will become the first step as the organization begins to adjust.

Source: Gray *et al*, 1993

of disclosure, from 28 companies in 1967, to 48 in 1972 and 69 in 1977. Kelly (1979) examined selected social responsibility disclosures from the annual reports of 50 selected Australian companies over the period 1969–1978. These results also confirm Trotman's findings of increased disclosure over the time period. Guthrie (1982) studied the annual reports of the top 150 listed Australian companies for 1980. Of the companies surveyed, 42% included some form of social responsibility disclosure. This analysis was extended using 1983 annual reports (Guthrie and Mathews, 1985). Guthrie found that in both 1980 and 1983, annual reports of 56% of the sample companies made some form of social accounting disclosure. Using the instrument developed by Guthrie, Gul *et al* (1984) studied a random sample of 136 annual reports of Australian companies. Due to the randomness of their sample, their results revealed that only 30% of the companies sampled made social accounting disclosures. Of the disclosing companies, 42% came from the construction industry and 32% came from the manufacturing industry.

Table 11.19 Major elements in an environmental audit or review

- Identify the most important of the organization's environmental interactions;
- Assess the degree of environmental impact;
- Learn about how to deal with and reduce or improve the organization's impact;
- Identify a priority list of interactions to be dealt with (this will develop, in part, from the first two and in part in response to actual and potential changes in law and in society's attitudes;
- Establish standards and policies;
- Identify responsibilities;
- Train staff;
- Change practices and put policies into action;
- Develop environmental information systems;
- Monitor performance and performance appraisal;
- Assess performance against standards;
- Reappraise this list, starting from the top, on a systematic and continuing basis.

Source: Gray *et al*, 1993

- In an earlier study in New Zealand, Robertson (1977) found that of the largest 100 companies (based on paid-up capital), 54 made some sort of social disclosure (ranging from major to very minor).
- In the United States, the best known studies of social reporting incidence were conducted by Ernst and Ernst (1972–78). A report was produced for each of the years 1972 to 1978 based on the annual reports of the Fortune 500 companies. By 1978, the survey was showing a small decline in the number of companies making social disclosures, but it was only a minor decline from 91.2% to 89.2% of surveyed companies making social disclosures.
- Somewhat less evidence is available concerning disclosure incidence in Europe and specifically the United Kingdom. However, research by Roberts (1991, 1992) suggests a situation of generally increasing levels of disclosure. Instances of extensive disclosure exist in reports from most European countries with disclosure levels being significantly higher in Germany that any other country. Roberts (1991) conducted a survey of a sample of 110 companies from five of the largest mainland European countries and found that 68% of them provided at least one item of environmental information in their reports. However, while the overall number of companies providing at least some information was fairly high, the level of disclosure of any sub-category of environmental information was generally low.

Overall, however, international studies suggest that a majority of companies have for some time been engaging in at least some form, however minimal, of social and environmental accountability disclosures.

Some studies have considered the amount of disclosure being made.

- Trotman's (1979) study found that in annual reports, the average pages per company report devoted to social accounting disclosures measured 0.08 in 1967, 0.30 in 1972 and 0.57 in 1977.
- In the study of annual reports of 1980 conducted by Guthrie (1982) the average number of pages devoted to social accounting disclosures per company was 0.68 of a page, with only 11% of companies in the sample devoting more than one page of their annual report to social disclosures. Of disclosing companies, 40% devoted less than 0.25 of a page to social disclosures. Similar results were obtained by Guthrie for 1983, with an average disclosure of 0.77 of a page per annual report.
- In a study of social reporting in Belgian organizations, Delmot (1982) studied a sample of 58 companies in 1980. The social information section of annual reports most commonly occupied a space of between two and four pages. Of the companies studied, 28% reported more than four pages and 19% reported between one and two pages.

Thus, it would seem from the evidence available, although patchy, the amount of space devoted within annual reports to social and environmental disclosures has been highly variable, although there are suggestions that on average it has been increasing.

11.7.2   Disclosure content

What is the content of these disclosures? Guthrie (1982) found that in 1980, Australian company annual reports made most disclosures with reference to human resources with the next highest number of disclosures being made about the environment. Community involvement followed as the third most popular category, with minor disclosures being made about energy and products. Gul *et al*'s (1984) study of Australian companies found that 36% of social disclosures related to human resources, 32% related to community involvement and 10% related to the environment. In New Zealand, Davey's (1985) study of 15% of firms listed on the New Zealand stock exchange as at 31 March 1992, found that 66% of companies reported on employment, 38% on corporate objectives, 3% on products, 16% on community support, 6% on environment and none on energy. Also in New Zealand, Ng (1985) studied the same sample of companies for the years 1981, 1982 and 1983. By identifying and discarding a lesser number of disclosures as being of a public relations nature than Davey did, Ng reported 88% of companies disclosing information about employment, 41% about corporate objectives, 28% about product, 19% about community support, 13% about environment and 3% about energy.

In the United States, the Ernst and Ernst (1972–1978) studies found that social accounting information most represented in corporate disclosures was related to environment and energy as well as fair business practices. These were followed to a lesser extent by human resources, community involvement and products. Types of disclosures made under these categories included:

(1) Environment	– pollution control
	– prevention or repair of environmental damage
	– conservation of natural resources
(2) Energy	– conservation
	– energy efficiency of products
(3) Fair business practices	– employment and advancement of minorities
	– employment and advancement of women
	– employment of other special-interest groups
	– support for minority business
	– socially responsible practices overseas
(4) Human resources	– employee health and safety
	– employee training
(5) Community involvement	– community activities
	– health-related activities
	– education and the arts
(6) Products	– safety
	– reducing pollution from product use

In Europe, Brockhoff (1979) examined reports of 300 German companies issued between 1 December 1973 and 30 November 1974. Of these, 205 published a social report during that period which included information on the social activities that had been made part of the objectives of the organizations, total number of employees, social benefits provided to employees, research and development and environmental protection. In the Netherlands, Dekker and van Hoorn (1977) investigated 64 social annual reports produced by Dutch companies in 1975. Most information provided, as has been common in continental European reports, related to employees and their interests. However other non-employee data included financial and economic expectations for the future and its consequences for internal organizational social policy, suggestion box information and impact on the environment. Roberts' (1991) survey of disclosures in France, Germany, Netherlands, Sweden and Switzerland showed that overall, 30% of companies disclosed an environmental protection state-ment, 28% provided process information, 39% provided product infor-mation, and 15% commented on energy usage. Health and safety information was provided by 24% of disclosing companies. While significant international differences in social and environmental reporting content are apparent, human resource disclosures, community involve-ment disclosures and more latterly environmental disclosures appear to be at the forefront.

11.7.3 Disclosure format

A further question arises as to the nature and format of disclosures being made over the past two decades. Trotman (1979) found that about half of all disclosures in Australian companies were qualitative in nature, while in 1980, Guthrie (1982) found that 60% of all disclosures were non-quantitative though 24% gave some non-monetary quantifications. Only 4% gave solely monetary disclosures and 12% made both monetary and non-monetary quantified disclosures. In New Zealand, Robertson (1977) found that of 54 disclosing companies he surveyed, 79 made qualitative disclosures, 17 made quantitative disclosures and 34 made monetary disclosures (obviously these figures include companies who used multiple types of disclosure).

- With respect to format, Pang's (1982) study of 100 companies listed on the Sydney Stock Exchange in 1980 found that 4 produced a separate report, 25 produced a separate section of the annual report, 18 provided separate headings in various reports and 32 provided social information as part of other major topics in the annual report.
- In his Australian studies, Guthrie (Guthrie 1982; Guthrie and Mathews, 1985) found that between 1980 and 1983, there was an increase in the number of disclosing companies willing to quantify disclosures, from 56% in 1980 to 82% in 1983. He found that social disclosures were located throughout annual reports with 45% appearing in the chairman's report. However, the majority of companies disclosed information in the general body of the annual report and no company provided a separate social disclosure booklet.
- In Canada, Zeghal and Ahmed's (1990) study of social disclosure media used by Canadian firms found that mass media vehicles of disclosure were used extensively but provided less information in quantitative and monetary form than did annual reports. The mass media vehicles also provided only a few information categories, with new banks and petroleum companies placing the highest importance on the human resources disclosure category with little intra-industry variation. These researchers found that the content of social disclosures was likely to be influenced by the medium of communication

employed (for instance, annual reports, brochures or advertisements). Brochures were also used to supplement the content provided in annual reports.

- In the United Kingdom, Harte and Owen (1991) analyzed the annual reports of 30 companies and found that 10 reported on environmental matters in a separately identified section of their annual report which was on average one page in length (ranging from half a page to two pages). Six companies provided some financial data about their social performance (such as clean-up costs, restoration costs, investments in energy improvement, treatment plants and research funding). Reporting of non-financial statistical information was less common than financial with only 3 companies providing such information. The majority of companies produced specific narrative comment on some environmental aspect of their business, usually relating to a product, process or service offered.

Overall then, the degree of quantification and the format employed in social and environmental disclosures remains at a fairly crude and elementary level with few companies' efforts that could be described as comprehensive. Much remains to be done in terms of development and more remains to be discovered through surveys and research of practices.

11.7.4   Factors influencing disclosure

Studies have also attempted to identify factors that appear to be related to social and environmental disclosures. Trotman and Bradley (1981) found statistically significant relationships between company size (total assets and total sales) and social responsibility – larger organizations tend to provide more social disclosures. They also found a positive correlation between the volume of social accounting information disclosed and the extent of social constraints faced by companies. Pang's (1982) study found that large companies tended to disclose socially related material more frequently than smaller companies, with her survey finding disclosure rates ranging from 92% for those with market capitalizations above A$500m to 75% for those less than A$100m. Gul *et al*'s (1984) study found that large companies made more disclosures about employees but disclosures about community involvement were spread across firms of all sizes.

In New Zealand, however, Davey (1985) and Ng (1985) did not find a correlation between social disclosures and size of organization. In Canada also Burke (1980) found that larger companies were likely to provide more meaningful social measurement disclosures. Interestingly however, Ingram's (1978) US study found that social information content depended to a large extent on the market segment involved. In another United States study, Cowen *et al* (1987) found that organization size had a significant impact upon environmental, energy, fair business practice and community involvement disclosures but had virtually no influence on human resources or product disclosures. Industry category only affected energy and community involvement disclosures. Human resource disclosures also appeared to be related to the presence of a corporate social responsibility committee within the disclosing company. Thus, while the size of organization appears to be in most cases significantly related to the level of social disclosures, the evidence is not absolutely conclusive and tends to suggest that the relationship may vary depending on the types of information content involved.

Further questions arise with respect to such observations as made by Trotman and Bradley (1981) that volume of social accounting information disclosed may be related to the extent of social constraints faced by companies. This may need further investigation given the admittedly only single case findings of Guthrie and Parker (1989) which traced the social reporting disclosures in annual reports of the major steel-making company in Australia, BHP Limited. They found that the disclosures did not react to social constraints and community pressures as might have been suggested by the legitimacy theory. On the other hand, Patten's (1992) study of social disclosures in US petroleum companies following the *Exon Valdez* oil spill in Alaska suggests that the legitimacy theory may yet explain social disclosures when major environmental catastrophes occur and induce widespread social disapproval. He found that a significant increase in environmental disclosures among petroleum companies occurred after that disaster and that the amount of change was related to firm size. Thus overall, organizational size appears to be a clear influence upon the organization's predisposition to make social and environmental disclosures with social pressure and social concerns being another possible influence but one whose potential impact requires further investigation.

11.7.5   International comparisons

By way of a final addendum, one of the few comparative international studies of social accounting disclosure has been undertaken by Guthrie and Parker (1990). They compared social disclosures in the annual reports of the 50 largest listed companies in Australia, the United Kingdom and the United States. Annual reports released during the period ended 1983 were examined with a view to investigating whether different nationalities sponsor different levels of social disclosure, whether there were significant differences in the incidence of corporate social disclosures between different companies and corporate social disclosure categories, and whether a particular method of corporate social disclosure was predominant. They found that 56% of Australian companies, 98% of UK companies and 85% of US companies disclosed social information. A statistically significant difference was found between the disclosure levels across these three countries. Disclosures were spread across six themes: human resources – 40%, community involvement – 31%, environment – 13%, energy and product disclosure – 7%, and others – 2%. The ranking of disclosure content themes was not significantly different between the three countries.

In the United Kingdom and the United States, the most popular form of disclosure was a mixture of monetary and non-monetary quantification, while in Australia a non-monetary disclosure method was the generally accepted form of disclosure. Again a statistically significantly difference in method of social disclosures therefore existed between the three countries. A significant difference also existed with respect to the location of social disclosure for the three companies.

- The director's report was the most popular in the United Kingdom, while in the United States a separate section (25%) or separate booklet (12%) was popular. In Australia, social disclosures were most frequently located in other sections of the annual report (64%).
- In terms of annual report space allocated to social disclosures, the United States had a weighted average number of 1.26 pages per annual report, Australia had 0.7 and the United Kingdom had 0.89 pages devoted to social disclosures. No significant difference was statistically observable between the three countries for the amount of social disclosure.

A number of further noteworthy observations were made by the researchers. British annual reports were re-examined to detect the extent of disclosure not related to requirements of government regulations (with respect to charitable donations, political donations greater than £200, disabled employee policy, conditions of South African workers, and employee consultation and communication policy). Compared with the 49 United Kingdom corporations originally to have found to have made social disclosures, the re-examination revealed that only 28 of them made voluntary disclosures beyond those required by regulations. This 56% voluntary British disclosure rate coincided with the Australian disclosure rate identified in the first instance. The three countries also appeared to give identical priority to information types as follows:

Rank 1   Human resources
Rank 2   Community involvement
Rank 3   Environment

Also of interest is the observation that all three countries included 'bad news' social disclosures in over 20% of their annual reports. Although subject to regulatory disclosure, United Kingdom reports had the lowest frequency of 'bad news' disclosure (22%), while the United States had the highest frequency disclosure (48%) of 'bad news'. Most types of 'bad news' related to job losses, environmental damage and equal opportunity infringements. The higher levels of disclosure in the US annual reports appeared to be largely prompted by private regulation in the form of FASB Statement of Financial Accounting Standards No. 5, *Accounting for Contingencies* and the AICPA Statement on Auditing Standards No. 12, *Inquiry of a Client's Lawyer Concerning Litigation, Claims and Assessments*. Overall, this comparative international study revealed that all three countries adopted a common ranking for the importance of major areas of social accounting content, but their social disclosure patterns differed markedly. Areas of difference identified included total disclosure levels, methods of disclosure and locations of disclosures in annual reports.

11.7.6 Social disclosures and market reactions

Quite a variety of studies have now been conducted on share price and shareholder reactions to social and environmental accounting disclosures. The conclusions as to the relationship between these variables are somewhat mixed. Indicators of social performance employed in these studies have ranged from rating systems to social involvement disclosure scales, to social accounting disclosures in annual reports, to pollution control indices and reports. Indicators of market performance have included net income in relation to sales or shareholders equity, growth in earnings per share, mean or median return on investment, stock price per share, risk adjusted return on equity, monthly closing stock prices, price/earnings ratios, profitability and systematic risk, and stock price movements (Mathews, 1993). Results of investigations of relationships between social performance and market performance have varied from the findings of no significant relationships: these include no meaningful difference in total returns to investors for high and low involvement firms; substantial positive effects on stock market prices for companies disclosing pollution data; expenditures on pollution control not automatically leading to high market returns; companies with better pollution control records having higher profitability, larger size, lower total and systematic risks, and higher price/earnings ratio than companies with poorer pollution control records. A sample of relevant studies of this type include Vance (1975), Belkaoui (1976), Spicer (1978), Abbott and Monsen (1979), Anderson and Frankle (1980), Stevens (1982), Shane and Spicer (1983), Mahapatra (1984), Freedman and Stagliano (1984, 1991), and Freedman and Jaggi (1986, 1988).

Mathews (1993) argues that while the studies do have results that are conflicting, it might be argued that on balance the evidence leans towards a view that a disclosure of social accountability information does have utility for shareholders and the security market because information content has often been established regardless of the direction in which share prices move. Thus, managers and investors may be able to make more rational economic decisions utilizing social accounting and environmental accounting information. It must be remembered, however, that these market-related studies are concerned with the traditional relationship between managers and investors. This relationship is an association rather than an implied one-way cause and may be complicated by as yet undiscovered intervening variables. While social accounting may be justified to shareholders as an aid to market efficiency and improved decision-making as already indicated in this chapter, its audience and motivating factors are rather broader than that. Employees, customers, public interest groups, government and the community all have concerns about social and environmental performance of organizations and the disclosure of that performance. Thus, market performance and market reaction studies only address relationships with one particular interest group and it is arguable that they do not cover the interests of much more important and powerful groups who will ultimately determine the cause of corporate activity and community survival.

11.7.7   Interest group concerns

Little is known about the accountability interests and activity of pressure groups in attempting to secure adequate reporting on corporate social and environmental impact. Wicks (1992) has discussed the activities of The World Wide Fund for Nature in raising funds from industry and commerce for its conservation program and its work with industry to help develop environmental policies. Tilt (1994) has undertaken one of the first studies of the influence of external pressure groups on corporate social disclosure. She has found that pressure groups are users of corporate social disclosures and do attempt to influence companies' disclosure practices. Her study of the environmental lobby groups in Australia finds that they consider current corporate social disclosures to be insufficient and low in credibility. Their preferred corporate social reports would include narratives and quantified terms appearing in the annual report and prepared by certified by, and/or held by a body external to the disclosing company.

11.8   THE ASIAN REGION EXPERIENCE

Social and environmental accountability of organizations operating in Asia represents an emerging subject about which not a great deal of evidence currently exists. Bedi (1992) argues that most Asian companies are decades behind their Western counterparts in accepting the concept of their social responsibility to society. However, he does point out that Asian managers are pragmatic but not devoid of idealism and that the relationship between business and society is changing. Nevertheless, he argues that this relationship is nowhere near as developed as it has become between Western companies and their own national societies. In his view, 'corporate citizenship is the most undervalued asset today in Asia' (Bedi, 1992, p. 116). Nevertheless, he argues that in a massively changing socio economic environment, Asian companies will find it necessary to develop their corporate citizenship and social responsibility in order to win continued social respect and the right to practice.

11.8.1 Evidence from Japan and Hong Kong

Yamagami and Kokubu (1991) have conducted a survey of corporate social disclosure in Japan examining mandatory and voluntary reports. The Japanese Commercial Code requires the production of the corporate annual report, termed the 'Business Report', including a balance sheet, income statement, business report, retained earnings appropriation and schedules. Voluntarily produced reports include the 'Operating Report', the 'English Language Version of the Annual Report' and the 'Public Relations Report'. The Operating Report is a pamphlet voluntarily sent to stockholders, based on the Business Report and being in the form of a newsletter. The English Language Version of the Annual Report is issued to raise funds in international markets or to seek publicity. The Public Relations Report appears in various formats and is designed for various purposes. It is not necessarily published annually and contains no financial statements.

Yamagami and Kokubu (1991) examined the voluntary reports of the largest Japanese companies among the 200 largest international companies included in the Fortune 500 biggest industrial corporations outside the United States in 1985. This resulted in the collection of voluntary reports in 1985–86 for 49 Japanese companies. In terms of quasi-social disclosures, the researchers found that the most frequently disclosed items were related to research and development (82.8% of companies sampled) and international activity (66.9% of companies sampled). Less frequent disclosures related to community involvement (27.6%) and environment (11%). Of the companies sampled, 34.5% made disclosures relating to their employee relations. The study found that the content of disclosure was scanty. It was generally found that disclosures were greater in the Public Relations Report, particularly in relation to environment (26.5%), community involvement (51%) and international activity (79.6%). Notably, chemicals, petroleum refining and industrial and farm equipment made extensive disclosures of environmental matters in their Public Relations Reports.

For the fiscal year ended 1989, Lynn (1992) examined the annual reports of 264 Hong Kong public companies. He found that only 6.4% of the sample made available any corporate social disclosure data in their 1989 annual report. Lynn observed that while almost 40% of the companies examined were in the property and construction field, that segment accounted for less than 1% of corporate social disclosure reporters. At the other end of the scale, two-thirds of utility companies employed corporate social disclosures and accounted for more than one-third of all Hong Kong companies making such disclosures. In relation to reporting themes, 11 companies disclosed information about staff development, 10 disclosed information about community relations, eight disclosed information about both of the above categories and only three disclosed information on environmental issues. Only six companies in the entire survey revealed both monetary and statistical numbers in their disclosures. Five companies gave no statistics at all and the rest reported on either expenditures or service statistics but not both. Most companies devoted about a page of their annual report to corporate social disclosures. As a group, the six utility companies examined exhibited the longest reporting history with an average of four years of corporate social disclosures. Overall, Lynn found that Hong Kong had the lowest degree of corporate social disclosure exhibited in studies worldwide as at the time of the study. Hong Kong companies appeared to have an extreme proprietorship bias reflected in reports being of interest only to owners and investors. Such reports were primarily oriented towards reporting only their financial results. However, a solid but small core of organizations had begun to express their corporate social disclosure responsibilities via their reports, and indeed the incidence of reporting appeared to have been increasing in recent years.

11.8.2 Singapore's activity

Singapore has a record of significant social and environmental improvement and concerns about social and environmental issues. This is reflected in such activities as 'Clean and Green Week', the Green Leaf Award, reforestation projects, wastepaper recycling, industrial pollution reduction, community tree adoption schemes, and corporate–community philanthropic projects (Anon, 1993abc). The Singapore government has identified noise pollution as another environmental area that will require attention as Singapore becomes more urbanized. Singapore has also introduced the Green Label Scheme to identify environmentally friendly consumer products. In addition, about half of the petrol sold in Singapore is unleaded. Furthermore, manufacturing and hotel industries have set up environmental committees to promote environmental friendly practices (Cherian, 1993). However, in relation to disclosure, Phua (1993) reported that social disclosures by local Singaporean companies related mainly to their involvement in community programs but that disclosure on environmental impact was less customary. Nevertheless, over the past decade, Singapore has had a National Energy Conservation Campaign (launched in 1984), a National Water Conservation Campaign (launched in 1983), and legislation covering areas such as the Environmental Public Health Act, the Water Pollution Control and Drainage Act, the Clean Air Act and the Sale of Food Act to assist in controlling pollution and environmental health (Low *et al*, 1985).

An examination of social disclosures in 1983 annual reports of 60 randomly selected Singapore companies was conducted by Low *et al* (1985). They found that 43% of the sample companies disclosed some form of social impact information, the most common type being the identification of social problems and the impact of material social events on a company's financial performance. In addition, 12% of companies reported statements of social objectives, 22% reported employee training and community activities, and 7% reported on employee retrenchments and accident rates. Disclosure rates appeared fairly consistent across industrial sectors.

A further study of corporate social disclosure in both Singapore and Malaysia was conducted by Foo and Tan (1988). Their study examined the reports of 299 of the 305 Malaysian and Singapore companies listed on the Singapore stock exchange as at the end of 1985. Of the 299 companies, 62% were incorporated in Malaysia and 38% were incorporated in Singapore. Only 36% of the 299 companies studied were found to disclose some form of social responsibility information. The sector making most disclosure was the finance sector (57%) with the mining sector being the lowest disclosing sector (13%). Of the Singapore companies studied, 43% made such disclosures compared to 31% of Malaysian companies. The researchers also found that largest companies in terms of market capitalization, asset value, paid-up capital, profit before tax and turnover had the highest incidence of social responsibility disclosures compared with smaller companies. Malaysian companies most frequently disclosed information about human resources followed by products and community involvement. The same pattern was evident for Singaporean companies. Much less frequency of disclosure was evident in companies from both countries with respect to both environment and energy.

More recently, Chiong *et al* (1993) examined the 1990 annual reports of a sample of 51 Singapore incorporated companies listed on the Singapore stock exchange as at 31 December 1990. They found that 48% of the companies (from all four industrial sectors studied) disclosed social information in 1990. These researchers observed that compared with the Low *et al* (1985) and the Foo and Tan (1988) studies, the number of companies disclosing social information in 1990 had increased relative to the 1985 study results but did not appear to have improved when compared with the 1983 study results. One difficulty in interpretation of these results, however, has been caused by the 1985 results being based on a study of both companies incorporated in Malaysia and Singapore. Again, larger companies had a higher incidence of corporate social responsibility disclosures that smaller companies. Types of information most frequently disclosed in 1990 were human resources (36%), products/ services/properties (24%), community support/philanthropy (16%), environment (6%), and corporate social objectives and/or policies (3%). Chiong *et al* (1993) found that social information was generally reported in an *ad hoc* manner with most companies using the Chairman's Statement to communicate such information (62%). Overall, the researchers found that while many companies in Singapore had still not disclosed social information in their annual reports, the trend was towards companies increasingly disclosing such information.

Given the different dates of studies, sample sizes and types of companies selected, it is difficult to make direct comparisons between various international studies of corporate social disclosure frequency. Nevertheless it can generally be said that on available evidence, Singaporean company social disclosures appear to match those of their Japanese counterparts and to be significantly in advance of companies in Hong Kong. In addition, when for example, compared with Guthrie and Parker's (1990) study of social disclosures by top 50 companies in Australia, the United Kingdom and the United States, Singaporean company disclosure frequencies in relation to social information as measured in the Chiong *et al* (1993, 1990) study are not incomparable with their counterparts in other countries. Guthrie and Parker's (1990) study of 1983 annual report disclosures revealed 56% of Australian companies making such disclosures, 85% of US companies making such disclosures and 98% of British companies making such disclosures (with only 56% of United Kingdom companies making disclosures voluntarily beyond those required by UK government legislation and regulation). Nevertheless, it is clear that in terms of corporate social and environmental accountability and related reporting, much yet remains to be done by Singaporean companies, as indeed it does by companies throughout the international business community.

11.9 SUMMARY AND CONCLUSION

This chapter has been designed to provide the reader with an introductory overview of international and Asian development, research and current practice in social and environmental accountability. As should by now be evident, this has involved the coverage of an enormous scope of practice, literature and research findings. Many of the issues canvassed herein would merit entire chapters or books in themselves. The comprehensive bibliography supporting this chapter attests to this assertion, and also provides the reader with a pathway towards investigating issues raised in this chapter in more detail.

On the evidence presented here, business and accounting both have a role to play in the further development of social and environmental accountability and related disclosures. Nevertheless they have clearly been slow starters in involving themselves in and contributing to such developments. Nor can it be said that they have been or will be the exclusive contributors to such developments, other important contributors being government regulatory bodies, public interest lobby groups and environmental and other professional consultants.

The rationales for corporate disclosure are quite varied and the rationale adopted depends largely upon the perspective of the adoptor. The perspectives may vary from corporate defender to corporate critic and the rationales may vary from complete self-interest in corporate survival and prosperity to a genuine desire to engage in full corporate citizenship in today's society. It is clear that disclosure of social and environmental accountability information may not be a costless exercise but the benefits in terms of positive contribution to our planet and human condition, cooperation with government and social priorities, and contributions to and support from local community are clear possible outcomes.

Over the last two decades, a variety of accounting and reporting models have been developed. Most of these represent theoretical prescriptions with lamentably few having been put to experimental test. Observation at this point would suggest that those models that are more practically feasible do carry with them significant information disadvantages. The production of financial data alone would appear to be unlikely to satisfy the social and environmental accountability requirements that society is increasingly placing on organizations. A more likely accounting and reporting development will include a combination of financial and operating statistics as well as qualitative information. It must also be said that further developments in accounting and reporting for social and environmental impact will almost inevitably be followed and reinforced by expansions in the attest function. This will take a variety of formats, as already indicated in discussions of social and environmental auditing in this chapter.

Studies reveal that corporate social and environmental disclosures have been increasing internationally over the last two decades, but it is also arguable that they remain at a minimal level in a number of respects. They tend to represent a relatively minor quantity of disclosure when compared with corporate financial disclosures; they are mostly comprised of narrative qualitative information with sporadic statistics included and are largely dispersed intermittently throughout traditional annual reports. They also place greater emphasis on human resource disclosure and still provide relatively low level disclosure on environmental impact. While studies reveal that managers and investors on balance do seem to take some account of corporate social disclosures, it is also arguable that constituents such as local community, public and environmental interest groups, government regulators and the general community will turn out to be the more important and influential demanders of such disclosures. It is to this audience that social and environmental accountability will owe its impetus for further development and the future shape of its structure and process. Within the international context, it would appear that Asian experience in terms of expanding corporate social disclosures is following the international trend. Nevertheless, on the available evidence, Singapore is showing definite signs of leading the way for Asia in this field.

REFERENCES

Abbott, W.F. and Monsen, R.J. (1979). 'On the Measurement of Corporate Social Responsibility: Self-Reported Disclosures as a Method of Measuring Corporate Social Involvement. *Academy of Management Journal*, 22, pp. 501–515

Adams, R. (1992). Green Reporting and the Consumer Movement. In D. Owen, ed., *Green Reporting: Accountancy and the Challenge of the Nineties*, London: Chapman and Hall, pp. 106–118

Anderson, J.C. and Frankle, A.W. (1980). Voluntary Social Reporting: An Iso-Beta Portfolio Analysis. *The Accounting Review*, LV, pp. 467–479

Anderson R.H. (1978). Social Responsibility Accounting: How to Get it Started. *CA Magazine*, September, pp. 47–50

Anonymous (1993a). Two NUS Students Win Awards In New Youth Category. *Straits Times*, Nov. 8

Anonymous (1993b). Residents to Get Pick of the Crop After Tending to Own Fruit Trees. *Straits Times*, Nov. 8

Anonymous (1993c). Recycled Items Main Draw at Flea Market. *Straits Times*, Nov. 8

Bebbington, J., Gray, R., Thompson, I. and Walters, D. (1992). Accountants and the Environment: Accountants' Attitudes and the Absence of an Environmentally Sensitive Accounting'. In *University of Dundee Discussion Papers in Accountancy and Business Finance*, December

Bedi, H. (1992). *Understanding the Asian Manager: Working With the Movers of the Pacific Century*. Singapore: Heinemann Asia

Belkaoui, A. (1976). The Impact of the Disclosure of the Environmental Effects of Organizational Behaviour on the Market *Financial Management*, pp. 26–31.

Blaza, A.J. (1992). 'Environmental Reporting – A View from the CBI. In D. Owen, ed., *Green Reporting: Accountancy and the Challenge of the Nineties*, London: Chapman and Hall, pp. 31–34

Brockhoff, K. (1979). A Note on External Social Reporting by German Companies: A Survey of 1973 Company Reports. *Accounting, Organizations and Society*, 4, pp. 77–85

Brooks, L.J. (1986). *Canadian Corporate Social Performance*. Toronto: Society of Management Accountants of Canada

Buck, J. (1992). Green Awareness: An Opportunity for Business. In D. Owen, ed., *Green Reporting: Accountancy and the Challenge of the Nineties*, London: Chapman and Hall, pp. 35–47

Burke, R.C. (1984). *Decision Making in Complex Times: The Contribution of a Social Accounting Information System*. Ontario: Society of Management Accountants of Canada

Cherian, G. (1993). PM: Singapore Committed to Protecting Environment. *Straits Times* 8 November

Chiong, T.T.S., Doh, J.C. and Meng, A.K. (1993). Corporate Social Responsibility Reporting in Singapore: An Update. *Nanyang Technological University School of Accountancy and Business SABRE Centre, Working Paper No. 14–93,* Singapore

Committee on Social Costs (1975). Committee on Social Costs. *The Accounting Review Supplement,* pp. 50–89

Cowen, S., Ferreri, L. and Parker, L.D. (1987). The Impact of Corporate Characteristics on Social Responsibility Disclosure: A Typology and Frequency-Based Analysis. *Accounting Organisations and Society,* 12, pp. 111–122

Davey, H.B. (1985). Corporate Social Responsibility Disclosure in New Zealand: An Empirical Investigation. *Occasional Paper No. 52,* Palmerston North: Massey University Department of Accounting and Finance.

Dekker, H.C. and Van Hoorn, Th.P. (1977). Some Major Developments in Social Reporting in the Netherlands Since 1945. *Discussion Paper,* Amsterdam: University of Amsterdam Department of Economics

Delmont, A. (1982). Social Written Information in Belgian Enterprises: Results of a Survey. *Working Paper,* Mons: University of Mons Department of Accountancy

Demers, L. and Wayland, D. (1982). Corporate Social Responsibility: Is No News Good News? *CA Magazine,* January pp. 42–46, pp. 56–60

Dierkes, M. and Preston, L.E. (1977). Corporate Social Accounting Reporting For the Physical Environment: A Critical Review and Implementation Proposal. *Accounting, Organizations and Society,* 2, pp. 3–22

Dilley, S.C. and Weygandt, J.J. (1973). *Measuring Social Responsibility – An Empirical Test. Journal of Accountancy,* pp. 62–70

Elkington, J. (1992). Industrial Applications of Environmental Impact Assessment. *Journal of General Management,* 7, pp. 23–33

Ernst and Ernst (1972–8). *Social Responsibility Disclosure: Surveys of Fortune 500 Annual Reports.* Cleveland: Ernst and Ernst

Estes, R.W. (1976). *Corporate Social Accounting.* New York: John Wiley

Foo, S.L. and Tan, M.S. (1988). A Comparative Study of Social Responsibility Reporting in Malaysia and Singapore. *Singapore Accountant,* 4, pp. 12–15

Freedman, M. and Jaggi, B. (1986). An Analysis of the Impact of Corporate Pollution Disclosures Included in Annual Financial Statements on Investors' Decisions. *Advances in Public Interest Accounting,* 1, pp. 193–212

Freedman, M., and Jaggi, B. (1988). Analysis of the Association Between Pollution Disclosure and Economic Performance. *Accounting Auditing and Accountability Journal,* 1, pp. 43–58

Freedman, M. and Stagliano, A.J. (1991). Differences in Social Cost Disclosures: A Market Test of Investor Reactions. *Accounting Auditing and Accountability Journal,* 4, pp. 68–83

Geddes, M. (1992). The Social Audit Movement. In D. Owen, ed., *Green Reporting: Accountancy and the Challenge of the Nineties,* London: Chapman and Hall, pp. 215–241

Gray, R.H. (1991). Corporate Reporting for Sustainable Development: Accounting for sustainability in 2000AD. *University of Dundee Discussion Papers in Accountancy and Business Finance,* August

Gray, R. and Bebbington, J. (1991). Global Environment and Economic Choice: A Role For Greener Accounting. *University of Dundee Discussion Papers in Accountancy and Business Finance*, November

Gray, R. and Bebbington, J. (1992). Can the Grey Men Go Green? *University of Dundee Discussion Papers in Accountancy and Business Finance*, November

Gray, R., Bebbington, J. and Walters, D. (1993). *Accounting For the Environment.* London: Paul Chapman Publishing

Gray, R.H. and Collison, D.J. (1991). Environmental Audit: Green Gauge or Whitewash? *Managerial Auditing*, 6, pp. 17–25

Gray, R., Owen, D.L. and Maunders, K. (1987). *Corporate Social Reporting: Accounting and Accountability.* London: Prentice-Hall

Gray, R., Owen, D. and Maunders, K. (1988). Corporate Social Reporting: Emerging Trends in Accountability and the Social Contract. *Accounting Auditing and Accountability Journal*, 1, pp. 6–20

Gray, R., Owen, D.L. and Maunders, K. (1991). Accountability, Corporate Social Reporting and the External Social Audits. *Advances in Public Interest Accounting*, 4, pp. 1–22

Gray, R., Walters, D., Bebbington, J. and Thompson, I. (1993). The Greening of Enterprise: An Exploration of the (Non) Role of Environmental Accounting and Environmental Accountants in Organisational Change, *University of New England Armidale Department of Accounting and Financial Management Working Papers*, 93–8, November

Gul, F.A.K., Andrew, B.H., and Teoh, H.Y. (1984). A Content Analytical Study of Corporate Social Responsibility Accounting Disclosures in a Sample of Australian Companies (1983), *Working Paper*, Wollongong: University of Wollongong

Guthrie, J.E. (1982). Social Accounting in Australia: Social Responsibility Disclosure in the Top 150 Listed Australian Companies 1980 Annual Reports. *Unpublished Masters Dissertation*, Perth: Western Australian Institute of Technology

Guthrie, J.E. and Mathews, M.R. (1985). Corporate Social Accounting in Australia. In L.E. Preston, ed. *Corporate Social Performance and Policy*, New York: JAI Press, pp. 251–277

Guthrie, J. and Parker, L.D. (1989). Corporate Social Reporting: A Rebuttal of Legitimacy Theory. *Accounting and Business Research*, 19, pp. 343–352

Guthrie, J. and Parker, L.D. (1990). Corporate Social Disclosure Practice: A Comparative International Analysis. *Advances in Public Interest Accounting*, 3, pp. 159–176

Harte, G. and Owen, D. (1991). Environmental Disclosure in the Annual Reports of British Companies: A Research Note. *Accounting Auditing and Accountability Journal*, 4, pp. 51–61

Harte, G. and Owen, D. (1992). Current Trends in the Reporting of Green Issues in the Annual Reports of United Kingdom Companies. In D. Owen, ed. *Green Reporting: Accountancy and the Challenge of the Nineties*, London: Chapman and Hall, pp. 166–200

Ing, B. (1992). Developing Green Reporting Systems: Some Practical Implications. In D. Owen, ed. *Green Reporting: Accountancy and the Challenge of the Nineties*, London: Chapman and Hall, pp. 265–293

Ingram, R.W. (1978). An Investigation of the Information Content of (Certain) Social Responsibility Disclosures. *Journal of Accounting Research*, 16, pp. 270–285

Kelly, G.J. (1979). Measurement of Selected Social Responsibility Disclosure Items in Australian Annual Reports and Their Relations to Temporal Changes Corporate Size and Industry, *Dissertation*, Armidale: University of New England

Laughlin, R.C. (1991). Environmental Disturbances and Organizational Transitions and Transformations: Some Alternative Models, *Organisation Studies*, 12, pp. 209–232

Laughlin, B. and Varangu, L.K. (1991). Accounting for Waste or Garbage Accounting: Some Thoughts from Non-accountants. *Accounting Auditing and Accountability Journal*, 4, pp. 43–50

Linowes, D.F. (1972). Socio-economic Accounting. *Journal of Accountancy*, pp. 37–42

Low, A.M., Koh, H.C. and Yeo, G.H.H. (1985). Corporate Social Responsibility and Reporting in Singapore – A Review. *Singapore Accountant*, 1, pp. 7–13

Lynn, M. (1992). A Note on Corporate Social Disclosure in Hong Kong. *British Accounting Review*, 24, pp. 105–110

Mahapatra, S. (1984). Investor Reaction to a Corporate Social Accounting *Journal of Business Finance and Accounting*, 11, pp. 29–40

Mathews, M.R. (1993). *Socially Responsible Accounting*. London: Chapman and Hall

Maunders, K.T. and Burritt, R.L. (1991). Accounting and Ecological Crisis. *Accounting Auditing and Accountability Journal*, 4, pp. 9–26

Ng, L.W. (1985). Social Responsibility Disclosures of Selected New Zealand Companies for 1981, 1982 and 1983. *Occasional Paper No. 54*, Palmerston North: Massey University Faculty of Business

Owen, D., ed. (1992). *Green Reporting: Accountancy and the Challenge of the Nineties*. London: Chapman and Hall

Pang, Y.H. (1982). Disclosures of Corporate Social Responsibility. *The Chartered Accountant in Australia*, 52, pp. 32–34

Parker, L.D. (1977). Accounting For Corporate Social Responsibility: The Task of Measurement. *The Chartered Accountant in Australia*, October 5–15

Parker, L.D. (1986). Polemical Themes in Social Accounting: A Scenario for Standard Setting. *Advances in Public Interest Accounting*, 1, pp. 67–93

Parker, L.D. (1991). External Social Accountability: Adventures in a Maleficent World *Advances in Public Interest Accounting*, 4, pp. 23–33

Parker, L.D. (1992). Social Accounting: The Grand Tour *British Accounting Association Summer School, Working Paper*, 1992

Parker, L.D., Ferris, K.R. and Otley, D.T. (1989). *Accounting for the Human Factor*. Sydney: Prentice Hall

Parker, L.D. and Guthrie, J. (1989). Corporate Social Reporting: A Rebuttal of Legitimacy Theory. *Accounting and Business Research*, 19, pp. 343–352

Parker, L.D. and Guthrie, J. (1990). Corporate Social Disclosure Practice: A Comparative International Analysis. *Advances in Public Interest Accounting*, 3, pp. 159–175

Patten, D.M. (1992). Intra-Industry Environmental Disclosures in Response to the Alaskan Oil Spill: A Note on Legitimacy Theory. *Accounting, Organizations and Society*, 17, pp. 471–475

Phua, K.K. (1993). Companies 'should disclose more info' on Social Impact of Activities. *Straits Times*, 10 July

Pizzolatto, A.B. and Zeringue II, C.A. (1993). Pacing Society's Demands for Environmental Protection: Management in Practice. *Journal of Business Ethics*, 12, pp. 441–447

Power, M. (1991). Auditing and Environmental Expertise: Between Protest and Professionalisation *Accounting Auditing and Accountability Journal*, 4, pp. 30–42

Puxty, A.G. (1986). Social Accounting as immanent Legitimation: A Critique of a Technicist Ideology. *Advances in Public Interest Accounting*, 1, pp. 95–112

Puxty, A.G. (1991). Social Accountability and Universal Pragmatics. *Advances in Public Interest Accounting*, 4, pp. 35–46

Roberts, C.B. (1991). Environmental Disclosures: A Note on Reporting Practices in Mainland Europe. *Accounting Auditing and Accountability Journal*, 4, pp. 62–71

Roberts, C. (1992). Environmental Disclosures in Corporate Annual Reports in Western Europe. In D. Owen, ed., *Green Reporting: Accountancy and the Challenge of the Nineties*, London: Chapman and Hall, pp. 139–165

Roberts, P., (1992). Business and the Environment: An Initial Review of the Recent Literature. *Business Strategy and the Environment*, 1, pp. 41–50

Robertson, J. (1977). Corporate Social Reporting by New Zealand Companies. *Occasional Paper* No. 17, Palmerston North: Massey University Department of Accounting and Finance

Rubenstein, D.B. (1990). There's No Accounting for the Exxon Valdez. *The CPA Journal* July, pp. 40–45

Sanyal, R.N. and Neves, J.S. (1991). The Valdez Principles: Implications for Corporate Social Responsibility. *Journal of Business Ethics*, 10, pp. 883–890

Schreuder, H. (1979). Corporate Social Reporting in the Federal Republic of Germany: An Overview. *Accounting, Organizations and Society*, 4, pp. 109–122

Shane, P.D. and Spicer, B.H. (1983). Market Response to Environmental Information Produced Outside the Firm. *The Accounting Review*, LVII, pp. 521–538

Shrivastava, P. and Scott, H.I. (1992). Corporate Self-Greenewal: Strategic Responses to Environmentalism. *Business Strategy and the Environment*, 1, pp. 9–21

Spicer, B.H. (1978). Accounting For Corporate Social Performance: Some Problems and Issues. *Journal of Contemporary Business*, pp. 151–170

Stevens, W.P. (1982). Market Reaction to Corporate Environmental Performance. *American Accounting Association Annual Conference*, San Diego

Tilt, C.A. (1994). The Influence of External Pressure Groups on Corporate Social Disclosure: Some Empirical Evidence. *Accounting Auditing and Accountability Journal*, 6, Forthcoming

Tinker, T., Neimark, M. and Lehman, C. (1991). Falling Down the Hole in the Middle of the Road: Political Quietism in Corporate Social Reporting. *Accounting Auditing and Accountability Journal*, 4, pp. 28–54

Trotman, K.T. (1979). Social Responsibility Disclosure by Australian Companies. *The Chartered Accountant in Australia*, 49, pp. 24–28

Trotman, K.T. and Bradley, G.W. (1981). Associations Between Social Responsibility Disclosure and Characteristics of Companies. *Accounting, Organizations and Society*, 6, pp. 355–362

Vance, S.C. (1975). Are Socially Responsible Corporations Good Investment Risks? *Management Review*, 64, pp. 18–24

Wicks, C. (1992). Business and the Environmental Movement In D. Owen, ed., *Green Reporting: Accountancy and the Challenge of the Nineties*, London: Chapman and Hall, pp. 102–106

Wilkes, A. (1992). BSE Briefing: The Business Implications of Future EC Environmental Policy *Business Strategy and the Environment*, 1, pp. 9–21

Yamagami, T. and Kokubu, K. (1991). A Note on Corporate Social Disclosure in Japan. *Accounting Auditing and Accountability Journal*, 4, pp. 32–39

Zéghal, D. and Ahmed, S.A. (1990). Comparison of Social Responsibility Information Disclosure Media Used By Canadian Firms. *Accounting Auditing and Accountability Journal*, 3, pp. 38–53

12 Consolidation Accounting: A Critical Review of the Relevant Statements of Accounting Standard in Singapore

Ng Eng Juan

12.1 INTRODUCTION

In Singapore, consolidation accounting is largely governed by four Statements of Accounting Standard (SAS). These are:

(1) SAS 20: *Accounting for the Effects of Changes in Foreign Exchange Rates*
(2) SAS 22: *Accounting for Business Combinations*
(3) SAS 26: *Consolidated Financial Statements and Accounting for Investments in Subsidiaries*
(4) SAS 27: *Accounting for Investments in Associates*

[SAS are issued by the Institute of Certified Public Accountants of Singapore (ICPAS) based on the International Accounting Standards (IAS) promulgated by the International Accounting Standards Committee (IASC). SAS 20, 22, 26 and 27 above are the Singapore equivalents of IAS 21, 22, 27 and 28 respectively.]

This chapter takes a critical look at the four SAS that govern consolidation accounting in Singapore. First, it reviews the provisions of

SAS 22 and SAS 26 for their consistency with consolidation theories; second, the provisions of SAS 27 are examined to discuss whether the cost-based equity or the pure equity method is required by SAS 27; and third, the provisions of SAS 20 are reviewed, particularly the methods used to translate financial statements of foreign subsidiary companies for inclusion into consolidated financial statements. Finally, this chapter examines two changes made recently in the revised IAS 22 *Business Combinations* in relation to consolidation accounting.

12.2   SAS 22 AND SAS 26: CONSISTENCY WITH CONSOLIDATION THEORIES

There are two theories underlying the preparation and presentation of consolidated financial statements: the parent company theory and entity theory. The main difference between the two theories lies in the underlying focus of reporting and, consequently, the interpretation and treatment of minority interest.

The **parent company theory** is based on the proprietary concept where the parent company owns the subsidiary. As owner, the parent company has control over the subsidiary's net assets and operations, while the minority interest does not. Thus, consolidated financial statements should be prepared and presented from the viewpoint of parent company shareholders. Under this theory, the minority interest is treated as outsider; it is therefore reported as a liability in the consolidated balance sheet and as an expense in the consolidated profit and loss account. The procedures under the parent company theory have evolved over a number of years from practice (Kam, 1986).[1]

The **entity theory**, on the other hand, was developed by Professor Maurice Moonitz and published by the American Accounting Association in 1944 in *The Entity Theory of Consolidated Statements*. In developing the entity theory for consolidated financial statements, Moonitz (1944) proceeded on the basis that 'consolidated statements are best fitted to reflect. . . the affairs of an entity composed of a group of closely affiliated companies'. The entity theory is thus based on the view that the consolidated financial statements should reflect the viewpoint of the economic entity in respect of all the companies in the group. No distinction is made between majority

---

[1] A derivative of the parent company theory is the **proprietary theory**, which views the business entity as an extension of its proprietor. When applied to consolidation, the proprietary theory results in 'proportionate consolidation'. It is, however, obvious that SAS 26 requires full consolidation instead of proportionate consolidation. SAS 26 specifically provides that 'the financial statements of the parent and its subsidiaries are combined on a line by line basis by adding together like items of assets, liabilities, equity, income and expenses' (para. 13). Thus, the proprietary theory of consolidation is not advocated in the standards.

and minority shareholders. The minority interest is therefore reported as part of shareholders' equity in the consolidated balance sheet and as a distribution in the consolidated profit and loss account.

Both the above two theories are based on the issue of what should be the focus of reporting for consolidated financial statements, to which Ma *et al* (1991) commented that 'there are no non-arbitrary criteria for choice'. Official pronouncements in the United States and the United Kingdom do not favour one over the other. Each of the two theories also has its fair share of criticisms, as discussed later in this chapter.

It is important to understand which of the two consolidation theories underlies the accounting standards. This knowledge will facilitate a better understanding of the provisions of the accounting standards. This knowledge is also useful so that the underlying theory could be applied to situations/transactions where the standards are silent, so as to achieve certain amount of consistency in practice. Accounting standards, by necessity, set out only the broad guidelines governing measurement and disclosure issues. It is impossible for any accounting standard to spell out the rationale underlying its provisions and the detailed treatments for all probable transactions. This is especially true for a complex topic like consolidation accounting. Thus, it is important to note the consolidation theory underlying the accounting standards so as to better understand the provisions therein and to have a consistent basis for inference.

12.2.1 Focus of reporting

Under the parent company theory, consolidated financial statements should be prepared and presented from the viewpoint of the shareholders of the holding company. Under the entity theory, consolidated financial statements are to be prepared and presented from the viewpoint of all companies in a group.

Accounting standards do not expressly state the focus of reporting. SAS 26, however, does allude to the purpose of consolidated financial statements as 'presenting financial information about the group as that of a single enterprise without regard for the legal boundaries of the separate legal entities' to meet the needs of 'users of financial statements of a parent' (para. 7). Thus, on the one hand, SAS 26 requires consolidated financial statements to present the financial information of a group as that of a single entity (consistent with the entity theory), and on the other hand, it also requires the consolidated financial statements to meet the needs of the parent company's financial statement users (in line with the parent company theory).

[This approach to consolidated financial reporting is not just confined to Singapore. In the United States, Accounting Research Bulletin No. 51 has a similar purpose statement:

'the purpose of consolidated statements is to present, primarily for the benefit of the shareholders and creditors of the parent company, the results of operations and financial position of a parent company and its subsidiaries essentially as if the group were a single company with one or more branches or divisions.'

Beams (1992) has commented that 'this appears to be a compromise between the parent company theory and the entity theory'.]

12.2.2 Presentation of minority interest

Under full consolidation, 100% of the net assets of the subsidiary are taken into the consolidated balance sheet irrespective of the extent of holding company's interest. Similarly, 100% of the profits of the subsidiary are also taken into the consolidated profit and loss account irrespective of the extent of holding company's interest. This being the case, the portion of the net assets and profits of the subsidiary that are not attributable to the holding company would have to be separately presented in the consolidated accounts as minority interest. The issue here is how the minority interest should be presented in the consolidated accounts.

Under the parent company theory, the interest of minority shareholders in the net assets of the subsidiary companies is presented in the consolidated balance sheet as a liability, and their interest in the operating results of subsidiary companies is presented in the consolidated profit and loss statements as an expense. Under the entity theory, all the shareholders of all the companies in the group are deemed to be equity shareholders. Minority interest in the net assets of the subsidiary companies is presented in the consolidated balance sheet as shareholders' equity in the same way that majority shareholders' interest is presented. Similarly, minority interest in the operating results of subsidiary companies is presented in the consolidated profit and loss account as a distribution.

SAS 26 requires minority interest in the net assets of subsidiary companies to be presented in the consolidated balance sheet 'separately from liabilities and the parent shareholders' equity' (para. 33). Thus, under SAS 26, the presentation of minority interest in consolidated balance sheet is neither consistent with the parent company theory (which requires minority interest to be presented as a liability), nor with the entity theory (which requires minority interest to be presented as part of shareholders' equity).

As for minority interest in the net income of subsidiary companies, SAS 26 provides that it should be separately presented in the consolidated profit and loss account (para. 33) and more specifically, 'adjusted against the income of the group in order to arrive at the net income attributable to the owners of the parent' (para. 13). Thus, under SAS 26, the presentation of minority interest in the net income of subsidiary companies in the consolidated profit and loss account is not consistent with the parent company theory (which requires minority interest to be presented as an expense); neither is it consistent with the entity theory (which requires the minority interest to be presented as a distribution).

12.2.3 Measurement bases for minority interest

There are two measurement bases for minority interest that arise immediately after a business combination: pre-acquisition carrying amounts of the net assets of the subsidiary company, and post-acquisition fair values of the net assets of the subsidiary company.

Under the parent company theory, minority interest in the consolidated balance sheet at the date of acquisition is measured based on **pre-acquisition carrying amounts** of the net assets of the subsidiary company. In this case, the subsidiary's assets and liabilities are consolidated at their book values, plus the parent company's share of any excess of fair value over their book value. In other words, subsidiary assets and liabilities are revalued only to the extent acquired by the parent. The minority interest in the subsidiary's assets and liabilities is consolidated at book value. While this approach reflects the cost principle, it leads to inconsistent treatment of majority-minority interests in the consolidated financial statements, and to a balance sheet valuation that reflects neither historical cost nor fair value.

Under the entity theory, minority interest in the consolidated balance sheet at the date of acquisition is measured based on **post-acquisition fair values** of the net assets of the subsidiary company. In this case, the subsidiary's assets and liabilities are consolidated at their fair values. The majority and minority interests in those assets and liabilities are valued consistently. But this consistent treatment is obtained through a questionable practice of imputing a total subsidiary valuation on the basis of the price paid by the parent company for its majority interest. On a conceptual basis, this valuation approach has considerable appeal when the parent company acquires essentially all of the subsidiary's issued share capital for cash. It has much less appeal when the parent company acquires a slim majority of the subsidiary's issued share capital.

SAS 22 provides that a minority interest that arises on a business combination should preferably be stated at the appropriate proportion of the 'post-acquisition fair values of the net identifiable assets of the subsidiary'. Alternatively, it may be stated at the appropriate proportion of the 'pre-acquisition carrying amounts of the net assets of the subsidiary' (para. 45).

It should be noted that SAS 22 limits the use of the post-acquisition fair values basis to identifiable net assets only. Thus, if the preferred treatment (post-acquisition fair value of net identifiable assets of subsidiary) is adopted, the consolidated financial statements will be based on a mixture of both parent company theory and entity theory. All the identifiable assets and liabilities of the subsidiary will be brought into the consolidated financial statements at full fair value (entity theory), whereas goodwill on consolidation, being a non-identifiable asset, will be valued based on the amount paid by the parent company only; minority shareholders' shares are not accounted for (parent company theory). On the other hand, if the pre-acquisition carrying amounts basis is used, the consolidated financial statements will be consistent with the parent company theory.

12.2.4 Unrealized intercompany profits and losses

In consolidation, intercompany profits and losses that are deemed to be unrealized have to be eliminated. This raises the issue of to what extent the unrealized intercompany profits and losses should be eliminated.

Under the parent company theory where minority shareholders are deemed to be outsiders, that portion of the intercompany profits and losses relating to minority interest should be considered as realized. Thus, only the parent's share of the intercompany profits and losses is deemed to be unrealized and eliminated. Under the entity theory, minority shareholders are deemed to be part of the shareholders. Thus, 100% of the intercompany profits and losses are considered unrealized and should therefore be eliminated.

SAS 26 requires that unrealized profits and losses resulting from intra-group transactions are to be 'eliminated in full' (para. 13(b)). Thus, as far as the elimination of unrealized intercompany profits and losses is concerned, the provision in SAS 26 is consistent with the entity theory. However, the standard is silent on how the unrealized profits and losses are to be eliminated. Should they be eliminated against group profits alone or between group profits and minority interest proportionately? In his survey of the accounting practices among Singapore companies on this issue, Ng (1993) reports that different accounting policies are used. This diversity in practice could be attributed to the absence of specific guidance from accounting standards and the absence of a consistent underlying consolidation theory.

12.2.5 Practical implications

The above analysis reveals that the existing consolidation accounting standards are based on a mixture of the parent company and the entity theories of consolidation. They do not appear to be based on any single underlying consolidation theory; rather, they appear to be formulated more for the purposes of justifying current practices. Thus, where the standards are silent, it is difficult to deduce what appropriate treatment should be applied. On the other hand, given the lack of internal consistency, there may not be any appropriate treatment. Guidance on the acceptable treatment may be sought by referring to generally accepted principles in practice. In this respect, further empirical research in Singapore consolidation accounting practices may be warranted.

It may not be advisable to recommend that the standards should consistently adopt a single consolidation theory, given the drawbacks of both the theories. Ideally, the standards should strive to achieve consistency with the theoretical framework and the concepts of financial statements as promulgated in Singapore's Recommended Accounting Practice (RAP) 1A. Also, full disclosure on the accounting policies used, especially for those transactions where the standards do not provide specific treatment, may assist users in analyzing financial statements.

12.3   SAS 27: COST-BASED EQUITY OR PURE EQUITY METHOD

SAS 27 governs accounting for investments in associates. It requires the use of the equity method to account for investments in associates in consolidated financial statements. Generally, there are two variations to equity accounting: the cost-based equity method and the pure equity method.

The issue of interest is whether SAS 27 requires the use of the cost-based equity method or the pure equity method of equity accounting.

Before the provisions of SAS 27 are analyzed, it may be appropriate to discuss the major differences between the two methods of equity accounting.

The major difference between the two is in the carrying amount of the 'investment in associated company' account. Under the **cost-based equity method**, the investment account balance at any point in time is equal to the cost of acquisition plus the investor's share of the post-acquisition retained profits of the associated company. The resultant carrying amount of the investment account cannot be interpreted, being a hybrid figure made up of cost and equity adjustments, and thus neither reflects the historical cost nor measures the underlying worth of the investment. To overcome this shortcoming, the pure equity method is advocated.

Under the **pure equity method**, the investment account balance would always be equal to the investor's proportionate interest in the net assets of the associated company.[2]

---

[2] The terms used for the two methods are very appropriate. Under the first method, the investment account balance is carried at cost plus equity adjustments, thus the term cost-based equity. Under the second method, the investment account balance ignores the cost figure, but always reflects the investor's equity interest in the underlying net assets of the investee, thus the term pure equity.

In terms of accounting entries, there are two major differences between the cost-based equity method and pure equity method:

(1) Treatment of the difference between the cost of acquisition and the investor's share of the fair values of the net identifiable assets (referred to as goodwill). At the date of acquisition, the entire cost of acquisition will be debited to the investment account under the cost-based equity method. However, under the pure equity method, only the investor's share of the fair values of the net identifiable assets of the associated company is debited to the investment account; the goodwill element is accounted for separately. For example, assume that A Ltd acquires 30% of B Ltd for a cash consideration of $40,000 when the fair value of B Ltd's net identifiable assets is $100,000. Under the cost-based equity, the journal entry required is debit Investment $40,000 and credit Cash $40,000. Under the pure equity method, the journal entry required is debit Investment $30,000 (30% × $100,000) and goodwill $10,000 ($40,000 − $30,000), and credit Cash $40,000.

(2) Revaluation of the associated company's assets. In this regard, the investment account under the pure equity method will have to be debited for the investor's proportionate share of the increase in the value of the associate's assets (revaluation surplus). However, no accounting entry is required under the cost-based equity method. Thus, where the associated company's assets are revalued, the investment account under the pure equity method would also be increased so as to be carried at an amount that is reflective of the investor's proportionate interest in the associated company's net assets. Under the cost-based equity method, the investment account would continue to be carried at cost (plus equity adjustments), unaffected by the revaluation exercise of the associated company.

The provisions of SAS 27 are now analyzed to examine whether the cost-based equity method or the pure equity method is intended.

In the definitions section of SAS 27, the equity method is defined as 'a method of accounting whereby the investment is initially recorded at cost and adjusted thereafter for the post acquisition change in the investor's share of the net assets of the investee' (para. 2). There is no mention of the treatment for goodwill and revaluation. However, it states that the investment is initially recorded at cost, which by definition includes the goodwill element. Therefore, it appears that as far as this part of the definition is concerned, the cost-based equity method is intended. However, the other portion of the definition that requires adjustment for post acquisition change (which may be defined to include revaluation) in the net assets of the investee seems to favour the pure equity method. Thus, even in the definitions section of SAS 27 is unclear whether the cost-based equity method or pure equity method applies.

Paragraph 6 of SAS 27 provides that:

'the investment is initially recorded at cost... Adjustments to the carrying amount may also be necessary ... for changes in the investee's equity... arising from the revaluation... and from the adjustment of differences arising on business combinations.'

Clearly the provision for adjustment to the carrying amount of the investment account for the revaluation of the investee's assets is consistent with the pure equity method. However, the adjustment to the carrying amount of the investment account for 'the adjustment of differences arising on business combination' requires the use of the cost-based equity method. This is because adjusting the investment account for 'the adjustment of differences arising on business combination' (which is either the amortisation of goodwill or the write-off of goodwill) implies that goodwill has to be initially accounted for in the investment account. (If goodwill were to be initially accounted for separately, then the goodwill account rather than the investment account will be subsequently adjusted for the 'adjustment of difference arising on business combination'.) It thus appears that para. 6 also gives a mixed indication as to whether the cost-based equity method or pure equity method should be used under SAS 27.

Paragraph 14 of SAS 27 provides that:

'on acquisition of the investment any difference (whether positive or negative) between the cost of acquisition and the investor's share of the fair values of the identifiable assets of the associate is accounted for in accordance with Statement of Accounting Standard 22.'

As SAS 22 requires goodwill be accounted for separately, para. 14 appears to require the pure equity method to be used.

From the above analysis, it appears that SAS 27 does not provide a clear indication as to which method is to be used. In fact, it may be inferred that SAS 27 does not make a distinction, either intentionally or unintentionally, between the cost-based equity method and the pure equity method. This absence of clear direction may result in reduced comparability and readability of consolidated financial statements. It is, therefore, imperative that SAS 27 contain an expressed and unambiguous provision as to whether the cost-based equity or the pure equity method should be used to account for investment in associated companies in the consolidated financial statements.

12.4   SAS 20: TRANSLATION OF FOREIGN FINANCIAL STATEMENTS

SAS 20 deals with, among others, the translation of financial statements of foreign operations into the reporting currency of the parent company 'for the purpose of including them in the financial statements of the reporting enterprise' (para. 1). This covers the translation of the financial statements of foreign subsidiary and associated companies for preparing consolidated financial statements.

Under SAS 20, the method of translating financial statements of foreign subsidiary and associated companies is determined by an assessment of the operational and financial characteristics of those operations. For this purpose, SAS 20 classifies foreign subsidiary and associated companies into two categories:

(1) Foreign subsidiary and associated companies whose activities are an integral part of those of the parent company; and
(2) Foreign subsidiary and associated companies whose activities are not an integral part of those of the parent company (referred to as 'foreign entities').

SAS 20 requires the use of the **temporal method** in translating the financial statements of those foreign subsidiary and associated companies whose activities are an integral part of the parent company, and the use of the **closing rate method** in translating the financial statements of foreign entities. (Fundamentally, the provisions of SAS 20 of segregating foreign operations into 'integral' type and 'independent' type are similar to the concept of functional currency in FASB Statement No. 52). This section of the chapter examines the appropriateness of the provisions of SAS 20 in relation to translating the financial statements of foreign subsidiary and associated companies for purposes of consolidation.

Based on the concept of circumstantial differences (Jennings, 1964), SAS 20 should be commended for recognizing differences in foreign subsidiary and associated companies (integral versus foreign entity), and providing for different accounting methods, each associated with the different foreign subsidiary and associated companies. However, certain aspects of SAS 20 may be called into question.

The concept of foreign entity may not be consistent with consolidation concepts. Consolidated financial statements are prepared for companies under a common control. Conceptually, control and independence are not compatible. Thus, it is difficult to imagine situations where a company that is under the control of the parent company can be independent from the operations of the parent. It must also be the exception rather than the norm that a parent company that has control over a foreign operation would only be interested in the net investment instead of the composition of the assets and liabilities of the foreign operation.

SAS 20 justifies the use of closing rate method as follows:

'to preserve as far as possible the results and the interrelationships of amounts appearing in the foreign financial statements (because) these results and interrelationships are regarded as providing the most meaningful indicator of the performance and financial position of the foreign operations for inclusion in the consolidated financial statements' (para. 17).

It may, however, be argued that 'preserving the results and the interrelationships of amounts appearing in the foreign financial statements' is inconsistent with consolidation concepts. In consolidation, no distinction is made for transactions entered into by individual companies in the group; all the transactions of subsidiaries are deemed to have been entered into by the parent company itself. Thus, preserving the results and the interrelationships of amounts appearing in the foreign financial statements contradicts the principles of consolidation. Preserving the results and interrelationships of the amounts appearing in the foreign financial statements may be desirable if the translation is for purposes of comparing financial statements of local and foreign companies for investment decisions, but definitely not for the purposes of consolidation.

Another comment about the closing rate method as provided in SAS 20 is that para. 32 provides that balance sheet items (except shareholders' equity) are to be translated at the closing rate, whereas the income statement items may be translated either at the closing rate or at historical rates (or average rate). However, in order to preserve the interrelationships (which is the underlying rationale for using the closing rate method), it is obvious that all the items (in the income statement and in the balance sheet) must be translated at the same rate (the closing rate). For example, if the various items in the income statement are translated at various historical rates, the interrelationships of income statement items (such as profit margins) will not be preserved. Also, it is clear that if the income statement items are translated at the various historical rates (or average rate) and the balance sheet items are translated at the closing rate, then interrelationships like the rate of return on assets in the foreign currency financial statements would not be preserved in the translated financial statements. It is only when all the items in the financial statements are translated at a single rate (closing rate) that the interrelationships are preserved.

Thus, para. 32 of SAS 20, under which the balance sheet items are to be translated using the closing rate and the profit and loss items are to be translated using either the closing rate or the historic rates, would not achieve results that are consistent with the underlying rationale for using the closing rate method. (Some accountants argue that profit and loss account items should, because of their incurrance over the whole reporting period, be translated using the average rate. However, this may be refuted on the ground that the same line of argument would require some balance sheet items (for example, machinery) which were acquired throughout the reporting period to be translated using the average rate, which is not in compliance with the provisions of SAS 20).

The concept of integral foreign subsidiary and associated companies and the required use of the temporal method to translate financial statements, on the other hand, is in line with consolidation concepts.

Generally, in translating financial statements of foreign subsidiaries and associated companies to incorporate individual items into the parent company's financial statements, it is appropriate to achieve the same effect as if all transactions of the foreign subsidiary and associated companies had been entered into by the parent company itself. The temporal method will give the above effect, and is therefore consistent with consolidation principles.

However, the accounting consequences of translation under the temporal method may not be consistent with the underlying economic consequences. To illustrate this, assume that S Ltd (a company incorporated in Singapore whose currency is S$) acquired 100% interest in F Ltd (a company incorporated in a foreign country whose currency is F$) on 31 December 19 × 1. The balance sheet of F Ltd as at 31 December 19 × 1 is as shown in Table 12.1 (see next page). Assume that F Ltd has not entered into any transactions for the next two years and also that the exchange rate has moved from F$1 = S$2 on 31 December 19 × 1, to F$1 = S$3 on 31 December 19 × 2, and to F$1 = S$1 on 31 December 19 × 3. The translated balance sheets under the temporal method of F Ltd as at 31 December 19 × 2 and 31 December 19 × 3 are shown in Tables 12.2 and 12.3 respectively.

It may be noted that as at 31 December 19 × 2, when the F$ becomes stronger *vis-à-vis* the S$, S Ltd is deemed to have made a good investment in that it benefits economically from a stronger F$. However, as Table 12.2 demonstrates, the accounting consequences of translation under the temporal method shows that there is an exchange loss (which will on consolidation be charged against the consolidated profit and loss account). On the other hand, as at 31 December 19 × 3, when the F$ becomes weaker *vis-à-vis* the S$, S Ltd suffers economically arising from its investment in F Ltd. However in Table 12.3, the accounting consequences of translation under the temporal method shows that there is an exchange gain (which will on consolidation be credited to the consolidated profit and loss account).

Tables 12.4 and 12.5 (see next page) demonstrate that under the closing rate method, the accounting consequences of translation is consistent with the underlying economic consequences of a change in exchange rates.

Thus, the accounting consequences of translation under the temporal method is inconsistent with the underlying economic consequences of a change in exchange rates.

Given the deficiency of both the closing rate and temporal methods, two fundamental questions have been raised in accounting literature.

- Whether the exchange rate is the correct basis of the translation process. Patz (1977) has proposed the use of a **Purchasing Power Parity Index** (PPPI), defined as the purchasing power of the domestic currency divided by the purchasing power of the foreign currency.

Table 12.1   Balance Sheet of F Ltd as at 31 December 19 × 1

Share capital	F$100	Land	F$200
Bank loan	F$100		

Table 12.2   Translated Balance Sheet of F Ltd as at 31 December 19 × 2
(Temporal method)

Share capital	S$200	Land	S$400
Loss	S$(100)		
Bank loan	S$300		

Table 12.3   Translated Balance Sheet of F Ltd as at 31 December 19 × 3
(As above)

Share capital	S$200	Land	S$400
Gain	S$100		
Bank loan	S$100		

Table 12.4   Translated Balance Sheet of F Ltd as at 31 December 19 × 2
(Closing Rate Method)

Share capital	S$200	Land	S$600
Gain	S$100		
Bank loan	S$300		

Table 12.5   Translated Balance Sheet of F Ltd as at 31 December 19 × 3
(As above)

Share capital	S$200	Land	S$200
Loss	S$(100)		
Bank loan	S$100		

Patz maintained that 'the objective of a firm is the maximization of command over goods and services locally, not maximization of command over domestic currency. Consequently, the focus of reporting should be this local command over goods and services'. For the moment, however, the use of PPPI in translation remains a completely theoretical issue. If the use of PPPI were to become acceptable, attention would need to be given to the practical problem of constructing objective and accurate indices. [In this respect, it is noteworthy that in 1993, the International Monetary Fund (IMF) has adopted purchasing power parity instead of the traditionally used exchange rate as the basis of comparing the per capital income of different countries.]

- Whether the financial statements of foreign subsidiary companies should be consolidated into the group accounts. For example, Mathews and Perera (1991) contend that there are grounds for serious doubts about the benefits of consolidated financial statements in an international context, owing to confusion about their purpose and the significant aggregation problems involved. In their survey of international practices, Nobes and Parker (1991) report that it was the practice in many European countries (such as Germany) for financial statements of foreign subsidiaries to be excluded from the consolidated financial statements.

12.5 SAS 22: AMENDMENTS IN THE REVISED IAS 22

The IASC has issued the revised IAS 22 which supersedes the existing IAS 22 (on which SAS 22 is based) in December 1993. Two amendments are of interest to the issues raised in this chapter and are discussed below.

12.5.1 Measurement basis for minority interests

SAS 22 provides for two alternative bases for measuring minority interest in the consolidated balance sheet immediately following a business combination namely (a) 'pre-acquisition carrying amounts' of the net assets of the subsidiary, and (b) 'post-acquisition fair values' of the net identifiable assets of the subsidiary (paragraph 45). While SAS 22 states its preference for the 'post-acquisition fair value basis', the revised IAS 22 adopts the 'pre-acquisition carrying amounts' basis as the benchmark treatment.

It is interesting to examine why there is a change of preference in the IASC standards.

The choice of the measurement bases centres around the argument of whether the net assets of the subsidiary should be reported in the consolidated accounts at their respective fair values imputed by extrapolating the price which the parent company has paid for its proportionate interest.

- Under the **pre-acquisition carrying amounts basis**, the subsidiary's assets and liabilities will each be measured on a hybrid basis (parent company's portion at current fair value and minority's portion at historic carrying amount), and the minority interest will be measured based on the pre-acquisition carrying amounts of the subsidiary's net assets.
- Under the **post-acquisition fair values basis**, the subsidiary's assets and liabilities will be stated at their respective imputed fair values

and the minority interest will be credited for its share of the fair values and measured based on the post-acquisition fair values of the subsidiary's net assets.

Thus, the main rationale for measuring minority interest based on the pre-acquisition carrying amounts is historical cost convention. Proponents of this basis argue that the post-acquisition fair values basis is not in compliance with historical cost convention. They also argue that the minority's proportion of the net assets has not been acquired by the parent company, and therefore, it is inappropriate to impute the fair value thereon. On the other hand, the post-acquisition fair values basis is justified on the ground of fair value reporting. The proponents of this basis argue that it is consistent with the purchase method of accounting for business combinations (see SAS 22) and with the economic entity concept of consolidation adopted in SAS 26. It is also argued that measuring minority interest on the pre-acquisition carrying amounts basis will result in the same asset being measured on a hybrid basis.

The change of preference in the IASC standard to the pre-acquisition carrying amounts basis was justified on the ground that 'current world practice favours this approach because it is argued that it accords more closely with the historical cost basis of accounting' (para. 179 of Exposure Draft or E32). The emphasis that IASC places on historical cost convention in its choice of the pre-acquisition carrying amounts as the benchmark treatment may reflect the influence of historical cost purists in its standard-setting process. Nevertheless, it is noted, as discussed above, that the post-acquisition fair values basis is more consistent with the overall framework of consolidation accounting adopted in the IASC standards.

12.5.2 Accounting for negative goodwill

SAS 22 provides for two alternative accounting methods for negative goodwill, namely **recognition in income method** and **immediate write-off method** (para. 40). Under the recognition in income method, SAS 22 further provides for two alternative treatments: treatment as deferred income with systematic amortization, and allocation over individual depreciable non-monetary assets acquired in proportion to their fair values (para. 42).

The revised IAS 22 provides for a benchmark treatment under which any negative goodwill is allocated over individual non-monetary assets acquired in proportion to their fair values. It should be noted that the benchmark treatment of 'allocation over individual non-monetary assets acquired' as provided in the revised IAS 22 is not conceptually the same as the 'allocation over individual depreciable non-monetary assets acquired' treatment as provided in SAS 22 (even though the two treatments are differentiated only by the word 'depreciable').

- The **allocation over individual depreciable non-monetary assets acquired treatment** is based on the rationale of recognizing the negative goodwill in income. It is one of the two recognition in income methods provided in SAS 22. It may be appreciated that both the recognition in income methods provided in SAS 22 (treatment as deferred income with systematic amortization and allocation over individual depreciable non-monetary assets acquired) have the same income effect.
- On the other hand, the allocation over **individual non-monetary assets acquired** method of the revised IAS 22 is not consistent with the recognition in income method of SAS 22. For example, if one of the assets acquired is land (which is non-depreciable), then after the allocation under the benchmark treatment of revised IAS 22, a portion of the initial negative goodwill (which has been allocated to land) will never be credited to income, unless and until the land is sold.

The rationale for using the allocation over individual non-monetary assets method is, as stated in E32, 'in order to determine their historical costs' (para. 172). Thus, the adoption of allocation over individual non-monetary assets method in the revised IAS 22 has changed the underlying rationale for accounting for negative goodwill from 'recognition in income' to 'historical cost convention'.

12.6 CONCLUSION

Upon analysing the four SAS that govern consolidation accounting in Singapore, the following observations may be made:

(1) The provisions of SAS 22 and SAS 26 are not consistent with any underlying consolidation theory: certain provisions of the standards are based on the parent company theory while others are based on the entity theory. The absence of interconsistency in the underlying theory may cause inconsistency in practice. However, until and unless the debate over the two consolidation theories is settled, it may be unwise to suggest any recommendations to make the standards more interconsistent. A more practical suggestion at this juncture would be to call for more disclosure; specifically, full disclosure should be made of the accounting policy adopted for transactions for which the standards do not provide specific guidelines (for example, the measurement basis for minority interests). In this respect, further research should be carried out to

ascertain what additional information need to be disclosed in aiding users in their analysis of consolidated financial statements.

(2) On the issue of whether the cost-based equity or the pure equity method is required by SAS 27, an examination of the provisions reveals that SAS 27 does not provide a clear indication. In fact, it may be inferred that SAS 27 does not make a distinction, either intentionally or unintentionally, between the cost-based equity method and pure equity method. For the sake of comparability of financial statements, it is recommended that SAS 27 should expressly and unambiguously state whether the cost-based equity or the pure equity method is to be used. Before the choice is made, however, further research on the merits of each method may be warranted.

(3) On the translation methods used to translate financial statements of foreign subsidiary companies for ultimate inclusion into consolidated financial statements under SAS 20, there are serious deficiencies in both the closing rate method and temporal method. To overcome these problems, more thought should be given to two questions raised in the accounting literature: whether exchange rates should be used as the basis of translation, and more fundamentally, whether the financial statements of foreign subsidiaries should be translated and consolidated. Given the differences in the economic environment, there is avenue for further research into these two questions in the Asian context.

(4) Finally, of the two changes made recently in the revised IAS 22 (namely, the measurement basis for minority interest and accounting for negative goodwill), it is interesting to note that in both these two amendments, the historical cost convention appears to reign supreme.

REFERENCES

American Institute of Certified Public Accountants (1959). *Consolidated Financial Statements* (Accounting Research Bulletin No. 51). New York: AICPA

Beams, F.A. (1992). *Advanced Accounting* 5th ed. New Jersey: Prentice Hall

Chambers, R.J. (1968). Consolidated Statements Are Not Really Necessary. *The Australian Accountant*, February 1968

Financial Accounting Standards Board (1981). *Foreign Currency Translation* (FASB Statement No. 52). Stamford: FASB

Institute of Certified Public Accountants of Singapore (1990). *Framework for the Preparation and Presentation of Financial Statements* (RAP 1A), Singapore: ICPAS

Institute of Certified Public Accountants of Singapore (1986). *Accounting for the Effects of Changes in Foreign Exchange Rates* (SAS 20). Singapore: ICPAS

Institute of Certified Public Accountants of Singapore (1987). *Accounting for Business Combinations* (SAS 22). Singapore: ICPAS

Institute of Certified Public Accountants of Singapore (1990). *Consolidated Financial Statements and Accounting for Investments in Subsidiaries* (SAS 26). Singapore: ICPAS

Institute of Certified Public Accountants of Singapore (1991). *Accounting for Investments in Associates* (SAS 27). Singapore: ICPAS

International Accounting Standards Committee (1989). Exposure Draft 32 Comparability of Financial Statements (E32). London: IASC

International Accounting Standards Committee (1993). *Business Combinations* (Revised IAS 22). London: IASC

Jennings, A.R. (1964). Opinions of the Accounting Principles Board. *Journal of Accountancy*, August 1964

Kam, V. (1986). *Accounting Theory*. New York: Wiley

Ma, R., Parker, R.H. and Whittred, G. (1991). *Consolidation Accounting* Melbourne: Longman Cheshire

Mathews, M.R. and Perera, M.H.B. (1991). *Accounting Theory and Development*. Melbourne: Thomas Nelson

Moonitz, M. (1944). *The Entity Theory of Consolidated Statements* New York: Foundation Press

Ng, E.J. (1993). Minority Interest in Consolidated Financial Statements: Measurement Issues. *Singapore Accountants*, October/November 1993

Nobes, C. and Parker, R. (1991). *Comparative International Accounting*. New York: Prentice Hall

Patz, D. (1977). A Price Parity Theory of Translation. *Accounting and Business Research*, Winter 1977

Rosenfield, P. and Rubin, S. (1985). *Consolidation, Translation, and the Equity Method*. New York: John Wiley

Rosenfield, P. and Rubin, S. (1986). Minority Interests: Opposing Views, *Journal of Accountancy*, March 1986

13 Depreciation Accounting: A Historical Perspective

Richard Low Siew Siang

13.1 INTRODUCTION

Of the many terms and concepts which have puzzled students in Accounting, the most perplexing is most probably **depreciation**. This concept appeared in the accounting literature as early as 1588 in an English text *A Briefe Instruction* by John Mellis and was referred to as 'lost by decay' of household implements. However, over the next four centuries, it has metamorphosed into something quite unrecognizable by even Mellis himself. Over the years and at different periods in time, depreciation has meant different things to different people. Even to this day this chameleon-like term has continued to provoke debate as to what it really means. It has not been difficult to find the problems relating to depreciation in the accounting literature. Even in Singapore we have not been spared from the haunt of this creature, and as late as August 1992, there was an article in the *Singapore Accountant* entitled *The Case for Not Depreciating Certain Fixed Assets: A Relook at the Depreciation Issues*. There are textbooks still available where the authors had claimed erroneously that in certain situations, depreciation could be a source of funds. For instance, '. . . depreciation . . . is a flow of funds under the working capital concept, being a release of services from fixed assets. . .' (Han, 1982, p. 103).

The confusion caused by this term could have been lessened and perhaps even eliminated if a better understanding of the metamorphosis of this concept were achieved, and more importantly, of the underlying circumstances resulting in the changes. This approach, in my opinion, would be superior to that of compromising in the mistaken belief that by treating the problem as one of definition (as is typical of Hendriksen's (1977) approach to accounting theory), the problems relating to depreciation could be avoided. This definitional approach (especially an incomplete one) has also been adopted by the Institute of Certified Public Accountants of Singapore (ICPAS). This has culminated in the adoption of the Statement of Accounting Standard (SAS) on depreciation (para. 2 and para. 13 of SAS 4 (1991), adapted from the International Accounting Standards (IAS) 4) which defines depreciation as follows:

> 'Depreciation is the allocation of the depreciable amount of an asset over its estimated useful life. Depreciation for the accounting period is charged to income either directly [as period expense] or indirectly [as expensed product cost].'
> 'The depreciable amount of a depreciable asset should be allocated on a systematic basis to each accounting period during the useful life of the asset.'

It would appear that the SAS has opted for an arbitrary method of depreciation so long as it is consistently applied (interpreted by most accounting bodies, which had adopted or adapted the IAS, as being preferably the straight line method). This definition does not explain what depreciation should be. Instead, it merely attempts to estimate, or more precisely, to account for a depreciation amount. This has been called depreciation accounting. Such an incomplete definition fails to define or explain the essence of depreciation. Rather than resolving the confusion, it has helped to create even more confusion.

The recognition of depreciation has become necessary only because of the need for periodic income determination of entities having an indefinite economic life. Depreciation would need to be recouped before profits can be determined. For any venture with a limited (or short) life span, the gains can easily be determined at the end of the venture after disposing off the remaining non-cash assets. In such situations, there would be no need to recognize depreciation.

Depreciation in its complete sense has two facets, that is, recoupment and consumption. Recoupment is the recovery of the shortfall, resulting from the difference between the outlay and the salvage value, if any, over the asset's useful life. The reasons for the need to recover could be to maintain adequate capital for operational effectiveness (that is, capacity), or efficiency, or to maintain the financial capital or merely to replace the asset. The reasons for the shortfall, which is due to a decline in value, could be because of consumption resulting in a loss in service potential or price changes.

This chapter attempts to achieve a better understanding of depreciation through a review of the historical development of the nature of depreciation. The next section reviews the nature and the various meanings that depreciation has taken on over time evolving into what it is today. The third section examines the different methods which have been developed to account for depreciation and concludes with a recommendation of a choice method. The fourth section discusses the criticisms that are often levelled against accounting for depreciation based on a cost allocation method, while the arguments in the defence of such criticisms are presented in the last section. We conclude the chapter with a summary of the findings from the review.

13.2   HISTORICAL DEVELOPMENT OF THE NATURE OF DEPRECIATION

Under the historical cost context, the objective of accounting information is to assist in the evaluation of the stewardship function, which is the accountability of the managers to the owners on what funds and the manner in which they are utilized.

The nature of depreciation over the years has taken on different meanings, such as the following:

(1) Decline in value
(2) Loss in service potential
(3) A charge necessary to maintain capital
(4) Annuity or provision charges over a period of time to create a replacement fund
(5) Provision charges to create a reserve
(6) Allocation of costs
(7) Recoupment of capital outlay

13.2.1   Decline in value

Depreciation can be defined as a reduction in price or value. According to May (1915, p. 149) the causes for this decline could have arisen from:

(1) Fall in value due entirely to external conditions and not caused in any way by age or change in conditions of use of the property (that is, price changes),
(2) Exhaustion through age or wear of the property, or
(3) Obsolescence or being superceded by superior types or methods.

Depreciation when defined as purely a decline in value could be determined by the difference in the valuations or values of the asset over different periods. As such, it would be possible to use market prices provided that comparable assets were available and the price changes were not temporary fluctuations. This would also mean that depreciation could be applied to determine the value of the asset. If valuation of the asset or property were the objective, then this approach to ascertaining depreciation would be most appropriate. However, if the objective of depreciation were to ascertain a charge out of earnings before the true operating profit could be determined, then the valuation of the asset would be irrelevant. Most of the developments relating to the nature of depreciation have been inclined towards this objective.

13.2.2 Depreciation as a loss in service potential

As early as Mellis' *A Briefe Instruction* in 1588 (Littleton, 1988, p. 223), depreciation was regarded in a number of bookkeeping texts from an economic point of view. This means that since all things were subjected to the ravages of time, there would be a fall in value due to wear and tear. The 'lost by decay' of household stuff would be charged to the profit and loss account (John Fleming, *Bookkeeping by Double Entry*, Littleton, 1988, p. 226). Depreciation was recognized in the earlier periods as a loss rather than as an expense.

Other examples (Littleton, 1988, pp. 223–241) where depreciation was treated as a decline in value due to wear and tear are as follows:

- In 1675, Stephen Monteage published *Debtor and Creditor Made Easie* where 'Horses impaired by a year's use' was charged to the Loss and Gain Account (that is, the profit and loss account).
- In 1801, *Book-keeping in the True Italian Form* by William Jackson supported this meaning of depreciation. This was evidenced by his explanation for a credit entry to reduce the asset value and charge to profit and loss which was 'for wearing, age etc'.The balance was called present value.
- By 1861, in *Bookkeeping* by W. Inglish, the term 'depreciation' was actually used. Depreciation was charged to trade expenses (not as a loss) with 'a yearly deduction of 5 and 10% requires to be made from original cost, to allow for deterioration or wear and tear' for accounts such as buildings and machinery.

This definiton of depreciation in its economic sense was adopted by the Interstate Commerce Commission in the United States when it defined depreciation as 'the lessening in cost value due to the smaller number of service units in the property than as found in the same property new'. This definition has been interpreted to include not only wear and tear but obsolescence as well, and in our present day parlance, as loss in service potential.

The Committee on Concepts and Standards of the American Accounting Association endorsed this definition in 1957 when it recommended that 'any decline in the service potential of plants and other long term assets should be recognized in the accounts in the periods in which such decline occurs'. It further suggested that the 'service potential may decline because of . . . gradual or abrupt physical deterioration, consumption of service potential through use even though no physical change is apparent or economic deterioration because of obsolescence or change in consumer demand'.

The assumption underlying depreciation as loss in service potential is that the initial cost representing the value of a storehouse of services can be released over the life of the asset. The advantage of this meaning of depreciation is that although the depreciation is based on the original investment which is static in nature, yet it recognizes that the loss in service potential may be irregular. This irregularity might not have been forseen at the time the asset was acquired.

13.2.3   Depreciation as a charge necessary to maintain capital

The development of the railways with their very capital intensive nature and the need to distribute profits resulted in encouraging a better understanding of depreciation. The *American Railroad Journal* in 1841 reproduced an article from *The English Railway Magazine* suggesting a better conception of the relationship between depreciation and net income. According to Littleton (1988, p. 227):

> '. . . emphasis is given to the necessity for carefully and periodically ascertaining the precise comparative degree of wear and tear so that only *bona fide* net income will be apportioned to the shareholders. In calculating the profit really available for distribution, it was stated that current expense should include the whole expenditure in every shape and not merely expenses paid . . . so that future proprietors are not left responsible for any portion of the expenditure which has been in fact incurred and exhausted in earning the present apparent dividend. And again the object should be to avoid heaping an unusually large expenditure on particular periods for wear and tear going on gradually during a whole series of years.'

Although this view of depreciation was still basically an incorporation of the earlier economic concept of decline in value due to wear and tear, what was new is the extension to the determination of the distributable profits. Profits must be accounted for in such a way that future proprietors were not left to bear past incurred expenses and this would mean that profits should be determined only after capital had been maintained. Thus, depreciation (expenditure in every shape and not merely expenses paid) was a charge necessary to maintain capital.

There were situations where fixed assets were valued and the declines in values were recognized as expenses. Some of these valuations were done annually such as that of the annual valuation done by the Grand Junction Railroad which was reported in 1841 (Littleton, 1988, p. 228). Other valuations were done less frequently like that of the Boston and Providence where an estimate of the present value of the cars and engines was made and the accumulated depreciation for the previous 10 years was 'charged . . . to income account and . . . deducted the same from the cost of construction' (Littleton, 1988, p. 230).

Other methods used to maintain the capital were extremely conservative. These included not recognizing the yet-to-be consumed service potential of fixed assets and charging them to current expenditures on acquisition, as in the case of the Liverpool and Manchester Railroad (reported in 1841) (Littleton, 1988, p. 228) where new engines were charged to current expenditures.

Depreciation based on capital maintenance is a broader concept than that of a loss in service potential. This concept is that income would result only if the invested capital at the end of a period exceeds that at the beginning of the period provided capital transactions and dividends are excluded. Capital maintenance is, however, an ambiguous term since the capital to be maintained can be interpreted in the following ways:

(1) Original monetary investment as in the AICPA definition in APB Statement No. 4 *Basic Concepts and Accounting Underlying Financial Statements of Business Enterprises* (1970).
(2) Service potential or equivalent in terms of the original cost of services as in the AAA Committee of Concepts and Standards (1957).
(3) Operating capacity or physical capital, that is, current replacement cost as in the 1963 AAA Committee of Concepts and Standards where depreciation was defined as the expiration of service potential of the asset but must be based on the current cost of restoring the service potential consumed during the period.
(4) Purchasing power of the capital.
(5) Replacement costs based on that necessary to ensure an equivalent level of efficiency in operations.

Since capital can mean anything from original monetary investment to operating capacity at current replacement costs, the concept of capital maintenance is so flexible that it permits the recognition of changes in the value of the dollar and the changes in the specific replacement prices. It also allows the recognition of the original monetary investment to be the capital to be maintained. This concept, however, has its disadvantage. Unless other additional criteria are introduced, it would result in a failure to permit a separation of operating income from extraordinary gains and losses. This is because so long as capital is maintained, the reasons for the excess, whether from non-operating or from extraordinary (such as holding) sources, cannot be differentiated.

13.2.4   Depreciation as annuity or provision charges over a period of time to create a replacement fund

This idea of a replacement fund was conceived in the 19th century. Early in that century, railway companies had begun to report the creation of such replacement funds. A replacement fund was perhaps a natural progression from the recognition of a decline in value and the desire to maintain capital by making good the assets when they had ultimately expired.

Examples of replacement funds (Littleton, 1988, p. 228) include the creation of:

(1) Depreciation fund by setting aside for repairs an annual percentage over and above the ordinary charge (reported by London and Birmingham Railway).
(2) Annual provisions for asset renewal by calculating an annuity for 12 years which would accumulate to the necessary total (reported by Baltimore and Ohio).
(3) An annuity to pay interest on first cost of certain baggage cars and to replace the principal at the end of five years (reported by Columbia and Philadelphia).

This historical link between depreciation and replacement fund appears to have resulted in a misunderstanding that depreciation is a source of funds. This misconception was further reinforced when depreciation was regarded as a charge to create a reserve.

13.2.5   Depreciation as a charge to create a reserve

From the provision for replacement, depreciation evolved into the concept of storing away in times of prosperity. In 1843, Charles Elliot Jr. in the *American Railroad Journal* (Littleton, 1988, p. 231) wrote that 'companies . . . making money' should have 'a contingent fund to prepare them for a contingency which as surely reach them as the next year' and that 'the money that is earned at the expense of the rails, cars and machinery should be hoarded to replace those things'. He recommended that 'every company should annually store away in times of property and should their profits not permit that reservation', then investors should avoid investing in those shares.

13.2.6   Depreciation as allocation of costs

Seen in the light of the confusion over the nature of depreciation, especially during the tumultuous railway era, a compromise was inevitable. By the 20th century the compromise was evident when the AICPA's

Committee of Terminology defined 'Depreciation Accounting as a system of accounting which aims to distribute the cost or other basic value of tangible capital assets less salvage (if any) over the estimated life of the unit (which may be a group of assets) in a systematic and rational manner. It is a process of allocation, not of valuation . . .'.

This definition related to depreciation accounting but in time depreciation itself took on this definition. Today, the most commonly accepted definition of depreciation which has been enshrined in the International Accounting Standards (the SAS 4 in Singapore) is very similar to the AICPA's definition above.

This concept of depreciation as an allocation of costs is not without its shortcomings. It is a static concept where the initial cost or other value is not changed during the life of the asset and the sum of all depreciation charges should be equal to the initial value less any salvage value. Another shortcoming of this definition is its failure to define what is meant by 'systematic and rational'. However, current practice has been to accept the straight line method which is an equal allocation of costs over the life of the asset as the preferred method.

Sprouse and Moonitz in AICPA's Accounting Research Study No. 3 suggested that replacement cost would be a more appropriate basis than historical cost because depreciation based on current replacement cost allows a better matching of current costs against current revenues. This would then result in a current net operation concept of income, and gains and losses arising from holding of assets due to current input value changes could be accounted for separately. This would also mean a better evaluation of the relative efficiency of current operations. Nevertheless, the problems of allocation would still be present. There was also the problem of determining the current values of assets when comparable assets were not available. This was further compounded by changes in the purchasing power of money. Technological changes could make the current value of the assets less valuable even though their replacement costs might have increased.

In the United Kingdom, attempts have been made (for example, SSAP 16) to allow changes in the value to be allocated by incorporating current replacement cost. However, this applies only to supplementary accounts and not to the audited annual report. The intention was probably for current replacement cost to ultimately replace historical cost. However, by the mid 1980s, the new contender, current replacement cost, had lost out. This method would have been less static than the original cost concept.

13.2.7 Depreciation as recoupment of capital

Before profits can be determined for distribution, the capital should be maintained (that is, excluding any capital transactions during the period) which means that any decline in values should be recouped from revenues.

Perry Mason in *Illustrations of the Early Treatment of Depreciation* commented as follows:

'It would be difficult to believe however that the fundamental facts of depreciation – the exhaustion of capital investment due to physical or functional exhaustion of service capacity and the necessity of recovering capital investment before any profit on a venture could be claimed – have not always been understood'.

The dual concept of depreciation with consumption and recoupment of capital outlay was understood early, for Littleton (1988, pp. 236–237) quoted from Edwin Guthrie's 1883 lectures as follows:

'Because the profit of manufacturing is the difference in value of that which is consumed and the value of that which is produced, it is important to ascertain accurately the value or cost of that which is consumed. The values consumable within the period, he indicated, are raw materials, stores, direct labour and outside services, and those consumable over a number of years are machinery and buildings. The object of this accounting for values consumed is stated as the recoupment of capital outlay'.

From the discussion above, it can be seen that in depreciation, there is a need to provide for the consumption of assets and the recoupment of capital outlay before profits can be determined. If the fall in value due to consumption of assets can be determined, the necessary recoupment will be a simple recognition of this fall in value. However, the fall in value due to consumption is not easy and often impossible to determine since the market value, whether entry value or exit value, is the result of interactions between demand and supply. This implies that the fall in value is not only a reflection of the consumption of the service potential. This is to say that the consumed value cannot be independently determined. Therefore, any attempt to determine a value for recoupment (that is, the depreciation) based on an estimate of the fall in value due to consumption may be impractical and any recoupment must by necessity be done through allocation of some value over the life of the asset.

If one were to accept that the amount of depreciation includes the price changes and not merely the consumption of the service potential (that is, the all inclusive concept referred to by May) then this would mean that the decline in market value would need to be ascertained. However, market values are not always easily obtainable, even when comparable assets are available. It is also not economically feasible to conduct periodic revaluations of assets. Furthermore, price changes can be temporary. Until the price changes have become sufficiently permanent, such changes should not be recognized. As such, the development of depreciation accounting and even the concept of depreciation itself must naturally be based on recoupment of capital outlay.

Having defined depreciation as the recoupment over the life of the asset so as to maintain capital, the question of what should be the capital to be maintained will determine the amount that should be recouped. The capital outlay of the asset can mean:

(1) The original outlay adjusted or unadjusted for changes in purchasing power
(2) The replacement value of the asset to maintain its operating effectiveness (or capacity)
(3) The replacement value of the asset to maintain its operating efficiency
(4) The net realizable value of the asset to maintain the purchasing power of the firm

The concept of capital maintenance to ensure operating effectiveness has long been rejected because of the inequitable consequences that could result. This is evidenced in the railway situations where although the trains could still run without adequate improvements, the profitability of the lines fell over the years. This resulted in the earlier shareholders receiving more than their fair share of the profits at the expense of the later shareholders. If replacement values of the assets had been adopted, the inequity of this concept might have been minimized. The problems of determining the replacement values, especially where no comparable assets were available, have been the main factor discouraging the general acceptance of this concept. The difficulties associated with changes in purchasing power and the problems of ascertaining the net realizable values have made these concepts just as unpopular.

Under a strict interpretation of the historical cost concept, the cost of an asset to be recouped can only mean its original outlay. This is also advocated in practice, not only because of the implementation problems of other concepts of capital, but also because of the simplicity of this concept. At one time, the idea of adjusting for changes in purchasing power (Current Purchasing Power concept) was in vogue and was then the recommended practice in the United Kingdom under PSSAP-7. This concept has since fallen out of favour.

Financial reporting has always been constrained by the laws pertaining to business operations. These laws, especially company law, developed from the era of the business venture. Ventures were originally set up to achieve certain short term goals and would end with the completion of these goals. At the end of each venture, all the proceeds would be distributed to the venture partners. Profits could also have been ascertained. An example of a venture would be sending a ship equipped with merchandise to the East and returning with other goods from the East to be resold. Once the goods from the East were resold, the remaining proceeds after deducting the costs incurred for operating the ship would be distributed. In such situations, there would be no necessity to ascertain profits or gains. However, should there be a wish to do so, there would be no need to differentiate operating profits from holding gains.

There could be situations where the partners might have decided to continue with new undertakings and not distribute the assets. The capital of each new undertaking would be the partners' share of the value of the assets at the end of the last undertaking. This would mean that the new capital would be the previous capital increased by the additional gains or reduced by the losses. This would require the entire assets of the venture to be revalued. A new venture is deemed to have started and new goals to be undertaken under new conditions. Under such conditions, revaluations would be done to ascertain the new capital and there would be no need to account for depreciation.

With the advent of businesses having an indefinite life, this has resulted in complexities in accounting for the consumption of the service potential of long life assets. The ventures of old have acquired an indefinite life resulting in each venture comprising a series of one-year ventures. Dividends which are to be paid out of profits with the on-going venture will mean that these profits will have to be ascertained.

As long as the venture is on-going, the determination of profits must be done on a regular basis. This means that wear and tear, deterioration and obsolescence of assets will have occurred, and should be recouped before the profits can be ascertained at the end of each one-year venture. The recoupment is to ensure that the original capital will be maintained.

An illustration of the effects of recouping the original costs of the assets in the following example (say on an equal basis) will explain the rationale for the development of company laws.

Example

A company invested $1,000 in a fixed asset from the capital raised. The asset is expected to have a five-year life span. The company is expected to earn $500 before depreciation charges per year. Funds derived from the firm's operations would be reinvested in assets with a five-year life span.

Year 1
Net profits = $500 - $200 = $300

Balance sheet

	$		$
Capital	1000	F.A.(X0)	800
Profits(X1)	300	F.A.(X1)	500
	1300		1300

Year 2

Net profits = $500 - $300 = $200

Balance sheet

	$		$
Capital	1000	F.A.(X0)	600
Profits(X1)	300	F.A.(X1)	400
Profits(X2)	200	F.A.(X2)	500
	1500		1500

From the illustration above, it can be seen that even if the profits were distributed, the original capital would still be maintained. The profits were associated with each year or each one-year venture. This would be similarly applied to losses.

The above illustration also helps to explain the law in relation to capital and the distribution of profits. The law permits the distribution out of profits from any year (that is, any one-year venture) although there may still be unrecouped losses from other years. This is in keeping with the interpretation that losses from ventures had in essence been charged against the opening or previous capital. Similarly, any profits represent the gains resulting from the excess over the opening or previous capital.

On the exceptional occasions where revaluations are done on the long life assets, the resulting gains (losses) would be the profits (losses) of the venture. The gain or loss could have been the consequence of price change or the incorrect estimate of the life or salvage value of the asset. Such an unrealized gain or loss would be subject to a degree of uncertainty greater than if the asset had been disposed off. Thus, it would appear reasonable that the unrealized gains should be differentiated from other realized gains or profits and the remaining unrealized gains would lose this special status once realized. However, losses would be deemed as realized even before disposal, by virtue of the principle of conservatism. The result of a revaluation should be that the assets would then assume the new values like the situation of the valuation or revaluation of such long life assets in a venture that was completed but the assets were used to start a new one.

From the above, it would appear that the laws on ventures have been incorporated into the present day company laws. The definition of capital as prescribed by the Company's Act includes issued capital. This definition is consistent with other sections in the Act which attempt to safeguard creditors from a reduction in capital resulting from events other than a loss from operations. The Act disallows even repayment of the premium on preference shares unless it is from unappropriated profits or from the share premium account. It is thus understandable that in compliance with the definition of capital and also to avoid the problems associated with capital based on other concepts of maintenance, the definition (of what is to be recouped) adopted by the Singapore accounting standards is based on the original capital outlay.

Due to the impracticality of determining the consumption or fall in value of an asset, depreciation can only be treated as recoupment. Thus, we can say that *depreciation is the recoupment of capital from revenue. It is a charge against revenue (like any other expense) in order to ascertain any excess of revenues over expenses and the owners' entitlement to any distribution of the excess.*

13.3 METHODS OF DEPRECIATION

The historical development of depreciation reviewed in the earlier section reveals the fact that over time, different methods had been in use to account for depreciation. The objective of these methods appears to have been to achieve the perceived ends of reducing the net distributable profit so as to prevent excessive dividends rather than maintaining the operating capital.

The methods that had been used include the following:

(1) No accounting for depreciation
(2) Retirement method
(3) Inventory method
(4) Eclectic method, that is, based on the ability to bear
(5) Annuity and sinking fund methods
(6) Creation of depreciation as reserves
(7) Allocation on a variable charge method
(8) Allocation on a systematic basis (time-based) such as:
    (a) constant charge, that is, straight line basis
    (b) decreasing charge, that is, the decreasing balance methods and the sum of the years digits from the largest to the smallest
    (c) increasing charge, that is, sum of the years digits from the smallest to the largest.

13.3.1 No accounting for depreciation

In the early days, depreciation was ignored and the decline in value of the asset was recognized only at the time of disposal. In some ways, this was the simplest approach and was appropriate in accounting for ventures or where the amounts of fixed assets were insignificant.

13.3.2 Replacement or retirement method

Under the replacement or retirement method, depreciation was not directly accounted for. It was recognized that depreciation did occur due to wear and tear but it was unnecessary to account for it since the renewals and repairs were deemed to be adequate to maintain the standard operating effectiveness of the firm.

Lardner in *Railway Economics* in 1850 (Littleton, 1988, p. 228) stated that 'In rolling stocks the natural progress of repairs and renewals is such that no gradual deterioration exists which is not made good. As such nothing is lost and even old material is used in other equipment and never totally disappears from the road.'

Under the replacement method, repairs and renewals would be charged as current expenses. The accounts would then carry the original values of the assets. The Liverpool and Manchester Railroad (Littleton, 1988, p. 228) in the United Kingdom in the mid 19th century charged their new engines to current expenditure as an expense.

Even when railroad regulations in America became national in scope, the second annual report (a form of company report) of the Interstate Commerce Commission in the United States reported that renewals and repairs were classified as operating expenses with no mention of depreciation. Preference then was to charge renewals and repairs as expense unless the expenditures were obviously for an expansion of the total property where a new asset account would be created.

Therefore, under this method, depreciation would be accounted for but only when the asset was retired. The original costs of the asset would be capitalized and on retirement, the replacement costs less the salvage value of the retired asset would be charged to depreciation. The accounts would maintain the asset's value at the original cost indefinitely. The assumption underlying this method was that the renewals and repairs would be a good replacement for the loss due to wear and tear. In reality, this could only occur by sheer chance.

This method of depreciation was thought to be a sound way of dealing with depreciation because if all plants were kept 'in thorough repair' and in addition if an amount of money were set aside each year, this will in a number of years enable 'the purchase of an entirely new series of machines' (Littleton, 1988, p. 239).

This method also assumed that the retirement of assets would occur fairly constantly for each asset category, resulting in regular depreciation charges. This might be appropriate where the assets were of small value such as tools, and in the case of railroads and public utilities, for assets such as poles, telephones and ties.

The difference between this method and no accounting for depreciation was that at the time of an asset's renewal, the new (replacement) cost of the asset would be charged to the profit and loss account, usually as current expenditures, whereas in the latter method, the original cost was charged to the profit and loss account.

13.3.3   Inventory method – valuation

By the mid 19th century, a number of situations had arisen where a variety of fixed assets were treated like merchandise accounts. Examples of these assets include the following:

(1) *Real estate:*
    the real estate account was debited with purchase money, repairs, taxes, etc, and credited with rent, sales and the value of what remained unsold and the remainder in the account was treated as loss or gain on real estate (Fulton and Eastman in *A Practical System of Bookkeeping*, 1853, Littleton, 1988, p. 226).
(2) *Steamboat:*
    the account was debited with the costs and charges and credited with 'sale, freight or passage' (Fleming, J. in *Bookkeeping by Double Entry*, 1853, Littleton, 1988, p. 226).
(3) *Railway stocks and real estates:*
    these were grouped with stocks such as cotton so that profit or loss could be determined (Jones, T. in *Parodoxes of Debit and Credit Demolished*, 1859, Littleton, 1988, p. 226).

By 1861 (Inglish, W. in *Bookkeeping*, 1861, Littleton, 1988, p. 226), depreciation was recognized as an amount to allow for the deterioration or wear and tear of buildings and machinery. The idea of different treatments on assets for non-retail purposes (that is, those not for sale) and those for business use were better understood (Pilsen, J. in *Complete Reform in Bookkeeping*, 1877, Littleton, 1988, p. 226).

Authors such as Matheson (1986) have suggested that the most effective method is to revalue all assets at stated intervals. However, there were doubts as to the feasibility of such a practice. The fall in value of an asset was deemed to be due only to wear and tear or the loss due to deterioration. Where assets of small values were involved, this method might be appropriate since allocation of small costs would be impractical. The problem with valuation, however, was the subjectivity involved, and should the market or liquidation value be available for use, it would inadvertently incorporate a value other than that which was due only to wear and tear or loss due to deterioration. A valuation method to derive the depreciation of the period would result in the balance sheet approach to income. This combines the operating expenses (that is, the depreciation due to wear and tear which was from operations) with the non-operating gains and losses (that is, the holding gains and losses due to price fluctuations). Such a method would not result in a systematic assignment of service cost or value to the periods.

Another objection to this method from the historical cost perspective is that market valuation would be a violation of the historical cost concept.

13.3.4   Eclectic method or ability to bear

In late 19th century, it was suggested that a fixed proportion of profits could be used to provide for the depreciation. However, even Matheson (1986) is of the opinion that such practices are unsound as deterioration would still go on even when no profit is earned.

The ability to bear method inadvertently results in businesses failing to consistently apply a fixed proportion of profits to depreciation. Instead, the depreciation charged would be based only partly on the profits earned. Matheson (1986) himself suggests that high rates of depreciation should be charged in the years of full operation to make up for the idle years where little or no profits would be earned. Garcke and Fells (1986) are also of the opinion that the norm of the day (that is, the 19th century) was for the amount of depreciation to be varied according to the conditions of the firms' businesses.

13.3.5   Annuity and sinking fund methods

The distinction between the annuity and the sinking fund methods is in the type of secondary assets that are involved. Secondary assets refer to those assets acquired from funds not distributed. This could be because of the reduced profits as a result of the deduction of the depreciation charge. The sinking fund method usually implies that external investments such as bonds would be set aside to create a sinking fund, whereas for the annuity method, no sinking fund would be created. Besides this difference, the two methods are the same in principle.

When these methods are used, an annual depreciation charge consisting of an annuity would be made. This annuity would theoretically be invested at an assumed interest rate so that the sum of the annuities and the interest accumulated over the life of the asset would be sufficient to recover the depreciated cost. Such a method was applied in the Baltimore and Ohio Report of 1883 (Littleton, 1988, p. 230) which provided for the tie renewals by calculating an annuity for 12 years which would in their opinion accumulate to the total of the cost.

In the Columbia and Philadelphia (Littleton, 1988, p. 230) case an annuity was charged to pay interest and to replace the principal at the end of five years. A modification of this method was that instead of providing adequate funds to recover the original cost of the asset, provision was made for the replacement cost of the new asset.

A problem with this method was that with fast technological changes, the new assets acquired could be very different from those they were to replace. Even if the replacement costs of the previous assets had been accounted for, they could still be insufficient to replace the assets concerned. On the other hand, the advantage of this method is that for businesses which were subjected to revenue controls by governments (such as in the public utilities in certain countries), they would be able to earn a constant rate of return on their total investment.

This approach of creating a sinking fund may have been responsible for the confusion that depreciation is a source of funds. In fact, this method in substance is similar to the concept where depreciation is seen as a means to create reserves.

13.3.6   Depreciation as reserves

Depreciation has not always been treated or understood as an allocation of cost or a provision for wear and tear. At times, it has been treated as a 'contingency which will surely reach in time' and as such, it is best to 'store away in times of prosperity' by formation of a contingency fund (an article by Charles Jnr Elliot in the *American Railway Journal* (1843), Littleton, 1988, p. 231). Thus, depreciation has at times been treated, not as an expense but as a reserve.

Charles Elliot (1843) recommended that:

'It can be shown that every company should annually store away, in times of prosperity, while their work is new, at least 6 cents for every mile travelled by their engines, 1 cent for every ton conveyed by 1 mile, and 200 dollars for every mile of road, to replace decayed materials, and injured iron and machinery. If their profits will not permit that reservation, then the prudent man will avoid their stock . . .'.

This perhaps had led to the mistaken idea at one time, and even as late as the 1970s, by some people that depreciation was or could be a source of funds. Even to this day, there are those who argue that it can be a source of funds, especially if depreciation were charged to manufacturing overheads which would then be allocated to inventory. This erroneous conclusion can be attributed to the fact that as the allocated overhead appears to have caused an increase in stock values, that is, an application of funds, depreciation which was part of the overheads must then have been the source. A better understanding of accounting for stocks would have clearly explained where the source of funds had arisen from. Stocks would have been valued at the lower of cost or market because the principle of conservatism has dictated that when stocks are to be valued, the realizable value of the stocks should be at least as high as if not greater than their cost. When goods were processed, the value of these goods would appreciate as their realizable value was deemed to have increased by at least the direct material costs and the conversion costs which would include the overheads. Therefore, the increase in the value of the stocks arose because of an increase in the realizable value and not the incurrence of overheads *per se*. The source of funds that had resulted in the increase in the stock value arose from an increase in the realizable value of the stocks. This would be similar to any other recognized gains from assets held resulting from an increase in the asset's value.

13.3.7   Allocation of cost as a variable charge

Once it is understood that depreciation is an allocation of the cost of the asset, the next problem is to decide the basis of allocation. Some actually opted for a policy based primarily on the ability to bear and provided depreciation based on whatever they felt they could afford.

Another method was to link the depreciation to the units of production or consumption based on the assumption that the service potential consumed, and thus the revenue produced, were related. This method would require that the total quantum of services be reasonably estimated and the value of the assets be in proportion to its remaining service potential. In other words, the assets' values would decline as a function of use rather than due to the passage of time. Obsolescence should also not be an important factor in the determination of the asset's life. Even the revenues as well as the costs of repairs and maintenance should be proportional to use.

13.3.8   Allocation of cost on a time-based systematic basis

Within this approach there are three main ways in which depreciation is treated as a charge against revenue: a constant charge, a decreasing charge and an increasing charge.

Constant charge

Among the various time-based systematic allocation methods for accounting of depreciation, the simplest is the **straight line method**. The depreciation charge in each period (year), D, is determined as follows:

$$D = \frac{1}{n}(C - S) \tag{1}$$

where C = original cost
       S = salvage value
and n = number of periods in the useful life

The effect of this method is an equal charge per period for the acquired asset during its useful life. The difference between the original cost and the accumulated depreciation is the net book value.

Assuming that the estimates of the salvage value and the life of the asset were correct, this method would still not yield a net book value which would reflect the market value at any time other than at the end of the asset's useful life.

This method could be justified if the discounted total future benefits were to decline as a function of time rather than of usage. It might also be acceptable if the revenues, the costs of repairs and maintenance as well as operating efficiency were relatively constant over the asset's useful life. Another applicable situation would be if the interest factor could be ignored or could possibly be offset by other factors.

Decreasing charge

There are at least three possible methods of treating depreciation as a decreasing charge, namely:

(1) Fixed percentage of the diminishing balance
(2) Double declining balance
(3) Sum of the digits

These methods would be appropriate for assets whose service potential declines more in the earlier periods or years and progressively less with time. Assets which are affected by fast technological changes would fall under this category. These methods could be justified where the assets would incur increasing repairs and maintenance costs or when the assets are expected to have a pattern of decreasing operating efficiency and revenues. High uncertainty of revenues in the later periods may also support such methods.

In the **fixed percentage of the diminishing balance method**, the declining net book value at the end of each period would be written down by a constant rate, r. This r, being a fraction of 1 (that is, a value between 0 and 1) is computed as follows:

$$S = C(1 - r)^n \tag{2}$$

where C = original cost
       S = salvage value
and n = number of periods in the useful life

The depreciation charges would be greater in the earlier periods and would decline with time. If S, the salvage value, were small and n, the life span, were short, then the first period's charge would tend to be relatively large. This would result in a very steep decline in the net book value of the asset. Under this method, the net book value at the end of the asset's useful life should approximate the net realizable value if the earlier estimates of useful life and salvage value were correct.

Another method which uses the fixed percentage is the **double declining balance method**. The rate that would be applied here is double that of the straight line method with the salvage value set at zero.

The rate, r, is calculated as follows:

$$r = 2 \times \frac{1}{n} \tag{3}$$

where n is greater than 2 (otherwise the method would not be applicable). The declining net book value in each period is reduced by this constant rate, r. The pattern of the depreciation charges, that is, progressively less with time, would be similar to that of the fixed percentage diminishing balance method. However, under this method, the net book value would approach but theoretically never reach zero.

The last of the previously mentioned three methods is the **sum of the digits method**. Under this method, the digits is the number of the periods (such as months or years). The resulting charges tend to be more gentle than the previous two methods.

A decreasing fraction, f, would be applied for each period. This fraction is computed for any period as follows:

$$f_i = \frac{N_i}{\sum_{j=1}^{n} j} \tag{4}$$

where N = the digit in the reverse order to the sequence of the periods
   i = the period of the depreciation charge
   j = the digit of each period
and n = number of periods in the useful life

Example

For a period of 4 years, f for each year is as follows:

$$Year\ 1 = \frac{4}{1 + 2 + 3 + 4} = \frac{4}{10} \tag{5}$$

$$Year\ 2 = \frac{3}{1 + 2 + 3 + 4} = \frac{3}{10} \tag{6}$$

$$Year\ 3 = \frac{2}{1 + 2 + 3 + 4} = \frac{2}{10} \tag{7}$$

$$Year\ 4 = \frac{1}{1 + 2 + 3 + 4} = \frac{1}{10} \tag{8}$$

The depreciation charge, D is:

$$D = (C - S)f_i \tag{9}$$

Increasing charge

Under this approach, the sum of digits method would be used in reverse. This would mean that the weightage for the earlier periods would be less, and thus, the depreciation charges for each period would increase progressively with time. The methods which are interest-based, such as the annuity method and the sinking fund method, would also have this similar effect of increasing depreciation charges.

Methods which would result in an increasing charge would only be appropriate for assets whose service potential or earning power and operating efficiency are expected to increase or where the future discounted benefits are expected to increase as a function of time. An example where this method could be applied is in the case of a hotel where earnings can be expected to increase with the hotel's rising reputation. The increasing charge methods may also be applied in situations where repairs and maintenance costs are expected to be constant or decreasing over the life of the asset.

The justifications for these approaches (that is, constant, decreasing or increasing charges) would only be acceptable if it is assumed that a relationship between depreciation and net revenue contributions exists.

13.3.9 The choice method

Since most financial accounting systems currently record only historical costs, it would be more cost effective to use information already available in the system. The use of additional information such as market values or replacement costs of assets should only be made when the additional benefits exceed the costs of acquiring the information. Even if it were feasible to obtain the market values, it might still be difficult to ascertain the portion that is due to price level changes and that which should be charged as depreciation (if it were interpreted as the consumption of service potential). Furthermore, since we live in a world of uncertainty, an accurate estimate of the fall in value of individual assets in every period would be impossible.

Given the costs of obtaining additional information not normally collected in the accounting system and uncertainty over the future, it would seem that the most economically feasible method of recouping capital outlay is to recoup the original cost equally over the asset's useful life. The basis of equal allocation is also supported in other disciplines such as in decision science, where under conditions of uncertainty, the use of equal likelihood is a well accepted approach. This method of recouping capital equally over time forms the basis for the straight line method of depreciation.

The nature of depreciation as implied in current practice has taken on the meaning of recoupment of capital outlay, deemphasizing depreciation as a fall in value due to loss in service potential. The loss could have been the result of wear and tear, deterioration or obsolescence. Accepting the fact that some loss in service potential would inadvertently have occurred by the end of the asset's useful life, the exact timing of the occurrence should be of less significance than that of the recoupment of the capital outlay.

If this interpretation of depreciation were accepted, then many if not all of the criticisms of depreciation as practised would not exist. These criticisms have been the consequences of imputing meanings to depreciation which were inappropriate for the commonly adopted measurement system, that is, historical cost.

13.4 PROBLEMS IN ACCOUNTING FOR DEPRECIATION

Accounting for depreciation as currently practised has often been criticized. These criticisms include the following:

- Depreciation is merely an allocation and as such it is arbitrary. The implication of this criticism is that if a method were unsupported by rationale but chosen at will, its results would be as good as that of any other method randomly chosen.
- The net book value, that is, the original outlay less the accumulated depreciation which had been charged off against revenues, would have no real meaning other than an arbitrarily derived amount which was unallocated.
- The effects of depreciation on the profit figures and the net book value would result in a return on assets called the book yield (Solomon, 1975) which may be different from the true yield. Moreover, the book yield using straight line depreciation for even a single asset would not be constant over the life of the asset (Hendriksen, 1970, p. 399).
- In special situations where assets are revalued, controversial treatments for depreciation may arise.
- In circumstances where the assets are expected to have a residual value greater than their original cost (such as in buildings), why should there be a need to depreciate?
- If recoupment is deemed to be the purpose of depreciation and since buildings are to be depreciated, then why should land not also be subject to depreciation?

13.5   DEFENCE AGAINST CRITICISMS

Based on the earlier review of the historical developments of the nature of depreciation, we have concluded that:

- Depreciation could result from a number of causes, such as wear and tear, deterioration, loss in service potential, obsolescence or just price changes.
- The consequence of depreciation is a reduction in value at the end of an asset's useful life.
- Due to the uncertainties that prevail, an estimate of the real fall in value at a point in time for every period would not be feasible as the estimate might be distorted by temporary market conditions.
- Given the assumption of going concern, there would only be a need to account for this expected fall in value in total over the asset's life.
- Under conditions of uncertainty, it is suggested that an expectation of equal outcomes would be an acceptable premise.
- Assuming that there is a need to recoup or depreciate, an equal amount in each period would be an acceptable approach. This implies that the straight line method would be the most appropriate.

Once the treatment for depreciation has been understood, the criticisms can be easily defended.

13.5.1   It was not an irrational method

Allocation does not necessarily have to be arbitrary if the choice were based on rational considerations. The choice of the straight line method for depreciation can be attributed to the uncertainties prevailing over the determination of the fall in values of the assets resulting from wear and tear. It follows then that the obvious rational choice would be to recoup the outlay that is expected to be lost during the asset's useful life.

13.5.2   The net book value, the unrecouped outlay

The **net book value** of an asset is the amount of the outlay not yet recouped. If the method were arbitrary and without rationale then the resultant net book value would have no useful meaning. However, since depreciation is meant as the recoupment of the capital outlay, the net book value would then represent the unrecouped amount.

13.5.3 Use of book yield justifiable

Given the uncertainties of the future, the use of book yield would be sufficient to satisfy the objective of the historical cost system. The book yield has often been termed the **Return on Net Investment** which is defined as follows:

$$\text{Return on investment} = \frac{\text{Net profit after depreciation}}{\text{Net book value}}$$

Undeniably, the book yield would not be the same as the **true yield** (or also known as the internal rate of return) in most situations, since the true yield must be based on cash flows whereas the book yield is based on accrual accounting.

True yield or internal rate of return (IRR) is derived from:

$$I = \sum_{i=1}^{n} \frac{X_i}{(1 + r)^i} \tag{10}$$

where I = initial cash outlay
X = net cash inflow
i = period of inflow
n = number of periods in the useful life
and r = internal rate of return (IRR)

The book yield may be significantly different from the true yield. However, the true yield can be ascertained only at the end of the project. Otherwise, the computation of the true yield would be but an estimated value based on expectations in a world of uncertainty. For a firm with an indefinite life, that is, a going concern, and with changing combinations of projects that may be interdependent or interrelated (each of which involving several different individual assets), the only means to accurately determine the true yield would usually be as late as the end of the firm's life, and not just the life of the asset. Thus, the true yield at any point in time before the end of the investment can never be determined with certainty. The uncertainties arise from the amount and the timing of the cash flows and the difficulty in relating the cash flows to an investment due to the synergistic effects amongst investments and even amongst assets within each investment. This estimation would be so riddled with uncertainties that any estimate would be of questionable usefulness. The book yield may then be the most feasible alternative as it can be objectively determined.

Since the objective of the historical cost accounting system is to satisfy the stewardship function, that is, accountability for the acquisitions, holdings and disposals of the entity's resources, the need for accountability would override the need to determine the yield.

An objectively determinable yield is particularly important, especially for enterprises that are subject to governmental controls over their returns. These controls over the rate of returns are accepted in exchange for the right to operate in businesses under special conditions, such as in a monopoly. Since the returns would be subject to control, they must be based on what has happened and not on what might happen. Therefore, the only uncertainty that could be allowed in the computation is the unrecouped portion of the outlay. If the decline in values in each period could be feasibly determined (that is, the benefits of obtaining this information exceed the costs), then it should obviously be accounted for directly in the computation of returns. Where this is not feasible, then there is a need to use an allocation such as the straight line method to recoup the outlay. Generally, the uncertainties present in the business environment would be such that an equal basis would be the most feasible.

In view of the above, it can be expected that government agencies would prefer the use of the book yield over a non-objective and unreliable estimate of the true yield. This is because it enables these agencies to control indirectly the prices of the services or products supplied by such enterprises. The above arguments apply equally to other enterprises in the performance of their stewardship function towards their shareholders.

It should be understood that the depreciation charged against profits is not intended to determine the true yield which is based on the cash flows over the life of the assets but to recoup the loss that is expected from the use of the assets by the end of their useful lives.

13.5.4 Revaluation controversies

Controversies over depreciation of assets which have been revalued have arisen because of the misunderstanding over the nature and purpose of depreciation. An asset is revalued when management is of the opinion that the prevailing circumstances have caused a non-temporary change to the value of the asset. Usually, upward revaluations are made only for long term assets when it is expected that the asset value is unlikely to fall below the book value during its remaining useful life, as in the case of freehold land. A revaluation exercise for such long term assets would imply that the capital of the firm has been changed due to significant changes in the asset values resulting from permanent changes in circumstances.

The UK Companies' Act (1980), prior to the 1980 amendments deemed that such gains from revaluation are unrealized and should not be distributed as dividends. On the other hand, any unrealized losses on revaluation done on only some assets should be recognized immediately. If the revaluation were done for all assets then the loss on an individual asset would be treated as unrealized. The Act also required that depreciation should be based on historical cost. The UK Companies Act (1981) amended this requirement to permit depreciation chargeable to profits to be calculated on the new values of the assets. However, it continues to allow the use of depreciation under the historical cost system.

The Singapore Companies Act is silent on the treatment of such revaluation. However, common law, as evident in cases such as *Dimbulla Valley (Ceylon) Tea Co Ltd.* v *Laurie, Bishop* v *Smyrna and Cassaba Railway Co*, and *Ammonia Soda Co Ltd.* v *Chamberlain* does not appear to disallow the distribution of such unrealized gains as dividends. This need not imply that such gains are not capital in nature, since all gains whether capital or revenue in nature, are all distributable so long as there is cash available for distribution. If the directors are of the opinion that such gains should not be distributed and wish to declare them as such, they can reclassify these gains to capital reserves. The view that the revaluation gains are capital in nature and can only be distributable in cash when these gains are realized is also recommended in the Singapore Accounting Standards, SAS 14. Paragraph 32 of SAS 14 allows the transfer of such gains to retained earnings (which are distributable in cash) only when the revalued asset has been disposed off, that is, when the gains have been realized.

Once assets have been revalued, the assets should assume the new values which would then replace the net book values. Any new value should then become the new capital outlay to be recouped over the remaining useful life of the asset and depreciation should be charged on an equal basis in accordance with the earlier arguments.

The approach described above results in a treatment similar to that of an asset at the end of a venture in earlier times. This is because when a revaluation has been carried out, the new book value is not a composition of the undepreciated or unrecouped old net book value plus the revaluation gains: the revalued amount represents the amount of the assets that should be recouped.

Authors such as Nobes (1985) recommend the use of a 'split' depreciation, one for the undepreciated original portion and another for the revaluation gains. The depreciation from the historical cost would be charged to the profit and loss account. The gains from the revaluation would also be subject to depreciation but they would be charged against the reserves created from such unrealized gains. Any unamortized unrealized gains in the reserves when the asset is finally disposed off would be brought to profits.

Nobes (1985)'s rationale for 'split' depreciation is that historical cost accounting usually ignores price changes until the assets are disposed off. When assets are revalued, the subsequent depreciation charges are also 'revalued'. This would affect the comparability of the profit figures across time and amongst firms. To facilitate comparability, he proposed the adoption of 'split' Depreciation.

Nobes (1985)'s rationale can be challenged since asset revaluations are done only as a result of significant changes in conditions affecting the firm. Therefore, comparing depreciation under historical cost, where it is assumed that there are no significant changes in conditions affecting the assets, is inappropriate. In fact, the problems of non-comparability do not exist.

The question as to how to treat the depreciation arising from a revaluation arises only because of a failure to understand the rationale for a revaluation. It was stated earlier that a revaluation is only done if and when there are circumstances leading to a permanent change in value of the assets. Once a revaluation has been carried out, the asset is stated as if it is a new asset. The revalued amount then represents the new capital outlay to be recouped over the remaining useful life of the asset.

13.5.5 Residual value higher than cost

There are occasions where the residual values of fixed assets exceed their costs. These costs can be the net book values or even the original costs of the assets. It is not unusual for such assets to have disposal values higher than their net book values but generally this would have been due to inaccurate estimates of the depreciation over the useful lives of these assets. It is also possible that in certain cases the residual value of a fixed asset may be even higher than the original cost. However, this would only arise if circumstances have changed significantly from that expected at the time of the acquisition.

If circumstances have changed so significantly that the residual value is higher than originally expected or even above the original cost, then the asset should be revalued once the change in value is likely to be permanent. A common example of such an occurrence is in the case of buildings.

Without significant changes in circumstances, market factors alone will not give rise to a situation where prices of buildings remain indefinitely higher than the original cost. This is partly because when a building is to be acquired, if it is known with certainty that the building will be sold off in the future at a price above original cost, then resources should be put into the purchase of buildings, as long as the profits are expected to be above the cost of financing. The resulting increase in demand will then lead to increases in prices until an equilibrium is reached where the expected future prices are less than their purchase costs.

Thus, there is still a need to account for depreciation on buildings because there is a possibility of a shortfall in value that has to be recouped at the end of the useful life of the building. Furthermore, buildings in themselves have a limited physical life span, and once uninhabitable, would have a negative value if demolition were to become necessary. Unlike land which has almost infinite life span, buildings cannot be owned for an unlimited period and when not sold or occupied they deteriorate rapidly, with their salvage values often falling to below zero.

Unless there are significant changes in circumstances from that expected at the time of acquisition of the fixed assets, the residual values of most fixed assets will be lower than their original costs. If the residual value of any asset is higher than the net book value at the time of disposal, this can only be due to an inaccurate estimate of the residual value. In fact, any material difference when anticipated should have been corrected during the life of the asset by revaluation or by re-evaluating the amount of depreciation to be charged per period. This in essence would concur with our definition of depreciation as recoupment of the shortfall resulting from the decline in value of the capital outlay.

13.5.6 Rationale for not depreciating land

Since the objective of depreciation is to recoup the fall in the value of an asset over its useful life, there must be a fall in value between the time of acquisition and the end of the asset's useful life. The fall in value must be significant enough in comparison with its useful life.

In the case of land, it is highly likely that its disposal value would be higher than original cost if held sufficiently long, since land generally has a useful life long enough to meet this expectation. However, land should not be depreciated because of its infinite useful life, and not so much because of the possible appreciation of its value in the future.

Two reasons why land should not be depreciated are as follows:

(1) There will be no shortfall in value in the long term. However, in the case of mining land, a fall in value is highly probable and should be depreciated accordingly.
(2) As the useful life of land is very long (almost infinite) the amount to be depreciated per period will be insignificant. In the case of leasehold property with a remaining short lease term, depreciation is required as the amount to be recouped each period would be material enough.

Buildings, on the other hand, have a limited physical life and a possibly shorter economic life, as evidenced by the number of buildings being demolished and rebuilt or extensively refurbished. Therefore, buildings should be depreciated.

13.6 CONCLUSION

Historical developments in accounting and business laws have been mainly responsible for present day accounting practices. Thus, an analysis of these developments would provide a better understanding of accounting practices such as depreciation.

The nature of depreciation has assumed a number of different forms over different time periods and even during the same periods. Depreciation has been interpreted in various ways including the following:

(1) The all inclusive decline in value from any cause
(2) A loss in the service potential from wear and tear, deterioration or obsolescence
(3) Charges to:
    (a) maintain capital,
    (b) create a replacement fund, or
    (c) create a reserve

Due to prevailing uncertainties in the business world, depreciation was defined as an allocation of costs. This present day definition of depreciation can perhaps be attributed to the emphasis on the methods used to account for depreciation or depreciation accounting, and this could have accounted for the two terms often being used interchangeably.

Depreciation as a decline in value has been entwined with the concept of depreciation as the recoupment of capital outlay. Over time, 'recoupment' had overshadowed the 'decline in value'. Business prudence has dictated that the accounting for depreciation should emphasize recoupment to avoid inappropriate distribution of profits.

Available methods of depreciation have been diverse and many. Depreciation was determined through valuation or by making a provision. Such provisions were based on time, interest or consumption. The most obvious and direct method is to ascertain the decline in value due to consumption or loss in service potential. However, due to market forces resulting in price changes that bear no relation to the loss in service potential, it would be impractical if not impossible to ascertain this decline in value.

Economic realities and the uncertainties in the business world have resulted in the recoupment of capital outlay being achieved through an allocation of the asset's cost on an equal basis. Given the state of uncertainty, an equal likelihood assumption would be justifiable. It should also be appreciated that although the asset's cost has been allocated to ascertain the amount to be charged to depreciation each period, the amount itself allocated is not the depreciation but merely a means to recoup the asset's cost.

If it were feasible to ascertain the decline in value due to depreciation with a reasonable degree of accuracy, then the amount to be recouped should be the decline in value. Methods adopted should serve the intended objective and not dictate or amend the objective.

For depreciation methods other than by valuation, different circumstances dictate which is the most appropriate method. However, if these circumstances involve future patterns of revenues, expected costs of repairs and maintenance as well as the interest costs, the determination of these revenues and costs would be subjective. Thus, unless such information can be ascertained with a reasonable degree of reliability, the choice of methods based on such factors would be questionable.

A reconciliation of the many controversial areas in depreciation can be achieved by focusing on depreciation as the recoupment of capital outlay. Due to the practical difficulty of determining the decline in value, a surrogate measure is the straight line method.

Once it is understood that the straight line method of depreciation is meant to recoup assets' cost on an equal basis, the depreciation charge would not represent a meaningless figure in the books or an irrational charge against profits. Furthermore, the rate of return based on profits affected by depreciation using the allocated costs would, in almost all cases, be different from the true yield. The true yield can be computed reasonably accurately only at the end of the investment. However, rates of returns are used to satisfy the stewardship function or to control the pricing of on-going investments or firms. For such purposes, objective estimates based on past data will be more relevant.

Revaluations of assets have often led to controversies but with a better understanding of depreciation and its developments, such confusions may be easily clarified. In fact, the resulting conclusions appear to support current accepted practices.

The need for depreciation arises only if there is a need to recoup capital outlay and unless the amount is material, recoupment on a regular basis will not be required. This would explain the difference between the treatment of land and building. This chapter concludes with the observation that there should have been very little confusion if there had been a proper appreciation of depreciation and its historical development.

REFERENCES

Baxter, W.T. (1981). *Depreciating Assets: An Introduction.* London: Gee and Co. for The Institute of Chartered Accountants of Scotland

Brief, R.P. (1993). *The Continuing Debate over Depreciation, Capital and Income.* New York and London: Garland Publishing

Fowler, R.F. (1970). *The Depreciation of Capital: Analytically Considered.* Nendeln/Liechtenstein: Kraus Reprint

Garcke, E. and Fells, J.M. (1986). Fixed Capital; Chapter 6 of The Factory Accounts (1887). In *Reporting Fixed Assets in Nineteenth-century Company Accounts* (J.R. Edwards, ed.), pp. 1–25. New York and London: Garland Publishing

Grady, P. (1982). Principles of Depreciation. In *Accounting Principles Through the Years: The Views of Professional and Academic Leaders 1938–1954* (S.A. Zeff, ed.). New York and London: Garland Publishing

Hatfield, H.R. (1989). What They Say About Depreciation. In *Studies in Accounting* (W.T. Baxter, ed.), pp. 337–350. New York and London: Garland Publishing

Han, K.H. (1982). *Cost and Management Accounting.* Singapore: Singapore Institute of Management

Hatfield, H.R. (1989). Defining and Accounting for Depreciation. In *Studies in Accounting* (W.T. Baxter, ed.), pp. 351–361. New York and London: Garland Publishing

Hendriksen E.S. (1977). *Accounting Theory.* Illinois: Richard D. Irwin Inc

Johnson, J.M. (1981). *Handbook of Depreciation Methods, Formula and Tables.* Englewood Cliffs, NJ: Prentice-Hall

Littleton, A.C. (1988). *Accounting Evolution to 1900.* New York and London: Garland Publishing

Mason, P. (1986). Illustrations of the Early Treatment of Depreciation (1933). In *Reporting Fixed Assets in Nineteenth-century Company Accounts* (J.R. Edwards, ed.), pp. 79–88. New York and London: Garland Publishing

Matheson, E. (1986). The General Practice of Depreciation; Chapter 1 of The Depreciation of Factories (1884). In *Reporting Fixed Assets in Nineteenth-century Company Accounts* (J.R. Edwards, ed.), pp. 89–124. New York and London: Garland Publishing

May, G.O. (1971). The Problem of Depreciation (1915). In *Twenty-five Years of Accounting Responsibility 1911–1936* (B.C. Hunt, ed.), pp. 149–162. Houston: Scholars Book Co

May, G.O. (1971). On a Proposed Definition of Depreciation (1922). In *Twenty-five Years of Accounting Responsibility 1911–1936* (B.C. Hunt, ed.), pp. 163–165. Houston: Scholars Book Co

May, G.O. (1971). A Confusion of Terms (1927). In *Twenty-five Years of Accounting Responsibility 1911–1936* (B.C. Hunt, ed.), pp. 166–167. Houston: Scholars Book Co

May, G.O. (1971). Railroad Depreciation (1927). In *Twenty-five Years of Accounting Responsibility 1911–1936* (B.C. Hunt, ed.), pp. 168–169. Houston: Scholars Book Co

May, G.O. (1971). Further Thoughts on Depreciation and the Rate Base (1930). In *Twenty-five Years of Accounting Responsibility 1911–1936* (B.C. Hunt, ed.), pp. 219–230. Houston: Scholars Book Co

Nobes, C. (1985). *Depreciation Problems in the Context of Historical Cost Accounting.* London: Certified Accountant Publications Ltd for The Chartered Association of Certified Accountants

Solomon, E. (1975). Return on Investment: The Relation of Book-yield to True Yield. In *Information for Decision Making, Quantitative and Behavioral Dimensions* (A. Rappaport, ed.), New Jersey: Prentice-Hall

Taylor, J.B. (1982). Valuation of Fixed Assets and Principles Related to Write-ups and Write-ins. In *Accounting Principles Through the Years: The Views of Professional and Academic Leaders 1938–1954* (S.A. Zeff, ed.), New York and London: Garland Publishing

14 Management Accounting: Historical Developments and Future Directions

Chung Lai Hong

14.1 INTRODUCTION

Management accounting as a paradigm has evolved significantly over the past century. The changes are numerous, and the shifting demands for management accounting information have been precipitated by the changes in competition, the transformation of the manufacturing environment and the impact of innovations in management practice. Many would agree that management accounting has evolved, but remain cautious when suggesting that perhaps a revolution or a 'paradigm shift' (Kuhn, 1970) has occurred (Bromwich and Bhimani, 1989).

This chapter will begin with a brief overview of the historical development of management accounting. Next, the impetus for the development of management accounting will be identified. Then, current developments in management accounting will be discussed. The next section presents a framework that classifies the various stages in the evolution of management accounting. Finally, the future directions for management accounting and a possible research agenda will be outlined.

14.2 HISTORICAL DEVELOPMENT

A comprehensive, chronological review of management accounting development in America is provided by Johnson and Kaplan (1987) who argued convincingly that management accounting has lost its relevance. Other reviews include Kaplan (1984a), Scapens (1984), Bromwich and Bhimani (1989), Anthony (1989), Horngren (1989), and more recently Birnberg (1992) and Spicer (1992). Since these reviews provide various insights into the historical development and are sufficiently detailed, this paper only highlights important milestones in the development and the reasons for movements from one stage to the next.

14.2.1 Cost accounting

During the *first half of the 19th century*, the need for information for internal planning and control arose when firms, such as textile factories and railroads, required internal administrative procedures to coordinate the multiple processes involved in their operations. New accounting techniques and **conversion cost systems** were developed to meet the desire of management to control the rate at which resources were converted to the final product. Of particular concern to management was the cost of labour since the work of labourers were centralized in the factory and wage contracts were substituted for market piece-rate contracts.

When mass distribution and mass production became possible *later in the 19th century*, the conversion cost systems which originated in the textile mills were refined and expanded. Andrew Carnegie was a pioneer in the use of **cost sheets for control** in his Carnegie Steel Company. Essentially, a voucher system of accounting was employed whereby each department listed the cost of materials and labour used on each order. These cost sheets were used to evaluate the performance of employees, to check the quality and mix of raw materials, as well as to price and evaluate process improvements (Chandler, 1977). During this period, accounting information was used in a sophisticated manner to control the operations of large, single-activity manufacturing concerns such as Carnegie Steel. However, the focus was exclusively on direct labour and materials, with little attention directed at overheads and capital costs. At this stage, cost accounting did not include the allocation of fixed costs to products or periods (Kaplan, 1984a).

From about *1880 to 1910*, development of **standard costs** occurred with the impetus provided by the scientific management movement in American industry (Chandler, 1977). The search for information to assess and control the financial and physical efficiency of processes and tasks in complex, metal-making firms motivated a systematic analysis of factory productivity. Engineers and accountants used standards for three purposes: to gauge the potential efficiency of tasks or processes; to control operations using variances between actual and standard costs and to simplify inventory valuation.

In the *early 1900s*, vertically integrated firms such as Du Pont Powder Company appeared as a result of the wave of mergers. In a vertically integrated firm, the functions of production, purchasing, transportation and distribution are centrally managed through departments. Prior to the advent of vertical integration, these activities were mediated through the market by scores of specialised firms (Johnson and Kaplan, 1987). In order to facilitate the control and coordination of a firm's diverse activities, reliable and useful information must flow to top management. The centralized accounting system allowed top management to rationalize operations and monitor efficiency.

By *1910*, Du Pont Powder Company was employing nearly all the basic methods that are currently used in managing big businesses. **A centralized accounting system** facilitated the flow of information through the company's complex departmental structure. Daily and weekly data on sales, payroll and manufacturing costs were required by the home office in order to rationalize operations and monitor efficiency. **Return on investment** (ROI) was used innovatively by Du Pont as a means of evaluating the performance of its departments and as a measure of the financial performance of the organization as a whole. Du Pont devised a ROI formula that shows how return on investment is affected by changes in the operating ratio and the turnover ratio. Information from the accounting system also enabled top management to carry out two capital planning tasks: the allocation of new investment among competing activities and the financing of new capital requirements (Johnson, 1975). The criterion used for evaluation of investment projects was ROI.

The *early 1920s* saw the creation of the **multi-divisional organization.** The viability of large integrated industrial firms such as Du Pont and General Motors (GM) was threatened by the complexities that arose as these firms expanded into new product lines or new geographic areas. GM was founded in 1912 through the integration of several units, each of which manufactured and sold a unique line of automobiles or parts. The founder, William Durant, failed to resolve the problems arising from managing a diversified company. With Du Pont's substantial investment in GM threatened, Pierre Du Pont succeeded Durant as company president in 1920. Under his leadership and with the help of Alfred P. Sloan, one of Durant's executives, GM's well-known multi-divisional structure was developed. The structure allowed top management to coordinate, appraise and plan the organization's diverse operations while full responsibility for operating performance was placed on the divisional managers. In other words, top management had the task of strategic planning while the managers were delegated the task of coordinating and controlling the operating activities for each division.

GM's management accounting system performed three tasks, described as 'centralized control with decentralized responsibility' (Brown, 1927): first, an annual operating forecast compared each division's *ex ante* operating goals with top management's financial goals; second, sales reports and flexible budgets were employed to compare actual and planned results; and third, both resources and managerial compensation were allocated among divisions on the basis of uniform performance criteria (Johnson, 1978). The management accounting system at GM incorporated various features aimed at aligning the interests of divisional managers and owners. For example, the **incentive plan** which awarded bonuses in the form of GM common stock was based on divisional performance. Further, a **market-based transfer pricing policy** among divisions was adopted to preserve a true competitive situation that makes divisional performance measurement possible.

By *1925*, Du Pont and GM had developed many of the managerial control practices that are widely used today. These include decentralisation via a multi-divisional organization, ROI as a performance measure, capital budgeting, flexible budgets, profit-sharing incentive plans and market-based transfer pricing (Kaplan, 1984a).

Since 1925, developments in cost accounting have been relatively sparse (Kaplan, 1984a). Nevertheless, a couple of innovations during this period are noteworthy. In the 1950s, the **discounted cash flow approach** for the evaluation of capital investments was devised by the consulting firm Joel Dean and Associates (Dean, 1951). Another development was the **Residual Income** (RI) extension to ROI, generally attributed to General Electric Corporation. The RI criterion overcame one dysfunctional aspect of ROI, whereby managers had an incentive to reject investment projects that yielded returns that were below the division's current ROI, but were greater than the firm's cost of capital. However, RI has not been widely adopted.

The transfer pricing problem received some attention in the *mid-1950s* through the publication of three articles by Cook (1955), Dean (1955) and Stone (1956) that described the full range of available practices. Hirshleifer (1956, 1957) developed the micro-economic foundations of **transfer pricing** and demonstrated the optimality of using the **opportunity cost rule** under certain conditions.

14.2.2 Management accounting

Before World War II, the primary focus of internal accounting was cost determination, with particular emphasis on product costing and the evaluation of efficiency of direct labour, direct materials and overheads. This was the era of cost accounting which was the response to the need for precise measures to monitor, measure and report costs of goods sold and manufactured in industrial production (Flamholtz, 1992). Precise measures were made possible by applying principles of scientific management.

In the post-war period, there was an increasing awareness that accounting information should consider the needs of users (Crossman, 1958). The era of management accounting began with the realisation that accounting information could be used more widely in managerial planning and control (Shillinglaw, 1980). Moreover, with the growth of service industries, such as Federal Express, Merrill Lynch and JP Morgan, it was recognised that cost accounting was not readily applicable and changes would have to be made. Broadly, two different schools of management accounting can be identified during this period: the behavioural school and the information economics and agency theory school.

Behavioural

The systematic investigation of management control processes and their behavioural implications began in the *post-war period*. Simon *et al* (1954) explored the motivational and control problems of decentralized organizations, and their findings had a profound impact on the perceived role of accounting information for managers. They identified three important uses of accounting information: score card-keeping, attention-directing and problem-solving. Concern for the behavioural impact of management accounting practices and particularly the dysfunctional consequences that could occur was voiced by researchers such as Argyris (1952), Ridgeway (1956) and Bruns (1968). The behavioural assumptions underlying management accounting were examined by Caplan (1966). These concerns with behavioural implications led to a wide variety of studies on the role of accounting information in budgeting, performance evaluation and control.

The initial emphasis of behavioural accounting research was on individual information processing and decision making (Hofstedt, 1975; Libby, 1981; San Miguel, 1977). Subsequently, calls were made to consider external validity in studies and particularly to study accounting in its organizational context (Hopwood, 1978; 1980; 1983; Flamholtz, 1983). Increasingly, organizational theory has been applied to study accounting issues. For example, the contingency theory approach to management accounting, which is based on the premise that there is no one universally appropriate accounting system for all organizations, has its roots in organizational theory (Otley, 1980; Cooper, 1981). Management accounting is viewed as a powerful means of ensuring organizational control and therefore must be studied in its organizational context.

One way of viewing the control process in organizations is provided by Anthony's (1965) hierarchical framework. He classified the planning and control functions performed by organizations into strategic planning, management control and operational control. During this period, a large number of textbooks and cases that described contemporary management control practice were written by researchers in the Harvard Business

School, notably John Dearden, Richard Vancil and Robert Anthony, among others. The behavioural problems with using ROI as a performance evaluation tool were identified (Dearden, 1960; Anthony, 1965; Solomons, 1965). Other issues addressed by behavioural accounting research included participation (Brownell, 1981) performance evaluation and incentive schemes (Hopwood, 1972; Otley, 1978).

Information economics and agency theory

During the *late 1960s*, a different school using the information economics approach was formed. This approach views the management accountant as choosing an information system in an uncertain environment to aid in decision-making (Feltham, 1968; Feltham and Demski, 1970). The value of an information system is derived from a formal model based on the utility of the information for decision-makers relative to the cost of providing the information. An important contribution of information economics research in management accounting is that it encouraged researchers to identify separately information system choice and information system design (Sundem, 1981). However, the research was essentially concerned with single-person information system choice.

An extension of information economics approach, the agency theory recognises that accounting information is not only useful for decision-making, but also forms the basis for contracting between economic agents.

> 'In agency theory, the firm is viewed not as an individual, but merely as an overlapping set of contracts among principals and agents, each of whom is assumed to be motivated solely by self-interest' (Baiman, 1982).

The owner (principal) has to provide incentives for the employee (agent) to pursue and achieve organizational goals. The agency model assumes that all individuals are motivated purely by self-interest but does not preclude the existence of a common interest among members of the firm (Fama, 1980).

In management accounting research, the agency model is used to identify the combination of employment contract and information system that will maximise the principal's utility function, subject to the behavioural constraints imposed by the self-interest of the agent. The principal–agent relationship is governed by a contract specifying what the agent should do and what the principal must do in return (Demski and Feltham, 1978). However, this relationship is fraught with problems arising from limited information, more particularly uncertainty and information asymmetry, and bounded rationality. The cooperative behaviour agreed upon ignores motivational problems and may not be enforceable due to the agent's self-interest. Therefore, an employment contract must be designed to mitigate the divergence between the cooperative behaviour that will maximise the welfare of the individuals and the self-interested behaviour that is achievable (Baiman, 1982). This divergence arises from two agency problems, namely, moral hazard and adverse selection. Both problems stem from 'information asymmetry', that is, the two parties to the contract have unequal information (Ross, 1973; Stiglitz, 1974). Adverse selection occurs because job applicants know their 'type' (such as training or skills) but the information that the employer has is incomplete. The result is less than optimal recruitment in that the owner is likely to hire lower skilled applicants who falsely claim the requisite skill level (Akerlof, 1970). Similarly, moral hazard occurs because the principal cannot fully observe the effort put in by the agent and therefore cannot be sure that the agent is not shirking on the job (Alchian and Demsetz, 1972).

Baiman (1982, 1990) provides useful surveys of research in the field since 1975. Agency theory offers some insights into the nature of management accounting. It highlights the roles of management accounting both as a control system and as an aid to decision-making. It demonstrates the importance of accounting information in the motivation of organizational participants and the need to consider behavioural consequences in system design and choice. It also emphasizes the importance of risk-sharing in the design of management accounting systems.

14.3   IMPETUS FOR CHANGE

Undoubtedly, work by Johnson and Kaplan has stimulated management accounting researchers to seriously consider the question of relevance of the extant management accounting practices. With the publication of *Relevance Lost* by Johnson and Kaplan (1987), debate has intensified over the issue. Most researchers would agree that a change in management accounting, if not a total revolution, is long overdue. The changes particularly over the last 15 years or so that have culminated in the present debate are transformation of the manufacturing environment due to technological innovations, changes in the nature of competition given the increasing level of globalisation, and impact of innovations in management practice such as Total Quality Management (TQM), learning organizations, high involvement management and networks.

14.3.1   The new manufacturing environment

'Traditional cost accounting data is obsolete in a repetitive manufacturing environment . . . cost accounting's dual purpose of planning and control must be redesigned' (Neumann and Jaouen, 1986, p. 132).

To achieve their goal to become world-class manufacturers, many companies have turned to **Automated Manufacturing Technology** (AMT). Many organizations perceive AMT as the appropriate strategic device in meeting this challenge (Currie, 1992). AMT is the basis of the 'factory of the future' and is making new demands on accounting and control systems. Organizations using advanced production techniques have seen significant changes in the manufacturing cost mix. The percentage of direct labour cost to total manufacturing costs has declined over the last century (Miller and Vollman, 1985). At the same time, overhead costs as a percentage of manufacturing costs have increased steadily. Accounting for overheads becomes more problematic for these organizations as they need to understand the causes of fluctuations in overhead costs (Howell *et al*, 1987).

The manufacturing environment has been transformed by technological innovations such as Just-in-Time systems (JIT), Flexible Manufacturing Systems (FMS), Computer-Aided Design (CAD) and Computer-Aided Manufacturing Capitalise Systems (CAMCS). Accounting and control systems in their present forms are outmoded and irrelevant in this new environment. In the management of process technology, the choice of performance measures used is critical as performance measures should be carefully assessed to ensure that timely and accurate information is available to assist in decision-making. More specifically, the use of AMT is unlikely to yield financial benefits in the short run. Therefore, performance measures must include non-financial aspects. Currie (1993) found that UK and US manufacturers concentrated heavily on short-term financial measures to assess the performance of AMT, while the Japanese and West German firms included strategic, operational and technical measures in their portfolio. This difference also reflects the perception of the Japanese that AMT operates in the context of a manufacturing strategy and not in isolation. Non-financial performance indicators include improved process and product quality, teamwork, more effective supplier and customer relationships, and reduction in plant space (Currie, 1992).

Just-in-Time systems (JIT)

In 1952, Toyota pioneered a new production system for producing automobiles that continued to evolve over the next 20 years. The **Toyota Production System** produced cars with higher quality at less cost, and in less time than the traditional mass production systems used by Toyota's competitors. During the 1970s, North American manufacturers, particularly in the automotive industry, were looking for ways to improve their operations. They focused on the Japanese system for reducing their inventory investment. Since its inception, the Toyota Production System has spread to industries far removed from the automobile industry. It has been referred to in many ways, including Just-in-Time, Lean Production and Zero Inventory.

JIT is a manufacturing philosophy of eliminating waste in all stages of the manufacturing process, from purchasing through to distribution. JIT attempts to have all work processed continually, without interruptions. By doing so, throughput times and inventory holding costs will be minimised, and large gains will be realised in productivity and quality. JIT is an approach to achieving excellence in a manufacturing company based on the continuous elimination of waste, where waste is defined as any non-value adding activity (Goddard, 1988).

JIT comprises two separate sets of activities:

(1) JIT purchasing, which attempts to match the purchase and receipt of materials with the time when inventory level reaches zero; and
(2) JIT production, whereby a pull–system is used to ensure that production occurs when there is a demand for the final product (Bromwich and Bhimani, 1989).

The elements that are necessary to ensure success of a JIT operation are people involvement, high emphasis on quality, excellent control on scheduling, excellent vendor performance and control, reducing order quantities and set up times, and cellular manufacturing (Goddard, 1988). Companies using JIT as a strategic tool were found to enjoy a greater degree of success as compared to those companies who merely used JIT as a cost reduction or inventory control tool (Hay, 1988). JIT has become an integral part in the drive to improve manufacturing techniques and product quality. It allows businesses to improve their inventory management, transportation systems, product scheduling, internal response time, and costing systems (Shephard, 1993).

Research on the JIT issue has been conducted using multiple research methodologies, including surveys (Cobb, 1992), case studies (Patell, 1987), laboratory experiments (Griffin and Harrell, 1991; Young, Shields and Wolf, 1988) and principal–agent models (Milgrom and Roberts, 1990). These studies have improved our understanding of the technical issues of JIT and the implementation problems, but have revealed little about the management and behavioural implications of the system (Young and Selto, 1991).

Computer-Aided Design (CAD) and Computer-Aided Manufacturing (CAM)

CAD emphasizes cost minimization and product simplicity through the computerisation of design, drafting and testing of products. The aim is to maximise the utilization of existing parts and reduce the design time phase of the product. CAM uses computerized technology to plan, implement and monitor the manufacturing processes.

The implementation of CAD/CAM and FMS (see below) is made possible by the expanded use of digital computer production technology which has important implications for the manufacturing processes. The substitution of machine processing for direct labour processing dramatically decreases direct labour costs as a percentage of total product costs. Due to the need for software engineers, programmers and computer technicians, most of the manufacturing costs have become fixed (Johnson and Kaplan, 1987).

An investigation of management's perceptions of the introduction of CAD before and after implementation was carried out by Currie (1989). The sample consisted of managers from 20 UK-based firms. She found that successful implementation was more likely when CAD was introduced as part of an overall corporate strategy. On the other hand, lack of awareness of the strategic use of technology and using CAD as an *ad hoc* response to falling profits, extended lead times, or reduction in productivity created problems in implementation. Successful implementation demands skills that are not necessarily technical but strategic.

Flexible Manufacturing Systems (FMS)

FMS refers to a production system which consists of a wholly automated group of self–setting–up machines with automated material carriers that load and unload jobs and a central computer that operates the entire process. Ideally, the need for support personnel is limited to maintenance and replacement of tools (Mackey, 1991). The main advantages of FMS include the ability to produce different varieties and volume levels using the same technology, quick customer response and lower labour costs (Bromwich and Bhimani, 1989). The purpose of such a system is to produce a large variety of parts at low to medium volumes at the lowest cost per unit. This is possible by concentrating on families of parts with similar characteristics and the support of CAD/CAM systems. Mass production of homogenous output in order to decrease setup times and costs are no longer necessary. Instead, mass customization or the ability to produce a customised batch at mass production prices is now feasible. This is achieved through short cycle times, flexible automation, and the ability to do quick changeovers with little or no production stoppage or cost penalty (Ross, 1990). All activities such as setup, scheduling and inspection are minimized and carried out under computer control (Jaikumar, 1986). This environment supports the JIT philosophy as low inventory levels are possible.

Direct cost reductions resulting from FMS implementation have been documented in various studies. A study by Salomon and Biegel (1985) revealed direct cost reductions up to a maximum of 66%. Similarly, in a study of 50 UK manufacturing companies, Bessant and Haywood

(1986) found reductions in lead-time (74%) and work-in-process inventories (66%), and increases in machine utilization (63%) and inventory turnover (3.5 times).

FMS provides benefits not only in terms of direct cost savings, but also in indirect strategic benefits (Sriram and Gupta, 1991). In industries where meeting customised schedules are critical, the increase in flexibility provided by FMS offers a significant competitive advantage. To capitalize on the competitive advantage offered by FMS, existing reporting structures in firms must be changed to meet the demands of the automated factory environment. With the introduction of FMS,

> 'management reports must focus less on measurements and control of individual cost centres and more on providing information useful to evaluating and supporting the long-term manufacturing strategies of the firm' (Sriram and Gupta, 1991, p. 36).

Attributes such as improvements in quality, productivity, product life-cycle and reporting timeliness impact cost and profitability and are of strategic importance in the FMS environment.

Foster and Horngren (1988) investigated the cost management implications of FMS by visiting 25 firms in the United States. A diversity of uses of FMS was found. Variations in accounting for costs, performance and cost measures devoted to quality, and operating performance were identified.

14.3.2 Nature of the competitive environment

The transformation of the manufacturing environment, made possible by advances in computer technology, has reshaped the basis of competition. Attention should no longer be directed solely at achieving economies of scale through possessing a significant market share and spreading fixed overhead costs over a large volume of products. In today's competitive environment, firms need to compete by achieving economies of scope, that is, the savings attributable to the ability to produce a wide variety of products using the same equipment. As more and more companies embraced the new manufacturing philosophies, the rules of competition were inevitably changed to include simultaneous achievement of flexibility, quality and low cost (Brimson, 1991). Those who fail to adopt the new manufacturing philosophies found it increasingly difficult to maintain their market share and survive.

With the advent of new technologies of world wide communications, data sharing and transportation, the players in the economic field and the nature of competition have become global. Globalization means that American industries not only compete against the European (or EC) and Japanese industries, but increasingly with industries emerging in countries such as Taiwan, Mexico, Singapore and India. Moreover, companies have found it worthwhile to relocate their production facilities to countries that offer much lower labour costs than in their home country. The worker is thus not only threatened by advances in technology that seek to replace labour, but is faced with competition for the job by workers in other parts of the world that offer more competitive wage rates.

In summary, today's competitive environment is characterized by increased uncertainty and volatility due to the existence of global competitors. Moreover, demand is customer-driven. This characterization contrasts with that of earlier competition: stable environment, few competitors and captive market. Another key element in the new manufacturing environment is time compression (Brimson, 1991). All functions in the value chain must be restructured to reduce time through the elimination of waste. Time compression is central to JIT production, and CAM/CAD manufacturing strategies. Reducing process cycle time, and the development time required to bring products to market become important to 'time-based competition' (Stalk, 1992).

14.3.3   Innovations in management practice

Organizations are faced with a new manufacturing environment in an increasingly competitive and global economy. The old paradigm of competition and management that worked under the old regime is replaced with a new paradigm of management that revolves around concepts like total quality management, learning and empowerment (Hodgetts, Luthans and Lee, 1994). The innovations in management practice impacts management accounting by providing different frameworks for viewing the role of accounting in organizations. Given that management philosophies and practices have shifted, a corresponding shift in management accounting should follow.

According to Ross (1990), the revolution in technology created a parallel revolution in management. The emerging 'hi-flex' organization is more organic than the traditional structure. In 'hi-flex' organizations, employees are in direct contact with, and at close proximity to the customers. In traditional hierarchies, people are many layers removed from the market-place. Relationships with suppliers and customers are emphasized, again in line with the JIT philosophy.

Total Quality Management (TQM)

Total quality can be defined in at least three ways:

(1) The first is in terms of its unifying principle which forms the basis of the firm's strategy, planning and all its activities. The principle of total quality management translates simply to 'total dedication to the customer' (Ciampa, 1992).

(2) Another definition focuses on the desired outcomes of TQM. These outcomes relate to higher customer satisfaction, minimisation of response times, better work climate, and a general ethic of continuous improvement.

(3) Finally, total quality can be discussed in terms of the tools and techniques that lead to the desired outcomes. Traditional tools like Quality Control, Statistical Process Control and Material Requirements Planning are some of the components of TQM efforts.

Ciampa (1992) describes total quality in terms of four components:

- The first component, **technical**, has evolved from techniques such as Statistical Process Control and Material Requirements Planning used in the 1950s and 1960s to Computer Integrated Manufacturing and Just-in-Time popularized in the early 1980s. These techniques are aimed at reducing cost, eliminating wastage and continuously improving quality.
- The second component, **people**, emphasizes the behavioural and organizational aspects of TQM and is largely based on Organizational Development (OD). OD concentrates on the values, attitudes and organizational climate in understanding the human side of organizational life (Bennis, 1969). OD is dedicated to human learning, management training and adult education.
- The third component stresses that total quality attention must be directed at the **strategic imperatives** of the business. In turn, the processes that these imperatives depend on should be identified and form the focus of quality improvement activities. Employees are thus made aware of what is important to the business and what to concentrate their efforts on.
- The fourth component puts the **customer** into the total quality picture. The driving force behind TQM should be the customers and efforts made at meeting their needs and expectations in order to create customer loyalty.

In Summary,

'total quality describes the state of an organization in which all the activities of all functions are designed and carried out in such a way that all external customer requirements are met while reducing internal time and cost, and enhancing workplace climate' (Ciampa, 1992, p. 41).

One of the important contributions of TQM efforts has been its focus on learning by emphasizing the identification of customer requirements and activities such as benchmarking aimed at enhancing an understanding of 'best practices'. These activities are useful in improving capabilities and skills within the organization. It is this emphasis on continuous improvement and enhancement of the organizational skill base which is at the heart of building a competitive corporation. This emphasis echoes Juran's (1974) approach to quality management, which focuses on serving customer needs and has several important implications (Grant, Shani and Krishnan, 1994).

Firstly, it provides an externally focused goal (that is, the customers) to the entire company. Secondly, the customer focus is a mechanism that unifies organizational processes. The requirements of the final customer drives the demand–pull sequence of relationships. Finally, quality management is a philosophy that integrates the entire management of the company. Juran's (1974) approach links quality improvement to quality planning, thus extending it from the realm of operations into that of strategic planning, thereby placing primary responsibility on top management. TQM affects an organization through its effectiveness in promoting coordination and integration of productive activity.

Unfortunately, many of the TQM efforts are more inwardly focused and an obsessive emphasis on quality alone will ultimately cause the organization to lose sight of other critical factors such as meeting customer needs. For instance, in the competition for the Baldrige Award (the US quality award), it has been suggested that there is excessive focus on the processes of quality rather than the results. For instance, in evaluating candidates for the award, only 300 out of a total of 1,000 points are allocated for the results of the quality effort (Garvin, 1991). Moreover, an organization can improve quality by 'single-loop' learning, that is, by adapting in response to changes in the environment, without being able to anticipate and stay ahead of change (Hodgetts, Luthans and Lee, 1994). Learning organizations (see next page), on the other hand, are characterized by their ability to anticipate changes.

A survey of Australian companies that are actively implementing TQM processes provides some insights into the organizational impact of TQM (Fisher, 1993). In many cases, the expectations regarding the benefits from implementation and the reported benefits accruing to the actual implementation were identical. An overall financial benefit-to-cost ratio of 4:1, starting from the first year of implementation was reported. Other benefits include reduced waste and improved productivity. Most respondents (65%) expected TQM to result in an organizational culture change: improved morale, teamwork, communications and employee involvement. However, only 29% of respondents indicated that the culture change actualised. As a result of their experiences with TQM, a majority of the respondents believe that TQM is essential for all companies.

Grant, Shani and Krishnan (1994) believe that TQM inevitably conflicts with established Western management practices because its assumptions and theories are inconsistent with those underlying conventional practices. Thus, they argue that TQM efforts will succeed in a company only if existing management practices are transformed. System-wide changes that are necessary include the redesign of work, redefinition of managerial roles, redesign of organizational structure, and learning of new skills by employees.

Learning organizations

Emphasis on continuous learning and meeting customer needs are reflected in the learning organization (Senge, 1990; Mills and Friesen, 1992). A learning organization is one that is able to sustain consistent internal innovation or learning in order to enhance profitability and succeed in today's turbulent environment. The immediate goals of learning responsiveness is to improve quality, enhance customer relationships, and more effectively execute business strategy. A learning organization has been defined as an organization that is skilled at creating, acquiring and transferring knowledge and at modifying its behaviour to reflect new knowledge and insights (Garvin, 1993). An important way in which an organization learns is through the individuals who make up the organization. In addition, organizations learn by routinising knowledge through encapsulating them in rules, processes and procedures. Another means of learning is by merging with other organizations. The knowledge embodied in the other firm's processes and personnel are thus absorbed into the organization.

Mills and Friesen (1992) identify three key characteristics of a learning organization:

(1) It must make a commitment to knowledge. Since an organization learns through its individuals, a crucial aspect of this commitment to knowledge involves the selection of personnel. Another aspect is the development of learning through avenues such as research, discussions and seminars that attempt to capture individual learning and make it accessible to other organizational members.
(2) A learning organization must possess a mechanism for self-renewal, that is, for creation of negative entropy. Processes and procedures that were initially essential for learning may become too rigid and thus hinder further learning and creativity. Mechanisms must exist so that the organization can intervene by abolishing or transforming these outdated procedures and creating a new critical mass.
(3) An organization that is committed to learning must be open to the outside world. Openness is required so that the organization continues to be responsive to the needs of customers, suppliers and other major stakeholders.

Management in a learning organization are trained to see the big picture, escape linear thinking and understand the subtle interrelationships within the organization (Senge, 1990). To meet the requirement of openness to external parties, firms are reorganizing themselves so that employees are put into direct contact with outside parties. Instead of a functional hierarchy, **flatter and delayered structures** are designed to make it easier for the organization to learn. A 'cluster organization' (Mills, 1991) consisting of interdisciplinary teams focused on customer needs, is evolving. No clear lines of reporting are established, but close communication between teams is encouraged. This new form encourages entrepreneurial behaviour, flexibility and adaptability by allowing employees to exercise their initiative in performing their jobs.

Some of the techniques used by learning organizations include dialogue, scenario analysis and business process re-engineering (Hodgetts, Luthans and Lee, 1994). **Dialogue** is a technique for helping individuals recognise and put aside basic differences among members of different groups within the organization, such as departments, divisions and levels of management. **Scenario analysis**, used by organizations such as Shell, forces managers to think through their response under different possible future scenarios as part of the strategic planning exercise. **Business process re-engineering** represents a fundamental rethinking and redesign of organizational structures and management systems. The power of information technology is harnessed to radically redesign the business processes in order to dramatically improve performance (Hammer, 1990). Operations are organized by process and not by function in order to do things right.

High involvement management

The advocates of this approach contrast the traditional approach or paradigm of management, based on bureaucratic norms and mass production technologies, with an approach based on committed workers and knowledge-intensive work.

The approach makes a number of humanistic assumptions about employees. For example, Lawler (1988) suggests that employees are knowledgeable, intrinsically motivated and are capable of a considerable amount of self-control and self-direction. While such a view has a long tradition in the management literature (Eccles and Nohria, 1992), the impetus for re-establishing its position lies in the increasingly interdependent, complex and knowledge-intensive industries that are characteristic of modern societies. Traditional, bureaucratic, control-oriented management styles are deemed to be not responsive enough to the new competitive realities. The core assumptions underlying this management philosophy are that staff are intrinsically motivated and that people-based skills are sources of competitive advantage.

Network organizations

Network organizations (Miles and Snow, 1992; Lei and Slocum, 1992), mirroring the *kieretsu* in Japan or *chaebol* in Korea are increasingly seen around the globe. A network overcomes complexities in its operations and exploits technology by organizing itself as sub-units that are connected, not with hierarchical mechanisms like plans, schedules and transfer prices, but rather with market mechanisms like contracts, franchises, and other exchange agreements. It represents an intermediary between single firm and market, that is, it consists of two or more firms, which due to the intensity of their interaction constitute a subset of one or more markets (Thorelli, 1986).

A network may be viewed as both vertical integration and diversification. Through a network structure, a firm can operate both efficiently and innovatively by focusing only on those things it does well and meeting the remaining resource requirements by contracting with other firms (Snow, Miles and Coleman, 1992). Given that the changes in organizational structure in the past have precipitated change in management accounting, the creation of network organizations will undoubtedly necessitate modification in the information provided by the management accounting system.

14.4 CURRENT DEVELOPMENTS

Accounting innovation has lagged manufacturing innovations (Kaplan, 1985; Dunk, 1989). The use of traditional accounting and control systems in today's manufacturing and competitive environment creates problems for the organization: first, the methods used for overhead allocation distort product costs: second, the system does not produce non-financial measures required for efficient and effective operations (Kaplan, 1984b; 1985).

The traditional cost accounting systems were developed when the market was dominated by labour-intensive industries. Understandably, direct labour was the focus of cost control while overheads were not a major component of the product cost. Thus, it was reasonable to use a single volume-related cost driver to allocate overhead costs to product. However, in the highly automated manufacturing environment of today, factory overhead costs increase while direct labour costs decrease as a percentage of total manufacturing costs (Miller and Vollman, 1985; Horngren and Foster, 1987). In addition, since mass production is no longer the norm, allocations using volume-based drivers lead to inaccurate product costing. Traditional methods of overhead allocation are inherently biased to under-cost low-volume, speciality products and over-cost standard, high volume products (Chenhall, 1991). Activity based costing is a recent accounting innovation that overcomes this problem. Accounting must become more than simply recording, summarising and reporting the financial aspects of the firm's operations (Brimson, 1991).

Traditional management accounting systems have mostly generated financial measures of an organization's performance. These measures do not adequately reflect all the aspects of an organization's activities that are necessary for it to succeed in today's manufacturing and competitive environment. Some of the current developments in the field which address these problems are briefly described below.

14.4.1   Strategic Management Accounting (SMA)

Bromwich (1990, p. 28) defines SMA as 'the provision and analysis of financial information on the firm's product markets and competitor's costs and cost structures and the monitoring of the enterprise's strategies and those of its competitors in these markets over a number of periods'.

Simmonds (1981, p. 26) sees the use of the management accounting data as

'the means of developing and monitoring the business strategy, particularly relative levels and trends in real costs and prices, volume, market share, cashflow and the proportion demanded of a firm's total resources'.

Theoretical support for the involvement of accountants in strategic management is derived from the economic perspective that sees economic goods as bundles of attributes. The accountant's role is to cost these attributes and monitor their performance over time. These costs are crucial to the sustainability of the firm's product strategies (Bromwich, 1990). Another source of support is derived from the theory of contestable markets that gives the conditions for a firm's price and output strategy to be sustainable in the face of potential competition, focusing on cost conditions (Baumol *et al*, 1982).

Shank (1989, p. 50) defines SMA, which he refers to as strategic cost management as 'the managerial use of cost information explicitly directed at one or more of the four stages of the strategic management cycle' (that is, formulation, communication, implementation and control). There are three central themes in strategic cost management: value chain analysis, cost driver analysis and competitive advantage analysis (Shank, 1989; Shank and Govindarajan, 1993).

(1) The value chain starts from raw materials to end-users and has an external focus. The firm is seen in the context of the overall value-creating activities, of which it is only a component.

(2) Cost driver analysis seeks to understand cost behaviour by understanding the complex interplay of the set of cost drivers at work. This is the focus of Activity-Based Costing (ABC), which is discussed in p. 360.

(3) Competitive advantage analysis is based on the premise that the role of cost analysis depends on how the firm chooses to compete. For example, the firm can either compete by being a low cost producer, or by effectively differentiating its product (Porter, 1985). Depending on the chosen strategy, the relevance and emphasis of cost analysis will differ. For example, an organization pursuing a low cost strategy would require more detail in reporting production costs and analyses of customer profitability than an organization pursuing a differentiation strategy (Shank, 1989).

Various studies have suggested that there is a link between the way firms achieve competitive advantage and the design and use of management accounting and control systems, pointing to the relevance of strategic management accounting. One of the earlier studies (Khandwalla, 1972) found increased use of accounting-based control systems as a result of increased competition in an industry.

Based on questionnaire and interview data, Simons (1987) concluded that management control systems differed significantly between prospector and defender firms. For example, prospector firms emphasize tight budgets and monitoring outputs more than defender firms. Subsequent studies by Simons (1990; 1991) revealed that interactive management control systems focus organization attention on strategic uncertainties and therefore guide the strategy formulation process to ensure continuing competitive advantage. Top managers focus on systems that produce and monitor information on strategic uncertainties that are associated with their visions (Simons, 1991).

A study of electronics and electrical manufacturers in Singapore found support for the thesis that management control systems do follow strategy (Chung *et al*, 1994). In particular, there are differences in emphasis placed by defender firms and prospector firms with respect to budget goals, cost control and planning.

Govindarajan and Shank (1992), using Porter's (1980) typology of strategy, argue that the role of management accounting and control depends on the strategy being followed. For example, carefully engineered product standard costs are more likely to be important for a firm that follows a cost leadership strategy than for a firm that follows a product differentiation strategy.

Expanding on the strategy typology of Porter (1985), Bruggeman and Van der Stede (1993) made a distinction between cost leadership, differentiation in a standard product environment and differentiation requiring short term flexibility (customised products). Based on an investigation of 18 companies (32 business units) in Belgium, the researchers concluded that the choice of competitive advantage affects the type of control to be used and the flexibility of the budget during the year. Only differentiation strategy based on product flexibility required loose budget control and allowance for budget revisions during the year. Tight control is optimal for the remaining two strategy types.

14.4.2 Activity-Based Costing (ABC)

ABC has been defined as

'a methodology that measures the cost and performance of activities, resources and cost objects, assigns resources to activities and activities to cost objects based on their use, and recognises the causal relationships of cost drivers to activities' (Computer Aided Manufacturing International, 1990).

ABC focuses on the activities performed to produce products. The costs of the activities are traced to products based on the consumption of the activities by each product. The 'cost driver', or in conventional terms, the allocation base, is a measure of the activity performed (for example, number of setups, material handling hours), and not a measure of volume of production (Cooper, 1990). ABC is basically a two-stage process: costs are first traced to activities performed, and then these costs are traced (allocated) to the products using the identified cost drivers. Product costs thus computed are more accurate than those reported using the conventional cost systems. Product costing is enhanced by the more discrete tracing of the cost of building a product, supporting a customer, or any other necessary activity. This is done by identifying all traceable activities and determining how much of each activity's output is dedicated to the cost objective (Brimson, 1991).

Technological advances and cost reduction programmes have focused largely on direct costs while adding significantly to overheads. There is a shift away from direct labour and towards more costly overhead resources. Traditional costing systems allocate overheads to products on the basis of direct labour hours, or some other volume-related activity. One major problem with these costing systems is that they tend to over-cost large, high-volume products and under-cost small, low-volume products when there is product diversity (Cooper, 1988). ABC overcomes this problem and produces better information for both operational and strategic decisions (Cooper *et al*, 1992). Moreover, the information itself causes managers to change their activities and processes to make the organization more competitive. ABC is most effectively implemented as a component of a framework of change and continuous improvement, for instance in conjunction with business process re-engineering, TQM and performance measurement (Sharman, 1993b).

Turney (1993) uses the term 'workforce activity based management' to describe the integration of ABC into the world of work teams and TQM. The availability of activity-based information to the workforce plays an important role in the continuous improvement process by providing relevant information about cost, time and quality and therefore allows fact-based decisions about improvement priorities. Furthermore, focus is achieved by providing workers with a clear, complete and measurable set of goals and performance measures. ABC is ideally suited to TQM because it encourages management accountants to analyse activities and determine their value to the customer (Steimer, 1990; Turney and Stratton, 1992).

Some authors (Sharman, 1993a; Cooper *et al*, 1992; Clark and Baxter, 1992) and some organizations (for example AT&T and IBM) refer to the concept not as ABC but as 'activity based cost management' (ABCM) or **Activity-Based Management** (ABM). ABM refers to the integration of ABC information into an overall management process which guides efforts to adapt business strategies to meet competitive pressures as well as to improve business operations (Turney, 1992). Advocates recognise that ABC does not merely improve the costing system, but in addition, it can improve business management. ABM's aim is to provide management with a method of introducing and managing process and organizational change (Clark and Baxter, 1992). It provides an essential link to TQM and its concept of 'continuous improvement' by directing resources to activities that yield the greatest profitability and helps to improve the way work is carried out (Turney, 1992).

A study of the United States' airline industry indicated that while output and volume are primary cost drivers, other factors reflecting product diversity and complexity were important secondary cost drivers (Banker and Johnson, 1988). In another study using cross-sectional data from US multinational electronics companies, actual manufacturing overheads were associated with volume, complexity and efficiency-based variables, but the volume-based variables had the most influence (Foster and Gupta, 1990).

Armitage and Nicholson (1993) conducted a survey of over 700 large Canadian organizations and received 50% returns. The results indicate that ABC is in different stages of development in different industry sectors and in organizations of different sizes. For instance, large organizations and manufacturing firms are more likely to have implemented ABC than small organizations and those in other industry sectors. Two results are especially important:

(1) ABC has had a high acceptance rate from organizations that have assessed it. Almost 80% of respondents that had assessed ABC had implemented ABC systems.
(2) Organizations that have adopted ABC indicated that their expectations have been met. Their expectations regarding the benefits of ABC were:
    (a) More accurate profit analysis by product,
    (b) More accurate information for product costing,
    (c) Improved insight into cost causation,
    (d) Improved performance measurement, and
    (e) Improved cost control.

The impact of ABC has generally been an improvement in quality of information in these areas. These results regarding expectations and impact of ABC are consistent with those reported by a similar UK study by Innes and Mitchell (1991).

Some evidence of the application of ABC in Singapore is beginning to emerge. Two surveys of the electronics industry reported by Schoch *et al* (1994) revealed that only a small proportion of firms in the industry are currently using the system. However, there are positive indicators that more firms are likely to consider the adoption of ABC in the near future: there is a general awareness of ABC and there are many firms which possess characteristics suited to the ABC system. There is some evidence that whether a firm is aware of new innovations such as ABC is partly dependent on strategy. In a study of management controls used by electronics and electrical firms in Singapore, it was found that prospector firms are more likely than defender firms to keep informed of new management accounting practices such as ABC (Chung *et al*, 1994).

14.4.3 Qualitative and non-financial performance measures

Kaplan (1984b) points out that the financial measures generated by traditional cost accounting systems do not provide an adequate summary of a company's manufacturing operations. The emphasis on financial measures alone undermines the effectiveness of strategies that the firm must pursue in order to survive. Faced with global competition and demands imposed by a changing manufacturing environment, organizations must consider non-financial measures such as quality, innovation and workforce involvement (Kaplan, 1983; 1984b). 'Quality' is the buzzword at the movement and is at the forefront of efforts to improve performance. The TQM movement has gained considerable momentum over the past decade, with the presentation of the Baldrige Award, ISO certification and countless books and articles written on the issue. Given the importance of quality as a competitive edge, firms must measure quality and attempt to understand how it can be improved. Similarly, innovation and workforce involvement are important factors that shape the competitiveness of the firm and thus should be measured and monitored.

The specific measures that are relevant to a firm are driven by the firm's manufacturing strategy (Kaplan, 1988) and differ over the product life cycle (Richardson and Gordon, 1980). Taylor and Graham (1992) suggest that the appropriate internal or external non-financial information will depend on the industry the firm operates in and the strategy pursued by the firm.

There is a critical need to directly measure specific characteristics of manufacturing which provide competitive advantage for the firm (Chenhall, 1991). In the new manufacturing environment, operating measures such as rates of unexpected equipment failures, ratios of preventive and corrective maintenance to total maintenance and reject rates are required to guide the firm in achieving its manufacturing goals and thereby sustain its competitive advantage (Schonberger, 1982; Chenhall, 1991). Operating measures in the new manufacturing environment can be categorised into the following: quality, inventory, material/scrap, equipment/maintenance and delivery/throughput (Howell and Soucy, 1987). Kaplan (1988) points to the inadequacy of operational control in the traditional management accounting system. Managers need rapid feedback on efficiency and performance but existing reports are usually on a monthly basis and provide only an aggregate level of information. There is no reliable, accurate and timely feedback provided by the management accounting system.

The traditional measures of operating performance such as equipment use, workcentre efficiency, direct and indirect labour ratios may be less useful in the JIT environment. For example, there is no ideal ratio for direct labour, or overheads in a JIT production system as JIT seeks to eliminate all non-value adding activities. Instead, performance is measured by tracking factors such as reductions in actual costs and improvements in quality (Management Accounting Guidelines, 1993). Innes and Mitchell (1988) in their survey of 10 electronics companies in Scotland found that factors driving costs such as quality, technical process and service activities were receiving increasing emphasis in costing systems. At the same time, performance measures were beginning to emphasise non-financial factors such as product quality, delivery and customer satisfaction.

Nanni, Dixon and Vollmann (1990) outlined the contingencies that determine when cost accounting measures fit the needs of organizational control in manufacturing firms. Their observations were based on the results of a survey of about 150 managers at four operating plants at Northern Telecom Incorporated, a multinational manufacturer of telecommunications equipment. Managers were presented with a list of performance measures and asked to rate the importance of each item to the long-term survival of the firm. The results show that the higher the management level of the respondent, the higher the perceived importance of financial measures. Moreover, accounting-based financial measures were considered more important in plants with stable market environments. This result is consistent with other studies such as Govindarajan (1984) and Govindarajan and Gupta (1985). The authors argued that global competition will lead to more dynamic markets which pose the need to change from the current emphasis on accounting-based performance measures. New management accounting systems must produce costs that mirror the manufacturing process, identify waste, isolate cost drivers and provide visibility to quality improvements (Brimson, 1991).

Despite the calls for including non-financial measures, the dissatisfaction with performance evaluation remains widespread. This sentiment is reflected in one of the findings of a recent study by the Economist Intelligence Unit and KPMG Peat Marwick. The majority of the respondents believed that performance measures were too financially-oriented, too focused on the inner workings of the company and too lacking in detail (Geanuracos, 1994). At highly profitable companies, satisfaction with performance evaluation was significantly higher (46% compared with 30% of all companies surveyed).

The key performance indicators that provide a more complete and balanced picture of the factors that determine long-term success can be classified into the following four areas: customer, internal processes, innovation and learning, and financial (Kaplan and Norton, 1992). This 'balanced scorecard' complements the traditional financial measures with operational measures that are the drivers of future financial performance. The scorecard brings together, in a single management report, many of the potentially conflicting elements of a company's competitive agenda. It guards against suboptimisation by forcing managers to consider all the measures collectively. Performance measures should monitor whether the strategic objectives of an organization are achieved. This is accomplished by incorporating all 4 perspectives:

(1) The customer perspective requires managers to measure factors that matter to customers. Typically, these involve time, quality, performance and cost.
(2) The internal perspective focuses on what the firm needs to do internally in order to meet customers' expectations. The factors that have the greatest impact on customer satisfaction include cycle time, quality, skills and productivity. The core competencies of the company must also be identified.
(3) A company's ability to survive in the face of global competition hinges critically on its ability to innovate and learn continually.
(4) The financial performance measures indicate if the company's strategy and operations are contributing to the improvement of profits, growth and shareholder value.

Operating performance improvements must ultimately translate to financial performance improvements. By employing the balanced scorecard, the organization's strategic objectives which are the central focus are translated into a coherent set of performance indicators that are designed to pull the employees toward the overall vision. Companies that are using the scorecard to measure performance and set strategy include Rockwater, Apple Computer, Advanced Micro Devices and FMC Corporation (Kaplan and Norton, 1993).

14.4.4 Target costing

Although the link between management accounting and corporate goals is stronger in Japan than in the West, marketing objectives are more important than manufacturing factors in establishing product costs in Japan (Hiromoto, 1988). A new product is designed and marketed at its target cost (that is, what it should cost if it is to achieve corporate goals, such as attaining a particular market share) and not at its actual product costs (Berliner and Brimson, 1988). Unlike the traditional case where product costs determine market costs, the causation is reversed. Target costs are based on the cost that the market can bear (using estimates of a competitive market price, if available). These target costs are based on estimates of what a product should cost in order to compete effectively (Morgan, 1993; Merchant and Shields, 1993). The target cost is usually below currently achievable cost and thus employees are encouraged to make continual improvements in order to attain the target (Hiromoto, 1988).

Target costing is sometimes called cost planning or cost projection. It can be defined as

> 'a cost management tool for reducing the overall cost of a product over its life cycle with the help of the production, engineering, R&D, marketing, and accounting departments' (Sakurai, 1989, p. 41).

Planning and designing of high quality products which match customer needs are followed by value engineering and cost reduction exercises aimed at attaining the target cost (Sakurai, 1989).

Since its introduction around 1988, numerous articles have been written by Japanese researchers on the topic. The more recent publications include Tanaka (1993) and Yoshikawa *et al* (1993). Researchers outside Japan have began to write about the topic. Cooper (1994) described how four Japanese firms use target costing systems in different ways.

14.5 EVOLUTION OF MANAGEMENT ACCOUNTING

The evolution of management accounting can be traced through the changing needs of control as organizations evolve from structures of a single function to functional, divisional and multinational. The evolving organizational structure imposes new information and control requirements on the management accounting system. It would be interesting to see how and when management accounting will change if new organizational forms, such as network organizations, take root.

Apart from the change in organizational structure, other factors that are instrumental in shaping our perception of organizational control include changes in perspectives about the environmental impact, nature of organizational goals, objective of control and the role of accounting

Table 14.1   Assumptions underlying management accounting and control perspectives

Assumptions and focus	Structural: Cost Accounting	Behavioural: Management Accounting	Environmental: Strategic Management Accounting
Environment: Internal	Structures of communication	Structures and social relationships	Structures and social relationships
External	Closed system; stable	Closed system; stable	Open system; unstable
Nature of Goals	Organizational goals: known, well-defined, prespecified	Organizational goals and individual goals may differ	Organizational goals and individual goals may differ
Objective of Control	Efficiency	Effectiveness	Learning
Role of Accounting Information	Answer machine	Ammunition machine	Learning machine

information. Each set of assumptions characterizes a paradigm by providing a specific focus and objective of control. A summary of the underlying assumptions of each of the three paradigms is presented in Table 14.1 and forms the outline for the subsequent discussion.

14.5.1   Paradigm I: Structural view/cost accounting

The traditional view of control is that it operates in an organization that is a closed system, that is, the organization disregards differing organizational environments and the nature of the organizational dependency on the environment (Katz and Kahn, 1966). The organization interacts with its environment only to the extent that it engages in open market transactions. Consequently, accounting information is collected to ensure that internal operations are functioning efficiently. In other words, the focus is on *cost accounting*. The approach concentrates on the information and communication aspects of a control system and is rooted in the early work on cybernetics (Weiner, 1969). Control is thus defined as the problem of designing optimal information networks, including accounting systems, that is aimed at attaining efficiency in operations. The model treats the response of the manager as flowing automatically from the nature of the communicated information in a rational manner. It fails to recognise that managers do not respond mechanistically because they process information based on their personal goals and perceptions, and not necessarily based on the organizational goals embedded in the control system.

Yet another problem with traditional cost accounting is that it assumes structured operations that must remain stable and buffered from environmental exigencies. However, with a Juran (1991) approach to production and quality improvement, control over operations can no longer be closed, but must include elements of human and social behaviours and the environment. For example, a Volvo-style autonomous work group is not only responsible for operational efficiency but is also responsible for areas such as maintenance, work design and quality control. Moreover, advances in technology, such as flexible manufacturing system, is making variety at the technical core economically viable (Jaikumar, 1986). Therefore, the technical core no longer needs to be buffered so as to remain stable. The current emphasis on high-involvement management (Lawler, 1988) and total quality control (Ciampa, 1992; Juran, 1991) suggests that a division between the so-called operational and managerial activities may be moot. Increasingly, employees at the shopfloor are given more opportunities to participate in setting goals, changing processes, and making decisions that were once the purview of middle managers.

The structural approach to control also assumes that goals are certain, homogenous and clearly defined. Therefore, control is directed at the operating level and people are treated as part of the process of transforming inputs to desired outputs. The accounting system provides information to coordinate and control the multiple processes involved in the operations of the firm. The objective of management accounting is to provide information regarding the efficiency of operations.

Based on the model of 'economic man', the primacy of rationality was initially unquestioned and taken as granted. Actions are chosen by relating consequences of alternatives systematically to pre-determined and well-defined goals. These goals are, in turn, assumed to be given and immutable. This assumption is congruent with the economic perspective of control where decision-making rules and models are based on economic theory (Birnberg, 1992). Management accounting systems provide the necessary information which is objective and neutral. Thus, the role of accounting is largely one of an 'answer machine' (Burchell *et al*, 1980).

14.5.2   Paradigm II: Behavioural view/management accounting

Recognition of the social relationships that exist in organizations and the purposeful goal-oriented behaviour of people prompted movement away from the structural approach. In other words, the impetus for the change from the structural paradigm is the basic assumption about goals. It is recognised that individuals have goals, and that these may differ from prescribed organizational goals. A different approach, the *behavioural* approach, emphasises the human and social process by which an organization achieves its goals (Tannenbaum, 1964). Apart from its focus on informational and communication aspects of operations, control in an organization also involves the process of influencing individual behaviour. The recognition that accounting has behavioural and motivational impact saw the move from the cost accounting era to the management accounting era. The purpose of an accounting and control system is to motivate people to make choices favourable to the organization, or to engage in actions that are consistent with organizational goals. The problems encountered in trying to achieve this are recognised in this paradigm.

The behavioral paradigm of control focuses on the process of influencing human behaviour and the potential for dysfunctional behaviours arising from inappropriate accounting and control system design. Problems arise from attempts at structuring a well-coordinated system of sub-goals within the organization, motivating managers, and evaluating their performance. The role of the control system extends beyond the provision of information for decision-making into the arenas of motivation and performance evaluation. The function of a management control system is to influence individuals so that they achieve organizational objectives (Flamholtz, Das and Tsui, 1985). The emphasis is no longer on efficiency of operations, but on effectiveness of individual actions in relation to organizational goals. Accounting serves as an 'ammunition machine' by providing information that supports desired actions (Burchell *et al*, 1980).

14.5.3 Paradigm III: Environmental view/strategic management accounting

With the rapidly changing and unpredictable environments facing organizations, it is no longer possible for an organization to focus internally and ignore environmental factors. An open system perspective that emphasises the close relationship between a structure and its external environment is essential. To support the open system stance of the organization, the accounting and control system must be externally-oriented. The advent of **strategic management accounting** recognizes this need for an external focus. Thompson (1967) conceptualizes organizations as open systems consisting of three major sub-systems: technical, managerial and adaptive.

(1) The technical or production sub-system is concerned with the throughput, the energic or informational transformation process whose cycles of activities comprise the major functions of the system. This corresponds to the operational level of the organizational hierarchy or the level of the core technology (for example, patient care wards and treatment rooms in a hospital). In order to remove uncertainty and environmental influences on this technical core, the organization will attempt to insulate it through the use of buffering mechanisms such as slack creation (Cyert & March, 1963; Thompson, 1967). This is important because operational efficiency requires conformity to a process, relatively high predictability and an emphasis on maintaining the *status quo* in order to be able to reproduce the task at a consistent level.

(2) The managerial sub-system comprises the organizational activities for controlling, coordinating and directing the many subsystems of the organization, for procuring inputs and disposing of outputs, and for securing and allocating personnel. It is required because of the need for stability and predictability in the cooperative efforts toward a common objective. Its role is to mediate between the relatively open adaptive and the closed technical levels and this requires flexibility. Thus, this sub-system emphasises the less formalised and more political organizational activities.

(3) In order to survive in a changing environment, an adaptive sub-system is required. It is outward-looking and permits the organization to exploit changing environmental opportunities. It is at the institutional level that the organization relates to its wider environment, determines its domain and establishes its boundaries. This is akin to the strategic planning process which involves an assessment of environmental conditions and the identification of opportunities and threats. An important distinction between operational and strategic control is the degree of openness required. At the operational level, attempts are made to close the system and isolate it from environmental effects. However, at the strategic level, interaction with the environment is essential in order for the organization to adapt and respond to changing conditions.

The current developments in management accounting fall into this paradigm. Strategic management accounting stresses the importance of generating external information such as information about the firm's product markets and competitors' costs. Strategic management accounting recognises that efficiency and effectiveness of operations are not sufficient for a firm to sustain its competitive advantage. There is a critical need to learn and adapt to changing environmental exigencies. Such an orientation is reinforced by the drive to become a learning organization (Senge, 1990). The objective of management accounting and control is to encourage continuous improvement and learning (McNair, 1993). Therefore, accounting essentially functions as a learning machine. In supporting this learning imperative, target costing calls for continuous reduction of costs of a product over its life cycle. Target costs are set at a level that the market can bear, and not at the level of actual product costs. To set target costs, the organization must be open to its environment and be aware of the market forces and customer demands. The importance of accurate product costs is also evident in the move to use activity-based costing systems. The product information may be used to inform strategic decision-making. To sustain its competitive advantage, firms must monitor the performance of key manufacturing characteristics that provide that competitive advantage. The move away from emphasis on financial measures in management accounting to non-financial and operational measures reflects this concern.

14.6 FUTURE DIRECTIONS: A RESEARCH AGENDA

Given our past experiences, it is perhaps appropriate to pause and reconsider the research agenda for management accounting. In order to facilitate management accounting innovation that moves with the times, it is believed that a few elements are critical to the research agenda.

Firstly, some research must be inter-disciplinary. To understand strategic management accounting and apply its concepts to organizations, the management accounting researcher needs insights from strategic management and organization theory. In order to identify the appropriate cost drivers in a manufacturing firm, collaboration with researchers and/or practitioners in the field of engineering or production management is crucial. The current fixation on quality suggests that knowledge about production processes and quality improvement techniques becomes critical. The management accounting researcher can attempt to be knowledgeable in all these areas that are outside the traditional purview of accounting. However, except for a few, the rest will have less than complete knowledge in these areas, and will benefit from collaboration with researchers in other disciplines.

Secondly, apart from learning from other disciplines, the researcher can also learn from practice. An organizationally-grounded approach to research that seeks to describe and explain the world as perceived by both organizational participants and the researcher has an important role in enhancing learning between academics and practitioners (Glaser, 1978). In studying management practices, case or field-based research provides an effective means of learning from practice and enhances our ability to address the issues and problems faced by practitioners. The aim of such qualitative research is to suggest appropriate theoretical constructs and develop ideas about their likely relationships. It is used at the exploratory stage of research and is more concerned with inductive generation of theory than with verification.

Case study research is defined as 'an empirical study that:

- investigates a contemporary phenomenon within its real-life context; when
- the boundaries between phenomenon and context are not clearly evident; and in which
- multiple sources of evidence are used' (Yin, 1984, p. 23).

A distinction is made between case study research and site visits which are brief visits to firms with the goal of gathering information that provides an overview of the subject of interest (Young and Selto, 1991). Field or case studies, on the other hand, encompass intensive, detailed investigations requiring attention to case research design issues and the commitment of considerable time and effort (Spicer, 1992). The case studies methodology remains an under-exploited research tool in management accounting research. Objections to case studies include firstly, its small sample size, which restricts the application of statistical techniques of theory verification, and secondly, its descriptive nature coupled with the limited attempts made by researchers to generalise their findings (Otley, 1984: Yin, 1984). The first objection presents less of an obstacle if cases are used for theory generation and the second objection can be overcome by using comparative case studies.

Spicer (1992) describes some recent cases in management accounting research that describe and/or explore changes in cost and management accounting practices in response to innovations in manufacturing. He further illustrates how case study research can be used to:

- Help choose between received theory and a plausible rival,
- Determine if theoretical predictions about conditions under which a particular accounting technique are likely to be observed are supported by observations of practice,
- Challenge textbook theory and build alternative explanations,
- Provide analytical evidence in support (or refutation) of a specific theory,
- Inform the design of other empirical research in a context where there is a substantial knowledge base of theory and empirical work.

Thirdly, a triangulation of research methods is recommended to allow researchers to be more confident of their results. Triangulation refers to 'the combination of methodologies in the study of the same phenomenon' (Denzin, 1978, p. 291). One means of triangulation is achieved by using multiple methods to examine the same dimension of a research problem. When two or more distinct methods yield comparable data and are found to be congruent, there is cross validation which enhances our confidence that the results are valid and are not methodological artifacts (Jick, 1979). The alternative means of triangulation is to use multiple techniques within a given method to collect and interpret data. For example, in survey research, multiple scales or indices focused on the same construct can be employed. This within-method triangulation involves cross-checking for internal consistency or reliability.

Triangulation can be applied to better understand management accounting problems. From the results of qualitative research (such as comparative case studies), appropriate theoretical constructs may be developed and their inter-relationships specified. After this exploratory phase, quantitative methods of research can be used to more precisely measure the constructs and test the hypothesized relationships.

For example, the issue of new management accounting developments such as ABC or SMA can be studied by a research strategy that includes both qualitative and quantitative methods. Surveys could be distributed to employees in firms that have implemented the new accounting systems to investigate issues such as their acceptance of the new systems, their perception of the usefulness of the systems and the problems faced. To complement this data, a sub-sample of employees could be selected for the purpose of semi-structured, probing interviews. Case studies of a few firms in the sample can be conducted to provide a richer data set. Archival data such as company files, minutes and newspaper clippings can be collected where relevant to reveal the espoused reasons for change and to provide a better understanding of the context within which the management accounting system change occurred.

Finally, the call for relevant research is strong given the current lag in management accounting innovation and its failure to address problems and changes in the organization. The practical relevance or usefulness of research must be assessed from the frame of reference of the practitioner (Dubin, 1976; Mitroff et al, 1974). Thomas and Tymon (1982) identified five components of research relevance:

- Descriptive relevance refers to the accuracy of the research findings in capturing the phenomena encountered by the practitioner in his or her organizational setting. In management accounting research, the use of laboratory experiments in isolation to understand an organizational phenomenon, such as budgeting behaviours, is subject to the criticism that it lacks descriptive relevance.
- Goal relevance refers to the correspondence of the outcome variable of a study to the outcome of concern to the practitioner. Without interaction with practitioners, management accounting researchers are likely to choose dependent variables that diverge from the concerns of the practitioner.
- Operational validity concerns the ability of the practitioner to implement action implications of a study by manipulating its causal

variables. Although some studies are descriptively valid, they may be useless to practitioners because their independent variables cannot be manipulated without causing harmful consequences to the organization (Pondy, 1974).

- Nonobviousness refers to the degree to which a theory meets or exceeds the complexity of common sense theory already used by a practitioner. In other words, research findings must not be trivial or simply commonsensical.
- Timeliness is the requirement that a theory be available to practitioners in time to use it to deal with problems.

With the current lag in management accounting research and the rapid change in the environment, the phenomenon of study may be supplanted by other phenomena before researchers are able to draw prescriptive implications from their research findings. The emphasis on rigour in research must be balanced by the need for research relevance. The move towards more field-based research is aimed at addressing the question of relevance. Academics have begun to accept studies that employ more qualitative methodologies and have provided additional publication outlets (for example, Journal of Management Accounting Research, Advances in Management Accounting) for the dissemination of research findings arising from such studies.

14.7 CONCLUSIONS

Management accounting research and practice is at the centre of significant transformation. As the system charged with the mandate of providing relevant information for planning and control, management accounting plays a crucial role in ensuring that the organization remains competitive. Given that organizations are besieged with changes both internal and external to the organization, existing management accounting systems are unable to meet the new demands imposed on them. External changes are brought about by globalization of the market place and increasing competitiveness, while internal changes are the result of the changing paradigm of management practices and advances in manufacturing technology.

Management accountants must revolutionize their thinking and practice to remain relevant. We have begun to see some encouraging developments in the form of strategic management accounting, activity-based costing, target costing and broader performance measures that include qualitative, operational and non-financial indicators. However, much more remains to be accomplished. Many of these concepts address the problem partially and a synthesis is required to provide a comprehensive framework for management accounting theory and practice. Our research agenda suggests how we can move towards this elusive goal of gaining acceptance of a management accounting framework that is relevant to practitioners and researchers alike. The research agenda accepts both qualitative and quantitative approaches to research, includes learning from practitioners as critical and encourages collaboration with experts from other disciplines. A more eclectic approach is required as management accounting seeks to regain its relevance.

REFERENCES

Akerlof, G. (1970). The Market for 'Lemons': Quality Uncertainty and the Market Mechanism. *Quarterly Journal of Economics*, August, pp. 488–500

Alchian, A. and Demsetz, H. (1972). Production, Information Cause, and Economic Organization. *American Economic Review*, 62, pp. 777–795

Anthony, R. (1965). *Planning and Control Systems: A Framework for Analysis.* Division of Research, Graduate School of Business Administration. Boston: Harvard University

Anthony, R. (1989). Reminiscences about Management Accounting. *Journal of Management Accounting Research*, 1, pp. 1–20

Argyris, C. (1952). *The Impact of Budgets on People.* Controllership Foundation. Ithaca, New York: Cornell University

Armitage, H. and Nicholson, R. (1993). *Management Accounting Issues Paper 3: Activity Based Costing*, The Society of Management Accountants of Canada

Baiman, S. (1982). Agency Research in Managerial Accounting: A Survey. *Journal of Accounting Literature*, Spring, pp. 154–213

Baiman, S. (1990). Agency Research in Managerial Accounting: A Second Look. *Accounting, Organizations and Society*, 15, pp. 341–371

Banker, R. and Johnson, H. (1988). *Cost Driver Analysis in the Service Sector: An Empirical Study of the US Airlines. Carnegie Mellon University Working Paper*, Pittsburgh, PA

Baumol, W., Panzar, J. and Willig, R. (1982). *Contestable Markets and the Theory of Industry Structure.* San Diego: Harcourt Brace and Jovanovich

Bennis, W. (1969). *Organization Development: Nature and Origins.* Reading, MA: Addison-Wesley

Berliner, C. and Brimson, J. (1988). *Cost Management for Today's Advanced Manufacturing.* Boston, MA: Harvard Business School Press

Bessant, J. and Haywood, B. (1986). Flexibility in Manufacturing Systems. *Omega: The International Journal of Management Science*, 14, 6, pp. 465–473

Birnberg, J. (1992). Managerial Accounting: Yet Another Retrospective. *Advances in Management Accounting*, 1, pp. 1–19

Brimson, J. (1991). *Activity Accounting: An Activity-Based Costing Approach.* New York: Wiley

Bromwich, M. (1990). The Case for Strategic Management Accounting: The Role of Accounting Information for Strategy in Competitive Markets. *Accounting, Organizations and Society*, 15(1/2), pp. 27–46

Bromwich, M. and Bhimani, A. (1989). *Management Accounting: Evolution Not Revolution.* London: The Chartered Institute of Management Accountants

Brown, D. (1927). Centralized Control with Decentralized Responsibilities. In *Annual Convention Series, No. 57.* New York: American Management Association, pp. 3–24

Brownell, P. (1981). Participation in Budgeting, Locus of Control and Organizational Effectiveness. *Accounting Review*, October, pp. 844–860

Bruggeman, W. and Van der Stede, W. (1993). Fitting Management Control Systems to Competitive Advantage. *British Journal of Management*, 4, pp. 205–218

Bruns, W. (1968). Accounting Information and Decision Making: Some Behavioral Hypotheses. *Accounting Review*, July, pp. 469–480

Burchell, S., Clubb, C., Hopwood, A. and Nahapiet, J. (1980). The Roles of Accounting in Organizations and Society. *Accounting, Organizations and Society*, 5, 1, pp. 5–27

Caplan, E. (1966). Behavioral Assumptions of Management Accounting. *Accounting Review*, July, pp. 496–509

Chandler, A. (1977). *The Visible Hand: The Managerial Revolution in American Business.* Boston, MA: Harvard Business School Press

Chenhall, R. (1991). Strategic Management Accounting. *Accounting Communique* No. 26, Australian Society of Certified Practising Accountants, pp. 1–4

Chung, L., Lim, L., Sng, S. and Tan, M. (1994). Management Control Systems and Business Strategy: An Empirical Study of Electronics and Electrical Firms in Singapore. In *Proceedings of the Pan Pacific Conference XI*, Bangkok, Thailand, 2–4 June

Ciampa, D. (1992) *Total Quality.* Reading, MA: Addison-Wesley

Clark, A. and Baxter, A. (1992). ABC + ABM = Action: Let's Get Down to Business. *Management Accounting*, June, pp. 54–55

Cobb, I. (1992). JIT and the Management Accountant. *Management Accountant*, February, pp. 42–44

Computer Aided Manufacturing International (1990). *The CAM-I Glossary of Activity–Based Management*, Arlington, Texas

Cook, P. (1955). Decentralization and Transfer Pricing Problem. *Journal of Business*, April, pp. 87–94

Cooper, D. (1981). A Social and Organizational View of Management. In *Essays in British Accounting Research* (Bromwich, M. and Hopwood, A. eds.), pp. 178–205, London: Pitman

Cooper, R. (1988). The Rise of Activity-Based Costing-Part One: What is an Activity-Based Cost System. *Journal of Cost Management, Summer*, pp. 45–54

Cooper, R. (1990). Cost Classification in Unit-Based and Activity-Based Manufacturing Cost Systems. In *Emerging Practices in Cost Management* (Brinker, B. ed.), Boston: Warren, Gorham and Lamont

Cooper, R. (1994). How Japanese Manufacturing Firms Implement Target Costing Systems: A Field-Based Research Study. *Proceedings of the Management Accounting Research Conference.* American Accounting Association, pp. 1–23

Cooper, R., Kaplan, R., Maisel, L. and Oehm, R. (1992). From ABC to ABM. *Management Accounting*, November, pp. 54–57

Crossman, P. (1958). The Nature of Management Accounting. *Accounting Review*, April, pp. 222–227

Currie, W. (1989). Investing in CAD: A Case of Ad Hoc Decision Making. *Long Range Planning*, 22, 6, pp. 85–91

Currie, W. (1992). The Strategic Management of AMT in Japan, the USA, the UK and West Germany, Part 1. *Management Accounting*, November, pp. 32–36

Currie, W. (1993). The Strategic Management of AMT in Japan, the USA, the UK and West Germany, Part 3. *Management Accounting*, January, pp. 56–58

Cyert, R. and March, J. (1963). *A Behavioral Theory of the Firm*. Englewood Cliffs, NJ: Prentice Hall

Dean, J. (1951). *Capital Budgeting: Top Management Policy on Plant, Equipment and Product Development*. New York: Columbia University Press

Dean, J. (1955) Decentralization and Intra-Company Pricing. *Harvard Business Review*, July/August, pp. 65–74

Dearden, J. (1960). Problems in Decentralized Profit Responsibility. *Harvard Business Review*, May-June, pp. 79–86

Demski, J. and Feltham, G. (1978). Economic Perspectives in Budgetary Control Systems. *Accounting Review*, 53, 2, pp. 336–359

Denzin, N. (1978). *The Research Act*. New York: McGraw Hill

Dubin, R. (1976). Theory Building in Applied Areas. In *Handbook of Industrial and Organizational Psychology* (Dunnette, M. ed.), pp. 17–39, Chicago: Rand-McNally

Dunk, A. (1989). Management Accounting Lag. *Abacus*, 25, 2, pp. 149–155

Eccles, R.G. and Nohria, N. (1992). *Beyond the Hype*. Boston, MA: Harvard Business School Press

Fama, E. (1980). Agency Problems and the Theory of the Firm. *Journal of Political Economy*, April, pp. 288–307

Feltham, G. (1968). The Value of Information. *Accounting Review*, October, pp. 684–696

Feltham, G. and Demski, J. (1970). The Uses of Models in Information Evaluation. *Accounting Review*, October, pp. 623–640

Fisher, T. (1993). The View from the Top: Chief Executives' Perceptions of Total Quality Management. *Australian Journal of Management*, 18, 3, pp. 181–195

Flamholtz, E. (1983). Accounting, Budgeting and Control Systems in Their Organizational Context: Theoretical and Empirical Perspectives. *Accounting, Organizations and Society*, 8, 2/3, pp. 153–169

Flamholtz, E. (1992). Relevance Regained: Management Accounting-Past, Present, and Future. *Advances in Management Accounting*, 1, pp. 21–34

Flamholtz, E., Das, T. and Tsui, A. (1985). Toward an Integrative Framework of Organizational Control. *Accounting, Organizations and Society*, 10, pp. 35–50

Foster, G. and Gupta. M. (1990). Manufacturing Overhead Cost Driver Analysis. *Journal of Accounting and Economics*, January, pp. 309–337

Foster, G. and Horngren, C. (1988). Cost Accounting and Cost Management in a JIT Environment. *Journal of Cost Management for the Manufacturing Industry*, Winter, pp. 4–14

Garvin, D. (1991). How the Baldrige Award Really Works. *Harvard Business Review*, 69, 6, Nov/Dec, pp. 80–95

Garvin, D. (1993). Building a Learning Organization. *Harvard Business Review*, 71, 4, July, pp. 78–91

Geanuracos, J. (1994). The Global Performance Game. *Crossborder*, Winter, pp. 18–21

Glaser, B. (1978). *Theoretical Sensitivity: Advances in the Methodology of Grounded Theory.* New York: The Sociology Press

Goddard, W.E. (1988). *JIT: Surviving by Breaking Tradition.* Essex Junction, VT: Oliver Wright Inc

Govindarajan, V. (1984). Appropriateness of Accounting Data in Performance Evaluation: An Empirical Evaluation of Environmental Uncertainty as an Intervening Variable. *Accounting, Organizations and Society,* 9, 2, pp. 125–135

Govindarajan, V. and Gupta, M. (1985). Linking Control Systems to Business Strategy: Impact on Performance. *Accounting, Organizations and Society,* 1, pp. 51–66

Govindarajan, V. and Shank, J. (1992). Strategic Cost Management: Tailoring Controls to Strategies. *Journal of Cost Management,* 6, 3, pp. 14–26

Grant, R., Shani, R. and Krishnan, R. (1994). TQM's Challenge to Management Theory and Practice. *Sloan Management Review,* Winter, pp. 25–35

Griffin, L. and Harrell, A. (1991). An Empirical Examination of Manager's Motivation to Implement Just-in-Time Procedures. *Journal of Management Accounting Research,* 3, Fall, pp. 98–112

Hammer, M. (1990). Reengineering Work: Don't Automate, Obliterate. *Harvard Business Review,* July/August, pp. 104–112

Hay, E. J. (1988). *The Just-in-Time Breakthrough: Implementing the New Manufacturing Basics.* New York: John Wiley and Sons

Hiromoto, T. (1988). Another Hidden Edge: Japanese Management Accounting. *Harvard Business Review,* 66, July/August, pp. 22–26

Hirshleifer, J. (1956). On the Economics of Transfer Pricing. *Journal of Business,* July, pp. 172–184

Hirshleifer, J. (1957). Economics of the Divisionalized Firm. *Journal of Business,* April, pp. 96–108

Hodgetts, R., Luthans, F. and Lee, S. (1994). New Paradigm Organizations: From Total Quality to Learning to World-Class. *Organizational Dynamics,* Winter, pp. 5–19

Hofstedt, T. (1975). A State-of-the-Art Analysis of Behavioural Accounting. *Journal of Contemporary Business,* Autumn, pp. 27–49

Hopwood, A. (1972). An Empirical Study of the Role of Accounting Data in Performance Evaluation. *Empirical Research in Accounting: Selected Studies,* pp. 146–182

Hopwood, A. (1978). Towards and Organizational Perspective for the Study of Accounting and Information Systems. *Accounting, Organizations and Society,* 3, 1, pp. 3–14

Hopwood, A. (1980). Discussion of 'Some Inner Contradictions in Management Information Systems' and 'Behavioural Implications of Planning and Control Systems.' In *Management Accounting 1980: Proceedings of the University of Illinois Management Accounting Symposium,* (Holzer, H. ed.) University of Illinois at Urbana-Champaign

Hopwood, A. (1983). On Trying to Study Accounting in the Contexts in which it Operates. *Accounting, Organizations and Society,* 8, 2/3, pp. 287–305

Horngren, C. (1989). Cost and Management Accounting: Yesterday and Today. *Journal of Management Accounting Research,* 1, Fall, pp. 21–32

Horngren, C. and Foster, G. (1989). *Cost Accounting: A Managerial Emphasis* 6th ed. Englewood Cliffs, NJ: Prentice Hall

Howell, R., Brown, J., Soucy, G. and Seed, A. (1987). *Management Accounting in the New Manufacturing Environment*, Montvale, NJ: National Association of Accountants

Howell, R. and Soucy, G. (1987). Cost Accounting in the New Manufacturing Environment. *Management Accounting*, August, pp. 42–49.

Innes, J. and Mitchell, F. (1988). *Management Accounting Innovation in Electronics Firms*. CIMA Report. London: CIMA

Innes, J. and Mitchell, F. (1991). ABC: A Survey of CIMA Members, *Management Accounting, UK*, October, pp. 28–30

Jaikumar, R. (1986). Post-Industrial Manufacturing, *Harvard Business Review*, Nov-Dec, pp. 69–76

Jick, T. (1979). Mixing Qualitative and Quantitative Methods: Triangulation in Action. In *Qualitative Methodology* (Van Maanen, ed.), pp. 135–148, Beverly Hills, CA: Sage Publications

Johnson, T. (1975). Management Accounting in Early Integrated Industrial: E.I. du Pont de Nemours Powder Company, 1903-1912, *Business History Review*, Summer, pp. 184–204

Johnson, T. (1978). Management Accounting in an Early Multidivisional Organization: General Motors in the 1920s. *Business History Review*, Winter, pp. 490–517

Johnson, T. and Kaplan, R. (1987). *Relevance Lost: The Rise and Fall of Management Accounting*. Boston, MA: Harvard Business School Press

Juran, J M (1974). *Quality Control Handbook*. New York: McGraw Hill

Juran, J M (1991). *Juran on Quality By Design: The New Steps for Planning Quality into Goods and Services*. New York: The Free Press

Kaplan, R. (1983). Measuring Manufacturing Performance: A New Challenge for Managerial Accounting Research, *Accounting Review*, 57, 4, pp. 686–705

Kaplan, R. (1984a). The Evolution of Management Accounting. *Accounting Review*, 29, 3, pp. 390–418

Kaplan, R. (1984b). Yesterday's Accounting Undermines Production. *Harvard Business Review*, July-August, pp. 16–20

Kaplan, R. (1985). Accounting Lag: The Obsolescence of Cost Accounting Systems. In *The Uneasy Alliance: Managing the Productivity–Technology Dilemma* (Clark, K., Hayes, R. and Lorenz, C. eds.), 195–226, Boston, MA: Harvard Business School Press

Kaplan, R. (1988). Relevance Regained, *Management Accounting, UK*, September, pp. 38–42

Kaplan, R. and Norton, D. (1992). The Balanced Scorecard-Measures that Drive Performance. *Harvard Business Review*, Jan/Feb, pp. 71–79

Kaplan, R. and Norton, D. (1993). Putting the Balanced Scorecard to Work. *Harvard Business Review*, Sept/Oct, pp. 134–147

Katz, D. and Kahn, R. (1966). *The Social Psychology of Organization*. New York: John Wiley

Khandwalla, P. (1972). The Effect of Different Types of Competition on the Use of Management Controls. *Journal of Accounting Research*, Autumn, pp. 275–285

Kuhn, T.S. (1970). *The Structure of Scientific Revolutions*. Illinois: The University of Chicago Press

Lawler, E. (1988). Transformation from Control to Involvement. In *Corporate Transformation: Revitalizing Organizations for a Competitive World* (Kilmann, R., Covin, T. and Associates eds.). San Francisco: Jossey-Bass

Lei, D. and Slocum, J. (1992). Global Strategy, Competence Building and Strategic Alliances, *California Management Review*, Fall, pp. 81–97

Libby, R. (1981). *Behavioral Decision Theory Research in Accounting.* Englewood Cliffs, NJ.: Prentice-Hall

Mackey, J. (1991). MRP, JIT and Automated Manufacturing and the Role of Accounting in Production Management. In *Issues in Management Accounting* (Ashton, D., Hopper, T. and Scapens, R. eds.), pp. 193–218, New York: Prentice Hall

Management Accounting Guidelines (1993). *Number 19: Implementing Just-In-Time Systems.* Society of Management Accountants of Canada

McNair, C. (1993). Form over Function: Toward an Architecture of Costs, *Advances in Management Accounting*, 2

Merchant, K. and Shields, M. (1993). When and Why to Measure Costs Less Accurately to Improve Decision Making, *Accounting Horizons*, June, pp. 76–81

Miles, R. and Snow, C. (1992). Causes of Failure in Network Organizations. *California Management Review*, Summer, pp. 53–72

Milgrom, R. and Roberts, J. (1990). The Economics of Modern Manufacturing: Technology, Strategy and Organization, *American Economic Review*, June, pp. 511–528

Miller, J., and Vollman, T. (1985). The Hidden Factory, *Harvard Business Review*, Sept/Oct, pp. 142–150.

Mills, D. (1991). *Rebirth of the Corporation.* New York: John Wiley and Sons

Mills, D. and Friesen, B. (1992). The Learning Organization, *European Journal of Management*, 10, 2, pp. 146–156

Mitroff, T., Betz, F., Pondy, L. and Sagasti, F. (1974). On Managing Science in the Systems Age: Two Schemas for the Study of Science as a Whole Systems Phenomenon, *Interfaces*, 4, 3, pp. 46–58

Morgan, M. (1993). A Case Study in Target Costing: Accounting for Strategy, *Management Accounting*, May, pp. 20–24

Nanni, A., Dixon, R. and Vollmann, T. (1990). Strategic Control and Performance Measurement. *Journal of Cost Management*, Summer, pp. 33–42

Neumann, B., and Jaouen, P. (1986). Kanban, Zips and Cost Accounting: A Case Study. *Journal of Accountancy*, August, pp. 132–141

Otley, D. (1978). Budget Use and Managerial Performance. *Journal of Accounting Research*, Spring, pp. 122–149

Otley, D. (1980). The Contingency Theory of Management Accounting: Achievement and Prognosis, *Accounting, Organizations and Society*, 5, 4, pp. 413–428

Otley, D. (1984). Management Accounting and Organizational Theory: A Review of their Interrelationship. In *Management Accounting, Organizational Theory and Capital Budgeting: Three Surveys* (Scapens, R., Otley, D. and Lister, R. eds.), pp. 96–164, London: MacMilan

Patell, J. (1987). Cost Accounting Process Controls and Product Design: A Case Study of the H-P Personal Office Computer Division. *Accounting Review*, July, pp. 808–839

Pondy, L. (1972). A Reviewer's Comment. *Administrative Science Quarterly*, 17, pp. 408–409

Porter, M. (1980). *Competitive Strategy*. New York: Free Press

Porter, M. (1985). *Competitive Advantage*. New York: Free Press

Richardson, P. and Gordon, J. (1980). Measuring Total Manufacturing Performance. *Sloan Management Review*, Winter, pp. 47–58

Ridgeway, V. (1956). Dysfunctional Consequences of Performance Measurements. *Administrative Science Quarterly*, September, pp. 240–247

Ross, G. (1990). Revolution in Management Control, *Management Accounting*, November, pp. 23–27

Ross, S. (1973). The Economic Theory of Agency: The Principal's Problem. *American Economic Review*, 63, pp. 134–139

Sakurai, M. (1989), Target Costing and How to Use It. *Journal of Cost Management*, Summer, pp. 39–50

Salomon, D. and Biegel, J. (1985). Assessing Economic Attractiveness of FMS Applications in Small Batch Manufacturing. In *Computer Integrated Manufacturing Systems: Selected Readings* (Nazemetz, J., Hammer, W. and Sadowski, R. eds.) pp. 252–277, Norcross GA: Industrial Engineering and Management Press

San Miguel, J. (1977). The Behavioural Sciences and Concepts and Standards for Management Planning and Control. *Accounting, Organizations and Society*, 2, 2, pp. 177–186

Scapens, R. (1984). Management Accounting: A Survey Paper. In *Management Accounting, Organizational Theory and Capital Budgeting: Three Surveys* (Scapens, R., Otley, D. and Lister, R. eds.), pp. 15–95, London: MacMillan

Schoch, H. Teoh, H.Y., Lee, M.H. and Ang, K.B. (1994). Activity-Based Costing in the Electronics Industry: The Singapore Experience. *Journal of Small Business and Entrepreneurship*, 11, 2, pp. 28–37

Schonberger, R. (1982). *Japanese Manufacturing Techniques: Nine Hidden Lessons in Simplicity*. New York: Free Press

Senge, P. (1990). *The Fifth Discipline: The Art and Practice of the Learning Organization*. New York: Doubleday

Shank, J. (1989). Strategic Cost Management: New Wine, or Just New Bottles, *Journal of Management Accounting Research*, 1, pp. 47–65

Shank, J. and Govindarajan, V. (1993). *Strategic Cost Management: The New Tool for Competitive Advantage*. New York: The Free Press

Sharman, P. (1993a). Activity-Based Management: A Growing Practice, *CMA Magazine* March, pp. 17–22

Sharman, P. (1993b). The Role of Measurement in Activity-Based Management, *CMA Magazine*, September, pp. 25–29

Shephard, N. (1993). JIT: Less Means More Service to the Customer. *CMA Magazine* December/January, pp. 14–17

Shillinglaw, G. (1980). Old Horizons and New Frontiers: The Future of Managerial Accounting. In *Management Accounting 1980: Proceedings of the University of Illinois Management Accounting Symposium* (Holzer, H. ed.), 3–16, University of Illinois at Urbana-Champaign

Simmonds, K. (1981). Strategic Management Accounting, *Management Accounting. UK*, April, pp. 26–29

Simon, H., Guetzkow, H., Kometsky, G. and Tyndall, G. (1954). *Centralization Versus Decentralization in Organizing the Controller's Department.* New York: Controllership Foundation

Simons, R. (1987). Accounting Control Systems and Business Strategy: An Empirical Analysis. *Accounting, Organizations and Society,* 12(4), pp. 357–374

Simons, R. (1990). The Role of Management Control Systems in Creating Competitive Advantage: New Perspectives. *Accounting, Organizations and Society,* 15(1/2), pp. 127–143

Simons, R. (1991). Strategic Orientation and Top Management Attention to Control Systems. *Strategic Management Journal,* 12, pp. 49–62

Snow, C., Miles, R. and Coleman, H. (1992). Managing 21st Century Organizations. *Organizational Dynamics,* Winter, pp. 5–20

Solomons, D. (1965). *Divisional Performance: Measurement and Control.* New York: Financial Executives Research Foundation

Spicer, B. (1992). The Resurgence of Cost and Management Accounting: A Review of Some Recent Developments in Practice, Theories and Case Research Methods. *Management Accounting Research,* 3, pp. 1–37

Sriram, R. and Gupta, Y. (1991). Strategic Cost Measurement for Flexible Manufacturing Systems. *Long Range Planning,* 24, 5, pp. 34–40

Stalk, G. (1992). Time-based Competition and Beyond: Competing on Capabilities. *Planning Review,* September-October, pp. 27–29

Steimer, T. (1990). Activity-Based Accounting for Total Quality. *Management Accounting,* October, pp. 39–42

Stiglitz, J. (1974). Incentives and Risk-Sharing in Sharecropping. *Review of Economic Studies,* 41, pp. 219–255

Stone, W. (1956). Intracompany Pricing, *Accounting Review,* October, pp. 625–627.

Sundem, G. (1981). Future Perspectives in Management Accounting Research, Paper presented at the *Seventh Accounting Research Convocation at the University of Alabama*

Tanaka, M. (1993). Target Costing at Toyota, *Journal of Cost Management,* Spring, pp. 4–11

Tannenbaum, A. (1964). Control in Organizations: Individual Adjustment and Organizational Performance. In *Management Controls* (Bonini, C. *et al* eds.). New York: McGraw-Hill

Taylor, B. and Graham, C. (1992). Information for Strategic Management, *Management Accounting, UK,* January, 70, pp. 52–54

Thomas, T. and Tymon, W. (1982). Necessary Properties of Relevant Research: Lessons from Recent Criticisms of the Organizational Sciences. *Academy of Management Review,* 7, 3, pp. 345–352

Thompson, J. (1967). *Organizations in Action.* New York: McGraw-Hill

Thorelli, H. (1986). Networks: Between Markets and Hierarchies. *Strategic Management Journal,* 7, pp. 37–51

Turney, P. (1992). Activity-Based Management: ABM Puts ABC Information to Work, *Management Accounting,* January, pp. 20–25

Turney, P. (1993). Beyond TQM: With Workforce Activity-Based Management. *Management Accounting,* September, pp. 28–31

Turney, P. and Stratton, A. (1992). Using ABC to Support Continuous Improvement. *Management Accounting,* September, pp. 46–50

Weiner, N. (1969). *Cybernetics.* Cambridge: MIT Press

Yin, R. (1987). *Case Study Research: Design and Methods.* Beverly Hills, CA: Sage Publications

Yoshikawa, T., Innes, J., Mitchell, F. and Tanaka, M. (1993). *Contemporary Cost Management.* London: Chapman-Hall

Young, S. and Selto, F. (1991). New Manufacturing Practices and Cost Management: A Review of the Literature and Directions for Research. *Journal of Accounting Literature*, 10, pp. 265–298

Young, S., Shields, M. and Wolf, G. (1988). Manufacturing Controls and Performance: An Experiment. *Accounting, Organizations and Society*, 5, pp. 607–618

Index